WHILE WAITING FOR RAIN

While Waiting for Rain

Community, Economy, and Law in a Time of Change

John Henry Schlegel

UNIVERSITY OF MICHIGAN PRESS
ANN ARBOR

Published in the United States of America by the
University of Michigan Press
Manufactured in the United States of America
Printed on acid-free paper
Open access e-book first published August 2022;
Additional formats first published November 2022

A CIP catalog record for this book is available from the British Library.
Library of Congress Cataloging-in-Publication data has been applied for.
ISBN 978-0-472-07561-4 (hardcover : alk. paper)
ISBN 978-0-472-05561-6 (paper : alk. paper)
ISBN 978-0-472-90297-2 (open access ebook)

DOI: https://doi.org/10.3998/mpub.12158309

Funding is provided by the Andrew W. Mellon Foundation, as part of the Sustainable History Monograph Pilot.

The University of Michigan Press's open access publishing program is made possible thanks to additional funding from the University of Michigan Office of the Provost and the generous support of contributing libraries.

When you cite the book, please include the following URL for its Digital Object Identifier (DOI):
https://doi.org/10.3998/mpub.12158309

CONTENTS

Digital materials related to this title can be found on the Fulcrum platform via the following citable URL: https://doi.org/10.3998/mpub.12158309

PREFACE

This book has been a long time coming. I once thought that it started back in the early nineties when I tripped over a review in the *Wall Street Journal* of Verlyn Kinkenborg's book, *The Last Fine Time*, about Polish Buffalo, New York in the fifties. Intrigued, I bought a copy. The book taught me about a world I had never experienced in almost twenty years of living here. I began to wonder how and why the physical, economic, and social devastation that I saw all around me had happened. Research followed and eventually this manuscript came together. Except that this sequence of events is just not right.

This manuscript started way earlier, in the summer of 1949 when I was seven and my parents took me to the grand, expansive, exciting "Railroad Fair" held on Chicago's waterfront. I was knocked out by all of the steam engines and various types of freight cars on display. A few years later, my father gave me a silver dollar. He explained that on a business trip his train to New York City, the Twentieth Century Limited, had been one minute late getting into Grand Central Station and passengers on this train always received a silver dollar for every minute the train was late, though it had never happened to him before. Right there and then I was hooked on trains. I looked forward to the times when a train blocked a road and stopped our car, or when driving along tracks a train came the other way. In either case, I watched the passing engines and freight cars for the names of the railroads emblazoned on the side, always hoping to find one from a line I had never heard of.

A few years later my family attended a Christmas party for the families of the employees of the spring company that my father worked for. It was held at the firm's factory and included several manufacturing demonstrations. One of the company's products was the suspension springs for railroad car trucks, the part under the car that contains the wheels. These enormous springs had to be coiled out of hot steel rod. I can still see the two men who used huge tongs to catch the heated rods as they came out of a furnace and then fed them into the coiler. But most of all I remember the man on the other side of the coiler who caught the still hot spring with tongs and threw it over his head into a tank of oil where it landed with an impressive splash and an appropriate shower of sparks. I was now also hooked on manufacturing and soon would scour the AAA guides to see if there were any factory tours in any place we were visiting. Occasionally my badgering of my parents succeeded, and we went on one of those tours.

In contrast, in the mid-fifties, maybe 1956 or 1957, the family trooped out to O'Hare Airport to meet my father, again returning from a business trip in the East. Though brand new, the place seemed tiny when compared to Chicago's big airport, Midway Field. We could almost drive up to the terminal. At the top of the escalator, there were only two ticket counters and apparently two gates. I never became as fascinated by airplanes as I was about trains, except for the wonderful old DC-8's whose wing tips would slowly rise as the plane gathered speed. Air travel was antiseptic. You could see trains close up; you could see manufacturing, though not quite so close. I could not get close enough to airplanes to fall in love.

Later, in 1960, I reversed the usual pattern for a college-bound student; I stayed in Chicago while my family moved away. Still, like many other kids I took the train home for Christmas. What I noticed most about this, and many following trips, was how dingy and crowded the trains were compared to those of my dreams of train travel. I spent seven years at school in Chicago, always traveling the Illinois Central to the family home. As I went back and forth, I watched passenger travel slowly get worse as first, the wonderful dining car with the white linen tablecloths and napkins and the nice china and heavy silver (surely plate) service disappeared, then the parlor car with individual swiveling seats vanished, and finally even the club car was gone.

During these years and the five when I played lawyer in Chicago, I also watched the beginning of the slow collapse of manufacturing in the Midwest and the even further decline in the fortunes of the railroads. When I got to Buffalo in the fall of 1973, I saw much evidence of the decline in manufacturing in the Northeast. I also had occasion to sample train travel again. Every other week in the spring of that academic year I went by train to visit my wife, who was finishing a degree at Yale. I left from Buffalo's glorious 1929 railroad terminal, its enormous concourse reduced to near silence as but two of the original twenty-five tracks, one from the east and one from the west, were still in use. The only good part of that depressing set of trips was the Oyster Bar in the basement of the Biltmore Hotel right next to Grand Central Station, a throwback from an earlier time (a tip from my father I might add). By then I should have understood that I was going to write about law and economy in the Twentieth Century. I was just too dumb to know it yet.

It should be reasonably obvious to anyone who has read this far that I grew up in a solid middle class American family—one of the few kids in my urban public high school who "went away" to a private school for college. From a young age it was expected that I would do so. My father, though not a college graduate, was a divisional accountant all of his life. And though it was said that he knew how to fix cars, I never saw him do any work that might have required getting his hands dirty, other than check the oil or change a tire, which he never did again after driving me to college the first time, as he more than once reminded me.

One grandfather, trained as a baker, worked most of his life for the postal service. He ended his career as head of the dead letter office in Chicago's main post office because he was unwilling to stump for the Democratic Party, which was a requirement for promotion. In contrast, my other grandfather was a plumbing salesman who represented the Democratic Party as an alderman in Chicago. I doubt that the two got to know each other.

Neither grandmother ever worked outside the home. My mother, who had a bit more college education than her husband, worked for several years as the personal secretary to the president of the Benjamin Moore Paint Company. After she was married, she worked many days, but was never paid for doing so.

While by upbringing, I could be expected to be, and in fact was, interested in finance—though as was the case with all good middle-class families then, money was never discussed at the dinner table—it is important to understand that for me, manufacturing and the men who did it were an essential part of middle-class life. I never wanted to toss that hot-wound coil spring up over my head and into the oil bath and so make the sparks. That was hard, dirty, dangerous work, and I had no interest in it. But it was honest labor done by honest men.

These men were an important part of the economy; their lives and families were too. It was a triumph for the United States to make a bunch of working stiffs into members of the middle class, if only barely. Doing so stilled the fear that all of the paper pushing—of financing, of management, and of law—was not really very real. Steam engines and the boxcars full of the products of manufacturing that got put in them had a comforting tangibility. Diesels, like airliners, were incorporeal in their bloodlessness.

It did not hurt that my father was always more comfortable with the guys in the factory than with the other managers, and he made this perfectly clear to me at least as often as he told me he would never again change a tire. I, too, prefer talking with the grunts who make the work move and with the middle managers such as my father whose jobs consist of translating between the workers and the leaders. My good friend, Tom Headrick, understood where value was to be found in organizations, though he never put it quite this way: Paint the fence; paint it very well. However, remember; it still is just a fence. Someone worked hard to put it there.

Family and class are thus among the most important values that have shaped this manuscript. Thomas Wolfe was right when he wrote, "You Can't Go Home Again," which is a good way of putting the historian's deep sense of the pastness, the foreign-landness, of the past. So, I write first to explain to those who did not experience firsthand an America that I knew, and that I saw mostly disappear from the passing scene, how its economy came together and why it fell apart. Second, I write for those who, sensing that something vital in our society has been lost, are trying to bring what they call "economic development" to what were once vibrant areas dominated by steam transportation and heavy manufacturing. Both groups profess that they understand that you can't go home again, but seem not to understand why. Hopefully, revisiting that past for insight into how economies form and are transformed will help each to advance their separate projects in present economic circumstances.

So much for my past and intentions. It is time to work for my readers.

WHILE WAITING FOR RAIN

Man lives from choice in the framework of his own making, trapped in his former achievements for generations on end.

—Fernand Braudel, Civilization and Capitalism
15th–18th Century

Economic life develops by grace of innovating; it expands by grace of import-replacing.

—Jane Jacobs, Cities and the Wealth of Nations

Introduction

On Common Misconceptions and More

IN THE MIDDLE OF the no longer recent great collapse of the American economy, Tom Toles, the wonderful *Washington Post* editorial cartoonist who started his career in Buffalo, produced a cartoon occasioned by the grand reopening of the American History Museum in Washington. In the cartoon, people gather around a domed exhibit, a model of a common suburban house with mom and dad and two kids standing for a formal portrait outside the front door, their two cars in the open garage. The legend on the exhibit reads, "The Postwar Boom 1946–2007." In the corner, a child asks her parent, "Did that really happen?"[1] This is a great bit of cartooning, except for one fact. The postwar boom gave out by 1973, if not earlier. By about 1985, the American middle-class family experienced economic life significantly different from the way that their postwar forebears did.

Similar common misconceptions about our national economy abound.

1. The Fifties[2] economy demonstrates the unmatched ability of American manufacturers in producing quality consumer goods inexpensively.
2. The decline of the American manufacturing economy is the result of greedy unionized workers who wished to be well paid for doing little.
3. The rebirth of the American economy would be guaranteed were we simply to reduce taxes and eliminate regulations.
4. The rebirth of the American economy would be guaranteed were we to stop the financial gutting of American companies by executives, banks, hedge funds, and private equity investors.
5. The future strength of the American economy can be guaranteed by investing heavily in (fill in this blank with your favorite newness).

Many partisans of local economies similarly believe "a lot of things that just ain't so." Consider Buffalo. Most of the locals believe:

1. In the Fifties, the City of Buffalo had a great, sustainable economy that unfortunately went downhill when the New York State Thruway, the Saint Lawrence Seaway, the suburbs, and high labor costs sapped its vitality.

2. The Buffalo area has lost the manufacturing jobs essential to a growing economy.
3. The decline of the City of Buffalo's downtown impeded growth in greater Buffalo because a healthy downtown is essential to any thriving community and so the recent modest revival of downtown Buffalo is evidence that growth is returning to the area.
4. The undertaking of great public works—parks, buildings, bridges, stadia—is an essential catalyst for economic growth in this or any other area.
5. The decline in the Buffalo economy that has caused young adults to leave the area must be remedied by building an economy that will motivate them to stay.

These days misconceptions are most often attacked by either scholarly apparatus or by tendentious argument. There are other possibilities. One is the essay, and this book may be best seen as a very long essay. But what kind of an essay? It is not an essay about the economic development of either the United States or Buffalo. Rather, it is simultaneously about the American economy and Buffalo's too. To understand either, one needs to look at both. Each story illuminates the other, for it is the contrast between them that raises questions about the process of economic change and possibilities for community economic redevelopment, aided, as is always the case, by governments, and so by law. Thus, as a book that is simultaneously about community, economy, and law, it is an essay that attempts to think about what can be learned from within such disciplinary categories, but without the limits that each separately imposes on understanding.

This book is structured around two questions that have occupied Americans for thirty-five years or longer. The first is: What happened to the Fifties economy and the communities that experienced it, and why? This question is essentially historical because effective action directed toward redevelopment requires an understanding of both local economic history and that of the larger entity within which it is located.

The second is: Why have we have been unsuccessful at recreating the Fifties economy and those communities that thrived in it, despite our attempts to bring about economic redevelopment? This question is essentially a matter of political economy—a mash-up of economic, historical, legal, political, and sociological understandings of lived experience—because effective redevelopment requires an understanding of the present circumstances, both national and local, and of those economic activities that might be taken for development but are inimical to it.

The answers to these two questions are presented in five Parts of variable lengths. Each of the first two Parts present a relatively long story and accompanying commentary that attempts to answer the first question. The final three Parts attempt to answer the second question, initially by understanding how economic development takes place, and thereafter by exploring both national and local conditions since, for good or ill, most communities experience economy locally. A brief conclusion follows.

All five Parts are framed by two epigraphs. The first is from the great historian, Fernand Braudel: "Man lives from choice in the framework of his own making, trapped in his former achievements for generations on end," which makes it clear why accurately understanding ones' economic past is important to shaping an economic future. The second is by the great urbanist, Jane Jacobs: "Economic life develops by grace of innovating; it expands by grace of import-replacing," which, by linking the economic concepts of innovation and import-replacement with the discordant concept of grace, clarifies that a history of growth and development is not sufficient to explain the episodic structure of economic life.

Part I—Law and Economic Change in America

This Part tells the story of the intermittent economic growth and equally intermittent decline of the United States after the Civil War. These years saw repeated efforts by producers of goods and services—first industrial, later consumer—to control competition in order to avoid the risk of bankruptcy resulting from the introduction of new products or services, especially transportation services. These modestly successful efforts created various merged, then oligopolistic structures, sometimes supported by law. Despite periodic declines in overall economic activity, and one real depression, the national economy continuously expanded and the middle class too. Then, after World War II, the domestic economy flowered gloriously. Identified with high wages, low unemployment, and high-priced goods, this Fifties economy saw continued expansion of the middle class and the upper reaches of the working class became middle class too.

However, this success at creating a stable economic structure was dependent on the nation's relative insulation from the world economy following WW II. That force for stabilization had disappeared by 1980. Recurrent efforts to reestablish such stability have regularly failed. As Braudel would have predicted, it is the Fifties economy that most haunts the United States.

Part II—Community and Economic Change in America: Buffalo, Queen City of the Great Lakes

This Part tracks the development of the Buffalo economy over the same time period. Once a gateway to the West and later a great rail hub, Buffalo's history parallels that of the nation up through World War I. Like most of the cities in the Northeast, as Buffalo's industrial and consumer manufacturing base grew, its population exploded with immigrants. These individuals gathered in dense ethnic/religious pockets. However, mergers and a growing oligopolistic market structure left Buffalo without the headquarters of any large corporation. In effect, it became a branch-plant town. After the Fifties most of the branch plants closed, just as they did elsewhere in the Rust Belt. Growth occurred primarily in government and service jobs. As Braudel would have predicted, it is also the Fifties economy that that most haunts Buffalo.

Part III—Thinking about Economic Development

This Part explores suggestive bits of political economy written by the urbanist Jane Jacobs in her books *The Death and Life of Great American Cities*, *The Economy of Cities*, and *Cities and the Wealth of Nations* in order to construct an understanding of economic change, of growth and decay. Jacobs focuses initially on the role of a city's innovations and exports as the means for bringing economic life to local communities. She considers the assistance that others may offer, particularly subsidies paid to poorer regions and the promotion of trade between advanced and backward economies, to be as "transactions of decline." Four troubling concepts underpin Jacobs understanding of economic change: *nature* as the ordinariness of productive tinkering; *grace* as a gift or blessing that is unknowable, unbidden, and undeserved; *the invisible hand* as a possible force in innovation; and *drift* as a fact of economic life.

After examining each of these concepts, the strongest pieces left in her analysis are the importance of export creation and the necessity of avoiding transactions of decline and the political impossibility of not engaging in such transactions in a relative democracy. In the end, the inability to specify the circumstances under which economic development takes place makes it difficult to identify redevelopment strategies. One palatable alternative might be focused on making any community attractive to all of its residents, in recognition of their collective participation in rebuilding that community. Such a strategy has the advantage of possibly ensuring that a community's attractiveness to the middle classes, admittedly not the most attractive or needy group of residents, who might bring economic development with them. Such a strategy can best be seen as action taken while "waiting for rain;" as such, it reappears in the final two Parts.

Part IV—Consider Buffalo

This Part begins by first comparing Boston's economic history to that of Buffalo, Cleveland, and Pittsburgh, as part of a broader attempt to identify the economic, social, and political conditions of Buffalo and its region, the position that Braudel identifies as being "trapped in . . . former achievements for generations on end." After the city's branch plant economy disappeared, the region's ethnic communities remained, though almost all but the African Americans dispersed to the suburbs. Voter demand for the replacement of lost jobs pushed elected officials into a continuing search for branch plants; the decline of the local tax base led those same officials to rely on transfer payments from federal, state, and even county government. As Jacobs might have predicted, these "transactions of decline," designed to shore up an employment base in poor or lower-middle class neighborhoods, failed to rebuild Buffalo's economy, exactly as was the case in other Rust Belt cities. Limited strengths, structurally difficult politics, and an, "I get mine too" mentality only made things worse. And so, the Buffalo community has been left to wait for the possibility of "grace," or as the title puts it "rain," even though local politics have created an imperative to act.

What then might Buffalo do were there at least modest funds available for investment into the community? If Jacobs is correct, the two possibilities that come most quickly to mind—investment into the poor, the neediest class, or the lower middle or working class, the most directly affected by the collapse of the local economy—are unlikely to do much toward making Buffalo or similar Rust Belt cities an attractive place to live and work. More plausible would be to attend to the wants, though not needs of the upper parts of the middle classes, a not particularly attractive target for governmental largess. Still, attention to their demand that their communities be safe, clean, and beautiful and that their children be well schooled by a government that does its regulatory job quickly and predictably, might redound to benefit all citizens by providing a reason for the individuals who might create opportunities for economic development to come and stay, while at the same time making the region more attractive for those left behind should such "rain" never come.

Part V—What Then about America

This Part also begins, as Braudel might, with a recapitulation of the economic history of the United States from Part I, in order to identify the economic, social, and political conditions in which Americans find themselves. This review notes the country's limited strengths—agriculture, transportation, education—great weaknesses—oligopoly, reliance on finance—and fractious political structure, as well as the difficulty of maintaining a consumer economy, dependent on imported goods for its continuation, without undercutting the economic opportunities of those whom it most benefits. Equally important, this Part makes clear that questions of economic change in such a large place as the United States are mostly reflective of local conditions—and their impact is largely local as well. Despite the overwhelmingly local nature of the economy, the fivefold division of social status nationwide—the poor, the lower-middle class, the middle-middle class, upper-middle classes, and the upper class—allows each group honestly to believe in the effectiveness its own set of federal level remedies to improve the economy, even though all remedies are likely to be ineffective on all but a few local levels.

After suggesting the implausibility of relying on both "do nothing" and the "do something" prescriptions for economic development as a substitute for Jane Jacobs's ideas, discussion turns to a contextual analysis of three common prescriptions offered in political debate—tax cuts, minimum wage increases, and subsidy removal. All are rejected because of their indeterminacy as a result of the marginal, and so limited, impact on various social segments, as well as the deeply situational distribution of these benefits. Such difficulties are an example of the real limits of law to structure markets and direct economic change.

When one goes to law to address an economic or social problem, only sometimes does law even pay attention. Often law delivers aid different from that requested. In either case, only sometimes does the aid delivered successfully address the problem. Delivery of the desired aid may even make the problem worse, just as the delivery of aid not sought, perhaps even resisted, may address the problem. Such seemingly random results are not evidence that going to law is a crapshoot; rather, the range of actual results shows that the interrelations between community, economy, and law are more complex than any form of policy analysis can comprehend.

In circumstances where legal action is likely to be overwhelmed by social structures, what action taken at the national level might be a sensible response to citizens' desire for economic redevelopment? Here, as in Part IV, national funding for local efforts to address the provision of middle-class amenities is a sensible starting place. If designed to make local citizens, both current and potential, feel welcomed with choices among safe, clean, and beautiful living conditions in which children are well schooled and government sensibly expeditious, such action would be a sensible use of federal largess. Indeed, such funding, were it implemented in the spirit of avoiding harm, offering help, and promoting change, while being sensitive to complexity, would be a plausible place to start in building the local economic resiliency that most communities thought they once had and still desire. And, at the very least, it may create a pleasant place to be "while waiting for rain."

Is Conclusion Even Possible?

The conclusion offers four observations. The first asserts that rooting analysis of economic growth and decline in communities, and not in larger entities, is important because it is in such communities that people build a hopeful, stable life. A key question for America going forward is why places like Buffalo, which so closely tracked the national economy, lost its tie to that economy. The second explains why the Fifties in Buffalo and elsewhere were anything but "The Last Fine Time," as Verlyn Klinkenborg put it, why rebuilding that past economy is impossible, and why building a new economy that, like its predecessor, would create a wage-earner or hourly middle class, would be a good, if difficult, thing to do. The third suggests that given the certainty that economic life will change, that economic development is a matter of waiting for rain, and that the uncertain effects of any action by law (which is to say government) may accomplish, it is probably best to seek government funds to make our communities better by supporting by a broad middle class. The fourth asserts that when choosing even this modest action, it is important to remember the time-boundedness of our present ideas, built as they are on past experiences, and so to be careful not to attempt to recreate a past that is but poorly remembered in order to meet a future that is quite likely to be unknown.

After this conclusion, comes "A Note for Historians."

In aid of those readers who are willing to continue even after reading this introduction, my good friends and readers Tom Disare and Phil Halpern have suggested that this is not a book designed to be read straight through. Rather, it is best absorbed in twenty-five or so page chunks and with clean breaks between the individual Parts. It is unlikely that they are wrong and so there are plenty of places where the reader may pause—subheadings and, within them, subsections identified with a typographical ornament, such as the one above.

PART I

Law and Economic Change in America

IN 1815, IT TOOK two-and-a half days for news of Wellington's victory to be transported from Waterloo to a British cabinet meeting in London two hundred miles away. If that battle were refought in 2022, Lord Liverpool's cabinet would be able to watch it on their cell phones in real time complete with commentary from on-scene reporters—"Yes, I'm right here with Uxbridge's Heavy Dragoons awaiting their call to battle. One of their officers is here with me. 'How does it feel to be facing off with the battle hardened French cavalry?'"—and analysis of its progress or prospects from assorted, assertedly expert, talking heads—"Well, in your opinion General, will Wellington's forces be able to hold their right flank at Hougoumont?" And had Andrew Jackson's troops been at New Orleans in 2015, CNN would have televised their rejoicing when they received notice of the signing of the Treaty of Ghent on December 24, rather than reporting on a battle fought two weeks after the War of 1812 was ended.

No one is unaware of the momentous changes of the past two hundred years, which is not to say that these changes have always been welcomed, much less always comprehended. Often, they are decomposed into changes in an economy, often understood as changes in technologies, and changes in social life, the lived experience of groups of humans, or the "community" of this book's subtitle. Of late, such decomposition often includes changes in law, usually understood as legal rules. And argument about the direction of causation between the various decomposed parts can be had for the asking.

In the interest of getting the basic story of community, law, and economy in America straight, it would be best to set aside arguments about causation and instead to treat change naturalistically, as something that just happens for obvious, even surface reasons, and to save the focus on community for the discussion of Buffalo in Part II. However, some preliminary matters cannot be put off so easily. It is important that readers know the particular, even "peculiar," sense in which I will use "the/an economy" and "law," so as to minimize any confusion with other possible meanings of these terms. By "the economy," I mean *a persistent market structure that is the fusion of an understanding of economic life with the patterns of behavior within the economic, political, and social institutions that enact that understanding.* In contrast, by "an economy," I mean such a market structure that at a time seems likely to be persistent but in retrospect turns out not to be so. Economic life thus may change, indeed does change all the time, without necessarily implying that there has been a change in "the economy," an enacted understanding of economic life. And by law, I mean *the many and variable actions undertaken by lawyers and other governmental officials, the formal and effective norms originating from the practices of these individuals, and the systematic presuppositions shared among them.* This is a broad definition of law, though not a boundless one.

Here, I wish to save my readers the time and trouble necessary to tease out five things that I generally believe.[1] First, I accept Schumpeter's assertion that capitalism is a constant process of "creative destruction."[2] To the extent that it is active, capitalism destroys the existing social and economic relationships of people and communities, creates new ones and, in the process, turns some previous winners into losers and some losers into winners. Other winners continue to win, and other losers continue to lose. There often are patterns to these wins and losses.

Second, capitalism is most intensely engaged in creative destruction at times and places where a concatenation of discoveries, improvements, structures and/or inventions come, or are put, together to form what Fred Konefsky, somewhat ironically, calls "a technology of freedom."[3] A good example of such a technology is the proliferation of bridges, canals, turnpikes, and water-powered factories in the northeastern United States in the first half of the Nineteenth Century. These created the mill town capitalism that doomed local artisanal production. The development of such a technology brings the freedom for some to engage in activities that could only have been dreamed of before, at the same time that it effectively extinguishes the freedom of others to continue their life as they knew it before, simultaneously creating and destroying worlds, just as Schumpeter would have it.

Third, humans attempt to channel or forestall the creative destruction of capitalism, and so maintain existing relationships or to build seemingly better ones, by group or governmental action based on economic/social/political models of what a proper economy looks like. Such models are often proclaimed as, or even after, they are instantiated, an example of model making as apology.

Fourth, in the Twentieth Century the model current at any given time was one seemingly designed to keep the broad middle class of that time reasonably happy and reasonably secure. This is what one would expect in a relative democracy.

Fifth, while capitalism creatively destroys and humans hopefully build, the vagaries of life—what Willard Hurst called "drift and default,"[4] and also wars and their consequences, inventions, the discovery of human or natural resources, changes in the economies of others—regularly interrupt the designs of humans and governments, as well as the seemingly settled course of any then current capitalism. The result is what we see in retrospect as the economic history of a time and place. A part of that history follows.

Before 1865: An Archipelago of Island Agricultural/Trading Economies

To understand the post-Civil War American economy it is best to first remember the economy that preceded it, ignoring arguments about when the American Industrial Revolution began. The economy of the Early Republic was essentially agricultural, especially for those farmers located at a distance from major cities or major navigable waterways. This is not to say that there was no commercial or manufacturing activity. Both could be found. Port cities—Boston, New York, Philadelphia, Baltimore, Charleston, Savannah, and New Orleans—thrived on international trade, importing manufactured goods for the benefit of themselves and their hinterlands in exchange for agricultural exports, at least the ones that could be brought to the city without spoiling. In inland towns, trade followed the same pattern, though on a more modest scale.

Manufacturing in the Early Republic was primarily for domestic trade, carried on in small shops where the traditional labor hierarchy—master, journeyman, apprentice—produced traditional goods—men's clothes, boots, tack, wagons and wheels, liquor, flour, and building materials. There was also a good deal of manufacturing outsourced under a system where "manufacturers" would secure the pieces for a task and then find workers in the countryside, often whole families, who would agree to undertake the manufacturing task, or at times only part of it. This system was prominent in the production of clothing and of woolen cloth in particular. Inland, there was some mining, smelting, ironworking, and of course, timbering.

The crucial matter was transport. Long-distance transport by stagecoach was possible, though very expensive; by wagon, significantly more difficult even with the improvements made by the growth of privately run toll roads and the expansion of the network of post roads. Effective long-distance travel was limited to water, either along the Atlantic coast or inland on navigable rivers. Factory-based manufacturing was similarly constrained to places where rivers or streams could be dammed, and waterwheel-derived power transmitted through a system of belts and pulleys that drove machines. Thus, in the early years of the Early Republic, the country was effectively an archipelago of small, island economies scattered along the seaboard and up rivers, largely insulated from interregional competition, and likewise protected by surviving notions of a "fair price," then often enforced by local law.

This set of relatively stable relationships was overlain by a series of innovations that would ultimately transform economic relations. First came Robert Fulton's steamship, soon thereafter the Boston Manufacturing Company's factory for the production of cotton cloth located up the Charles River in Waltham, the first factory that to modern sensibilities would seem to be such. Next came the Erie Canal and its imitators. Thereafter, came the railroads and finally, Morse's telegraph.

The steamship reduced travel time, at least on streams that could accommodate it. As a result, it brought inland cities such as Cincinnati, Louisville, and Saint Louis, effectively closer to nearby settlements. For port cities such as New Orleans, Savannah, Philadelphia, and New York, the steamboat both compacted and expanded the size of existing inland markets, by reducing travel time. A collateral result was that, for a while, growth in the Northwest Territory predominantly continued to move inland from the rivers rather than from the Great Lakes.

The Erie Canal and its many kin likewise opened up less expensive, less uncomfortable, and less time-consuming transportation in areas previously remote. Sparsely populated areas began to fill in as people and goods traveled more easily to neighboring markets and even quite distant markets. Here again, the extension of existing waterways—for that is what most canals were—most often benefited port cities. Thus, the most successful of the canals, the Erie, brought modest improvement to Buffalo, its western terminus, by opening a water route to the Great Lakes, an alternative route for populating the Northwest Territories, and eventually for shipment of its agricultural produce. However, the biggest beneficiary was the port of New York, which now had a greater inland economic reach for its stream of imports as well as a less expensive route for the transport of grain from the Genesee Valley, south of Rochester, an area that became America's breadbasket, for a while at least.

The canals were largely government funded. This was only occasionally true of the railroads, which often paralleled the canal routes. Government support was usually limited to the power of eminent domain, a not insignificant governmental benefit, even though it came with the obligation to pay the landowner fair compensation. Railroads often opened interior areas where navigable waterways or canals were non-existent or impracticable. Indeed, a map of early railroads demonstrates the degree to which they were designed to reduce the time of travel between cities and potential trading partners; or to divert trade, such as can be shown from the first long-distance railroad, the South Carolina Canal and Railroad Company, whose more than one-hundred-mile route from Charleston to the northwest was designed to draw Savannah River traffic from Savannah to Charleston.

Though trackage grew to more than nine thousand miles in the twenty years before 1850, the following decade saw an explosion to triple that amount. Maps show that by this time railroad trackage, especially in the states of the old Northwest Territory, rather than expanding the economic reach of particular cities, was taking a grid-like shape designed to make sure that all areas of a state were covered, opening new markets for manufacture and agriculture. Equally important, the expansion of routes between eastern cities and midwestern ones meant that agricultural products, once moved by steamboat on the Ohio and Mississippi Rivers to New Orleans, were now diverted to the principal northeastern ports, especially New York. Aiding this transfer was the expansion of telegraph communication along railroad rights of way. It made coordinating long-distance train movements practicable, though gauge differences between roads, especially between roads in different parts of the country, made for complex interchange between lines.

In contrast, factories did not grow as fast. Even after reliable high-pressure stationary steam engines became available, which meant that manufacturing activity was no longer tied to waterways, employment in most factories remained small. Part of the reason for slow growth was that large steam engines worked best where the power produced could be applied directly to large-scale processes—hammers, blowers, and pumps. Another reason was that the available belt-driven systems for the distribution of power limited the size of facilities. And yet a third reason was the inability to take advantage of that baseline aspect of factory production in an economy that was not consumer driven—interchangeable parts. Thus, with significant exceptions such as the production of cloth and armaments, most manufacturing remained on something close to a job-shop basis. Craft methods dominated.

At this point some readers might ask, "What's law got to do with it?" Everything and often nothing. Start with "everything"—the great, mostly silent work of law constantly refines understandings of mine and thine, of property and contract, and of the institutional structures within which all of life is lived. These refinements are most often marginal changes in law. Though sometimes over a long period of time, what was at first marginal may become transformative—for example the shift in married women's property rights or the slow, partial transformation of the law of master and servant into the law of employer and employee. In this country, such refinements occur mostly at the state level. Traditionally, it is the job of the legal historian to chronicle and fix these changes in the collective memory, lest change be obscured.

In these years before our uncivil war there was much of this silent work of law going on. The law of contract underwent refashioning, and the English law of property grew increasingly simplified. The corporate form began to be more generally available. Some of it has obvious importance for the shape of local economies—the law of property with respect to the taking of land when a stream is dammed to create a millrace is a good example of such change. Konefsky's marvelous explication of the Charles River Bridge case is a good example of the occasional reach the Supreme Court.[5] But most legal change passes silently, noticed only in retrospect as patterns become clear, the law as a vast janitorial organization cleaning up after life.

And then there is the "nothing." One might easily claim that law did little during these years. At the federal level there were the tariff and thus the federal budget, the postal service and its post roads, the maintenance of ports and navigable waterways, but in these activities were a part of the great silent background of law; though at least in theory tariffs supported nascent manufacturing enterprises and in fact raised Southern anger. At the state and local level, other than the digging of canals, little can be pointed to besides local governments occasionally investing in railroad enterprises in the hope that their particular station would bring local prosperity.

Given the limited ability of local governments to act beyond the specific powers devolved to them by their respective states, and the limited tax base of the states themselves, canal digging was financed with bonds sold under the promise that they would be secured by the tolls collected, tolls that almost never came close to the debt burden. So, "nothing" should not be surprising. Similarly, the federal government of constitutionally limited powers and equally limited sources of revenue succeeded at only one of the two economic activities it attempted—the various land acts in the years following 1785 that helped populate the Midwest. But the other—the creation of a national currency not based on the coinage of such gold and silver that it could acquire for minting—was simply beyond its ability to sustain. The separate creation of the first and second Bank of the United States and the demise of each created much political heat but seems to have made little overall difference in how the country changed. If there weren't enough specie for the economy, then some substitute would be found. Maybe there were lower cost solutions, but multiple circulating bank notes would have to do.

Now, it would be a mistake to assert the existence of the economy as defined above—a persistent market structure fusing an understanding of economic life with patterns of behavior within the economic, political, and social institutions that enact that understanding—in the United States in these years. Though by far the greatest number of people in the country were engaged in agriculture tied to coastal trading activity, the United States did not have an agricultural/trading economy. It had a series of agricultural/trading economies, an archipelago of such economies, each reaching out to its hinterland, as advances in transportation made it possible, and connected initially by coastal trade, and later by a few cumbrous interregional railroads.

There surely had once been an agricultural/trading economy (as defined above) in most of the thirteen colonies and those separable economies persisted largely intact into the 1820s. However, three circumstances destabilized these disparate economies. The first was simply the Constitution and the Federalist drive to integrate the separate economies into a national one. The second was the gradual growth of manufacturing in the North, aided as it was by the extension of canal and then railroad transportation as well as general population growth. Growth in railroads implied manufacturing growth. It would have been implausible to import all of the track and cars and engines that growth in trackage assumed. The third was more complicated, predicated as it was on the existence of slavery.

The degree to which the country was not yet an economic unit that might have had a national economy is made clear by recognizing the possibility that there might have been two different regional economies in the United States, both agricultural/trade economies, but one of them built on slavery in the area south of the Mason-Dixon line as extended by the Ohio River. The great political story of the years after the United States terminated the importation of slaves is the story of the South's attempt to maintain a market structure and to make it persist—that enacted an understanding of economic life—the planter understanding—with the institutions that gave meaning to plantation life.

Paradoxically, as slavery drove the Republic apart, it drove each of these two regions—slave and free—together. Somehow, the logic of even partial union supported the slow destruction of the individual agricultural/trade economies that had been established in the states. Because partial union required connection across political boundaries that had been heavily influenced by the geography of ports and drainage, any unification of the separate Northern and Southern economies was not going to be based on river, canal, and railroad trade with the agricultural hinterland. Instead, it would be based on links between the commercial parts, the centers in each economy, and eventually on manufacturing, first in the North, then in the South.

Still, manufacturing growth alone does not make an economy into the economy, any more than agricultural/trading growth does. Growth needs to settle into a persistent structure for there to be more than an economy. Such stability was not to be had in these years. And so the war that was fought over the persistence of the plantation is thus the best evidence that there was no single American economy at this time, or for at least another eighty more years.

The Eighteen Seventies and Eighties: Competition and Its Avoidance

The Civil War brought destruction and loss of life in settling a great moral and political question, while perhaps ignoring the just compensation clause of the Constitution that the North was fought to preserve. War does such things. It also brought a suspension of the bimetallic currency standard with the issuance of the first national currency, the so-called Greenbacks. It also brought an increase in the national debt and the National Bank Act of 1863, which allowed the federal chartering of banks, whose ability to issue bank notes backed by government bonds provided a significant market for the war debt. Together with the National Bank Act of 1864, which created the Office of the Comptroller of the Currency as the regulator of national banks, and the National Bank Act of 1865, which taxed the notes of state-chartered banks, these bits of federal legislation created the possibility of a national paper currency, but not yet.

As is common in martial conflict, the Civil War caused both a great, though not commensurate, increase in economic output by both sides and a similar, though again not commensurate inflation in the price of goods and services and in the level of wages. After the War, Congress attempted to return to the bimetallic standard, fumbled, and produced a great deflation, painful to farm debtors and wage earners. Those who most directly felt this pain confronted more following the economic collapse of 1873, a similar contraction in 1885, and an even greater contraction starting in 1893, knew these decades as the Great

Depression. For others, the matter was not so clear. During the Eighteen Seventies, economic expansion was limited, trending up only for a brief period that allowed the adoption of the gold standard in 1879. Then starting in 1880, the American economy trended sharply up with only a dip during the period from 1893 to 1896. And even during the Eighteen Seventies, significant expansion in limited areas, particularly in transportation, was noticeable.

It was clear after the carnage was over that railroad building had continued while everyone's attention was elsewhere. The most famous bit of railroad construction in these years was the completion of the congressionally authorized transcontinental route shared by the Union Pacific and the Central Pacific, but the more significant work was the increasing density of lines in the area outside the old Confederacy, especially the push of lines across the Missouri River and the outward expansion of lines in Michigan, Wisconsin, and Minnesota as they followed the increasing density of settlement in those states. The comfort of passenger service had been modestly improved with the development of the first dining car services and the first sleeping car service. Freight service was smoothed with the beginnings of through service over cooperating rail lines, and mail service sped up with the first postal car that permitted sorting of mail picked up between major postal destinations.

The Eighteen Seventies also saw the first significant increase in trackage density in the South and a push west across the Red and the Sabine Rivers into the Southwest so that rail service stretched to the edge of the Great Plains. And the Eighties saw the construction of four more transcontinental routes, the completion of the first north-south route on the West Coast, additional infill to the edge of the Great Plains and the South and expansion into Kansas and Nebraska. All totaled, the network had expanded from 30,000 miles to more than 160,000 miles. This expansion was made easier by the general adoption of a standard, 4 ft. 8 ½ in. gauge, replacing half a dozen different track widths that complicated the interchange of trains. Standard gauge also served as the catalyst for the adoption of a system of uniform—to the railroads at least—time zones to make long-haul scheduling easier.

This expansion was funded with the aid of British capital and federal land grants, particularly the main lines to and along West Coast and many lines traveling east to west in Minnesota, Iowa, and states to their south; Wisconsin and Michigan; and Mississippi, Alabama, and northern Florida. This program had earlier funded the Illinois Central Railroad's route south from Chicago, which had been essential to the North's cause in the Civil War. Under it railroads were granted alternate sections of land on either side of a line's right-of-way. As the line got built, the railroad company could sell its sections to farmers eager to move west and so recoup part of the cost of that line; the farmers in turn created a ready market for rail service augmented by federal sales of the remaining sections. This program, plus the Homestead Act of 1862, filled the farm belt areas served by major east-west trunk lines and soon brought north-south railroad connections, known as the short lines, to serve agriculture there too.

Farming, especially subsistence farming, is a scary occupation bedeviled with large capital investments, large amounts of personal labor, and absolute dependency on natural events for its success. It was also a lonely occupation before the availability of gasoline-powered trucks. Farming a quarter section or even an eighth meant that one's nearest neighbors were still quite far away. The railroads, which also required activity with large capital investments, made remote farming possible but also presented another large, fixed cost—the cost of the transportation of crops to market, or more accurately, the cost of dealing with the elevator operators who aggregated the crops of many farmers into carloads to be moved by train to market.

Farmers soon learned that railroads priced their service lower for long hauls—where either the cost of service was less because of fewer switching expenses or competition from other roads would hold down price—than short hauls, where switching costs were higher and there was no competition. They also learned that railroads gave rebates from posted prices to large customers—Standard Oil was the most notorious beneficiary—who entered into exclusive contracts. And, in Iowa at least, railroads entered into pooling agreements whereby they shared revenues to diminish the possibility of price wars and reduce competition. Farmer outrage over the difference between long-haul and short-haul rates, rebates, and revenue pooling, boiled over into the Granger movement that sought regulation of railroad rates. The Granger campaigns succeeded in securing state regulation of rates of intrastate traffic in several states and regulation of rates charged by their other nemeses, the elevator operators. Ultimately, such regulation was nationalized as well as weakened with the adoption of the Interstate Commerce Act of 1887, which required "reasonable and just rates," addressed the long-haul/short-haul problem and established the Interstate Commerce Commission to superintend these provisions.

All of the talk about agriculture and the railroads during these years hides the emergence of the more significant economic shift away from an agricultural base to manufacturing. While agricultural products and productivity increased, they increased proportionately less than manufacturing output and productivity. Both were driven by territorial expansion, immigration, and second-generation population growth. While both economic sectors increased their proportionate use of capital goods as against labor, the share of the workforce engaged in agriculture declined modestly, while that of manufacturing increased significantly because there was simply more manufacturing being done.

The shift from agriculture to manufacturing also represented a physical movement from rural to urban. That movement, slow as it was at first, meant an increase in the need of, and so the market for, consumer goods. The invention of the sewing machine before the Civil War, when combined with the development of mass production methods for making uniforms in that war, created a market for men's ready-to-wear clothing that reduced the cost and increased the size of wardrobes for men of modest means. Similarly, the development of methods for sewing leather by machine both before and after the war over time reduced costs for the boots and shoes worn by these same men.

The effects of improvements in the production of canned goods for fruits, vegetables, and meat products, and of the development of the refrigerator car for the transport of dressed meat slaughtered in central locations by disassembly-line methods are less clear, at least in a world where canned goods were a middle-class luxury, as were ice boxes necessary for perishable items, and root vegetables were winter staples for everyone. In urban areas, daily shopping by one's servants was still a necessary norm. The appearance of Quaker Oats, the first generally available breakfast cereal, was more of a portent than it was of a clear change in anyone's daily life.

More clear was the benefit of the five and dime—Woolworth's was the first with staying power—and of the much bigger department store—Macy's, Marshall Field's, and Wanamaker's—in these years. These stores made goods cheaper and shopping more convenient. They merged the growing consumer targeted manufacturing (and importing) sector in ways that wholesalers supplying general stores really could not, because general stores simply did not do a volume of business that allowed them to stock such a broad range of merchandise. Here was a niche that was soon filled by the mail-order houses, the first of which was A. Montgomery Ward, established in the early Eighteen Seventies.

By no means the most significant, but surely the most interesting, of the new consumer products was the bicycle. In the mid-Eighteen Seventies, Americans began to imitate the French by producing high wheel, "penny-farthing," bicycles, ones with a large front wheel on the axle to which the pedals were mounted and a small back wheel. These creations were highly dangerous because they were very unstable and quite jarring when ridden on cobblestone streets due to their solid rubber tires. But that did not stop young men with money from buying them to show off. Then, in the mid-Eighteen Eighties, came bicycles that we would recognize as such—two equal-sized wheels, chain-drive rear wheel propulsion, and pneumatic tires. In short order, this version of the two-wheeler, often mass produced with assembly-line methods, replaced the high-wheel bike. With the development of a frame design that accommodated women in skirts, a bicycle craze hit the country, at least among the young and nimble who could afford such.

Manufacturing, protected by a tariff wall, was slowly shifting away from its traditional center in the Northeast as the population moved west facilitated by lower transportation costs with the expansion of rail networks to move goods. Thus, iron and steel production, and the manufacture of goods reliant on these materials, began to move from the mid-Atlantic into the Midwest. The exception that secures the rule is the movement of cotton textile production from New England into North Carolina, closer to cotton agriculture. The increasing use of steam power that made these transfers possible also led to the growth in the manufacture of capital goods, especially various machine tools, facilitated mass production and, correspondingly, for the decrease in the percentage of skilled labor in many production processes.

The growth of manufacturing in these years interacted with a westward expansion of agriculture to make America a magnet for immigration. A significant portion came from Germany, Scandinavia, and the United Kingdom. They engaged in farming, skilled and unskilled manufacturing, mining and logging, but also professional work. All but the English experienced degrees of hostility based on strangeness of language, dress, and customs, as well as a sense by earlier immigrants that the newcomers were taking jobs away from "native" Americans, or worse, were keeping wages down by their availability. Some immigrants stayed, some returned. In the aggregate, they seem neither to have facilitated changes in the American economy nor retarded them.

Partisans of the American labor movement might disagree. Though constant dollar annual earnings in manufacturing rose by 40 percent during these years, the workday shortened a smidge, and the work week stabilized at six days, the cause of organized labor did not prosper. During the Sixties, local craft unions strengthened, as did national federations within particular crafts and local federations of disparate crafts; but during the prolonged economic depression that started in 1873, membership waned as bitter strikes, most memorably the railway strike of 1877, were not successful. Many national unions disappeared, and their locals often became more or less secret societies that protected members from the blacklist. Lockouts and refusals to negotiate were common.

The experiences of unions in the Eighteen Seventies did not dampen labor's quest for control over the conditions of the employment relationship. With the pickup of economic activity in the Eighteen Eighties, a movement toward one big national union, the Knights of Labor, began to grow. The Knights appealed strongly to workers in the new, mass production industries, though it sought to enroll workers of all kinds. Growth in membership accelerated during the economic contraction in the middle of those years, especially in the aftermath of a successful strike against railroads controlled by Jay Gould. However, after this early success, the Knights began to lose membership in the aftermath of the Haymarket Square riot, even though it took no part in that event. Meanwhile, craft unions that felt unwelcome in the ranks of the Knights of Labor formed the American Federation of Labor (AFL). This group started small and grew slowly until after the turn of the century.

Again, the question, "What's law got to do with it?" comes to mind. Even after briefly establishing a national paper currency, facilitating the expansion of railroads, populating of the lands west of the Mississippi, and beginning railroad regulation, this question persists. The answer depends on what "it" is. Robert Wiebe speaks of the fifty years between the Civil War and World War I as embodying a "search for order."[6] He is not wrong. One can see this search in the effective dissolution of the archipelago of agricultural/trade economies in the Eighteen Eighties when railroad transport had mostly filled in the settled areas of the country with short lines rather than just occasionally bridging the main routes.[7] Still, to treat railroad expansion as evidence of the dissolution of an old order, and so a law-aided search for a new order, cannot be done without ignoring most of the old Confederacy. So, there were searches for two kinds of order: an old order destroyed by the railroads, and a new one.

The old order was one where competition was kept in check by the effective isolation between mostly small towns. This is the world where living together, as well as apart from others, allowed social relations to deter the price gouging that would come from monopoly. This is the world of fair price and of guild-inspired cooperation among multiple small producers of consumer goods such as bread or shoes or meat. One can see the attempt to restore this old order among manufacturing concerns in the larger cities with the creation of companies that include the name "union." Local competition in an area served by multiple producers drove all closer to the point where marginal cost equals marginal revenue, a place where capital is seriously at risk, especially when improvements in production processes required the purchase of expensive machinery to even compete. This is not a fun place to be.

The great Granger fights with the railroads and elevator operators were a similar search for ways of restoring a lost local order. Social constraints on competition were ineffective with respect to the railroads because they were not local. Though providing local service function, grain elevators along railroads were originally owned by the railroads and later subsidized by them and as a trading business they participated in an economic world outside of local social pressures. The local regulation of the price of elevator services was upheld in *Munn v. Illinois* and later with respect to intrastate railroads but was limited in effect by the commerce clause of the Constitution.

Some union activity in the large towns and cities is of a piece. However, most union activity, particularly the activity of the railroad unions, is part of a different search, a search for a new order—implicitly based on the proposition that the old order cannot be restored. These new economic circumstances are primarily a result of the expansion of the area of effective competition brought about by the growth of rail transport.

An expanded area of effective competition, or even its elimination, could bring great cost savings to consumers. For example, between 1865 and 1870, the cost of kerosene for oil lamps, the primary source of light before the widespread availability of manufactured gas, dropped from fifty-eight to twenty-six cents per gallon because John D. Rockefeller and his associates bought out or drove out of business, most of the northeastern manufacturers, then closed the high cost plants, suborned the railroads to secure low rates for transportation of their product, and reduced the retail price to discourage new entrants. But when really effective, most competition brought marginal price so close to marginal cost as to be quite scary for producers. To try to keep price above marginal cost, manufacturers tried two methods. One was the traditional cartel of which the "Iowa Pool," formed by three of that state's east-west trunk lines and active with varying degrees of effectiveness between 1870 and 1884, is perhaps the best known. The participating railroads agreed to share revenues as a way of reducing the potential profits of an individual road from a reduction in price built in to increase traffic.

Pools or similar forms of cartels were ineffective in the long run because the agreements establishing them were not enforceable in court. Producer response to the enforceability problem was to seek another way of attempting to keep price comfortably above marginal cost. First, a trust was created, an example of the usually silent work of law being brought to the problem of establishing a new order. Then, firms in the industry would then exchange their stock for a proportional interest in the trust that would be run by a committee of trustees. Profits would be distributed according to each firm's proportional share in the trust. Standard Oil pioneered this use of the ancient device of the trust, though for a slightly different purpose—that of gathering control of several of its constituent parts into one centrally administered whole. But quite quickly, other trusts were formed, most famously the Sugar Trust that at one point controlled more than 95 percent of the sugar market in the country.

The establishment of both pools and trusts assumes that competition is likely to be at least regional, and over quite large regions, in whatever economy is going to emerge, which more honestly would be to say whatever economy is going be created, now that the railroad had upended competitive relations limited to quite local areas. It is evidence of a wish to control what emerged. But beyond this, little more can be said. There clearly is no "it" around about which one might ask, "What's law got to do with it?" A possibly emergent order is no "it," except in dreamers' eyes.

Which is not to say that there was no law. When there is trouble in their surround, people, at least American people, go to law. The Grangers went to state legislatures for relief of what they saw as unfair extractions by the railroads and elevator operators. And when they learned from the Supreme Court that there were limits on the ability of the states to reign in the practices of the interstate movement of goods by rail, they went to Congress and secured passage of the Interstate Commerce Act. Similarly, once the railroads saw the way that the financial success of the Illinois Central Railroad was assured by the grant of federal lands in support of its construction, other potential railroad projects asked for and so received similar, or even better, deals from Congress than did the IC's backers. This is just what boosters already located in the western lands did when they went to Congress to secure modification of existing statutes governing the sale of federal lands, after they found that such statutes did not make purchase sufficiently attractive to secure expansion as fast as they might have wished.

Less obviously, local competitors went to state law, most often state corporation law, to create their "union" firms just as would the railroads when they later decided to create "union terminal railways" to operate the switching facilities for interchange between lines or for shared terminal facilities. And they availed themselves of state contracts law when establishing pools and state trust law when creating trusts.

And all sorts of people who worried about "the trust problem," the growth of large interstate corporations unamenable to state regulation because such would conflict with the Commerce Clause, went to Congress to secure the passage of the Sherman Act in 1890. However, going to law was not a wholly successful strategy in these or any other years. Law sometimes helps, but often does not as it is limited in its ability to foreclose the possibility that human ingenuity will create other circumstances and other understandings that will allow escape from law's language. Labor was rebuffed by law so many times that some parts of the labor movement argued that going to law was a bad idea. And when law helps, it sometimes supplies what was asked for, but just as often supplies something quite different. What it delivers may have the intended results, but often it does not. Indeed, perversely, sometimes law makes things worse. Pools fell apart. Local union firms soon were overwhelmed by competition from farther away; indeed, often such firms became the building blocks for later established trusts. Trusts often turned out to be unwieldy and brought more negative public attention than their organizers expected or wanted. None of these attempts at order created the stable, profitable, modestly competitive environment that businessmen claimed that they wanted. Federal support for railroad finance may have worked to facilitate construction and provide a ready market of people eager to use the new lines' services, but not always, and from time to time, competing roads were successfully constructed without it. Neither the Interstate Commerce Act nor the Sherman Anti-Trust Act of 1890, which attempted to deal with the trust problem by declaring "every contract, combination in the form of a trust or otherwise, or conspiracy, in restraint of trade" to be "illegal," turned out to work exactly as their supporters wanted or their opponents feared. Law is an ambiguous tool in the hands of citizens.

The Eighteen Nineties and Teens: Trying to Tame Competition in the Real Economy[8]

The years between the great contraction of 1893 and American entry into the World War I, known then as the Great War, were essentially good years. Jeffrey Frieden calls these years the golden age of "global capitalism".[9] The term promises too much, but the American economy grew fairly steadily, marred only by the Panic of 1907 that eventually led to the Federal Reserve Act in 1913. At the time this was a modest change in the banking system.[10] Limited inflation replaced the deflation of the twenty years earlier. Employment increased, as did immigration. Exports increased greatly, though they were still primarily agricultural. The first hints of the development of a large economy based on consumer durables could be seen, at least in hindsight.

Significantly, the American railroad system continued to expand, reaching its greatest extent in miles of track in 1916. Most of the additional trackage was infill, especially in the West and Great Plains, but two major lines, the last two major lines—the Great Northern line from Duluth west along the Canadian border and Henry Flagler's Florida East Coast Railway from Jacksonville to Key West—were completed. However, most of the growth in America's transportation network would be found in the development of new modes of transportation—automobiles and airplanes.

Though the first recognizable automobiles could be found in Germany in the late 1880s and in the United States by 1893, they were much like the early personal computers, for enthusiasts only. Just after the turn of the century, the market exploded. Many of the brands we now know or still remember—Oldsmobile (the first successful mass market car and the first produced on a recognizable production line), Cadillac, Buick, and Ford emerged, as did some luxury brands that have not survived—Maxwell, Packard and Pierce-Arrow (eventually the Chrysler), and some brands that only auto freaks know—Hudson, Jeffrey (later Nash), Oakland, REO, Studebaker, and Western. Many of these pioneer automakers had simply shifted from the production of wagons, small carriages, or more often, bicycles, to the newest gadget. In the years just before the war, two other long-lasting brands appeared—Chevrolet and Dodge. The real game-changer was the Ford Model T, eventually the first car produced on an automated production line and the first successful product targeted at working-class buyers.

Less successful, probably because its use was less obvious, was the airplane. Though the Wright Brothers had flown in 1903 and there were lots of people trying to build planes, endless fights over the Wrights' patents as well as the search for a better design meant that mass production was still a plant run of ten planes over several years. The U.S. Navy funded the development of the float or seaplane; the U.S. Army, the conventional trainer; neither supplied appropriations of any size until after the beginning of World War I. Once the French and Germans demonstrated the importance of the plane for combat, wartime funds created the possibility that a few firms might have staying power. Still, most planes produced for both services were licensed designs of English or French manufacturers. And even then, existing firms produced a large number of airframes, but got little engine business, as that was directed toward existing automakers—Ford and Packard, under the proposition that they already had mastered mass production methods.

The Great War expanded the market for medium trucks and created a new market for the light truck. While truck manufacturers such as Mack date back to the turn of the century, the market for delivery trucks did not attract major auto companies until the need for troop and supply transport brought Ford and Dodge into the business of producing these medium-weight vehicles. Chevrolet developed the light truck from the frame for the field ambulance. The alteration of the body style of the ambulance into the familiar cab and cargo bed created the pickup truck, a vehicle that would transform rural agricultural life once it was married to Ford's first low-cost, mass-produced tractor.

Even without these advances and even with the loss of the populist campaign for the unlimited coinage of silver, agriculture entered what is more legitimately called its golden age as soon as the depression of 1893 worked its way out. The rising price of agricultural products brought by modest inflation was magnified by the overall increase in demand for the cereal grains that dominated agricultural production. This demand was a result of the increase in the nation's population, especially in urban areas. A significant reduction in the rate of growth of acreage under cultivation, combined with the growth of productivity based on increasing investment in farm machinery, significantly reduced the percentage of the population engaged in farming. That exports increased, though the major export remained cotton, did not hurt either. All these factors worked together to increase farm income faster than the prices of the goods that farmers needed for increasingly large-scale production.

Unfortunately, the war over railroad pricing and regulation that farmers had waged, was not over. The Supreme Court quickly emasculated the Interstate Commerce Act and it took a change in administrations to fix the resulting mess. First the Elkins Act of 1903 restored the prohibition on rebates and the Hepburn Act of 1906 restored the ability of the Interstate Commerce Commission to set maximum rates. Finally, the Mann-Elkins Act of 1910 restored the prohibition on charging less for long than short hauls. Which specific railroads were secretly in favor of changes that probably established a reasonably stable structure for competition is a much-mooted subject. However, the Supreme Court in the *Northern Securities* case upheld an injunction barring the merger of the Northern Pacific, Great Northern, and the Chicago, Burlington and Quincy on the grounds that the resulting combination would have a monopoly of the northern routes to the Pacific Coast, and so violate the Sherman Act. This ruling effectively cut off mergers as the route to railroad stability, and so the new set of rules administered by the Commission was at the least an adequate second best for almost everyone.

But to raise the Sherman Act is to broach a subject far wider than the railroads, for these years encompassed what Naomi Lamoreaux has called "The Great Merger Movement."[11] The precise sequence of events and their meaning, while of great importance to historians of corporate law and of antitrust, is of less importance than the evidence they provide for the searching among lawyers and clients for a legal form that would avoid "ruinous competition"—and at the same time survive attack under the Sherman Act. The solutions that the lawyers offered, either by digging into their well-worn green bag—the trust—or after securing legislative assistance—the holding company and thus the interstate corporate merger—all affirmed the idea that it was only through some variety of cooperation/consolidation that the competition loosed on their world by the railroad could be tamed. This drive seems to have been given hope by the earliest Supreme Court cases suggesting that while pools and like devices would not survive antitrust scrutiny, corporate combinations would. Whether this understanding turned on a misreading of a fine point of chancery pleading, or whether the Supreme Court changed its mind when cases brought during the Taft and Wilson administrations led the Court to find that both Standard Oil and American Tobacco were monopolies in violation of the Act is not critical either. Since both firms were to be broken into constituent pieces, the answer was that monopoly was not the answer to "ruinous competition." Another avenue would have to be sought.

The most important change in economic life in these years was electricity. Though manufactured gas had replaced kerosene for home lighting some years earlier, Edison's direct current system quickly become a challenge to gas. The first home that used both his system and his incandescent bulb had been J. P. Morgan's in the late Eighteen Eighties. However, the practical advantage of Westinghouse's alternating current system was made apparent at the World's Columbian Exhibition in Chicago in 1893; its superiority for the transmission of electric power was shown thereafter by the delivery of power from Niagara Falls to Buffalo. Soon, electricity began to replace manufactured gas for outdoor lighting. Then came the wiring of entire neighborhoods, and so electricity replaced manufactured gas for home illumination too. With this change also came the first electric appliances—the iron, the toaster, the fan, and the vacuum cleaner. The production of recognizable consumer durables for upper-middle class houses was well on its way.

Of the many changes in industrial processes and products in these years, two stand out. Electric power made the electric motor possible. The late Nineteenth Century had been an age of steam power—the steam ship, the steam locomotive, and the steam engine. The latter allowed the movement of industrial production from river falls to any place that coal could be directed. But steam technology implied a continuation of the use of centrally powered, belt-driven processes. The electric motor allowed the organization of processes pretty much any way that seemed sensible. It also had the advantage of not needing constant tending. It was always there, always available when called upon. As power sources, motors could be scaled up or scaled down and so, once installed, most could be moved and even be swapped in or out as needs changed. Flexibility was the central premise of capital investment in electrically powered machines.

In contrast, the open-hearth furnace for the production of steel was quite inflexible. It required an enormous and fixed investment, couldn't be moved, and unless continuously run, required expensive further investment to be restarted. Its advantage was that it produced enormous quantities of high-quality steel, far more than the existing Bessemer converter process. Of course, the increase in quantity fit well with the increase in demand for steel in industrial and consumer goods. Unfortunately, when demand dried up, enormous mills shut down, putting enormous capital investments in peril, not to mention an enormous number of jobs and the communities dependent on them. Still, steel made America great.

The slow but steady proliferation of the products of Alexander Graham Bell's telephone system influenced both consumer and commercial processes. The telephone increased the immediacy of commercial life and of upper-middle class social life as well. It did not put the postal service out of business, however. Indeed, during these years, the postal service began rural free delivery and parcel post service, both of which made significant inroads into the railroad parcel business and provided further support for catalog purchasing in parts of the country where general stores still offered few goods and little selection.

Meanwhile, at the lower end of the social scale, immigration continued, even increased. While the previous wave of migration was primarily from of Northern, Central, and Western Europe, this new wave was primarily from Southern and Eastern Europe. While the earlier group had been largely farmers and skilled tradesmen, the later group's farmers, faced with a lack of arable land, largely settled in urban areas as unskilled laborers. These men (and they were disproportionately men) were swallowed up in the growing mass production industries, often at wages that were frightfully low, yet were still an improvement over what might have been expected in the old country. Their willingness to accept such low wages created more than a small amount of friction with skilled and semi-skilled earlier immigrants who were seeing their jobs disappear as machine tools continued to replace labor.

There is little doubt that the availability of a large pool of unskilled workers depressed the wages of manufacturing workers and caused a significant amount of opposition to immigration on the part of labor. Yet during these years, the inflation-adjusted wage of manufacturing workers increased modestly, though less than the increase in the productivity of those workers as a result of the increase in the use of machine tools. Working hours also declined modestly, though clearly nowhere near the eight-hour day and forty-hour week demanded by labor. Job security was non-existent, not just because of the enormous number of uncompensated industrial accidents, but equally from the irregular layoffs in response to changes in economic conditions.

As workers organized to address these concerns, the friction between skilled and less skilled workers continued to play an unfortunate role. In the aftermath of the economic contraction in the middle of the Nineteen Nineties, the AFL began to grow. It relied less on law and more on reaching agreements with the smaller manufacturers who still depended on craft labor, particularly in the construction, printing, and other narrow trades—for example cigar-making, the trade of the group's longtime leader, Samuel Gompers. The failures of the Homestead strike against the Carnegie Steel Company in 1892 and of the Pullman strike in 1894, cemented the AFL's emphasis on "business unionism" and aversion to relying on law for gains by labor.

The AFL's dislike of law, or at least the judiciary, was quite understandable given the record of the courts, both state and federal, in labor matters was anything but supportive. The willingness of courts to enjoin strikes, picketing, and boycotts, and sentence union leaders for contempt, was notorious. And when legislation protecting a union's, or even an individual worker's, rights could be secured, the willingness of courts to find such legislation in violation of the due process or commerce clauses fueled one of the great causes of the Progressive movement in politics.

At the same time, the AFL was not completely averse to adding to its membership by admitting to its ranks certain large industrywide affiliates. Notable additions were the United Mine Workers and the International Ladies Garment Workers' Union, both of which worked most often with relatively small employers. And the miners mounted successful strikes in 1902, 1910, and 1912. Still, employers increasingly resisted unions in general, and the closed shop in particular, and were horrified by the activities of the recently formed Industrial Workers of the World, ("Wobblies"), like the earlier Knights, a movement for one big union. Overall, labor did not succeed in improving its lot significantly.

That law is part of this story of extraordinary industrial expansion is a given. What is not obvious is the why. Consider the Bankruptcy Act of 1898. One might argue that the availability of comprehensive federal bankruptcy legislation would make individuals more willing to commit personal effort and funds to economic activity, except for two things. First, by this time, the corporate form was generally available to any person for most business purposes and so, complete insulation from personal liability was easily available except in those few states, such as California and New Jersey, where in the event of insolvency, creditors could force stockholders to contribute an amount equal to par value in addition to the original subscription. Second, the statute had no provisions for corporate reorganization. Such problems were left to the federal equity receivership, whose procedures had been modestly perfected as part of the railroad bankruptcies that followed the panics of 1873, 1884, and 1893.

This statute was not passed to protect corporate investors in a few states from being hounded by corporate creditors. But if not, it only dealt with insolvencies among partners and individual proprietors who had creditors in multiple states but who did not wish to litigate their claims in state court. By 1898, the economic integration of the country had become such that almost any entity of more than trivial size was likely to have a creditor somewhere other than that entity's place of business. Business failures likewise rose precipitously whenever the current economy took a significant downturn, as in 1893; still the partnership form was in the process of disappearing. That the statute was intended to clean up problems disclosed by recent partnership failures, or to protect owners of very large single proprietorships, such as Andrew Carnegie, is possible but ultimately seems implausible.

David Skeel's history of bankruptcy legislation suggests the great driver of the legislation was none of these but was due instead to the unhappiness of Northeastern creditors.[12] As regularly applied, state insolvency law allowed debtors to prefer local creditors over the interests of these Northeasterners. Western and Southern interests favored state law for precisely these reasons and so wanted no bill. The compromise that allowed the legislation to pass was worked out wholly within the dominant Republican Party and focused entirely on the question of filing of involuntary bankruptcy petitions and the lists of predicate acts, one of which would have to be proven in order to secure involuntary relief. Minor issues involved whether to employ a permanent bureaucracy to administer the statute (a clear nonstarter), and how to pay the people involved if these officials were not permanent bureaucrats. Curiously, the resolution of this latter issue turned out to be the most significant effect of the legislation. It led to the formation of the specialized bankruptcy bar that continues to exist today and, one might add, whose fees continue to be a matter of public controversy.

Or, consider the Morrill Land-Grant College Act of 1862, which established grants of federal land that each state might sell to establish a college that specialized in "agriculture and the mechanic arts." Written at a time when colleges regularly enrolled students at sixteen and even younger, and when it was mostly upper-middle class White men enrolled, it is hard to believe that the author, a congressman from Vermont, could have known that he was establishing the core of state higher education, much less the grand rivalries that made college football a national obsession. What did he and Congress derivatively believe that they were doing? Most likely they believed they were modestly increasing the ability of the states to offer something more practical than the classical course of study that was the backbone of college education.

These two stories tell something about law's help when it is offered. The land grant colleges were only somewhat successful at promoting science and the mechanical arts until well into the Twentieth Century. Schools of agriculture proliferated, but schools of engineering are not exactly what their founders meant by the mechanical arts. In any case, both branches of learning were significantly dwarfed by other parts of these universities, ignoring the racial politics that turned the agricultural and mechanical (A&M) or agricultural and technical (A&T) schools into schools for African Americans. And whatever the intent of the Bankruptcy Act of 1898, it is doubtful that anyone ever meant for it to become an assembly-line process for dealing with consumer debtors, as it had by the Twenties, and creating a specialized bar as part of its ministrations.

Thus, when trying to understand the relationship between law and economy, it should be remembered that often law just does not work well when viewed as a matter of intent, which is not to say that going to law is not an important element of the relationship between law and economy. Precisely the contrary. The relationship might be understood more fully by looking not at specific products of that going—the Bankruptcy Act of 1898 or the Morrell Land-Grant College Act of 1862—but by revisiting two stories briefly told earlier, one about labor and the other about management.

Consider first labor in the years before World War I. The story that is usually told is that labor was exploited by management trying to destroy worker control over the nature and pace of work. Workers organized to fight management but found that law constantly frustrated their efforts. There is nothing wrong with this story; it is close to the truth. But there is another story that fits better with Samuel Gompers preference for self-help, thus avoiding law. Management found that changes in transportation made old forms of competition, forms that allowed skilled labor significant control of the nature and pace of work, quite difficult and so invested in capital goods that allowed a reduction in the cost of labor. Labor responded with all the tools at its disposal—strikes, picketing, and boycotts. Management, hurt by these tactics went to law. Law responded with injunctions. In response, labor went to law. In some places law responded by enacting statutes protective of labor and so in support of its desire for better working conditions. Management then went to law to nullify those statutory protections. Labor then withdrew from the field and went back to self-help.

Though the time sequence does not fit precisely, the point does not require precise fit. In a modestly democratic government, when people find themselves put upon by present circumstances that they see as wrong, not necessarily against the law, but nevertheless wrong, they go to law. Labor tried this first, relying on its presumed legal freedom to organize—joining together to act for its own benefit—and then, when that didn't work, to seek legislative redress. Management went to law as well, twice going to the judiciary. Management was more successful than labor, and this is why the first story is the one commonly told, but there is this other point. Economic actors seek law's help when they think law will help them. (Of course, they will accept the help of others when that help is supportive and convenient.) The Progressive movement tried to help labor achieve something close to its goals. But labor had its own interests, and when Progressive reforms were unsuccessful, labor went its own way.

Similarly, as the railroads altered the scope of the markets that made up an archipelago of economies, destroying the comfortable terms of competition between manufacturers, the manufacturers knew that they were in for an unpleasant ride. Competition drives price to the point where marginal cost equals marginal revenue and that is not a secure place to be. Social constraints helped keep competitors from being individually rapacious in each island in the archipelago. To respond to this new set of circumstances, manufacturers first tried to bulk up locally, often using the corporation, which was becoming more common as the century ground on. This run to the law of business organizations proved to be ineffective. The railroads, which also were strongly impacted by competition, first tried contract—the pooling agreement—to limit competition, but it did not work. Purchase, the law of sales, was the next alternative for the manufacturers. John D. Rockefeller bought out his competitors in order to create a monopoly for the production of kerosene in the Northeast, all while using less than savory tactics to reduce prices and thus make it profitable to shut down some of the production capacity he bought. Monopoly was a pretty good idea for moving away from a world where marginal price equaled marginal cost. Others tried it also using that old legal form, the trust, a form that limited the cost. What the trust promised to provide was an enforceable pool.

In response, particularly to the repeated efforts of railroads to pool revenues and the nasty tactics of Mr. Rockefeller and his ilk, rural communities and small manufacturers supported passage of the Sherman Anti-Trust Act. This legislation didn't stop anyone from trying to escape from the point where marginal cost met marginal revenue. Some of these attempts were successful. In the *EC Knight* case, the Supreme Court held that manufacturing alone was not commerce and so creating an effective monopoly in the manufacture of sugar in the northeastern United States was not prohibited. In so doing, the Court also helped sanction that wonderful new invention of New Jersey law, the holding company, which was based on the legal principle that a corporation might hold the stock of another corporation.

Holding companies began to sprout like dandelions. Most included names that contained words such as American, Associated, General, International, National, or United States. Promoters of such holding companies expanded the game of "watering" stock, that is, issuing stock in excess of the value of the constituent parts of the corporate entity, and then reselling this stock at a profit. Still, it soon became apparent that the holding company was not the real key to the ability to control price; in another railroad case, the Supreme Court disapproved of the creation of a holding company monopoly among the northern railroads. This decision seems to have killed the appetite for forming more holding companies. Even worse, the ones that had made it through the Panic of 1907 soon found that the Supreme Court again refused to approve of the holding company structure. This time, it ordered two such companies to be broken up—the newly redesigned Standard Oil and the American Tobacco Company.

So far, I have told a story about the doggedness of the Justice Department and the various United States Attorneys in pursuing the objectives of the people who sought the passage of the Sherman Act. Except that this is not whole of the story. The remedy imposed by the Supreme Court, while busting the eponymous "trusts," left behind the effectively oligopolistic structure of American industry that, for the next forty years, kept marginal revenue comfortably above marginal cost and so, on a national basis, recreated in certain segments of an economy the friendly competition that existed locally in each of the country's archipelago of economies. The farmers and the small manufacturers got close to nothing in the end, and the large manufacturers got something that they and their lawyers never imagined, but that turned out to be serviceable for a while. And the railroads? By submitting to regulation by the ICC, they too secured a stable scheme of pricing, of comfortable competition, and an audience before which to settle their internecine disputes. Samuel Gompers was not a fool to be cautious about going to law.

The Twenties and Thirties: An Associationalist Ideal

At the end of World War I, the United States was the largest national economy in the world. Its greatest strength, aside from a substantial natural resource base, was its enormous domestic market tied together by a strong railroad network that allowed the country to be a relatively insulated, self-sufficient economic entity. This is not to say that the United States did not participate in international trade and finance. It was a key player in both areas. Rather, the size of the domestic market and its relative affluence meant that most manufacturers, and many retailers, had a market so large that they could grow to an enormous size based on transactions within the domestic economy alone, protected of course from foreign competition by relatively high trade barriers.

Given these obvious advantages, the economy's overall performance in the following two decades was surprisingly erratic, but overall, disastrously weak. A sharp postwar inflationary spurt was followed first, by an equally sharp recession and then, by a somewhat frenetic period of genuine growth. Thereafter, a general recession that began just slightly before the famous stock market crash of October 1929 terminated a classic market bubble, turned serious, turned into the Depression. Four years later, when the economy bottomed out, the unemployment rate was about 25 percent; prices, particularly of farm products, had declined significantly; mortgage foreclosures had hit record levels, as had bank failures; and not surprisingly, industrial production had plummeted too. For the balance of the decade, the economy grew slowly, interrupted only by a decline in 1937, though not to the level of its pre-Depression high.

If one factors out the substantial amount of noise in the economic record of these years, several significant changes stand out. The most obvious is the growth of an extensive consumer electric (though surely not electronic) appliance industry. In addition to earlier products such as irons and vacuum cleaners, three new products—the radio, the refrigerator, and the electric (as opposed to the hand-cranked phonograph—appeared as electrical service was extended to most urban and increasing numbers of rural households. Equally noticeable was the great expansion in automobile ownership, though here the impact of this growth was more significant in rural areas where auto ownership provided a significant opportunity to reduce isolation than in urban ones and where existing transit networks and shops within walking distance made the cost of ownership seem more of a barrier to purchase.

More invisible, but in the long run equally significant, were three more changes. The first was the almost complete absence of investment in industrial plant and equipment during the Thirties. Overcapacity and lack of demand in a deflationary economy made the decision to defer capital expenditures an easy choice. Indeed, the deterioration of plant and equipment was extraordinary in transportation, especially the railroads; heavy manufacturing, especially the steel mills; so-called basic industries such as coal, copper, or petroleum; and commercial products. The only real exceptions were in airplane manufacturing where a modest technological push is apparent; in consumer electrical products, particularly the aforementioned radio, the one consumer product that managed to spread widely in those years; and in the movies, where the advent of the talking picture brought investment in the technology related to the sound stage.

The other two changes were more promising—the slow development of the commercial aircraft industry, whose major success with the DC-3 began the increase in air travel in the late-Thirties; and the expansion of consumer services, especially in the Twenties, both in the financial area with the growth of the installment purchase of autos and appliances, and in retail trades of all kinds. Nevertheless, as the Thirties drew to a close, the economy of the Northeast was still dominated by heavy industrial production, such as steel, autos, electrical machinery, and by rail transport, all of which employed enormous numbers of blue-collar, variously skilled workers, in accordance with late-Nineteenth-Century industrial norms. The South was still largely an agricultural economy and the West, an agricultural and mining economy. Both thus provided low-value goods to feed Northeastern factories and mouths. The whole was stitched together with a railroad system that had already begun to shrink.[13]

With immigration cut off in a nativist reaction to the Great War, the ethnic makeup of the population was largely settled; immigrants and their families from Eastern and Southern Europe provided much of the workforce in the large industrial plants. This was the backbone of the working class. Northern, Central, and Western Europeans provided much of the white-collar workforce, staff, and line, that thought it ran the predominantly dispersed, divisional structure of large industrial corporations. These individuals dominated the middle-and lower-middle classes that numerically overwhelmed the upper-middle class of professionals and local owners of shops and small factories. At the same time, the growth of clerical functions in large industrial corporations and in service industries brought an increase in female, particularly unmarried female, wage labor, beyond traditional work in textiles and apparel.[14]

Such an economic structure was not wholly surprising, given the persistence of the large, turn-of-the-century, industry-specific mergers designed to create effective product monopolies. The firms that had resulted from antitrust intervention before the war, devolved into relatively stable oligopolies, maintained their production processes, and grew vertically to control supplies and distribution. At the same time, "discounters" or "chain stores"—national retail organizations such as the Great Atlantic & Pacific Tea Company (the A&P), Sears, Roebuck & Company, or Montgomery Ward & Company—began to establish branches in order to infiltrate local markets that had been previously insulated from competition by the still-significant difficulties of greater-than-local passenger transportation. The simultaneous growth of distribution through nationally controlled, sometimes locally franchised retailing organizations caused much consternation to local elites unused to more than incidental competition at the retail level. As a result, these local elites began to utter the same variety of complaints about ruinous or destructive competition and predatory pricing that had been voiced by those large manufacturers who sought refuge in the Great Merger Movement twenty-five years earlier. These complaints, which continued to be heard from producers in much more competitive industrial segments such as lumber, coal, and cement, coalesced in a movement that is commonly called *Associationalism*.[15]

Many economic theorists who supported Associationalism in the Twenties and Thirties, sometimes referred to as "institutional economists," believed that economic instability was the result of excess production of goods and services coupled with relentless downward pressure on producer prices caused by "chiselers," who reduced prices and otherwise "cut corners" for temporary personal advantage.[16] These economists argued that downward pressure on prices could be resisted if producers banded together into groups that would work both to "coordinate" production (i.e., manage reduction and expansion) and to isolate and vilify chiselers, so as to enforce good—and thereby suppress "unfair"—trade practices. This theory also held that insufficient demand in poor times could be remedied by increasing, not decreasing, employment, and by providing Social Security and unemployment insurance so that the disposable income of wage earners, and thus demand, could be maintained—a Keynesian prescription before John Maynard Keynes.

Associationalism was essentially a Main Street theory. It hoped to maintain high wages through the high prices that would support the small, local retail or wholesale businesses that were being undercut by the growth of so-called "discounters," large regional or national retailers, as well as the more competitive sectors of the producer economy. That there were few such discounters around in the Twenties and Thirties, except in groceries where the growth of the dreaded chain store was slowly destroying small neighborhood grocery stores, even as they banded together in buying co-ops such as the IGA (Independent Grocers Association), should not be held against the theory. Associationalism wanted an economy of uniform, high prices, such as that found in more oligopolistic markets or as was enshrined in the steel industry's basing-point price system whereby all steel prices were quoted as if the product were being shipped from Pittsburgh. This system denied distant, local producers locational monopoly pricing ability, but at the same time allowed them to make up in freight charges collected, but not incurred, the costs associated with their smaller scale, and so higher cost, production processes.

Yet it was not laissez-faire in a different guise. Associationalism assumed some level of governmental involvement in the economy, as befits a theory whose public champion was Herbert Hoover, first as Secretary of Commerce under both Harding and Coolidge, and then as President. Supported by the Federal Trade Commission, the theory required a crabbed construction of the antitrust laws to permit associations to perform their regulatory and disciplinary functions and to provide legal support for suppressing unfair trade practices. It also seemed to require high trade protection for American industries, and indeed these ideas are popularly associated with the Smoot-Hawley Tariff of 1930. When reduced to legislation, Associationalism regularly echoed Progressive concerns about the protection of small producers and ordinary workers, as can be seen in the first New Deal of the Roosevelt administration, in which Associationalism spawned the National Recovery Act and the Agricultural Adjustment Act and such seemingly unrelated legislation as the Social Security Act, the Wagner Act, the Fair Labor Standards Act, the Federal Housing Act, and the Robinson-Patman Act.[17] The prevalence of agricultural marketing cooperatives and state retail price maintenance statutes are of a piece. Surviving bits of the self-regulatory norm inherent in the theory still can be found in the New York Stock Exchange and the National Association of Securities Dealers, predecessors to the Financial Industries Regulatory Authority as well as the numerous bodies setting industry standards that exist in fields such as plumbing and electrical equipment. The theory can even be seen in Karl Llewellyn's early plans for the sales article of the Uniform Commercial Code.[18]

The Associationalist diagnosis of the problems of local business in the Twenties and of the Depression economy of the Thirties seems remarkably inaccurate.

For example, the growth of the chain store was spawned by the growth of automobile ownership in middle-class families, and so of an increase in point-to-point transportation options. The presence of private, personal transportation meant that for some middle-class buyers the effective geographic dimension of the economic market had increased beyond that of the neighborhood, which because it was limited, also limited price competition. A geographically wider market meant that stores could stock an expanded range of products for the larger potential clientele, and that competition for that potential clientele was sharper because of the wider range of alternatives that the automobile made available. And increases in the availability of truck transportation made it possible to deliver larger quantities of any given item to the larger stores by integrated grocery suppliers, thus lowering unit costs and costs to the consumer.

Moreover, the continued growth of the downtown department store, an entity that by 1910 had offered an even wider selection of goods than did chain grocery stores, had already undercut the neighborhood economy for middle-class consumers. The downtown department store had grown with the improvement in public transportation that came with the development of electric street railways. Home delivery of purchases, available by about this time, eliminated the need to carry any more packages home than the customer wanted. By drawing people downtown, the department store pulled shoppers away from the smaller, local department stores found in most major city neighborhoods. The lesser objection to these developments seems to be based on the fact that even the downtown department stores were locally owned, not brought to town by outsider, national chains.[19]

Accurate or not, the managed, Associationalist market was a prominent economic ideal in the years between the wars. However, that ideal had another side. Stabilization of prices at high levels and control over the introduction of innovation protected the market position of large producers as well as small retailers. For such producers, Associationalist theory could be seen as justifying classic cartel behavior, behavior that in Europe led to collusion with large trades' unions and to industrywide bargaining, still epitomized by the metalworkers' union in Germany. The American version of the cartel model supported the relatively static competitive position of participants in the more oligopolistic markets, but ignored unions until the National Labor Relations Act tried to shoehorn them into the model when building on the first War Labor Board' policies in World War I. Under oligopolistic competition, leading firms, in effect, negotiated price publicly and then strove to avoid undercutting that price. Simultaneously, they used their research staffs and advertising to generate product differentiation that might alter market share in their favor, always dreading the possibility that a competitor would develop a breakthrough product that could remake current, reasonably stable relationships in unforeseen ways.

Although Associationalism, as a theory, preferred the private organization of markets implicit in the ideal of an association, it just as clearly recognized that stable economic relationships that yielded high prices, high wages, and continuous profits could be established by governmental regulation. Thus, it could support a regulatory response to the widely felt sense that a weak and speculative financial system was a contributor to the Depression. The extension of speculative credit, especially in the real property and securities markets, was viewed as unfair, as were widespread self-dealing, manipulation, and even fraud in bank lending practices and in the underwriting of securities issues and their trading in the stock market. These problems and the large number of bank failures and ineffective state bank regulation, led to significant federal legislation directed at boosting confidence in the financial system, legislation that, while often supporting the Associationalist ideal, supplemented it with a national regulatory role. The Banking Act of 1933, which included provisions known as the Glass-Steagall Act, requiring a separation of commercial from investment banking, and other pieces of legislation establishing the Federal Deposit Insurance Corporation, Federal Savings and Loan Insurance Corporation, Federal Home Loan Banks, and the Federal Farm Credit Administration, were all designed to increase the soundness of the banking system. They created the stable, profitable relationships among the providers of major sources of credit for an economy long favored by Associationalism's theorists. The legislation establishing the Securities Exchange Commission and securing for it the means for regulating the securities markets based on a principle of disclosure and of penalties for nondisclosure. The Securities Act of 1933, the Securities Exchange Act of 1934, and the Investment Company Act were structured similarly. Together, all of this legislation was designed to strengthen those institutions essential for the credit and investment expansion that would undergird recovery, and not incidentally, honestly finance both oligopolistic producers and Main Street merchants.[20]

The Twenties and Thirties further sharpen questions about the relationship between law and economic change. As one lists even a small part of the New Deal's legislation, one can quickly identify the response of law to economic dislocation. Local relief efforts were supplemented with funds supplied by federal programs mounted by the Works Progress Administration and the Civilian Conservation Corps, programs that are largely lost in the story of the economy in these years, but that were crucial for those whose hunger they reduced and shelter they supported. The great structural statutes in agriculture, banking, communications, labor, securities, and transportation that survived Supreme Court challenges as well as those that did not—the National Recovery Act and Agricultural Adjustment Act—also exemplify the way that law is mobilized in times of trouble. All were, or at least might have been, major changes in the doctrinal matrix. They can even be seen to have significantly aided the creation of the administrative state. That said, the role that these statutes played in economic change remains unclear.

Each of these great structural statutes changed the efficient market solution to a problem of supply and demand. Consider only two modest changes made by the Fair Labor Standards Act and the Trust Indenture Act. Both were classic Associationalist pieces of legislation based on that movement's diagnosis of underconsumption as the root of economic weakness and its penchant for picking up on unfinished Progressive causes. The Fair Labor Standards Act created the rule requiring time-and-a half for overtime for certain groups of workers. After adoption, it could be expected that such a rule would, at the margin, make employers respond to the opportunity to increase production by relying less on extending the hours of existing workers and more on increasing total employment. At the same time, the Fair Labor Standards Act's adoption of a firm rule worked toward minimizing the old problem of whether employers unfairly coerced employees to work long hours. The Trust Indenture Act yoked old problems even more directly to new objectives by establishing rules dictating fairer terms in the indentures that governed bond issues, terms with respect to trustee selection, notice to bondholders, and their consent to the restructuring of bond obligations. This was the only one of the New Deal securities acts that featured substantive regulation rather than mere disclosure. Such statutory provisions were expected, again at the margin, to increase the willingness of investors to purchase bonds because they knew that their interests would be more fully protected. However, the change in the efficient market solution to a problem of supply and demand at a hypothetical margin is like a tree falling in the forest unheard. Unless that margin is reached, legal change changes nothing in the economy. What passage of the law means is that a set of structures have been put into place that may or may not become relevant under future economic conditions, dependent as they are on future political, technological, even demographic occurrences.

But to notice the structural element in such legislation is to bring to the forefront the matter of the degree to which the New Deal statutory reforms enacted the Associationalist economy. Here, the answer is a resolute negative. The creation of potentially efficacious institutional structures is not enough to "enact" the economy. Consider the possibility that, contrary to fact, World War I had ended with a long-term truce among four or five countries whose manufacturing capacity remained in good shape and whose economies thus competed vigorously. There is little reason to believe that in such circumstances, circumstances in which relative insulation from the world economy would decrease as air and ocean transportation improved, the margin where any of these statutes would bite would ever be reached. These laws might well have been of antiquarian interest, but little else. Indeed, their notoriety today is a function of the fact that at some point, action within the institutions that they created actually took place, that the economic relations that they made possible came to pass.

Note, however, that even though a change of behavior at the margin may never take place, a change in legal entitlements may easily work a change in the distribution of economic resources. The Fair Labor Standards Act immediately made some employees wealthier, those whose wage gains were less than the cost of hiring additional employees, especially where slack demand or capacity constraints effectively turned the choice to hire additional employees into the choice to begin a second shift. And this increase in disposable income of individual workers may well have been enough to alter, as always, at the margin, the efficient market solution to other questions of supply and demand, most obviously those of clothing, food, and housing. But such an alteration is no more a change in an economy than would be the modest change in the market for legal services brought on by adoption of the Trust Indenture Act. Law changes lots of things in the details of economic life for the participants without bringing about a transformation of the economy, from one enacted understanding of economic life to another.

The Forties and Fifties: Associationalism at Work

Wartime mobilization, and then production, pulled the economy out of the Depression in ways that all the thinking and writing of economists and all the action of politicians could not manage. By taxing some, borrowing much, and spending it all to win World War II, the United States adopted a Keynesian solution to its economic problems, but out of necessity, not out of theoretical understanding, for such a theoretical solution was still rejected by most economists, as it had been during the Depression.

Total war meant that there were jobs for virtually everyone not actively engaged in the armed forces. However, the rationing and price controlling of most consumer products, combined with the termination of production of other products, meant that wartime wages were, by default, largely saved. Savings took place elsewhere, too. Investment in plant and equipment was directed solely to war production. Even there, investment was limited by a clear preference for lowest cost solutions to any problem. This preference often meant that firms made do with old technology, patched and mended, rather than invest in the new and possibly better, at least unless that technology met a critical war-related demand. Still, the innovations that the war spawned were notable—synthetic rubber, radar, sonar, separation of uranium isotopes using the hexafluoride compound, and the vacuum-tube-dependent ENIAC computer—but changed the daily lives of Americans very little during those years. Much more significant was the wartime spread of military installations and, to a lesser extent, war production plants in the South and West that began to break the agriculturally based colonial economy of the former, and the agriculture and natural resources-based colonial economy of the latter.

Wartime economic practice continued to support the Associationalist bent of the economic/legal understanding of the period that preceded it. If anything, the war accentuated this. Given the inflationary pressures that came with a sharp growth in total wages and the wartime price control mechanism that was designed to deal with those pressures, the existing structure of commercial relations was, if anything, reinforced. Not only did the large, established firms that secured the greatest portion of war-related contracts prosper, but also firm prices on rationed goods meant that small units of production and distribution prospered as well. Gas rationing increased the growth of railroad travel and made it seem as if the decline of railroads during the Depression was only a temporary setback. The war may not have been won on Main Street, but Main Street prospered as much or more than it had in the brief euphoria of the Twenties.

Labor also prospered. Though wage increases were drastically limited under the War Labor Board's fabled "Little Steel formula," at least union recognition and bargaining over working conditions were ensured. Strikes, like wages, were limited, at least in theory. In practice, the incidence of strikes increased over the course of the war. However, out of the wartime experience both labor and management understood that the country preferred industrial peace at a modest price. Acceptable were increased costs from modest wage increases, from the introduction of nonwage benefits such as the recognition of work rules that kept production expensive, but labor less onerous (a covert form of a wage increase), and from the proliferation time-and-a-half overtime guaranteed by law, a major source of increased prosperity for workers.

Overseas, American aircraft were attempting to destroy both European and Japanese industrial might. In retrospect, it is reasonably clear that strategic bombing accomplished much less than was thought. A surprising amount of industrial plant and equipment was left intact in Japan and Germany, even after Russian troops took a fair portion of what was to be found in their zone of occupation. Still, Europe, even victorious Great Britain, was prostrate with a combination of significant population loss and the destruction or exhaustion of industrial plant and equipment. In both war theatres, infrastructure was in shambles and the removal of captive sources of raw materials made resumption of the production of goods very difficult. In Europe, the destruction had been so severe that economic conditions were worse in 1947 than they had been in 1945, in part because agriculture remained in a terrible state.

Farm production, beyond local needs, was difficult to bring to urban markets for lack of transportation. Once there, it was difficult to sell for lack of currency. This lack of currency was due first, to the lack of a functioning government to establish and maintain that currency, and second, to the lack of jobs, a situation that was caused by the lack of industrial production brought on by the decline in the stock of available plant and equipment, a scarcity of raw materials, and the selfsame lack of currency, a vicious circle, if ever there were one. And in Germany, the United States military, the number one supplier of the ersatz currency of the times—the cigarette—was, except for occupation troops, being withdrawn as fast as the troop transports could be found to meet the call to "bring our boys home."

Even worse, much of the war production in both Germany and Japan and their respective occupied areas, had been a part of a command economy where goods were produced based on supplies delivered. Unfortunately, allied diplomats who planned for a postwar international order made such countries' switch to a market-driven economy more difficult. These efforts, that at Dumbarton Oaks led to the creation of the United Nations, at Bretton Woods outlined a new economic order. The Bretton Woods agreements partially reestablished the fixed rate regime for foreign exchange that Roosevelt had interred when he took the United States off the gold standard in 1933. Under the Bretton Woods gold exchange standard, the United States agreed to exchange dollars for gold at a rate of $35 per ounce, but only in transactions with foreign central banks. The currencies of the other states that participated in the system were then tied to the dollar or to gold at fixed rates, and states agreed to maintain their currency within a band (generally, 1 percent) of the fixed rate. The International Monetary Fund, also established at Bretton Woods, was designed to lend money to states that had insufficient gold or foreign currency reserves to keep the actual value of their currency at the agreed-on rate, usually because of an inability to cover their trade deficits.[21]

As a practical matter, under this system international trade needed to be done in currencies with sufficient gold, foreign exchange or, in the short term, credit at the IMF to ensure that they could be converted into any other currency in the system. The Axis powers were, however, stripped of their little remaining gold by the victors. Without a convertible currency, such countries were much less able to purchase foreign goods, including raw materials for the production of manufactured goods that, when exported, would generate foreign exchange. Thus, the production of goods for export to those countries that had a convertible currency with which to purchase manufactured goods was difficult, even where transportation was possible, unless all raw materials and capital goods needed for production were domestic, an unusual circumstance in the economies of these countries.

Paradoxically, Europe's rescuer was Russia, for the Communist takeovers of Poland, Czechoslovakia, Hungary, Yugoslavia, Bulgaria, and Romania, coupled with threats directed against Greece and Turkey, brought a response from the United States. In reaction to the creation of the "Iron Curtain," the Truman Doctrine poured money into Greece, and lesser amounts into Turkey. Economic conditions in the countries of Western Europe began to pick up when next the United States poured economic aid into them under the Marshall Plan, as well as military aid, always a prop to an economy, under NATO. Still, even with all this aid, Europe, and comparatively less-aided Japan, were restarting their economies from a very low level.

In contrast, the United States had won all the marbles. As the only truly functioning major economy north of the equator,[22] it held virtually all economic power in its hands and thought that it held all political power as well. Like Julius Caesar, it bestrode "the narrow world like a Colossus." The returning GIs cared little about such things, however. They needed jobs. Their needs brought about the replacement of women workers with men in many of the best-paying jobs, though this was only a temporary decline in female participation in the waged workforce. It was supported by the redeployment of an ideology that exalted the one-wage-earner family supported by a "family wage."[23] Although the decline of overtime in the immediate postwar years initially made the family wage quite difficult to achieve, the GI Bill, for a time at least, served to sop up much potential unemployment with its extension of benefits for servicemen who sought further education, including higher education, which the colleges were quick to supply and that in many cases brought people from unknown public schools in the Midwest to fancy places like Harvard, Columbia, and Yale.

Immediately after the war, the rise in consumer demand—fueled first by the simple absence of goods and services during the war, second by the disproportionately large savings that were accumulated in those years when high wages could find few goods to purchase, and finally by the developing baby boom—brought significant inflation. But by 1947 inflation subsided, with only a modest spurt in 1950 associated with the onset of the Korean War. Housing and autos led the postwar economic expansion. In addition, the United States was exporting goods, including farm products, at a very high level. These exports earned large, if not wholly meaningful, trade surpluses; they were financed with aid or credit from the federal government, for as indicated above, there was little that European countries and Japan had to export.

America's military and economic spending in Europe, the same kind that drove the American economy during the war, was modestly helpful in supporting domestic postwar expansion. Most Americans soon experienced fairly good times, though agriculture was a notable exception because the high farm prices supported under war-time regulation were difficult to maintain until we hit on the expedient of using surpluses they generated as instruments of foreign policy through Food for Peace and other federal programs. The reintroduction of wartime production that accompanied the Korean War meant that large-scale government stimulation of the economy returned for the better part of four years; it was accompanied by another dose of somewhat less generous GI Bill benefits. But Korea was not fought under conditions of "total war." This time, consumption was not particularly squeezed as a result of war mobilization.

Given that purchasing power was reasonably stable by 1951; that high savings by people still fearful in the aftermath of the Depression made capital reasonably plentiful; and that consumer goods were relatively plentiful and foreign sales large, the economy grew strongly for the entire decade and beyond. Labor was relatively free to seek wage increases or the addition of benefits under the theory, derived from World War II and enshrined in the Internal Revenue Code, that benefits were somehow not wages. Only agriculture continued to lag. Farm employment continued its wartime decline; farm size, its wartime increase; farm income, its relative stagnation. This is not to say that in urban areas the great postwar expansion was inexorably upward. Indeed, there were three modest recessions during the chronological fifties, the last coming at the end of the decade and contributing to the election of a Democratic administration in 1960. But these were rightly seen as good years by consumers, wage earners, and businessmen, fueled as they were by the insulation of the domestic economy from international competition originating in the still-recovering European and Japanese economies and by the interaction of this insulation with the practices of the Associationalist legal/economic model of a good economy.

The lack of international competition meant that American industry could raise wages and easily pay for such wage increases by raising prices modestly, relying on increases in demand to lower unit costs, and by deferring improvements in production processes, plant, and equipment. Nor was there any internal need to do otherwise. Industrywide bargaining meant that competitors were seldom differentially disadvantaged by increases in wages, increases that to some extent, may have reflected productivity gains. The prices of nonlabor product inputs were reasonably steady, and domestic companies controlled access to most raw materials, particularly petroleum, at low world prices. Stockholders were a quiescent, dispersed lot, as Adolf Berle and Gardiner Means had observed a generation earlier, who looked primarily for predictable dividends and less for capital appreciation. Disgruntled investors sold; they did not fight management.[24]

The continued authority of the Associationalist ideal of managed, rather than ruinous, competition seemingly protected retail business owners, though here the development of new national chains, such as McDonald's and Holiday Inn, and the expansion of discounting beyond groceries into hard goods, ought to have given careful observers pause. That ideal similarly protected members of the numerous oligopolistic industries by limiting them to "gloves on" competitive fights for market share. American industry had become big, cumbrous, comfortable, and more dependent for its prosperity on the gross level of demand derived from increases in total employment than on product improvement derived from capital investment. Such increases in employment were easy to find, for these were years when any new idea meant that more employees would be hired; no one would have suggested that existing jobs be rearranged so that both new and old tasks could be accommodated with the existing workforce.

In some ways the quiescent state of American industry in these years is counterintuitive. While producers were insulated from international competition, capital costs were unusually low because the United States maintained a sheltered market in credit growing out of the structure that New Deal legislation left behind. Checking accounts were largely limited to corporations and upper-or upper-middle class families, and there were few equally liquid investments offered elsewhere. Securities were effectively purchased by a similarly limited group, due in part to high and fixed minimum brokerage commissions, and in part to a lingering fear of the stock market that many middle-class people had learned from the 1929 crash. Savings for most people were channeled into time deposit savings accounts, often at savings and loan associations that were statutorily limited to paying low rates of interest—2 or 3 percent for most of these years—and similarly limited in their investment of these funds to home mortgages, often insured under the FHA or the GI Bill. This segmentation of the national pool of savings provided support for the housing market and a pile of corporate bank balances available for lending to corporate borrowers at rates that were secure from serious competition from the long-term, debt-oriented securities markets.

Under these circumstances, one might have expected that the relatively low cost of credit would have brought forth a torrent of investment in new product development, old product innovation, and the improvement of production processes to make up for the lack of such investment since 1929. But this did not happen on a grand scale. The only major improvement, even in the consumer economy, was the phenomenal growth in network television and in the production of ever-bigger television sets, often marketed as large pieces of wooden furniture known as consoles, just as had been the case with first phonographs and then radios. Two possible reasons for the lack of investment come to mind. First, vital competition often drives investment and there was no such competitive threat, domestic or international. Second, any investment in new plant and equipment would have meant, if not a total reduction in employment, at least a replacement of existing jobs with others, perhaps located elsewhere. Such a change in employment patterns, in some sense would have been unpatriotic, for it would have altered the lives of the veterans to whom we owed so much for their wartime service and around whom the anti-Communist ideal of the free and productive society was being built.

This is not to say that there was no investment in innovation in these years. Innovation was obvious in the mass production of the primarily suburban, new housing, modeled on Levittown, and in air conditioning, television, and the stereo. But the results of a lack of innovation were also already evident. In iron and steel, little investment in the new, basic oxygen process was made. In rails, new investment was limited to replacing steam with diesel power. This obvious improvement in technology drew attention away from the continuing decline in demand, both in terms of passengers and freight that the boom in heavy transport during World War II had obscured. Passenger rail travel declined with the proliferation of private autos and later with the growth of business air travel; freight declined with the increasing availability of truck transport, a circumstance obvious even before the war.[25] Indeed, the plans for what became the Eisenhower Interstate Highway System were first drafted in 1941. In 1957, the proposal was advanced on precisely the twin grounds unsuccessfully offered sixteen years earlier—a combination of national defense and highway congestion from increasing truck traffic.

The social consequence of what, in retrospect, was a hot-house economy, insulated from competition abroad and limited in competitive pressures at home, was a dramatic increase in the size of the middle class, both white and blue collar. This larger middle class was built on three things: first, reasonably high wages; second, low housing costs, aided by the nationwide adoption of the fully amortizable, thirty-year mortgage[26] (introduced on a mass scale by federal agencies during the Depression) available at interest rates intentionally kept low by the structure of banking regulation, and effectively lowered even further by the tax deductibility of mortgage interest in a time of high marginal tax rates; and third, the extension of college education—more a matter of increasing status than of improving skills—to groups who previously could not have afforded it. This was the "Quiet Generation," quiet because times were good, and families needed building.[27]

These new, middle-class Americans, traditionally segregated by ethnicity, sought to leave their familiar urban neighborhoods for the suburbs. Their reasons for doing so were many and conflicting. They sought to escape the rising tide of Black migration to Northern cities that had picked up during the war and further increased with changes in Southern agricultural practices, such as the introduction of the mechanical cotton picker that made the sharecropper's or tenant farmer's already precarious livelihood even more fragile. They also sought to escape the family pressure that was omnipresent in old ethnic neighborhoods of multiple family dwellings wedged closely together. Especially, they hoped to fulfill that quintessential American dream, sold endlessly in the popular press, as well as by producer advertising, of owning one's own home. In suburban enclaves, now segregated primarily by income, but to some extent by ethnicity usually tied to religion, and always by race, just as had been the case in the older, city neighborhoods, these individuals created a middle class that was different from both that of the classic bourgeois shopkeeper or professional of Nineteenth-Century Europe and America or that of the salaried middle manager ubiquitous in corporate life since the latter part of that century, and at the same time, far larger in scope than had ever been seen before. They were the first wage earner or hourly middle class. It was the first time that such workers had become citizens who counted, and their appearance was evidence of a social/political revolution that had taken place pretty much without shedding a drop of blood, at least in the United States.

Meanwhile, the combination of Marshall Plan aid and NATO-related expenditures in Europe, and similar economic aid and Korean War-related expenditures in Japan, plus low domestic defense expenditures in both areas, and incredibly high savings rates in Japan, meant first slow, then explosive growth abroad in the mid-Fifties. While Japan was effectively closed to foreign investment, opportunities for American companies to invest in Europe grew quickly. These companies encountered a policy, unlike that in the United States, of keeping interest rates high, largely because equities were traditionally held by family groups and their bankers, and thus high returns on debt provided income for the traditional *rentier* class. In the earlier years, risks also may have been high. Equally important, outside of the town home and rural estate of the most privileged classes, there was no real tradition of home ownership that governments might have supported through low mortgage rates.[28]

American companies earned their profits in European currencies that until 1958, were limited in their convertibility, and when convertible, were sometimes subject to unfavorable, fixed exchange rates. In the comparatively high-rate environment of Europe, American companies thus had real incentives to keep their earnings working in Europe by investing them at European interest rates, an incentive increased by the fear that the newly formed European Economic Community would use high tariffs to keep out American manufactured goods. In contrast, European companies increasingly earned easily convertible dollars for their exports, but had no reason to keep these earnings in the comparatively low-rate environment that characterized the American economy. However, in a gold exchange standard currency regime, when American companies chose not to repatriate their profits but to invest them, and European companies chose to repatriate their profits by transferring them to their respective central banks, these individually rational actions allowed a build-up of European dollar holdings that, in turn, created noticeable pressure on the American gold supply should European central banks decide to convert their dollar holdings into gold.

As a result of the growth in European exports, the American balance of trade, the measure of current exports as against imports, which had regularly shown a surplus, began to decline. Consequently, given the continuation of governmental expenditures abroad—largely military after economic aid was ended in the mid-Fifties, the declining positive balance of trade allowed the development of a negative balance of payments, the measure of total currency and gold outflows as against inflows.

Initially, that negative balance of payments was good for a world economy that still was short of payment reserves. It allowed foreign countries to build up reserves, particularly of dollars, the reserve currency of choice. However, what was once a good thing and remained so because an increase in reserves was essential for financing the continuing growth in international trade, by the late-Fifties came to be seen as troublesome, given that a sufficient increase in the American gold supply was not forthcoming. The first call on the American gold reserve was as fractional backing for the dollar as a domestic currency. The balance of the reserve was, under the gold exchange standard, held to guarantee the American pledge to redeem in gold the dollar holdings of foreign governments at the $35 per ounce ratio set by the Bretton Woods agreements. This guarantee of redemption was fine, so long as no foreign government sought to exercise the right to redeem its dollar holdings. Unfortunately, foreign governments, in order to rebuild their gold reserves depleted by wartime expenditures, did just that. The American gold reserve slowly was being depleted.

With outstanding dollar reserves exceeding the gold available to back them, the possibility that someone would be left without a chair when the music stopped began to worry foreign governments. These governments feared that the United States would devalue its currency, unilaterally increasing the price of gold and hence the amount of foreign dollar holdings required to be exchanged for a given amount of gold. At the same time, the U.S. government feared that devaluing the dollar would both spark domestic inflation and bring about an international economic crisis that could undermine the strength of the anti-Communist coalition that seemed essential for Western security. Thus began a period of intense official concern about the balance of trade, balance of payments, dollar outflow, current account, and other measures of a "problem" that most Americans couldn't understand, in part because the language used to describe the problem was so multifarious.

The first concrete and separable manifestation of that problem came in the early 1960's. With the gradual opening of capital markets worldwide, European companies discovered that they could take advantage of a regulated American banking market that, because of the New Deal reforms, kept capital costs in the United States significantly lower than they were in Europe. These companies would borrow dollars in New York and use them to pay for capital investments abroad. Such a sensible business strategy had the obvious effect of increasing the supply of dollars abroad, a private outflow of capital on top of the governmental outflow for military purposes, and so of increasing the deficit in the balance of payments and concomitant worries about the American gold reserve. In 1962, in an effort to reduce that outflow and the accompanying worries, the Kennedy administration introduced the Interest Equalization Tax. This tax was designed to increase the effective interest rate on bonds denominated in dollars and sold in the United States by foreign borrowers to the interest rate that would have been paid on similar bonds had they been sold in foreign markets. The idea was to discourage the issuance of such bonds by taxing American purchasers of the bonds.

The temporary success of this tax strategy is far less important to understanding the American economy in the immediate postwar period than two other things. First, the need to impose the tax serves to mark a significant change in that economy. For the first time in more than twenty years, international economic activities were having a negative impact on management of the American economy. The Interest Equalization Tax affirmed, though few understood this at the time, that the United States was no longer an economic island. Domestic economic policies would thereafter have to be recognized as having international effects and foreign economic policies recognized as having domestic economic effects. Within a few years, the impact of that fact on middle-class Americans, and especially their college student children, became apparent as Icelandic Airlines, not then a member of the North Atlantic fare cartel, offered cheap flights to Luxembourg (with an obligatory stop in Iceland offering a chance to buy things at the airport duty free shop), disrupted that cartel and made it possible for more Americans to vacation in Europe than ever before, especially more students and recent students.

Second, although the imposition of the Interest Equalization Tax largely ended the market for bonds denominated in dollars and sold in the United States by foreign borrowers, it did not dampen the demand of foreign corporations for dollar-denominated loans. Governments may have been worried about the American balance of payments, but borrowers were not. The Interest Equalization Tax could be escaped by keeping funds in dollar denominated investments abroad. And so emerged the Eurodollar market, a market initially specializing in making loans denominated in dollars to European borrowers, a market located really nowhere. That market, apparently born in the mid-Fifties when the Russian government wanted a place to keep its dollar earnings where the American government could not confiscate them, lends dollars deposited in banks located in various countries in which the dollar is not the national currency. Somewhat unaccountably, such deposits are not subject to bank reserve requirements, which means that these lenders can offer lower interest rates than would be asked for loans in their various national currencies. Though such rates were not as low as American rates, the difference was still sufficient to be attractive to European borrowers, and so in time, these deposits grew enormously. The establishment of this market meant that some portion of the monetary units at the root of our economy had escaped from the control of both the Treasury Department's fiscal policy and the Federal Reserve Board's monetary policy.[29] Even more important in the long run, the development of the Eurodollar market affirmed the dollar's central role in trade and investment worldwide, its role as a unit of account alternative to gold for settling international trade transactions or accumulating national currency reserves. Paradoxically, the dollar had become an effective reserve currency, even as governments were worried about its soundness. After all, the United States was still the largest economy in the world.

The most obvious indication that one is confronting economic life in full bloom is that there is almost nothing to talk about. There is almost nothing going on. Even a social/political revolution passes essentially unnoticed. The actors have settled into playing the roles that they seem to assume they will play. Law is quite silent as well. Such is the case with what I call the Associationalist economy of the Fifties.

After the adoption of the Labor Management Relations Act (Taft-Hartley Act) in 1947, which added unfair labor practices on the part of employees, such as jurisdictional strikes and secondary boycotts, to the unfair labor practices on the part of employers identified by the Wagner Act, there was but one significant piece of economic legislation in the succeeding fifteen years—the Interstate Highway Act of 1957. And that piece of legislation is more of a reflection of the impatience of the enlarged middle class with the limits on its ability to use its big cars and leisure time, its two weeks of paid vacation, than a reflection of any troubles that would cause those harmed to run to law for its uncertain succor. All of this is not to say that the organs of law shut down during these years. Rather, the legislative product—the expansion of the rice support program to two more counties in Arkansas where the possibility of such support made it newly plausible to grow rice or the creation of a public authority to extend an airport or maintain a port—was so trivial as to beggar the process.

The relative silence of law is, of course, misleading. Narrowly conceived as the formal and effective norms originating from governmental entities, especially the law of property, contract, and theft, of mine and thine, law is always there, the modest hum of a faithful dynamo. Looking at law more broadly conceived, as the many and variable actions undertaken by governmental actors, of discretionary action, as the traditional language of the law would have it, the matter is the same. Because in an enacted economy like that of the Fifties the formal and effective structures are in place, the work of the bureaucracy goes about its modest regulatory business constantly, but quietly. Yes, noise always emanates from narrowly interested parties and that noise bulks large in the business press, but when looked back upon, tempests and teapots come to mind. This is the real significance of the Interest Equalization Tax, buried as it was in an otherwise ordinary omnibus tax bill. Law was finally roused from its quiet work to attend to what, in the longer run, turned out to be a significant problem. The Associationalist economy was in trouble.

Sixties and Seventies: A Troubled Economy

For about the next twenty years, an increasingly troubled economy, centered in the production of consumer and heavy industrial goods, lurched downhill. After the invasion of the Volkswagen Beetle, it took a flotilla of inexpensive Japanese imports to make the automobile industry realize that its market had changed. "Voluntary" export restraints entered into by Japanese manufacturers, designed to give the industry time to get back to its fighting weight, didn't seem to help. Then there was the continuous decline of the steel industry that, once deprived of the stimulus provided by the Vietnam War and plagued with excess capacity devoted to an aged production process, ceded market after market to substantially cheaper imports and domestic upstarts, even while receiving trade protection. Similar stories might be told in the case of textiles (again despite significant trade protection), machine tools, clothing, footwear, and of course, the television set, that quintessential product of the Fifties life and economy. Most of the areas in which significant declines did not occur were industries where comprehensive federal or state regulation was in place, such as aviation, banking, communications, power, and securities. The only real growth industries in this period, other than entertainment—and for a while, the famous British invasion dominated parts of that as well—were real estate, plus the associated construction enterprises, and higher education, plus the associated spin-offs from the production of technological research conducted in medicine, electronics, and other science-and engineering-related fields.[30]

How did this state of affairs come about? Initially, foreign manufactured products were attractive simply because they were cheaper. The Associationalist model of a high-wage, high-price economy made it difficult for newly prosperous younger and lower-middle class consumers, the expanded middle class that the Fifties economy brought into being, to afford many things, especially small appliances and other electrical goods, or much of many things that were affordable only in small amounts, mainly soft goods. The new, larger discount stores that had begun to appear in the Fifties—stores like E. J. Korvettes that sold American-made hard goods at "discount" (i.e., less than the high list prices charged by the small Main Street retailers)—soon turned into specialty retailers, such as Pier 1, or into moderate-income department stores, such as K-Mart, Ames, or Hills—a development that eventually replaced the previous major outlet for foreign-made goods, other than luxury goods, "the five and dime," such as Woolworth's or Kresge's. This new kind of store was a place for the regular sale of first soft goods, later small appliances, eventually electronics. And with a place to shop, a segment of the market soon followed. Poor and working-class families could have more clothes in their closets and small, inexpensive appliances in their kitchens; eventually they could have cheaper electronics in their family rooms.

For such products, transportation costs, when combined with loss or damage from trans-shipping to boats and from boats to trains or trucks, were a significant expense, so that wage-rate disparities were the only thing that could allow foreign goods to be competitive. But, over time, transportation costs came down radically with the development of container shipping. For other products such as steel and autos, lower wages combined with an unexpected advantage that derived from the wartime destruction of industrial capacity in Europe and Japan. Overseas, once capital could be assembled to revive these industries, capacity was built with the newest, most efficient technology and work processes—production methods in advance of those existing in the United States. The same was true of South Korea and Taiwan, countries that previously lacked heavy manufacturing capacity. The combination of better methods and lower wages was sufficient to offset the quite significant cost of ocean freight for heavy, often bulky goods, unsuited to container shipping.

Eventually, foreign manufactured products were attractive because they were better. As foreign wages rose, first in Europe and then in Japan, producers there relied on technological advances that reduced costs for the mass production of new products—the Walkman stereo and the videocassette recorder are the best known—often actually invented in the United States. Faced with persistent consumer demand for inexpensive, newly available products, American companies, used to oligopolistic competition, were not able, or at least not willing, to compete. Their response was to cede the low-price market, as the steel industry had done, or to move production overseas. In either case, American companies eventually shrank domestic manufacturing capacity. Later, they tried automation, the choice to substitute increasingly sophisticated machines (often manufactured abroad) for labor, often unsuccessfully.

The delay in the introduction of automation raises the major conundrum concerning these years. Why did it take so long to abandon the Associationalist ideal that was the Fifties economy, when it was increasingly dysfunctional in the years after 1962? A priori, aggressive capitalists, if acting as traditionally pictured by advocates of labor and social welfare, should have remembered the economists' mantra that sunk costs are sunk, quickly closed plants, laid-off workers and redeployed such capital as was salvageable. Yet almost nowhere was this strategy followed. Most often, employment was ratcheted down slowly and capital, worked down as close to scrap as possible.

Part of the reason for this choice in heavily unionized industries such as steel and autos is reasonably obvious. Labor is a relatively immobile factor of production, tied as it is to family and community. Closed plants are never in its interest and so, its representatives, who have no personal interest in shutting down their business either, can be expected to fight hard to preserve jobs and wage structure in the short run, even if some other course of action would be more socially beneficial. On the other side, management, fat, happy, and always inordinately concerned about its prerogatives, is equally self-interested. It understands that conflict makes no one money, even if at the end of the inevitable conflict over eliminating productive capacity or expensive labor practices, capital wins. In the aftermath of a battle won, management is likely to find that there are disgruntled, not particularly productive workers in any remaining plants. Poor labor-management relations, forged from the notion of quid pro quo, rather than the notion of joint problem solving, bear some share of the responsibility, and thus also pushed in the direction of inertial choice.

The parallel choice to avoid putting off closing plants in thinly unionized and in nonunionized sectors is less obvious. Family and management ties to declining enterprises, a sense of obligation toward local communities, possibly a sense of continuing obligation to workers derived from their status as veterans, and of course Hurstian drift and default, all seem to have played a role. Taken together, what is significant is not that, in the end, the no-win scenario in labor-management relations was played out, but that in most cases, it was avoided for as long as possible. Such was the strength of the Associationalist model in the late Sixties and Seventies, long after it ceased its relevance to America's place in the world economy.

While the dysfunctional post-Fifties American economy slid comfortably downhill, five developments silently continued to transform the country. The first was the malling of suburbia. Initially, this process began with open malls, even in places such as Chicago with an inhospitable winter climate. Soon after, enclosed malls proliferated across the landscape, starting with the even more inhospitable Minneapolis.[31] This process largely destroyed the existing suburban versions of Main Street and continued the retail evacuation of the urban business core that had begun with the accelerated growth of the suburbs in the Fifties, a development that only hastened the residential evacuation of those same cities.

The second development accompanied the completion of the interstate highway system. Initially, the existence of these highways magnified the evacuation of urban areas by their White, newly middle-class population. Then, in the same way that the new highway system had opened large tracts of land for residential development, it opened similar tracts for the development of light industrial and expanding service employment, particularly in banking, insurance, and healthcare, all within easy reach of the new suburban housing. Thereafter, jobs followed housing and housing, jobs in a reinforcing cycle that created new suburban communities. Unlike the upper-middle class suburbs of the Twenties and Thirties, these new suburbs were surprisingly independent of the urban areas that had initially spawned them.

The third development was the continued evacuation of rural America, especially the Midwest. Though federal subsidies kept agriculture profitable, as farms increased in scale to pay for increasingly expensive hybrid seeds, chemical fertilizers, and equipment, the farm population declined.[32] This decline in population led to the decline of local retail trade, a circumstance that was accelerated as better highways for auto transport made it easier to shop in regional centers. And then families supported by local retail trade followed the departing farmer families to more urban areas. During these years, it was a real achievement for a rural community simply to maintain its population, even with recruited industrial employment, usually from firms attempting to escape a unionized workforce, unless luck placed a growth industry—higher education was the most obvious one—in the area.

The fourth development was the growth of the South and West. In the South, the out-migration of Blacks, displaced by the mechanization of agriculture, was offset by an even larger in-migration of Northerners escaping declining industries and chasing manufacturing jobs that were fleeing union labor contracts. In the West, aerospace and other military-related jobs were the draw. In both areas, the climate was made increasingly habitable by the perfection of air conditioning. And as cities grew, construction and service jobs grew in tandem.

The fifth development was a significant change in the structure of the American industrial firm. Traditionally, industrial corporations, vertically integrated to a significant extent, made one major product and a few closely related ones. Typically, individuals who started in plant management, and so thought like production managers, dominated these firms. Such firms grew from the investment of retained earnings, either internally or by merger with other firms in the same industry. Then, in the Sixties, this type of growth by merger was stymied by the Celler-Kefauver Amendment to the antitrust acts.[33] Some other method of growth would have to be found.

In these same years, the Ford Foundation decided that the state of education for management had been seriously neglected and began to pour money into its improvement, seen as making management training more scientific.[34] However, the only science that management schools knew, having ceded the remnants of Frederick Taylor's time and motion study to departments of industrial engineering, was financial management based on the elaboration of methods for the valuation of assets that had grown out of accounting practice. Soon, this branch of the management curriculum, relabeled finance, exploded. The simple notion that a diversified portfolio of stock market investments was, all things being equal, more likely to provide a more consistent return over a suitably long period of time than would investments concentrated in one narrow area, became a central part of the knowledge base of the untold numbers of graduates produced by the management school.

Consultants quickly took this idea and argued that the same could be said of investments in individual business, especially cyclical ones. With a so-called "cash cow," a company with predictably high profits, one could build an increasingly large and diversified stable of firms, buying and selling them to optimize one's portfolio and produce superior returns, or so the theory went. One needn't know anything about actually running these businesses; that was the job of their individual managers. All one needed to know to build a corporate empire was the temporal nature of the business cycle of the individual constituent firms and the proper methods for reading financial statements to see how one's investments were faring, offering capital to those that were prospering and disposing of those that were not.

Whether this theory led or followed corporate practice is not clear. Yet, starting in the Sixties, American corporations, recognizing the continued tax advantages of the retained, as opposed to distributed, earnings that they had always used for expansion,[35] but stymied by antitrust law from expanding through merger with competitors, and for some, still not clear reason unwilling to chance investment in internal expansion, began to use retained earnings captured in the form of new issues of common stock to build empires. They purchased strikingly diverse businesses, creating what were called "conglomerates," the most famous being Harold Geneen's ITT, James Ling's LTV, and Charlie Bluhdorn's Gulf & Western, later rechristened Paramount Communications. For the time being, it seemed as if the traditional industrial corporation, already under siege by foreign competitors, would be succeeded by another form of industrial organization.

The slow, downhill slide of the American economy that accompanied these social and economic changes was occasionally interrupted by less gentle lurches toward the bottom. The first such lurch followed from Lyndon Johnson's ultimately foolish decision simultaneously to fight a land war in Asia, build a Great Society, and maintain the free importation of goods lest the American standard of living decline. By pursuing a policy of producing both "guns and butter," but not raising taxes, he began a string of federal governmental deficits at a time when the economy was probably already operating at full capacity.

Unfortunately, during these years, the Federal Reserve had adopted a policy of seeking regular growth in the money supply, further augmenting that supply during each recession under the Keynesian theory, by then generally accepted, that such action would lower interest rates and so expand employment. Moreover, at the same time, though not for obviously related reasons, the growth in American economic productivity (total output per worker) began a steep decline from about 3 percent in the late Fifties, to nearly zero percent by the end of the Seventies; corporate spending for research and development declined similarly.[36] So too did the percentage of children who earned more than their parents when at the same age. The Fed's monetary policy and the productivity decline combined with the set of economic policies that Johnson left behind and Richard Nixon continued, though by diverting Great Society expenditures, and more than a few others, to the cause of Mars, created serious economic problems. Late in Nixon's second term the withdrawal of American troops from Vietnam allowed him to shift to a more "butter" and less "guns" focused policy. However, doing so did not ameliorate these problems, but rather demonstrated that Nixon was neither prepared for, nor capable of dealing with the economy at large. Unfortunately for the country, this fact distinguished him from no one.

The result was the beginning of the Great Inflation, which lasted close to a generation, and hammered manufacturing. By the time this event was over, it had reduced the value of the dollar by about two-thirds and the real value of wages by 20 percent. The newly broadened middle class was being seriously squeezed as interest rates increased significantly, especially on home mortgages; as the cost of common services, such as haircuts and dry cleaning, not to mention more complex services such as medical care, began to accelerate; and as prices in the grocery and drug stores moved from a trot to a gallop.

The combination of inflation and a system of fixed exchange rates occasioned the second lurch downhill. Domestic inflation meant that, from the perspective of foreign buyers, American exports seemed more expensive; from the perspective of American buyers, foreign imports seemed cheaper. This disparity in perception led to a sharp deterioration in the American balance of trade as foreign buyers cut back on the purchase of American goods and American buyers clamored for more imported goods. Simultaneously, the further restrictions on the outflow of funds that were imposed soon after the Interest Equalization Tax failed to solve the American balance of payments problems, problems that were augmented by the increased overseas military spending occasioned by the Vietnam War. This augmentation compounded the effects of the deterioration in the balance of trade. Quickly, foreign governments, especially France, threatened to convert their dollars into gold. In 1971, fearing that continuation of the outflow of gold threatened the "bankruptcy" of the country or, more properly, of the policy of guaranteeing the convertibility of dollars into gold at the fixed rate established by the Bretton Woods agreements, Richard Nixon, who had more than exacerbated the problem by intensifying the war in Southeast Asia, "temporarily" refused to honor the nation's commitment to exchange dollars for gold. Two years later, when circumstances had not improved, he abandoned the gold exchange standard entirely.

What no one seemed to notice was that the demise of the gold exchange standard and its replacement with a system of "floating" exchange rates involving the major international currencies—rates determined in the market for foreign exchange and not by the willingness of governments to exchange currency at stated rates—was not the disaster for the world economy that many had feared it would be. France may not have liked the result, but by 1971, the world had a sufficient quantity of a new reserve currency, the American dollar, thoughtfully placed at the world's disposal by the Kennedy administration. Indeed, from the perspective of international trade and finance, the problem with the inflated dollar in the late Sixties and early Seventies was that it had ruined a perfectly good reserve currency and medium of exchange. So, like the Interest Equalization Tax, the adoption of a floating exchange rate may have been more a symbol of the continued decline of the American economic island that had made possible the realization of the Associationalist ideal in the Fifties, than of much practical significance, given that the dollar continued to be freely accepted as a medium of foreign trade and indeed, as a reserve currency. The world had slipped back into the Nineteenth and early Twentieth Centuries' world of the free, this time almost weightless, movement of capital.[37]

In the world of floating exchange rates, the dollar was joined as a reserve currency by the Deutschmark, the Swiss Franc, ultimately the Japanese Yen, and to a lesser extent, the British pound. In a complex, but ultimately successful, worldwide effort, first centered in the forum provided by that previously not very important World War II creation, the International Monetary Fund, the international economy came to be managed as if it were still governed by a weak gold standard. In due course, this task was moved to the less cumbrous group of five treasury ministers, which initially included Great Britain for old time's sake, though eventually in recognition of the continuing relevance of London as a world financial center and included France solely for the sake of good NATO relations. But the system of floating exchange rates did not solve the problem posed for any country that attempted to protect its economy through the establishment of stable exchange relations. Such a country was subject to just the kind of strains on its currency that the American economy experienced when it was anchored to gold. The failure to deal with this problem would come to haunt the international monetary system more than once. At the time, however, everyone expected that the short-term consequence for the world and American economy would be a further increase in inflation.

Recognizing this expectation, when Nixon closed the gold window in 1971, he simultaneously took the unprecedented step of instituting wage and price controls in an allegedly peacetime economy, this to the astonishment of the assembled multitudes. Such controls were anything but unwelcome to the American people, unused to annual inflation rates of 6 or more percent. In addition to placing stress on family budgets, such inflation decreased disposable inflated income, as wage increases were also eaten into by marginal income tax rates as a result of moving to higher tax brackets. Controls, progressively weakened, were about as effective as could be expected, more so because they were not in force long enough to spawn a fully developed black market.

Inflation, however, continued unabated.[38] Next, the economy experienced two more lurches toward the bottom, each accompanied by a significant increase in inflation. In 1973 came the Arab oil embargo that followed the Yom Kippur War, which when lifted, was accompanied by the decision of the Organization of Petroleum Exporting Countries (OPEC) to quadruple the price of oil, largely in response to the failure or unwillingness of the United States to force Israel to give up the territory that it had secured in that war.[39] The unemployment rate hit 8.5 percent. Then in 1978 came a second shock, one from the loss of access to Iranian oil in the aftermath of the Iranian Revolution and from the further OPEC price rise that followed. Because the United States had become highly dependent on importing countless tankers of now very expensive oil, its balance of trade, already significantly negative, declined precipitously, and soon the world was awash with dollars.

Curiously, during these years, the most extraordinary—but usually unremarked—aspect of the American economy was the general inability of economists and policymakers to explain persuasively, much less to act on, the cumulative slide of that economy. How it came to be that inflation did not bring economic growth, its traditional accompaniment, but instead allowed the continuance of a relatively stagnant economy—the dreaded "stagflation"—was a mystery, and not a pleasant one. The public signs of this mystery are hardly memorable beyond the resort to talismanic objects such as the WIN—Whip Inflation Now—buttons prominently displayed in Washington during the Ford administration and the famous Carter lament about what the pundits eventually called "economic malaise," though he never used the phrase. The notion that inflationary expectations bred actions that produced inflation, a theory that was said to support wage price controls, is but one example of ineffective theories best forgotten. What could not be forgotten was that the largest economy in the world was in real trouble.

Watching any economy come apart is not a pretty sight, and the disintegration of the Associationalist economy during the Sixties and Seventies was no exception to this generalization. The bewildered and human pain that followed, as solid expectations of future life were completely unraveled—labor, management, adolescents, and old people alike in their pain, though not in their loss—is perhaps the most characteristic aspect of these years. Gasoline wasn't supposed to cost a dollar per gallon; wages weren't supposed to lag behind inflation; imports weren't supposed to threaten established supports of community life. And this disorientation included public life; America wasn't supposed to be a pitiful, helpless giant suffering from a "crisis of confidence," Jimmy Carter's actual words, a lesson that he learned to his dismay.

That the experts could make no sense of these events is an understatement. Arthur Laffer could take a cocktail napkin, draw a curve on it that linked declining income tax rates with increasing tax collections, and it became a theory, somehow just as strong a theory as Milton Friedman's theory about changes in the growth of monetary aggregates and inflation, based as his was on years of research in monetary history. Ideas for taming inflation as sensible, but unprecedented, as Richard Nixon's embrace of peacetime price regulation and as silly as Gerald Ford's distribution of WIN buttons, were both worth a try because no one could understand what was going on anyway. Maybe a conglomeration of companies was a good idea; if a group could be assembled so that the profits of its component parts experienced different temporal cycles, some always up when the others were down, so that the company as a whole would always be profitable. But then, maybe it was really dumb to assume that management by financial statement was better than management from the factory floor. Either was obviously arguable.

Law understood no more than the humans who used it. People felt pain, felt the times to be out of control, and so went to law in search of whatever nostrums seemed plausible at that *given* time and place. Trade protection made as much sense as did abandoning the gold standard, as did reinvigorating antitrust enforcement, as did price control, as did price decontrol, as did establishing a strategic petroleum reserve, as did airline price deregulation. As was the case during the Depression, people were hurting, and so law responded in such ways as the practical politics of the legislative process allowed.

Airline deregulation was a piece of the puzzle that only fit into *a, not the*, pattern. Although sensible people might have understood that the Associationalist economy was irrevocably coming apart, no one knew what kind of economy lay ahead or even when a new economy might come together. No set of structures existed, intentionally or accidentally, with which to forge the next economy, except in the sense that lots of structures might or might not prove important depending on what happened next. The two nostrums that were harbingers, the laughable Laffer curve and the deregulation of airline fares, do not loom particularly large in any sensible story of these years. Indeed, it is hard to see exactly why the notion that raising the effective return on invested capital would aid the economy or would have the same effect as reducing price rigidity, except on the goofy theory, belied by the good years that were the Fifties, that governmental regulation was somehow always and everywhere an economic mistake.

The Eighties and Nineties: Trying to Build an Economy

Two of the most significant changes in the American economy in the past forty years have their roots in the Seventies. As inflation increased and real wages declined, the severity of the impact of recessions on unemployment increased. In response to each increase of unemployment, the Federal Reserve Board of Governors acted to lower interest rates so as to expand employment. The result in each instance was an end to recession, but also to an increase in inflation. Then in October 1979, Paul Volcker, new chair of the Federal Reserve, decided that he had had it with inflation. He convinced the Fed to scrap conventional wisdom; it would no longer increase the monetary supply in order to stimulate the economy and would let interest rates rise and fall as they pleased. Soon, interest rates hit sky-high levels, and in 1981 the country dropped into a deep recession that lasted for two years. The unemployment rate reached 10 percent. About the same time, Ronald Reagan had the mad, but ultimately successful, idea of defeating the "Evil Empire" by spending it to death and simultaneously cutting taxes, producing enormous deficits in the federal budget.[40] These actions helped pull the economy out of the recession that Volcker had created, once again proving that Keynes was most useful to those who did not believe in him.

When the recession was over, the Great Inflation was over as well. It is not at all clear which of these events caused its demise, or indeed, whether it is important even to understand the phenomenon. It is possible that Volker used a psychological trick to undercut inflationary expectations; in the five years after 1979 monetary growth did not vary much from what it had been previously. However, it seems more plausible that the precipitous rise in nominal interest rates in the early Eighties interacted with a rise in real rates of return to boost investment in capital assets and bring a decline in the actual rate of inflation. Such assets, especially those implementing new technologies, related to computerization in manufacturing and service industries, changed the structure of production.[41] These technologies either increased entry-level skills needed to operate production processes and so widened the gap between those skills (and the wages appropriate to them), and the remaining grunt jobs; or as in the service sector, decreased the skill level and the absolute number of entry-level jobs. In either case, the Associationalist model of the economy was further undercut. A similar undercutting occurred in diverse segments of the economy.

The second significant change was at first less direct, but more circumstantial, and even a bit against the grain. The Sixties and Seventies were the high-water mark of social regulation in America, adding civil rights, consumer protection,[42] environmental quality, occupational safety, pension security (ERISA), and products safety to the list of New Deal regulatory programs. Among the ideas offered to explain the dismal economy was the proposition that it was rooted in excessive regulation. While questions about the costs of social regulation, particularly environmental quality and occupational safety, can and will be debated endlessly,[43] the notion that a root cause of the economic weakness of the Sixties and Seventies economy was regulation remains a curious idea. Although the most heavily regulated sectors of the economy—communications, energy, and transportation—were few and generally entailed only modest direct costs for either industrial producers or consumers, and the more lightly regulated sectors—banking and securities—arguably had been a crucial economic engine during the Fifties by keeping capital costs low, numerous legislative programs of deregulation were adopted during these years. The effect of these programs was, however, mostly felt in the Eighties.[44]

Classic price and entry regulation, like that imposed by the Civil Aeronautics Board or the Federal Communications Commission, was based on an implicit bargain between the regulators and the regulated. The regulators would guarantee that all existing participants in the market had a good chance of survival, essentially by acting as a force for stabilization of a cartel—limiting entry, parceling out new business, and seeing that price was sufficient to allow the least efficient producer to have a chance to survive economically. In exchange, the regulated entities agreed to a program of subsidization of service that was essentially too marginal to offer at a profit. In air travel, this was regular service to every little airport that had any political clout; in telephone, it was inexpensive local service supported by charging higher than "cost" rates for long-distance service.

The argument against this form of regulation was comprehensively formulated by Alfred Kahn, a Cornell economist who served as chair of the CAB under Carter. In his book, *The Economics of Regulation,* Kahn argued that price and entry regulation was a waste of resources, those resources that were devoted to subsidization of otherwise unprofitable service.[45] The argument seemed to have a certain plausibility, and soon it began to spread to various other realms. The precise temporal sequence of events here makes little difference. Examples are numerous. In air travel, first came the disappearance of the single-price airfare, always and at any time the same, and the proliferation of cheap restricted fares, an event that helped airline traffic grow into a mass-market phenomenon in ways that it never had been before. Then came bankruptcies, consolidation, and the development of a hub-and-spoke route system that worked both to lower costs and to make new entry difficult but allowed smaller niche players to thrive. A similar pattern developed in both truck and rail transport: lower costs, fewer, larger firms as a result of bankruptcy and merger, and small specialists. A more limited slice of the population experienced the end of fixed, uniform commissions for stock trading, a development that reduced the costs of trading for institutional investors more than it did for individual stockholders.[46] In all three areas, a large, government-stabilized cartel was succeeded by a smaller oligopoly, just as in the Twenties in the aftermath of Supreme Court curbs on monopolistic holding companies. In communication and finance, the sequence was different and the time frame longer, but the end point was much the same. First came lower prices—the decline in long-distance rates and the abolition of fixed commissions on stock trades—and then a great proliferation in new services: call waiting, caller ID, and cell phones; interest-bearing checking accounts and automatic teller machines. Eventually came consolidation into seeming oligopolies, mostly by merger. Perhaps such results were sensible, though it is doubtful whether they were intended.

The effect on the economy from deregulation was not quite what the theory predicted. Prices declined for most consumers, except for the road warriors of corporate sales departments who shifted from long boring rides in large comfortable cars ending at indifferent motel rooms, to shorter, cramped flights, boring waits in airports, and short drives in cramped rental cars ending at indifferent motel rooms. More significant however, in each deregulated industry the product or service seemed to change over time.

The simplest example is rail and truck transport, where the transformation of industry structure combined with the potential of computerization to produce just in time manufacturing and retailing, a concept that significantly reduced inventory costs and eliminated dozens of local distributors. Trucks, rail cars, and ocean freight containers, always on the move, became in effect the inventory function, serving as moving warehouses. Similarly, in communication, first the fax machine, then the dial-up modem, and finally cable and wireless technology, again combined with computerization, transformed the humble phone call into something else—a document delivery service, an information-retrieval mechanism, a real-time financial transactions network. These changes transformed the phone into bandwidth to be used for purposes essentially unrelated to inviting neighbors over for dinner and a friendly game of cards. Likewise, in banking and securities, the proliferation of products that are neither deposit taking nor lending, nor the purchase and sale of debt or equity interests in business entities—bank cards, money market mutual funds, securitization, derivatives, interest rate swaps—have created what can be seen as a new industry, rather grandiosely called financial services.

A significant portion of the economic growth in the late Eighties and Nineties came in these areas, though not without often-enormous costs. Though more complicated and ultimately expensive than in other industries, these costs are most obvious in bank regulation, a story that also had its roots in the Seventies.

The Great Inflation brought an enormous increase in unregulated interest rates. Soon there were complaints across the land that savings deposits were "eroding" because they were earning a regulated low return, a rate far below the rate of inflation. To make matters worse, the development of the money market mutual fund, a device that invested cash in short-term Treasury obligations and similar debt instruments issued by the most credit-worthy commercial borrowers—commercial paper—offered savers a heftier return than could savings accounts, because the rates on these investments were not regulated. In pursuit of such returns, savings poured out of deposit taking institutions. Banks called Savings and Loan companies found that they lacked money for making new mortgages. Commercial banks found that demand for corporate loans had declined as corporate treasurers issued the commercial paper that the money market funds craved, rather than visiting their local banker.[47]

The initial governmental response to this problem was to allow commercial banks to offer interest on checking accounts and savings and loans to offer higher rates on its deposits.[48] The commercial banks, left with a riskier portfolio of loans made to borrowers whose credit was not good enough for the commercial paper market, moved heavily into fee-generating activities to pay for the now more expensive deposits. The savings and loans had, however, a more embedded problem; the interest rates they were now paying for deposits were substantially higher than the interest rates on the portfolio of thirty-year mortgages they had made over time and still held. Thus, although these institutions had funds to loan, they were losing money with each transaction. Two changes followed.

The first was seemingly a great success, the invention of the collateralized mortgage obligation (CMO). Financial institutions would sell their mortgages to the New Deal's federal mortgage organizations—the Federal National Mortgage Association (Fannie Mae), primarily serving commercial banks, the Federal Home Loan Mortgage Corporation (Freddie Mac), primarily serving savings and loans, and the Government National Mortgage Association (Ginnie Mae) primarily serving mortgages insured by the Department of Housing and Urban Development, the Veterans Administration, and the Farmers Home Administration. These organizations had long sold their own bonds to provide funds that could be lent to the providers of home mortgages. Now they began to issue similar securities, CMOs, with their own, extremely valuable guarantee and moreover, collateralized by the newly purchased mortgages. This set of transactions allowed financial institutions to shift the risk of owning mortgages with fixed long-term rates to institutions thought to have less sensitivity to interest-rate shifts, such as pension plans and insurance companies.

The other change was anything but a success. In the name of maintaining fairness between different types of financial institutions, the Depository Institutions Deregulation and Monetary Control Act of 1980 and Garn-Saint Germain Depository Institutions Act of 1982 deregulated savings and loans and permitted them to engage in lending collateralized by other assets than home mortgages with the hope that these institutions would earn the greater returns that those forms of lending provided. This decision was followed by the savings and loan crisis of the late-Eighties, as savings and loans around the country folded because of bad, occasionally even corrupt, investments or continuing "negative spreads" between deposit interest rates and mortgage portfolio returns, or both, not to mention terribly lax regulatory oversight. The Treasury paid out billions on the claims presented by depositors who lost their savings in the process, an obligation that derived from the provision of deposit insurance by the Federal Savings and Loan Insurance Corporation (FSLIC), one of the little programs of the New Deal that had successfully enticed deposits back into a banking system that had imploded in the Twenties and Thirties.

The details of the savings and loan debacle are essentially uninteresting—a combination of greed, deception, and incompetence that is all too common in human affairs. To the extent that the problem was not the result of these causes, it came from the failure of the managers of these institutions to understand and so change practices in response to the changes in the market, identified earlier, that led to high and volatile interest rates. In the savings and loan business, as traditionally operated, predictable profits were made by the spread between the rate paid on deposits and the rate paid on loans; growth was secured by increases in volume. Changes in the economic life meant that this business was quickly transformed into one where profits were based solely on the now unpredictable spread between these two rates and growth came from improving that spread. Managers, bred in the culture of the savings and loans of an earlier era, did not understand how to operate in the new environment. They had little experience in making loans other than home mortgages, and so were regularly taken in by rosy scenarios painted by commercial real estate developers; were subject to extraordinarily lax regulation at a time when, because of changes in the market, they needed strict regulation most; and were also victimized by their parent companies in many cases. An entire industry largely disappeared into FSLIC receiverships as numerous investments, particularly those that were made as part of a real estate boom in the Southwest, soured. The cost to federal taxpayers was enormous, not just in terms of the payments made on deposit insurance, but also from the losses suffered by the federal agency, the Resolution Trust Company, that was created to dispose of the assets of the failed savings and loans.[49]

It is interesting that this debacle did not slow the rush to deregulate or create more than a passing recognition in the political process that classical price and entry regulation, or even more attenuated forms of regulation, such as were apparent in both banking and securities, create patterns of investment, and so of personal commitment, that are upset when regulation is removed. In the case of airlines and railroads, the casualties were firms that, and people who had located in particular places, and there depended on the existence of this particular mode of transportation, that in a deregulating environment, was uneconomical, given that the price of the subsidizing product was declining and so the availability of dollars for subsidy. In the savings and loan industry, the offending pattern was a large overhang of low-rate mortgages that bore face maturities of up to thirty years. The cost of removing this overhang was the end of an industry that had financed the postwar build-out of suburban America and an enormous bill for the taxpayers. In the securities industry, it was the much quieter and less appealing story of an industry turned upside down. Secure and promising careers were ended, and famous firms were swallowed whole as competition created the need for new products and new skills.

Numberless trees and barrels of other hydrocarbons have been spent on the question of whether deregulation has been good for American economic life. In truth, there is no way to know the answer, for there is no way to know what would have happened had deregulation not happened, though the persistence of the status quo was not likely. Deregulation was, however, only a part of what was going on in economic life in the Eighties and Nineties. Much of the rest was the continued destruction of the economic model that had made the Fifties economy such a spectacular thing, probably by accident, by being the right model for that particularly unforeseeable time.

Increasingly, the Associationalist model of high prices, high wages, and lifetime employment, at least for white-collar workers, came undone in a range of industries, whether trade-protected or not. Copper, tires, textiles, clothing, shoes, televisions, stereos, dishes, glassware, cookware, watches, pens, and even telephones slowly became mostly imported products; autos, somewhat less.

Manufacturers continued the process of first conceding the low-end products, then the oldest manufacturing facilities, and finally whole markets.

In some areas, technological innovation or the development of new processes entirely—steel mini-mills using scrap for feedstock is a good example—kept parts of old industries alive. But more than occasionally, these were markets where manufacturing costs were not yet matched by foreign producers. In still other markets, a slimmed-down industry survived in niches—autos that are particularly designed for the odd tastes of the American consumer or specialty steels. And thus, left behind was a landscape surprisingly denuded of former industrial icons, except for a few long-term survivors. IBM, as well as Boeing and the rest of the surviving oligopoly that is the aerospace industry, are the most obvious; General Motors, Ford and the, no longer named Chrysler, the most recurrently troubled. These were joined by Hollywood and Wall Street. Even the conglomerate alternative to the Fifties industrial behemoths passed from the scene, a victim of the Eighties junk bond craze that facilitated busting up such entities for fun and profit, a topic taken up soon.

As one examines this record of the decline of heavy industry, it becomes apparent that the broad increase in the standard of living that took place in the Fifties and early Sixties has been America's own version of the winner's curse. Americans have always searched for new markets and so have been alive to the world of international trade. Free trade, and thus the idea of comparative national advantage, has been a truly central part of the national consciousness since World War II. Free trade, really freer trade, was to be a way to avoid the recurrence of the Depression, to unite nations by means of growing mutual dependency, and to provide an object lesson for the Third World of the benefits of open economies, in contrast to the closed Communist economies in Eastern Europe and Asia. Foreign policy thus supported freer trade, though at times domestic considerations made freer trade look more like trade managed for strategic national advantage.

Freer trade interacted with the American standard of living in a crucial way. As the United States became less of an island, less capable of standing separately, maintaining the standard of living that was built in a high-wage, high-price economy became more difficult. In response, Americans fighting to remain a part of the enlarged middle class, did many things. They drastically curbed saving. They supported tax reduction, borrowing from an uncertain future. They chose to try to increase their income by working harder; the growth of the two-wage-earner household during the Seventies and Eighties surely cushioned economic decline for families who found that local industrial jobs had disappeared. And they found it easy to increase their acceptance of lower cost imports from an international arena with which they were familiar and in which they were comfortable, if not wholly dominant. That arena became the source for the goods that were necessary for membership in the lower-middle class and above. And the best evidence of this hypothesis is the great political upheaval in the Eighties and Nineties when changes in economic life began to pinch the middle class. Since prices were as low as could be expected—but for a shift in the return on capital, again discussed below—Americans sought the extension of our collective budget by further reducing taxes and justifying that reduction by reducing benefits provided to those who could be seen to use them for other than middle-class services, i.e., immigrants and welfare recipients.

Of course, because of America's economic dependence on imported oil—environmental concerns, a part of a middle-class standard of living, have kept coal and nuclear power from being winners—and because of American's addiction to computers and consumer electronics, there was really no other plausible choice than freer trade. Letting the dollar become a reserve currency, indeed even exulting in it becoming such, was like the middle-class standard of living, a mixed blessing. It made trade easy, but it made investment easy also. The Interest Equalization Tax had a hidden lesson in it. Capital seeks its highest returns consistent with its tolerance for risk. And its tolerance for risk pretty much dictates its time horizon—ultra short to rather long.

In the Sixties and Seventies, when returns on invested capital were compared worldwide, returns in the United States were rather low. The reason was simple: lower returns were both part of our Associationalist model of a stable economy and likely in an insulated market where competition is "gentlemanly," and no one has to work very hard to keep a firm going. The difference was not enormous; a good guess is that it was about 4 percent between the even more Associationalist Germany and the United States.[50] But the difference was enough to mean that return on domestic investment in equities, and so stock prices, was marginally lower and that those who could move their funds around the world found that, once the value of major currencies was no longer tied to a stock of gold, numerous investment opportunities, denominated in various currencies, became real alternatives to investments denominated in dollars that were being printed with a certain abandon to finance wars, domestic deficits, and imports. Looked at critically, returns on investments denominated in dollars simply did not stand up to those available elsewhere. And so, those American firms that could move their funds around the world found that more promising investments in plant and equipment were to be had elsewhere. Often, these investments were made in pursuit of lower labor costs, at other times in new production processes, especially those substituting lighter weight components for heavier, since the modest increase in the cost of production was less than the decrease in the cost of ocean freight and so, the resulting product was still salable in the United States. Though investment in new plant and equipment was concentrated elsewhere, buying was still an available alternative for middle-class Americans addicted to their standard of living; increasingly, manufacturing was not.

There was, as is often the case, a countercurrent. The United Sates was still the largest economy in the world, though the expanding European Union with its new single currency, the euro, was trying to overtake it. American addiction to a Fifties standard of living for the broadened middle classes, maintained with imported goods, meant that foreign producers rapidly acquired great piles of dollars, for most the reserve currency of choice. Those earnings had to go somewhere. Conversion to foreign currencies would only result in a further decrease in the value of the earnings. Thus, many producers of imported goods used their dollars to make portfolio investments in New York, the largest and deepest securities market in the world; to purchase tangible American assets, such as real estate, still-viable manufacturing companies, or almost any service business; or to duplicate their existing, overseas plant and equipment in America, thus saving the transportation costs and simultaneously making their products more attractive to domestic customers. Oddly, what seemed to many observers to be a dangerous tendency to live well beyond our means, proved to be not even a half-bad experience for many Americans.

As the remnants of the Associationalist Fifties economy were being destroyed, a successor economy seemed to be growing, developed out of America's real economic strength—higher education. Computers, or at least their software (the major names were, alphabetically, Apple, Hewlett-Packard, a reinvigorated IBM, Intel, and Microsoft), pharmaceuticals, healthcare products, electronic technology spin-offs from defense industries, advanced engineering processes—were all high-growth, high-return industries right here in America; they were significant sources of exports as well. It seemed as if Americans were going to do the world's research and development. Production was another matter. All major (and a surprising percentage of minor) American corporations purveying consumer or industrial goods had built or acquired many international facilities capable of producing goods for local markets and for export to the United States. Production would increasingly be done elsewhere.

Another source of growth was in the continuing expansion of service industries: banking, insurance, real estate, healthcare, "hospitality," travel, and government. This was particularly true in the South and West, areas that had already increased their light-manufacturing base and so could support a similarly increased population. In Florida, as well as in the Southwest where the natives had expanded water supplies through transport by canal, growing numbers of retirees fueled still larger increases in the size of the service economy. In a real sense, service jobs also were a product of the American system of education, though not necessarily one to be proud of, filled as they were by a small number of college and professional degree holders and many others who, at best, held associates degrees and were paid accordingly.

These examples were noticed by that other high growth, high return product of our educational system, the financial managers that the Ford Foundation, so kindly fed us. They ran the financial services industry. The proliferation of new, and modestly useful financial products coming out of Wall Street's version of Hollywood's dream factories, which took advantage of the breadth and depth of the American capital markets and tapped into international markets as well, made many men (but few women) rich. In the process, the financial engineering that Wall Street delivered to the various institutions that increasingly came to dominate American financial markets—insurance companies, mutual funds, pension funds, the private foundations of the wealthy, university endowments and, do not forget, hedge funds—transformed the financial landscape. Where once a solid dividend record was all that counted when measuring a stock's attractiveness, now institutions—many so large that they would find it very hard to sell their holdings in any given stock and others limited in their ability to do so by their choice to pursue indexing as an investment strategy—gave attractiveness an entirely new dimension, a dimension derived from the new high-growth, high-return industries. Total return, the sum of dividends received and stock price appreciation, was now the measure of investment success—that, and steady earnings growth. All one heard was the demand for "increasing shareholder value," a euphemism for raising a company's stock price. And so, a failure to increase per share earnings was punished severely. Capital price appreciation was the investment game.

Thus, at the end of the Nineties, the United States appeared to be left with an economy that consisted of the products of the American system of higher education; those things that were too heavy and too inexpensive to be effectively made and shipped from overseas; services that had to be delivered locally[51] including construction; entertainment, always a viable industry for any cultural hegemon; autos, an industry kept alive by the growth of foreign manufacturers who, afraid of trade protection legislation, chose to use profits earned here to create plants producing for a market once served from abroad; and the sale of the myriad products, including fancy food, that made up a middle-class lifestyle. While some argued that the industries reborn by deregulation had to be added to this list, it was more likely that, just as had proven to be the case with truck and rail transportation, unless the deregulated industries were tied to the products of the American system of higher education, their growth represented one-time opportunities. It seemed that the American preference for oligopolistic competition—a modest possibility of price control derived from branding and economies of scale, coupled with an endless fear of a competitor's "breakout" innovation—would assert itself in deregulated industries as well, with a modest difference from the Fifties version of Associationalism: It would be accompanied by a largely financial oligarchy as well.[52]

The notion that economic life would be better if law went away is anything but new to America in these years. It is the root of British political economy from Adam Smith to John Stuart Mill and beyond, a set of ideas that had much purchase here during the forty years before World War I. In England, the targets for these ideas were limitations on, and monopolies of, trade—especially those designed to protect agriculture, guild, and contractual control of employment, and residual examples of price control, a remnant of Christian just price theory. However, the associated idea that, with the disappearance of these types of regulation, a natural market would reassert itself was then, and is now, a useful political trope, but really quite silly. None of the advocates of deregulation ever suggested that the great silent work of contract, tort, and property law be dispensed with. Indeed, many contemporary followers of this strand of political economy advocate strengthening the rights of property and contract, if not the law of torts. Commercial law is never targeted for deregulation nor intellectual property law, much less water rights in the intermountain West or riparian rights is the well-watered East.

What all of these various bodies of law help one to see is that there is no such thing as a "natural" market, a market whose definition/structure is independent of law. A deregulated market is as constituted by law—its operation delimited and its outcomes influenced by the combination of law with the routine practices and resource endowments of the participants—as a regulated one, thus changes in any combination of law, practices, and endowments will alter economic outcomes and so shuffle winners and losers in that market, but that is all. It will, in this sense, result in economic change, often in predictable ways. However, any notion that such change therefore will bring economic growth rather than redistribution of existing rewards is rather iffy. Thus, while there were modest changes in law throughout the Eighties and Nineties, just exactly what those changes had to do with the mixed record of growth here and decline there is difficult to say.

As is often the case, law worked to ameliorate catastrophes such as the aftermath of the Savings and Loan Crisis, where the Federal Government funded an overwhelmed FSLIC that in turn picked up the pieces. Why less was done for the employees and investors whose respective jobs and savings were destroyed when the economics of production and transportation of goods brought the continued decline in long-standing industries, is not clear. Law's impact on growth in the services sector seems to have been marginal, though exactly how to measure that growth is a difficult question. What is never remarked upon is the fact that some of the growth in the services sector of the economy is magnified by the decline in manufacturing. Had manufacturing remained strong, the same growth in the services sector of the economy would have appeared to be far less remarkable. More significant for understanding law and economy is the fact that during these years when it seemed that the only sources of growth were in the American system of higher education, a system that continued both to be emulated abroad and to draw increasing numbers of international students, public support for higher education began slowly to be withdrawn, while its costs began increasingly to be pushed onto students and their families.

The slow decline of public support for higher education fits with a different pattern, however. It is part of the earlier noted fight on the part of the enlarged middle class to maintain a social position defined, as would be expected in a consumer economy, by consumption. The two-wage-earner family was a sensible, if not welcomed, response to the economic squeeze that was the Great Inflation. Families chose to save less and borrow more, particularly by using ubiquitous credit cards, applications for which arrived almost every day in the mail. As a way of coping with middle-class incomes that had effectively declined or only stagnated, families also chose to spend available funds on cheaper imported goods. The importance of such spending is evidenced by the fact that it did not decline when, in the Tax Reform Act of 1986, the deduction of nonmortgage interest was withdrawn. If debt could finance current consumption, it could just as easily finance the increasing cost of higher education.

The choice to save less, spend more and, when possible, increase the reliance on debt to finance current expenditures fits nicely with the drive to control the one cost that the middle classes, the most persistent group of voters, can modestly influence—taxes. The now going on forty years of agitation to lower-middle class tax rates, while often a canard of the more than middle class, resonates with the middle classes because for them, the reduction of their major taxes—income or real estate—somehow seems like a big increase in disposable, i.e., consumable, wealth. And if rate reduction forces curbs on spending, well so be it. It is mostly other people who use government services, or so the middle classes are regularly told. Thus, while patterns of change in this economy during these years are hard to decipher—perhaps reflecting the fact that no economy emerged in them, however much "The New Economy" was on every pundit's tongue—in terms of law's relationship to the economy, a rhetorical pattern that was aimed at reducing the tax burden on the middle classes seemed to be discernible.

The Twenty-First Century: And Then It All Collapsed

"Seemed," however, is an important word in the assessment of economic life in the late Nineties, for as the early years of the new century showed, that life was anything but what it seemed. To understand why, one must double back to the Eighties.

Research in finance at the management schools established that a diversified portfolio of below market grade, or "junk" bonds, might well outperform a similar portfolio of market-grade bonds, because there was no reason to assume that defaults in a properly diversified portfolio of junk bonds would be in any way correlated. With this understanding and some shrewd salesmanship by a gentleman named Michael Milken at the investment bank Drexel, Burnham & Lambert, numerous institutional investors were willing to add a few junk bonds to their portfolio while other, more aggressive firms were willing to hold great chunks of these bonds.

The creation of a market in junk bonds made possible the leveraged acquisition of large, multidivisional firms, the conglomerates of the Sixties and Seventies. Stock in these entities, even when bought at a premium, was cheap enough that a buyer might expect that a strategy of radically trimming the product mix and slimming the workforce of each of the remaining units, would raise that unit's return on invested capital enough so that each unit was ready for resale at a price that, when added to the price garnered for the other units, was far in excess of the purchase price of the whole. This was a winning business strategy for some buyers of conglomerates and a losing strategy for others, but in the end, the growth of the junk bond market destroyed the conglomerate model of industrial organization. Created with inflation-influenced stock prices by the financial engineers in the management schools and left to slog around in our economy, the conglomerates were destroyed by the children of those same engineers.[53]

While painful for the conglomerates and other multidivisional firms taken over, the junk bond craze fueled the growth of several telecom enterprises that, with the break-up of AT&T and the development of wireless, helped transform that industry. Thus, the entire episode seemed a positive development for the economy overall, even though ultimately Milken was jailed for securities violations, Drexel similarly pled guilty and was dissolved in bankruptcy, and Ivan Boesky, one of the major players in the takeover of these companies, was also convicted of securities law violations.

Less positive was the savings and loan crisis, discussed above, that had begun about the same time as the junk bond craze, but continued. Here, the different understanding spread by the financial market theorists—that deregulation would bring innovation and growth—seemed not to pan out as bankers, freed of regulation, were cast adrift in a world they did not understand. When they were not therefore taken in by thieves and charlatans, they often proved to be thieves and charlatans themselves. Again, many of these people ended up in jail.

The junk bond craze, the savings and loan crisis, and the subsequent financial crises were underpinned by economic/financial models that assumed perfect competition and a normal distribution of economic events. This is not, in itself, surprising. Such models can establish singular, stable, equilibrium market outcomes. Almost any other, even vaguely plausible set of assumptions would yield multiple equilibria, results that would lead to indeterminate policy prescriptions and so undermine the pretense of economics and finance to science. In addition, these two assumptions fit with the ideology of free-market capitalism and thus the results produced were easily capable of being identified as efficient outcomes, a label with a certain psychological kick in a world where inefficiency is regularly seen as costly.

About the time that the savings and loan debacle was winding down, two Nobel Memorial Prize-winning economists and a famous trader, once an executive at the investment bank Salomon Brothers, decided to try their hand at running a hedge fund. The economists had pioneered work on models for pricing options and so their firm, Long-Term Capital Management, planned to use these theories and the trader's ability to manage leverage with the intention of making high returns based on strategies that used option-like instruments. For three years, Long-Term Capital Management was fabulously profitable. In the fourth year, an economic crisis in Russia that led to a quick decline in the value of the ruble caused the firm to implode and thus imperil many Wall Street banks, its trading partners. These banks were "encouraged" by the New York Federal Reserve Bank to organize the rescue and ultimate liquidation of the firm. Apparently, these Nobel Prize-worthy economic models did not work as well in practice as in theory, for they were built on assumed distributions of events that were not duplicated in a real financial market.

While Long-Term Capital was unraveling, something else was going on over in the stock market, a frenzy over the potential of the then still new internet—think AOL and Google. For several years, venture capital firms primarily located in Silicon Valley, had been backing start-up firms attempting to exploit the potential of this new technology. When the initial public offerings of the earliest start-ups were made and returned, to say the least, generous capital gains, Wall Street was alive with interest in anything related to the internet. Venture capital providers sprung up like mushrooms in all sorts of places other than Silicon Valley. Interest extended to bandwidth builders such as Global Crossing and WorldCom, and any business model that could exploit the coming paperless world, such as Groceries.com and Enron, which itself had nothing to do with the internet other than using it for trading purposes, a possibility opened up by deregulation of energy markets and the breakup of vertically integrated energy companies. Even cable television providers, such as AOL Time Warner, but most notably Adelphia, got swept up in the euphoria of providing internet services over their cable feeds. Somehow Health South, a healthcare company, somewhat improbably got included too.

Soon, everybody wanted to venture their capital and any three computer geeks with a demo and what might pass for a business plan could get a hearing from men in suits. Actually, making money was not necessary to secure funding; a decline in "burn rate," the measure of how fast existing cash reserves were being burned through when bringing an idea to market, brought additional waves of investor interest. And so, many of these geeks got real money. The stock market soared to its highest point ever, at least until the mania began to subside. Those who did their IPOs early made out like bandits; some like Google did far better. In the aftermath, many of the investors in what were called "dot.com" stocks lost everything, as did many investors in venture capital firms that backed them. Then it began to appear that many of the businesses swept along in the euphoria, businesses that actually seemed to be making money, including stars like Enron, Global Crossing, WorldCom, Adelphia, and Health South, turned out to have structured their books to hide the fact that their business model was flawed. Though the internet continued to grow, the stock market crashed. Soon the country was experiencing a real recession for the first time in years. This time some people went to jail, including some Wall Street stock analysts, and a bit of legislation commonly known as SOX, the Sarbanes-Oxley Act of 2002, a mishmash of provisions, including ones establishing a regulatory oversight body for auditors, requiring senior corporate executives to assume personal responsibility for the accuracy of corporate financial documents, and creating enhanced reporting requirements for financial transactions was passed to remind corporations not to cook their books.

Unfortunately, here is where things got complicated. Quickly, the Federal Reserve, following the by then Keynesian orthodoxy, brought interest rates down with a crash and kept them there.[54] As was the case the last time this happened, during the stagflation of the Seventies and in the aftermath of the early-Eighties recession, real estate began to take off, particularly in the Sunbelt states. It was a classic bubble, though many including regulators, denied this characterization. Without the Savings and Loans around to extend mortgages, their role was taken over by individuals or firms called "mortgage brokers," who, *for a fee*, were willing to arrange to lend money to anyone with an appropriate risk profile, ultimately to anyone with any possible, or impossible, credit record, and for pretty much any real property, though especially for Florida and Southern California condominiums and Arizona and Nevada single-family homes. Of course, not all mortgagors were new homebuyers. Many were owners of existing homes who were refinancing, either to take advantage of the continuing decline in mortgage rates or to use the increase in home prices to justify an increase in the size of an existing mortgage that followed the decline of interest rates with the purpose of taking cash out of the refinancing and to use it for other purposes, or both. There were also investors buying multiple new homes for the purpose of resale. These individuals, and many of those in the other two categories, expected that rising home prices meant that a resale or another refinancing would repair any errors in judgment as well as produce profits on resale or more cash from yet another refinancing.

The buyers of all of these mortgages expected to sell them quickly to someone, most likely a bank, but occasionally a non-bank bank[55] like the mortgage lender Countrywide Financial, who, *for a fee*, would package them for the next buyer who would package the packages *for a fee* and then sell the packaged packages to the ultimate buyer who, like everyone before, was uninterested in any actual mortgage loan, but only in the package. Most of the packagers were Wall Street entities, often investment banks, but increasingly financial holding companies. These entities had a vehicle necessary for absorbing this entire "product." Indeed, they soon needed all the product that could be offered. They had taken the simple securitization model developed for Fannie Mae and Freddie Mac twenty years earlier and improved it by constructing a new generation of CMOs, this time complex securities designed to mirror the particular needs of various buyers. *Fees were taken* for this service too, while arguing to the credit-rating agencies that the economic notion, at the root of the junk bond craze, that diversification of investment could reduce risk was precisely what these securities represented and so they were worth the highest possible rating.

As if this were not enough, the same firms developed vehicles that seemed to take these mortgages off their own balance sheets while awaiting packaging; they were called Securitized Investment Vehicles (SIVs) and Conduits. Meanwhile, the need for product led to the development of securities called Collateralized Loan Obligations (CLOs) containing medium and large business loans and Collateralized Debt Obligations (CDOs) containing the lowest rated, and so most dubious, pieces of these CMOs, pieces of CLOs and other debt interests, including large commercial real estate loans and "leveraged" (junk or subprime) loans, often from private equity transactions undertaken at unheard-of levels of leverage, not to mention "synthetic versions of these securities.[56] And to assuage the fears of regulators or private entities, that for one reason or another were concerned about the riskiness of these or other securities, banks and other financial entities, *yet again for a fee*, created instruments called Credit Default Swaps (CDSs) designed both to "insure" against the possibility of default, and at the same time to not be securities within the meaning of the various Securities Acts, but futures regulated under the various acts governing commodities and futures exchanges or limitedly regulated, "over-the-counter" transactions.

What no one seemed to notice was that, while the circle of financial players in this game had become larger as European banks and American and European issuers joined the game, what Wall Street had created was the simultaneous replay of the crazed lending that characterized the savings and loan crisis, complete with the requisite thieves and charlatans, the interconnected liabilities of the Long-Term Capital Management disaster, and the accounting shenanigans of the dot.com hangers on, some of whom might have been described as thieves and charlatans too. There was, however, one difference. As a result of the adoption of the Gramm-Leach-Bliley, or Financial Services Modernization Act of 1999, which removed the barriers between commercial and investment banking dating back to the Glass-Steagall Act of 1933 and brought the dawn of an era of "light" bank regulation that echoed the deregulation ethos of the Eighties, the commercial banks (really financial holding companies and other financial institutions) had become complicated behemoths. Each tried to imitate the European model of the "universal" bank in the hope that, as a "financial supermarket," a classic buzz word of the era, each could both cross-sell products and cross-subsidize internal operations. Together these objectives would reduce costs and increase profits.

What is most fascinating about these entities *taking a fee* while passing product up or out of the chain is the question of who was ultimately providing the funding and who was bearing the risk of default—traditionally the same financial entity. In response to the dot.com bust, the Federal Reserve had tried to keep interest rates low. As a result, everyone and her brother was rabidly looking for higher yielding investments, and in so doing was accepting more risk than might have traditionally been the case. Whether the premium charged for accepting such additional risk was adequate was not particularly clear at the time. Private equity firms set the mark here. They bought assets, heavily leveraged the acquisition, and when lucky, sold in two or three years, from time to time collecting a large, debt-financed dividend along the way. Hedge funds mimicked this design with much success, but the two most desperate players were the banks and the money market mutual funds.

The money market funds, inventions of the Seventies, had turned into entities that gathered idle working capital from corporate treasurers seeking higher returns than the banks could afford to offer, even to large depositors. These funds had long invested in commercial paper, the short-term debt—no more than ninety days—issued by major companies. The banks that had lost this source of deposits were constrained from holding assets that had a desirable yield by the so-called Basel II rules, (an internationally negotiated standards for bank capital adequacy) enforced by various bank regulators, that related the amount and type of assets held to the necessary amount of a bank's capital. Like many such financial constraints, this one had a certain amount of wiggle room. Capital adequacy was measured, not by the face value of an asset, but by its risk weighted value, unfortunately initially measured by the bank itself. Still, it was a plausible assumption that more risky assets were more likely to default, and so required a greater capital cushion than less risky assets. Individual loans were deemed more risky; highly rated securities, i.e., certified as such by rating agencies, even CMOs, CLOs, and CDOs backed by the kind of loans that, standing alone would be risky, were deemed less risky, once again based on the reasoning that a diversified pool of assets would over time perform better than any single asset, chosen at random, in the pool.

The only assets seen as less risky than AAA securities were US Treasury notes and bonds, confusingly also rated AAA, long a staple of buy-and-hold investors.

However, with the Federal Reserve relentlessly driving interest rates down, banks had little reason to amass Treasuries, for the spread between their yield and a bank's cost of funds was shrinking. Banks had previously satisfied their day-to-day credit needs through the repo market, a market in ultrashort—one to nine days—loans. Credit in this market was inexpensive, because all lending was secured and formally evidenced by a matched pair of contracts—the present sale of a security, matched with an agreement to repurchase that security, or one identical to it, one to nine days later, at a price just slightly higher than the sale price, an increment that represented the interest on the loan. This was the market where the money market funds and other non-bank banks regularly "put to work," earn a return on, their otherwise uninvested funds. With Treasury yields low and yields on the highest rated—AAA—portions of CMOs, CLOs, and CDOs significantly higher, banks (and again other non-bank banks or large investors) came to understand that they could increase the spread between the returns on their assets and their cost of funds by switching from Treasuries to these other AAA securities. Money market funds were willing to provide funds to carry, in effect finance the purchase of these securities because the repo interest rate for such securities was higher—not dramatically, but still higher—than the rate earned on repos of Treasuries. And, if further risk reduction seemed appropriate or desired, these banks and other non-bank banks or large investors could protect their assets by purchasing Credit Default Swaps, supposedly providing protection against default, protection that was often extended by the same web of banks, non-bank banks, and large investors.

Pretty soon, banks were buying CMOs, CLOs, and CDOs issued by other banks[57] because bank regulators treated them as requiring a low risk weighted capital charge. The banks expected that these securities would be financed with overnight funds in the repo market, rather than just using that market for short-term cash needs. The banks were thus earning fees on the transactions leading up to the issuance of these securities, and then funding the purchase of similar securities issued by other banks at ultralow rates. They thus had turned what once were individual loans of little or no liquidity and bearing a high risk-based capital requirement, into seemingly liquid assets returning a lesser, but still significant rate that carried a low risk-adjusted capital charge. Thus, leverage could increase at little cost. Return on equity, roughly the measure of a bank's use of capital, could rise significantly. With greater earnings per share, bank stocks rose, and bankers were paid handsomely until the merry-go-round slowed and then suddenly stopped. What followed made the recessions of the early Eighties and the early Naughts seem like ordinary cloudy days and is now known as the Great Recession. Apparently, some of the products of the American system of higher education were not what they were cracked up to be, for as it turned out, products conceived under theories that emphasized risk dispersal/diversification turned to have concentrated ownership, undermining the assumptions of those theories.[58]

At first, the only hint of the soon-to-be disaster was the slowing of the growth of real estate prices. Then came a decline in mortgage originations starting in late 2005. This was followed by a rise in the default rates on recently issued mortgages and a worry about the value of various mortgage-backed securities on balance sheets. Funding of SIVs and Conduits started to become difficult and occasionally to fail with the result that their assets had to be returned to bank balance sheets. Banking insiders would have noticed a growing panic about getting mortgage loans off balance sheets and securities out the door.

In mid-2007, two investment funds marketed by Bear Stearns that contained CMOs and similar securities, had been forced to liquidate because a decline in asset values had led to financial problems. Then, various financial firms began to recognize losses on their portfolio of securities, showing large losses as part of their quarterly financial statements. These losses reduced their regulatory capital. Such a reduction in capital necessitated the sale of securities to remain within the Basel II rules, further depressing values. Rumors about various entities having funding problems began to be confirmed as funding crises were solved with massive loans. Then quickly, such crises could only be solved by the purchase of the failing institution by a stronger one—Bear Stearns, an investment bank, was the first; later came Washington Mutual, Countrywide Financial, and finally Merrill Lynch, a securities broker-dealer,—often with the aid of the Federal Reserve. Finally, Lehman Brothers failed and filed for bankruptcy, which caused the default on an issue of its own securities held by the Reserve Primary Fund, a major money market fund.[59] This loss caused the fund to "break the buck," to reduce the value of its assets below the numerical sum of its investors' stakes in the enterprise, and thus brought on real panic in the streets. If money market funds were no longer a safe investment, everything more risky was suddenly far riskier than before. The financial system ground to a halt.

After all the important people were done being amazed that it was a mistake to have let Lehman Brothers fail, both the Federal Reserve and the United States Treasury sprang into action. Almost all of their actions were designed to bolster the liquidity in and, more importantly the solvency of, the financial system. The Treasury secured a piece of legislation, TARP (Troubled Asset Purchase Program), that was supposed to fund the purchase of troubled assets; assets whose value had radically declined, from large and not so large banks. That program ran aground over questions about how to value the troubled assets and so morphed into a different program that allowed the Treasury to shore-up bank capital by purchasing nonvoting preferred stock. However, the Fed, with the help of its nominally independent New York branch, did most of the work.

After allowing the two surviving investment banks—Goldman Sachs and Morgan Stanley—to become commercial banks, subject to regulation as such (a small price to pay for access to Federal Reserve funding mechanisms when solvency was in question because of the lack of liquid markets) the Fed began to spread money right and left, most often by lending against collateral of dubious quality—for example money market fund commercial paper, commercial paper of business borrowers, collateralized paper of many varieties, and debt of both Fannie and Freddie.[60] All of these efforts provided liquidity in the aftermath of the Lehman bankruptcy. This program continued with regular purchases of the debt of the federal government. Two nonfinancial entities, General Motors and Chrysler, received direct Treasury investments in stock as part of a carefully engineered quick trip into and out of bankruptcy. A big insurance company, AIG, which turned out to have written the lion's share of Credit Default Swaps with respect to various issues of collateralized securities whose value had been drastically reduced, a classic example of misperceived risk, was forced to pay in full its obligations on those swaps. Paying these obligations was a way for the Fed to further shore-up AIG's counterparties, mostly large banks, by using funds provided by the Treasury, again for the purchase of AIG stock, this time nonvoting common stock.

While various pundits weighed in on the questions of the legality, necessity, effectiveness, and cost of all of these programs, the financial system slowly healed itself, paying off loans with profits, and avoiding equity dilution when replenishing capital. Unemployment peaked and took forever to decline. A bit of legislation, commonly known as the Dodd-Frank Act of 2011, increased the safety and soundness of the financial system by forcing banks to hold more capital and so decrease leverage;[61] it seems to have been as effective as SOX was in curbing financial accounting abuse. This time, no one seems to have gone to jail, except for ordinary Securities Act violations.

It took nearly a decade to finish the recapitalization of the largest banks in the increasingly concentrated banking system under the new, Basel III standards; curiously, this is about as long as it took to deleverage the banking system after the Panic of 1907 and then again after the onset of the Depression. It took just as long to bring employment back to the level it was before the financial crisis.

Wage growth was almost non-existent and overall economic growth lagged too. The explanations for the slow recovery from the Great Recession were as various and inconsistent as those given for the Great Inflation. From a worldwide perspective, one might have imagined economic blocs as if they were a group of boys at their first middle-school dance egging one another on about asking some arbitrarily defined, pretty girl to dance—"No, I'll join in, if your go first." Nationally, almost all one heard were the tired tropes coming from a badly polarized political system about the evils of "bail outs" and "job killing" regulation, as contrasted with necessity for, and the lack of, sufficient stimulus and the need to protect both consumers and the federal government from financial misbehavior of many kinds. Together with the endless assertions that proposed spending was unaffordable, even though seemingly lots of money was sloshing around in the economy, all of this language provided good clues that no one really had any idea about what might need to be done and why.

Meanwhile, income inequality continued to grow as the middle-middle and lower-middle classes continued to hollow out, especially outside of the urban areas on both coasts. The talk everywhere was about globalization, not that this had not been happening to humans for a very long time, though for Americans it had picked up speed first with containerization, then with various trade agreements, and most recently with the establishment of Permanent National Trade Relations[62] with China in 2000. Continued offshoring of production processes, a process that had begun in the Sixties and had made goods cheaper for American consumers, added to the job loss that came from the decline in American-made goods. Not surprisingly, alternative employment opportunities came with reduced wages.

Somehow mysteriously related talk about the growth of social media companies and various online services that came with stories of instant great wealth bestowed on twenty-somethings, did not advance the discussion of growing inequality. Talk about online shopping on Amazon and elsewhere that seemed to portend only more jobs with quite modest wages filling orders in cavernous, surely misnamed, "fulfillment centers," was not helpful either. Everywhere the need for more education was touted together with the promise of higher wages for graduates. Incongruously, accompanying stories about crushing student debt, modest salaries, and deadening employment routines did not note the irony deprivation at the root of the proffered remedy for job losers.

Still, all the talk about economic growth, always tied to the wired or wireless internet was not a phantom. Everywhere there were apps for the quickly ubiquitous smart phones that turned out to be both addictive and annoying deliverers of ads, the doings of friends and family, the importunings of business associates, driving directions, and a portable version of the old Yellow pages phone directory as well as being actual telephones. Financial markets kept bringing forth new "product" almost all designed either to increase fee income or decrease transaction costs, the proliferation of index funds being the best example of the latter. And the jabber about private markets being the new public markets seemed as best a distraction for remembering that public markets, except markets for corporate debt, never raised a lot of money for capital investments, and that what the private markets were really doing was providing a substitute for capital expansion in the absence of retained earnings and creating a way for early investors potentially to monetize the paper growth in the value of their capital investments.

Not surprisingly almost no one suggested that the Federal Reserve's continuation of very low interest rates might possibly result in a repeat of the boom-and-bust cycle that started with similar Fed actions following the dot.com bust of 2000. What was lacking everywhere, but in the world of start-ups, was the optimism that permeated the Nineties.[63]

To know something is to be able to name it.[64] If the Fifties instantiated an Associationalist economy, what name properly describes the American economy in the Twenty-First Century? The last two decades of the Twentieth Century did not see a return to the laissez-faire capitalism thought to have gripped the United States in the 1890s. For all the complaints about the costs of regulation, protections for the environment, food and drug, labor relations, occupational safety, pension, product safety, securities, and wage and hourly employment protections have not disappeared. Social Security and Medicare, unemployment, bank deposit, pension, and brokerage failure insurance survived largely intact. The economy did not emulate the Gilded Age financiers and break into an orgy of unrestrained, to-the-death competition. Nor is it likely that it will. Oligopoly is too much a part of the American and world experience now. Bigger is better because bigger has a better chance of controlling price in a world where branding counts for much and economies of scale are still believed to count for more. In this way what has happened in banking is no outlier. We are not turning backward.

For a while, it appeared that a namable economy began to emerge from the Eighties. During these and the following years, financial markets became incredibly disciplining. Companies had to deliver ever higher total returns on capital based on steady, predictable earnings growth or face pressure to cut losses quickly. This was an unforgiving economy, an economy where people with the labor market skills of the hour were pampered as never before, but only for as long as their star shone brightest. No longer Associationalist, the American economy seemed to have become Impatient.

The Associationalist economy promised that economic growth would increase the availability of leisure; in response, some commentators even began to worry that so much leisure time would become a social problem. By the Twenty-First Century, all that was past; now there would be no leisure time until retirement, should retirement ever come. The communications revolution meant that the global stock market, which operates around the clock, could be checked at any time in the day or night while on safari in Africa. First, courier largely replaced real mail; in turn, courier was replaced by fax; then, the on-time standard was email and text messaging, available essentially anywhere, anytime by mobile phone. Coast-to-coast and intercontinental flights had become staples of commerce, where once the pace of train and ocean travel—both with real sleep caught on the way—was once a break from the daily routine. The best production process was a just in time production process.

In the financial world, large "players" focused solely on asset price appreciation. Though often heavily leveraged, they were essentially risk adverse, and so eschewed both "speculation" and long-term investment, yet expected transactional liquidity supplied by buyers and lenders. They could move enormous amounts of money almost instantaneously, and pretty much without regard to national borders. The markets where some put their money to work were driven, not by earnings trends, but by quarterly earnings, or more often expectations about quarterly earnings, by expectations about the next Fed Open Market Committee meeting and not by the results of the meeting itself. Others came to see advantage in getting an infinitesimally small temporal jump on the competition to exploit fleeting discrepancies between market prices and thought that overnight was a long time to hold a position while instant liquidity was necessary and so often assumed.

Individuals came to think similarly about their own compensation. Such was best delivered in cash right now and in the largest possible amount. If it had to be in stock, it was better if it were saleable very soon, or if in options, "in the money" now. They seemed to understand that Marx was right when he noted that, in capitalism, it is always possible that, "All that is solid melts into air," and so, many craved the solidity of eight-figure, full floor penthouses in Manhattan.[65]

Yet, it soon became clear that what seemed to be the economy—a persistent market structure fusing an understanding of economic life with patterns of behavior within the economic, political, and social institutions that enact that understanding—was anything but. While impatience was seen in many places, as often in the case when capitalism is engaged in creative destruction, a persistent structure was nowhere to be found. Not surprisingly, CEOs, politicians and especially pundits, peddling their wares on talk shows in the hope of securing the requisite Warholean fifteen minutes of fame with its attendant monetary recompense, regularly tried to sell us on the idea that we finally did have the economy. However, for most citizens, especially those without education beyond high school, these assertions seem implausible.

The best evidence of the implausibility of such stories is the long list of financial disasters over the past thirty plus years. After junk bonds destroyed conglomerates, and bank lending practices plus regulatory mistakes destroyed the savings and loan industry, Long-Term Capital Management destroyed itself and strong-arm tactics on the part of the New York Federal Reserve Bank only averted wider damage to the economy. Then, in quick succession, came the dot. com boom and bust and a real estate securitization boom and bust, again facilitated by regulatory mistakes—most notably the Gramm-Leach Bliley Act's push into deregulation of the traditional structure of banking. Such is evidence of the absence of anything like a persistent market structure. Perhaps a more complete historical perspective may help understanding here.

Understanding Economic Change

It seems best to see this long story as one of change and growth in not wholly unpredictable, but hardly necessary, ways. Capitalism destroyed some of the postwar economic edifice, an edifice built out of earlier understandings of what made for a good economy and the accident of conditions at the end of World War II. But, in no sense was it obvious exactly how capitalism would work Schumpeter's "creative destruction," or to what end.[66]

What then of Fred Konefsky's "technology of freedom," the motive force of creative destruction? It is reasonably clear that no such thing was operative in the Fifties. The Quiet Generation was most notable because it was quiet. With hindsight, low birthrates in the Depression and the early war years resulted in a small cohort of new entrants into the workforce, and so economic opportunities did not have to expand at a fast pace to create a sense of good times. And, again with hindsight there were hints of something to come—television, the interstate highway system, and the move of both the Dodgers and the Giants to the West Coast pastures. But the Fifties were the end product of a stable economic formation.

In the Sixties and Seventies, on the other hand, one can see the breakdown of that stability, particularly in terms of changes in the international monetary system. Hints appear more densely—computers; malls with their ubiquitous national brands; the growth of air travel and containerized shipping; the silent growth of the industrial offshoots of higher education; and the flow of foreign autos, electronics, and oil. But the pain of those years, a rampant inflation, and an extraordinary decline in industrial productivity, was the pain of things falling apart, not the birth of a technology of freedom.

The Eighties, Nineties, and Twenty-First Century present a more difficult question. The past forty or so years have been in an intense period of what Schumpeter would have seen as creative destruction. The cumulative effect of changes in communication and transportation; the relative shift to an economy based more on services, particularly financial services, than on large-scale industrial production; the appearance of a truly national market in consumer goods and an international market in the products of the American entertainment and finance industries; and the spread of biotechnology and computer capacity, have together brought both creative and destructive change on an extraordinary scale. Fights over freer trade and income inequality evidence both that creativity and that destruction.

Thus, it is clear that Americans have a surfeit of technology. Freedom is another matter, for the concept of a technology of freedom implies a stable economic formation, a place for at least many, if not all, to experience the fruits of technology to express freedom. Americans have yet to see such stability for more than fifty years.

Perhaps it is too soon to expect to see the emergence of a stable economic formation. After all, the Associationalist economic stability took a long time to come together from its beginnings in the 1870s as the agrarian and artisanal manufacturing economy of the pre-Civil War years was destroyed and painfully replaced. First came a national railroad network and the shift from the earlier methods for the production of capital goods to industrial methods involving great hordes of unskilled workers. Then, this process was repeated in the production of consumer goods, which expanded rapidly with the extension of electric power and internal combustion engines. The whole process took about seventy-five years, but generated only about twenty years of economic stability, twenty years to enjoy the freedom made possible by technology. Measured on this Braudelian time scale, Americans still have twenty-five, maybe fifty years to go. Their unwillingness to wait needs to be damped down.

Rather than seeing this story about America as unfinished, it could be seen as one of rise and decline *simlpiciter*. However, doing so would ignore that it is a very ambiguous story. An attempt to maintain America's position of power, to remain as a colossus, would have required an isolationist course in the face of pressing reasons to do otherwise. Rebuilding Europe meant avoiding the debacle that a second Weimar Republic in Germany might have caused. Similarly, rebuilding both Europe and Japan was seen as necessary to match the advance of international communism. Both results are arguably good, whatever one thinks about the political motivations that prompted them. So at most, an honest story of rise and decline would more likely turn out to be, not a story of decline, but in decline brought about as a necessary part of seeking noble ends, of economic self-sacrifice.

It would be a mistake to see this story as one of rise and decline in another sense. The Fifties economy, which we take as the touchstone of a good economy, the economy that produced the optimism necessary for the great social and economic reforms of the Johnson years that now are being "rolled back,"[67] was a deceptive economy; it was not an economy of continuous upward progress. The Fifties had three recessions of its very own; but it was an economy accompanied by a sense of limitless prospect. Unfortunately, that sense was based on the absence of others in Europe and the Far East. Absences, whether in texts, discourses, or economies, distort perception. Implausible possibilities appear real and real likelihoods seem implausible. Decline from a distorted perception is a distorted perception of decline.

There are, however, three alternative meanings that merit a consideration more serious than an understanding of rise and decline. The first is Lenin's prediction of the inevitable shift of the West from industrial to finance capitalism.[68] Though such a story is part of a currently unfashionable intellectual tradition, in very real ways, it fits the evidence better than a story of rise and decline. The Fifties in America was without a doubt the apogee of the industrial economy. The present dominance of the United States' economy by financial institutions is unlikely to have peaked, however much one might hope otherwise.

The problem with the Leninist story is twofold. First and most simply, in the Fifties, capitalism was Associationalist; today, it is something else or maybe nothing at all. Since the Fifties, there has been a change in the way that capitalism thinks of itself, but the relationship between that thinking and economic activity in the world is less than tight. That capitalism thinks of itself as centered in asset price appreciation, that this is where the big money is to be made, does not make finance the center of the economy. Indeed, finance, standing alone, is a zero/sum game—my gain is your loss and then we add in the transaction costs. That finance understands this peculiar property is evidenced by its relentless attempt to reduce transaction costs and to maintain the ability to exploit information asymmetries, not to mention its attempt to earn fees multiple times as others shoulder financial risk. It is only by financing something else that it becomes barely possible for financial capital to yield a net economic gain.

Second, financial capitalism is hardly as dominant as it would have us believe. There still is an industrial capitalism with industrial production centered in the Sunbelt, not to mention all over the world. Why else the continuing outcry against impediments to union organizing efforts, sweatshops, and environmental degradation, staples of the Nineteenth Century's problems of an industrial economy? Industrial production seems to have departed mostly from the Rustbelt in the United States.[69] Again, this is a problem of distorted perception, a problem perhaps exaggerated by this story.

A second alternative meaning would focus on the transportation revolution that began in the Twenties with the decline of the railroads and the rise of interstate trucking, and, after the Fifties, continued with the great expansion of air travel and the rise of containerized shipping. Strangely, these changes were followed by the modest resurgence of a now largely unregulated, oligopolistic rail system, which may be in the process of uniting with the equally oligopolistic Canadian system. This revolution parallels the communications revolution that began years earlier with the decline of the telegraph, the rise of the long-distance telephone, then the intercontinental telephone, then microwave, cell phone, broadband, wireless and satellite communication, as all of these have interacted with the mainframe and the networked personal computer, the laptop, the tablet, and the smart phone. These twin revolutions are the most obviously positive aspects of "deregulation" in the United States, and both have transformed the economy in significant ways that skews any story of rise and decline or of a purported shift from industrial to finance capitalism.

Changes in transportation and communication have brought a reduction of distance in economic affairs. London or Tokyo is closer now than they were, even in 1950. This change has followed a shift of power away from local interests, from the guys (a word used intentionally) who visibly got together to decide about economic matters—local manufacturers, local labor leaders, local civic leaders—to more distant interests, again generally guys, who peer into one or more computer screens, situated everywhere and nowhere who make decisions about production and finance that are felt all over the globe.

However, there is a problem with the assertion that this story is all about transportation and communication. It is but a portion of the larger story of globalization, a story that may or may not start in East Africa but is underway by the time of the rise of the civilizations of the Tigris and Euphrates River valleys. What is a constant is an expanded consciousness of, and intersection with, places faraway, at least in terms of technologies of transportation and communication. What is new in this long story arc is the fact that, for the first time the effective world is pretty much the actual world.

For well over six thousand years, local economies have been upended as methods of communication and transportation have allowed the expansion of trade, and local dreamers have had their minds opened to new possibilities made available from that same expansion. Thus, the experience of a loss of local control or local life has been one of long standing. Loss of local control distorts perception by making local phenomena, in this case a clear shift in the dominant forces in economic life in the United States from industrial to financial behemoths, seem more important than they are in the expanded, effectively world, economy. Similarly, loss of local control draws too much attention to the messengers of change and too little to the underlying structural shifts that make these messages possible. Yet again, this is a problem of distorted perception.

Still a third meaning to the story of American economic life might be based on the assertion that the years since World War II have instantiated the triumph of consumerism in both its positive and negative senses. *Dinglichkeit* pervades the land in ways that simply weren't true sixty years ago.

The ability to tell a story about the triumph of consumerism in America is clear. The lives of Americans outside the lowest classes are filled to overflowing with goods, goods that are at best, transiently satisfactory. Just what will enter our lives after the departure of the double mocha decaf latte with a hint of cinnamon is not clear, but what ought to be clear is that in time, something else will come, just as something else came after wood oven-fired, goat cheese pizza. We hate our cars and can't repair them, but there is no reason to believe that we would consider acting on that dissatisfaction, any more than we would act on our unhappiness with the disruption in our lives that comes from cell phones going off in meetings, classes, cars, and concerts.

There is a clear isomorphism between consumerism and the rise of freer trade after World War II. Freer, never free, trade advantages consumers as a class over producers as a class, though not necessarily all consumers or all producers. It provides those local consumers, whose income it does not reduce, with more and cheaper and different goods than those provided theretofore by local, now disadvantaged producers. And freer trade and its seeming isomorph, consumerism, might both be linked to something as specific and obvious as the fear of a return of the Depression that we sought to hold off with a Keynesian emphasis on the production and consumption of consumer goods.

But the associations between freer trade and consumerism, and between both and the Depression, as obvious as they may be, are no tighter than the associations between the way capitalism thinks of itself and economic activity in the wider world. Freer trade would work without consumerism; it would just be based more on durable goods. Consumerism would work without freer trade; it would just be based more on locally produced goods. And fear of the return of the Depression might have been assuaged by freer trade in durables or by a local consumerism.

All versions of the story of the triumph of consumerism have a problem. Before the Fifties, there were consumers and a consumer society; in the Twenties, almost half of the twenty largest manufacturing companies produced consumer goods.[70] Before the Fifties, there were fewer middle-class consumers and fewer things to consume.

The Fifties expansion of the middle class downward to encompass a previously excluded group of both blue-and white-collar workers was, it should be remembered, intimately tied to the return of victorious veterans of World War II and then the Korean "police action." It was prolonged into the Seventies by their existence, though unfortunately probably not much by the addition of the new, Vietnam veterans to the ranks of the old. This expansion of the middle class created the possibility of consumption on a scale that was more noticeable than that provided earlier by the department store and the Sears, Roebuck catalog. What a buoyant economy, however deceptive was that buoyancy, changed radically was that it supported the development of mass consumption.

The growth of truly mass consumption is not something deserving of a sneer. It, together with the malling of America and the technical capacity provided by the transportation and communication revolutions, created a single country offering a single experience out of what previously was the geographic proximity of many local and regional tastes. The proliferation of national brands to such an extent that, in the mid-Eighties, children from Buffalo could feel completely at home the first time they visited a mall in Flagstaff, Arizona, created a national experience that simply was unavailable before. From a national experience might flow a national identity. But it seems wrong to see any consumer society as the cornerstone national identity, as if consumerism would define a people and its civilization.

All civilizations define themselves through what they produce and consume, whether it be art, olives, slaves, wheat, nobility, beef, steam engines, chilies, refinement, or oversized apple walnut muffins. Mass consumption does not alter this fact for good or ill. On the good side, it is desirable for the United States finally to have something approaching a national culture, even if it is a national culture based on branded apparel, hotel chains, and smart phones. More than two hundred years is a long time to wait. On the ill side, there is a certain ephemeral tackiness to our mass consumption. But that is not new. The extension of consumer goods through industrial production to the upper reaches of the slowly expanding middle class of the Nineteenth Century brought forth a similar wringing of hands, a cry of consumerism. We know that extension by the names given to the arts and crafts movement—Pre-Raphaelite and Roycroft—a movement that, whatever the acknowledged beauty of the objects that it produced, is easily understood as nostalgia on the part of a privileged class for an earlier time when the new consumers were anonymous workers and faceless servants. The present cry of consumerism risks validating a similar sense of the nostalgia for an earlier time on the part of a differently privileged class.

If no technology of freedom has emerged, if stories of decline *simpliciter* or a Leninist story of the inevitability of finance capitalism or one focusing on transportation and communication or another on consumerism are all unsatisfactory understandings of this story of our present American economy, what is left? When reading Romeo and Juliet for the first time, as late as Act III one would be hard pressed to decide whether Shakespeare had written a romance or a tragedy. At the same place in Hamlet multiple possible endings are still open. After Elizabeth Bennett refuses Mr. Darcy's offer of marriage in *Pride and Prejudice*, it is possible that Darcy will throw himself off a bridge and a remorseful Elizabeth will become a cloistered nun. In the middle of stories, it is always difficult to see how it will all work out.

It seems that this story has no obvious meaning because it is difficult to focus one's mind firmly on some thing or some story that is neither stable nor obvious. And such is the position Americans find ourselves in with respect to the trajectory of our present economy. Economic change is open-ended. Change may or may not lead to the stasis of the enactment of the (insert your favorite greatest hope) economy. If it does, Americans may get a happy ending, but then again, they may not. The best thing about America's position is that Americans do not know the ending and so might act in a way that would alter the trajectory of their story. The point of this book is to understand how economic development takes place, and so, how it might be sensible to act. Only after looking at the history of a particular economy, that of Buffalo in Part II, will it be appropriate to turn to questions of understanding and then action.

PART II

Community and Economic Change in America

Buffalo, Queen City of the Great Lakes

As the United States expanded west in the early Nineteenth Century, the development of an inexpensive, all-water route via lakes Erie, Huron, and Michigan that could bring immigrants to the upper Midwest and send Midwestern agricultural products back east, presented an interesting opportunity. Seizing it, DeWitt Clinton, Governor of the State of New York, convinced the state's legislature to fund the building of what came to be called the Erie Canal, or more colloquially, Clinton's Ditch. In part, the objective of this project was to strengthen the economic position of the state's Atlantic Ocean port city of the same name by building an alternative to the existing routes to "the West," one overland from Philadelphia through Harrisburg and Carlisle and on to Pittsburgh; another up the Potomac to the Cumberland Narrows, then overland to the Monongahela or Youghiogheny Rivers and on to Pittsburgh; and a third that swept south to breach the Appalachians at either the New River or the Cumberland Gap. All wended their way to the Ohio River and all routes favored the ports of Philadelphia or Baltimore, as well as seeded the development of Cincinnati and Pittsburgh.[1] A northern route needed a port at the eastern end of Lake Erie. Potentially, the port might develop into a major trade and transport center.

Of the choices New Amsterdam, now known as Buffalo, was not immediately obvious. Located about a mile south of the point where the lake drains north into the Niagara River, the river that eventually tumbles over Niagara Falls, near the junction between Lake Erie and Buffalo Creek, Buffalo did not offer a particularly attractive harbor. The serpentine course of the creek suggested it could easily silt up. Likewise, the prevailing southwesterly winds, together with the strong current created as the lake narrowed into the river's channel, suggested that so much sand could be dumped at the city's doorstep as to make harbor maintenance a continuing project. Alternative harbors could have been found four miles north, where Scajaquada Creek flows into the Niagara; or ten miles north, where Tonawanda Creek flows into that river. Unlike at Buffalo whose harbor is unprotected from the winds, both were protected by an island—Squaw, now Unity Island and Grand Island respectively; moreover, in these locations the entry to each harbor would have been swept clean by the strong current of that river.

Unfortunately for the settlements that grew up on Scajaquada and Tonawanda Creeks, there were rapids about two miles north of Buffalo Creek where the Niagara River passed over an up-tilted, erosion-resistant layer of Onondaga limestone. And so, the canal's designers faced the problem of whether to bring the sail-powered lake boats north to Scajaquada or Tonawanda Creeks or the smaller, shallower draft, mule-towed canal boats south to Buffalo Creek. Given the strong current in the Niagara River and the prevailing winds, they chose to build a small lock at the rapids and a protected, partly onshore, channel above and below them. In 1825, the Erie Canal would terminate at Buffalo Creek. Here the lake boats and the canal boats would exchange their differing cargos at a harbor that, like much of the canal, was frozen over anywhere from two to five months a year. Here, Buffalo Creek would be deepened and widened until that sluggish stream was transformed into the equally sluggish Buffalo River. The entrepôt at the east end of the Lake Erie would be known as Buffalo.

Buffalo's Geographic Setting

The geography that links Buffalo to Lake Erie and the Niagara River suggests that, while Montesquieu may have pushed the point too far, geography and geology sometimes partner in economic destiny. The shape of the Buffalo economy, and in a sense its whole social world, reflect his observations. Geography meant that, wherever the Erie Canal would terminate, the economy of its terminal city would initially be founded on trade and transport. Indeed, Buffalo's status as an entrepôt, was confirmed when, in 1843, the most western of the rail lines of the New York Central Railroad[2] followed the canal builder's flattest route from New York City, allowing trains from Albany to reach Buffalo.

Here again there was an alternative, a more mountainous route along the Pennsylvania border that ended about sixty miles southwest of Buffalo, at Dunkirk on Lake Erie. Dunkirk was a fourth possible anchor for the route to the Midwest, at least once rail transport was possible. However, this southern route, chosen by Jay Gould for his Erie Railroad, was completed later than the more northerly one because it was more difficult to engineer and more difficult for early trains to traverse. Dunkirk would therefore be less attractive to shippers because it did not offer alternatives for transport farther east—cheaper, but slower canal boats as against more expensive, but faster railcars—than Buffalo did. In time, the more northerly port would prosper while the more southerly would limp along.

Similar examples of Montesquieu's wisdom abound. The transport of grain by boat from the Midwest made Buffalo a major grain storage center. Faced with the expense and difficulty of unloading grain boats by hand, in 1842 a Buffalo merchant, Joseph Dart, developed the first steam-driven mechanical device for unloading the boats as well as the first grain elevator.[3] Associated development as a milling center also occurred. Someone would eventually try to arbitrage the difference between the freight rates for the transport of grain and of flour to the east, hoping that the cost of milling was less than the value of service increase in the freight rate for a given weight of flour, as against that weight of grain. This addition to the area's economy took quite a few years after the development of Dart's elevator to become significant.

The canal and the railroads brought immigrants—Irish, Swedish, Germans, Poles, Czechs, Hungarians, Slovaks, Croats, Serbs, Ukrainians, and Italians—to Buffalo on their way west, travel that increased as railroads expanded to Chicago and beyond, first along the south shore of Lake Erie, and later across southern Ontario. For some Buffalo was far enough. Weary of the journey, exhausted of funds, stuck in the city because the frozen harbor meant that moving on was impossible, or simply meeting others who spoke the same language, meant that some of the westward-moving stream settle in Buffalo. These dropouts provided the labor, ultimately unionized, which became the backbone of commercial and industrial life in the city and of its ethnic diversity. The Germans, the first group to arrive after the Irish (who are generally said to have helped to build the canal,) brought their metalworking tradition with them and their brewing skills, dependent on the local grain trade, and created a city full of breweries.

Here again, geography played a role. Foundries and other metal-shaping businesses grew in Buffalo starting in the 1840s. They relied on iron, and later steel, billets shipped to the city from the Adirondacks. Then, during the Civil War, the first blast furnace for the production of pig iron was built along Buffalo Creek. Others followed along Scajaquada Creek and the Niagara River near Tonawanda Creek. Eventually in 1901, large-scale steelmaking followed, drawn by the proximity to Lake Erie, the ability to move iron ore via lake boat, and the availability of coal brought to the city's port on new railroads from the south and southeast after the New York Central finished its route.

After the Civil War, these four resources—water, rail, grain, and metalworking—formed the basis for Buffalo's economy. It remained so until 1898 when local entrepreneurs used the inventions of Tesla and Westinghouse, who together had figured out how to deliver alternating current electric power reasonably safely over significant distances, to build a station in nearby Niagara Falls that could supply Buffalo with reliable, inexpensive hydroelectric power, the second such station in the country. This facility, and an earlier one providing direct current, together drew power-dependent industries, such as industrial chemical and carbide production, to the City of Niagara Falls. These industries rounded out the bird's eye view area's economy in 1900, a time when Buffalo was the eighth largest city in the United States. The city celebrated its growth by hosting the grand Pan-American Exposition. The backers of the exposition lost money, though it is doubtful that the assassination of President William B. McKinley was the cause of that loss. Indeed, neither event was a portent of things to come.

The Local Geography

The physical structure of Buffalo reflects the centrality of water and rail to the city's economy. As the following map shows, the city subtends an angle of about 150 degrees along the shoreline extending from Lake Erie into the Niagara River. Two street grids can be discerned. One is radial, from a point near the waterfront. This is the city's original plan, drawn by Joseph Ellicott, representative of the Holland Land Company, the original patent holder of Western New York's real estate. The other is rectilinear, seemingly centered on the same spot, but in fact centered on a street, Main Street, two blocks to the east. The Erie Canal slid in between the radial center and the waterfront, terminating at Main Street, effectively preferring the rectilinear grid, but without forcing adjustment to the radial one.

In the years after the canal was opened in1825, transshipment was the primary economic activity in Buffalo and that activity was centered on the waterfront, which in these early years, was a small portion of the shoreline from a point north of the mouth of the Buffalo Creek stretching a short distance around and down that waterway. By 1843, competition in this trade came from the railroads. The first railroad was an economically insignificant route to the north that began just west of the city center. It eventually reached Niagara Falls. Soon, two more, the New York Central and its bitter, more poorly financed rival, the Erie, entered the city from the east, then snaked their ways to a place north of the creek, close to the terminus of the Erie Canal and along the north side of a fetid extension called the Hamburg Canal, also built by the State of New York.

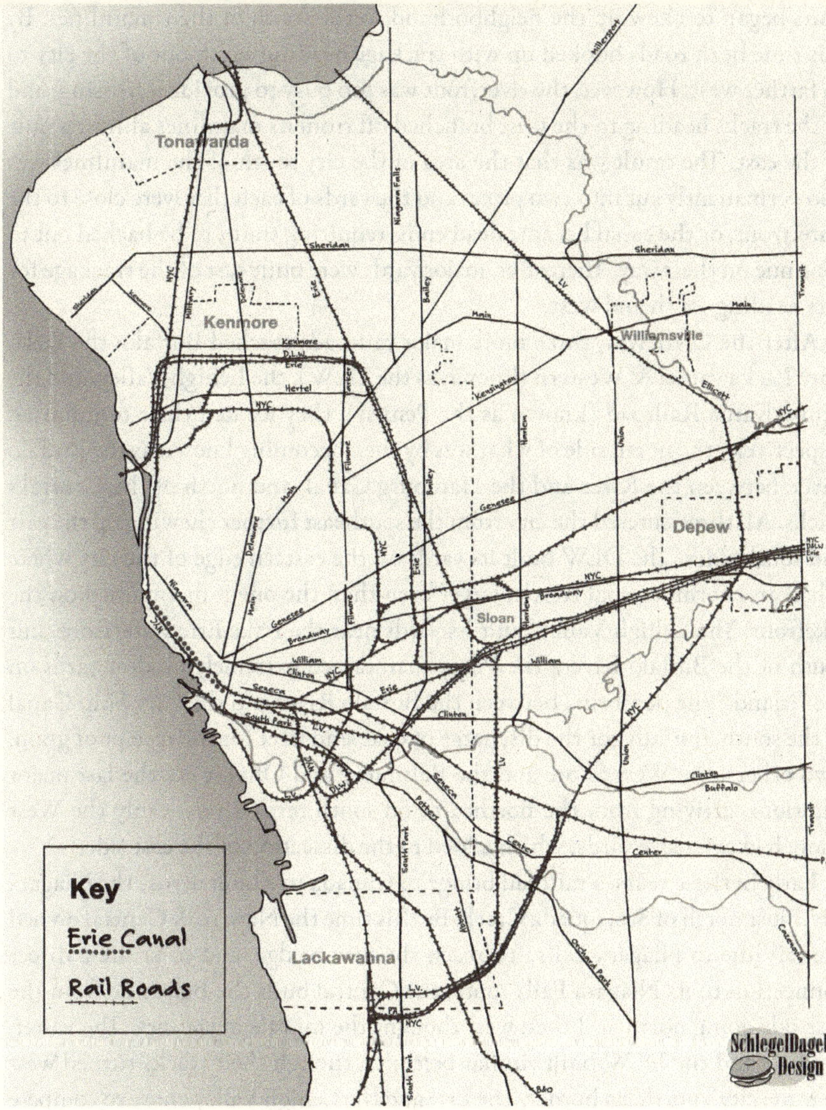

Figure 1. Map of Buffalo Showing Change over Time
John Henry Schlegel and Elizabeth Burnett

The rail routes ran east to west at street level all the way. They effectively cut the city in two, separating north from south.

Soon these railroads created spurs to the Buffalo Creek in order to be closer to the lake freighters. Each built large freight houses right at the edge of the creek designed for moving cargo from boat to rail or from rail to boat. These spurs began to chew up the neighborhood to the south of their mainlines. By this time both roads hooked up with trackage heading south out of the city to go farther west. However, the riverfront was too busy to provide a crossing, and so the tracks heading to the west branched off from its mainlines almost a mile to the east. The result was that the area of the city south of the mainlines was also permanently cut into two pieces and the yards of each that were close to the waterfront, or the canal became dead ends, requiring trains to be backed out to continue on their way. Thereafter, major yards were built east of the trackage for cars heading south and west.

After the Civil War, three more major railroads reached Buffalo: the Delaware Lackawanna & Western (known as the DLW), the Lehigh Valley, and the Pennsylvania Railroad (known as the Pennsy); they located their terminuses, respectively: the north side of what was by then becoming known as the Buffalo River, between the River and the Hamburg Canal, and north of the Central's tracks. All three entered the city from the southeast further chewing up the east and south sides. The DLW built its yards on the eastern edge of the city where it had an enormous coal trestle, larger even than the one it maintained on the lakefront. The Lehigh Valley built its yards near the Lake Erie waterfront, but south of the Buffalo River. The Pensy maintained extremely modest yards on the "island," the peninsula between the Buffalo River and the City Ship Canal to the south, initially for the discharge of coal, and later for the receipt of grain. Two others, the West Shore and the Baltimore and Ohio, were the last major additions, arriving from the northeast and south respectively. Only the West Shore had extensive yards, which added to the dissection of the east side.

Early in these years, a railroad bridge to Canada was built across the Niagara River just north of Scajaquada Creek. By this time the New York Central owned the rail line to Niagara Falls. To reach the new bridge, and to create a direct connection to its Niagara Falls route, the Central built the Belt Line from the east side going north and then west thought the middle of the city. Thereafter, the Erie and the DLW built similar beltlines, though their tracks turned west near the city's northern border. The Erie and the Lehigh Valley chose to compete with the Central for business to Niagara Falls and from there, on to Canada. The Erie built a line going diagonally from the point where its beltline crossed Main Street to the City of Tonawanda. The Lehigh Valley built a similar line, though it started east of the city and went more strongly diagonally northwest, again to the City of Tonawanda, where both companies had lines that followed the existing New York Central tracks to the falls.

Except for a stretch of William Street on the east side where the Erie and one of the New York Central yards, including its stockyards, were concentrated, the agglomeration of rail lines was noticeably misaligned with the original radial pattern of the streets. Moreover, the rail lines interfered with the modest attempt to place a gridded-street pattern over the radial design to the north and east of the central city area. On the east side, there were effectively only three north-south streets for a distance of two miles and only one of them, Bailey, the most easterly, extended the full length of the city.

The south side was remarkably isolated from the rest of the city by the combination of the river and the rail lines that entered the city from the east. Only one street connected the two pieces of the south side that were split by the dense mass of lines heading south of the city. The isolation of the south side made it sensible for the Lackawanna Steel, located on the waterfront directly south of the city's border, to create a commuter line down to the mills as a way of assuring sufficient employees.

Only the west side was well served because the radial plan there had established north-south streets. And even there, a remnant of a hamlet called Black Rock made hash of both the radial and the gridded-street plan. That place, part of which became part of City of Buffalo when it was first incorporated, had a street pattern oriented to the lakefront, and was thus on a diagonal to the grid. As a result, the residents of the area were also isolated to a surprising extent.[4]

Industrial employment followed neither the radial nor the gridded-street plan, but instead the water—the lake, both rivers, and the canal system—and the railroads. Thus, in addition to the areas around the rail lines and their yards on the east, southeast, and south sides, industry was clustered along the Erie, the DLW, and the New York Central beltlines and in the northwest part of the city where they all came together. Likewise, a belt of industry stretched from Tonawanda Creek south along the Niagara River and the Lake Erie shore as far as the steel mills in Lackawanna, along both sides of the Buffalo River and its dredged companion, the City Ship Canal, and along the Erie and Hamburg Canals.

Buffalo's Community Structure

The spatial configuration of employment in the context of the geography of the city meant that wherever one lived, getting to work was not easy, at least unless one worked in the neighborhood so that walking was possible. Thus, the chaotic overlay of street plans, railroads, and employment opportunities fostered the growth of strong, isolated neighborhoods. It was in these neighborhoods that the ethnic structure of Buffalo grew.

Three disconnected pockets, separated by the Buffalo River and several railroad tracks, comprised three Irish neighborhoods; a big swath of the east side north of these tracks was Polish. To the northeast, a similar swath was predominantly German; and west, near the harbor and along the Niagara River, was the Sicilian enclave. Isolated pockets to the north were Polish and Hungarian, respectively. A small Black neighborhood, a largely orthodox Jewish one on its southern border, and an ethnically distinct (Campobassini) Italian neighborhood lay still farther south, but just north of the oldest Irish neighborhood, fit snugly next to the east side of the downtown core. This area also included a small Greek community at the north end and a slightly larger Lebanese one at the south.

In these neighborhoods, most residents observed an ancient pattern, living near to where they worked and shopping near to where they lived. Working near where one lived was made relatively easy by the industrial activity along the railroad tracks, rivers, and canals that defined neighborhood boundaries. Shopping near where one lived was made relatively easy by the prevalence of strip commercial development along major thoroughfares in these neighborhoods. The rhythm of home life for the wage-earning classes who dwelled mostly in small houses or apartments with, at best, iceboxes for refrigeration, was marked by daily trips on foot to the baker, butcher, and grocer, not to mention the corner tavern. Of course, first the horse car, then the interurban railroad, and later the electric trolley made travel easier for the vast majority of people who were too poor to afford a horse, much less a carriage. Still, anyone who has ridden through Buffalo's older urban neighborhoods and looked carefully for the original uses of the buildings there will easily understand the degree to which the separation of industrial from residential uses is a Twentieth-Century idea.

Identifiably ethnic neighborhoods grew by accretion at the margins, as is obvious from the decreasing age of churches as one travels outward from the city's center. However, this accretion took a particular form. Marginal development was essentially a matter of what we today think of as a peculiarly 1950s American invention—suburban growth, sprawl even, though it took place within the city limits. Those who could afford to move away from the soot and grime and crowding of the older neighborhoods to the newer, roomier neighborhoods on the margin, did so.

This migration was made easier because most suburban areas within the city's political boundaries were developed as horse car and trolley lines were extended outward. Indeed, the developers either owned the transit lines and or subsidized their extension. Moving was desirable because in Buffalo, like much of the industrial Midwest, residential construction was primarily wood frame. Such construction requires regular maintenance; neglected, it declines in value quite quickly. Moving up, if possible to the newest development, or merely to a newer house, meant a significant improvement in a family's lifestyle, especially since technological advances in heating, plumbing, and electric power made significant differences between the oldest and newest construction.

Thus, the newest immigrants usually ended up occupying the oldest, most dilapidated housing. But these were not randomly selected immigrants; the newest immigrants were likely to be of the same ethnicity as the departed residents. However, most of these immigrants did not think of themselves as possessing an ethnicity, as Germans or Italians or Poles, but as Bavarians or Sicilians or Pozaniskers, people who came from a particular region, or even a particular city or village, and who all spoke the local dialect. Only in America, where an immigrant was a foreigner, did the underlying language form part of what today we think of as "ethnicity."

But language was only part of the sense of being a *landsman* or *compatriota* or *rodak*. Religious faith was an equally important part. In neighborhoods that were walkable by necessity (and not, as now, because it is cool) Christians of all stripes gathered around the local church and Jews the local synagogue in the same way that they gathered around the local saloon. These structures created social solidarity in a new land. For Catholics, the Latin Mass and a sermon in the native language was a public recognition of the small piece of the world they had abandoned. Sometimes, parishes were even more narrowly tied to particular regions with the result that neighborhoods occasionally had multiple parishes surprisingly close together, each serving a distinct subgroup of the overall ethnic community.

For Protestants whose native language was not English—mostly Germans and an admixture of Scandinavians—a service in the native tongue, hymns and all, provided a similar tie. These churches also were a part of the fabric of ethnic communities, though the fractiousness of Protestantism shows in the occasional gathering of churches of multiple denominations quite near to one another, often at the same intersection.[5]

A more subtle difference between Catholics and Protestants can be seen in another aspect of the location of churches. Ethnic Catholic churches tended to be embedded within their relevant communities in ways that Protestant churches were not. Thus, Catholic churches were less likely to be located on the arterial streets that often served as the boundary between neighborhoods; Protestant churches were seldom located anywhere but on arterials, often arterials that marked these seams between ethnic areas. Probably this difference reflected the lower density of denominational adherents in a specific area. It is likely that these differences also signified a certain attitude toward the larger world that was the city. Even when the denomination in question, for example, Lutheran or Evangelical or Evangelical and Reformed, was largely tied to a particular ethnicity, location suggested a looking outward when gathering.

No matter what the church might have been, communal meals, service societies, even English language classes, reinforced the ethnic bond, as did native language schooling for children, usually parochial,[6] but at some times, in some places, also public. Friday fish fry, served and shared at the local tavern, built the local Catholic community as well. For German Protestants, local specialties, like roast beef on a kimmelweck roll, served the same function. And, when an ethnic group gathered together in one area of a town, it became possible for neighborhood merchants to provide familiar foods that supplied a further tie to what eventually came to be felt as the old county.

Ethnicity provided a route to employment as well. In the days before equal employment opportunity, employers of a given ethnicity often felt an obligation to hire countrymen.[7] Most employers knew that ethnic homogeneity in a small plant or in a given department minimized the possibility of disruptive interethnic conflict. And given that, in many factories, the tradition of allowing foremen to hire was still alive, ethnic homogeneity was easy to maintain when new immigrants would turn up at the foreman's church all the time.

The great central, northerly trending swath of the city was the preserve of the White Anglo-Saxon Protestants, or so it is said. At the least, it was White and mostly Protestant, though a minority made up of upper-middle class Catholic professionals—doctors especially[8]—were part of the neighborhood as well. The term "Anglo-Saxon" most often meant that the family had spoken English for a long enough time and had earned enough money that questions of actual origin were irrelevant, as in the case of the German Schoellkopf family, who started first with a tannery, then a dye works, and finally a large electric power plant, and eventually became one of the city's first families.

It is in this center section that, in 1868, this elite secured the services of the young Frederick Law Olmsted to design a gracious network of parks and parkways that some believe still defines the city today.[9] At the very least, this network suggests the rhythm of life as it was split between the servants and the family. The lack of significant remnants of strip commercial life on the primary thoroughfare, Delaware Avenue (until that street enters the area of its Twentieth Century residential expansion,) shows that either the baker, butcher, and grocer delivered, or that a servant traveled to the city market at or to Main Street for provisions. The lack of corner taverns meant that drinking was done at home or at one's club; the lack of places of employment within walking distance meant that father traveled either in his own or a hired carriage. Mother remained at home when not visiting friends or doing good works. The parks and parkways provided appropriate places for families to spend weekend afternoons.

Before 1865: A Small, but Growing Place on the Niagara Frontier[10]

In the years immediately after settlement, Buffalo was just one of numerous isolated frontier towns. This place, incorporated in 1813 as the Village of Buffalo, was about one square mile in size, clustered around the center of the city's radial street plan, and comfortably away from both Buffalo Creek on the south and Lake Erie on the west. This little settlement was unalterably changed with the coming of the Erie Canal in 1825. Soon after in 1832, the village was reincorporated as the City of Buffalo, now encompassing about four-and-a-half square miles, extending its southernmost reach to the creek, west to the lakeshore, and substantially north and east of the preexisting village. The optimistic view of the area's potential, shown by the expansion of Buffalo's political boundaries, embodied a model of the economy suggested by the existence of the canal, that of an entrepôt, a place where transshipment occurs and where goods are traded. At that time, the model was based on the movement of goods, particularly grain, between lake boats and canal boats. And so not surprisingly, Buffalo thought of itself as one of the canal's two termini, the Queen City of the Great Lakes,[11] an identity that remained fixed until well after it was no longer true.

Still, this identity was not in the least foolish, for the immediate popularity of the canal was so great that the State of New York quickly undertook a program to widen and deepen it. Not wholly surprisingly, the municipality's population doubled in each of the three decades following the canal's completion. Emboldened by this increase and the state's enthusiasm, in 1853 Buffalo expanded its boundaries to encompass forty-two square miles, almost its entire current extent, and within the boundaries of a larger preexisting town first called Willink, then Clarence, next a town first called Buffalo, then Black Rock. Thus, the economic heart of the city would be found on a waterfront that stretched on either side of the place where the Lake Erie met the Buffalo Creek. That economic heart was expected to support a large place; and it did. By 1860, the city was the tenth largest in the United States. It was larger even than Pittsburgh, a place that had benefitted from settlement to the west via the Ohio River.

Improvements to the city's waterfront were made sporadically after the canal was opened. By the Civil War, the structure of the waterfront was largely complete. A large breakwater created a sheltered harbor and protected a set of slips that expanded the available wharf age. The City Ship, or Blackwood Canal had been created to do the same thing between the Buffalo Creek and the lake; here again, slips expanded even this area, as did two canals that were designed to connect the river to the Hamburg Canal. Freighter transit up what by then was called the Buffalo River, expanded as well.

Not all of Buffalo's citizens thought that an economic identity based on waterfront commerce was wise. Quite early, voices argued that Buffalo's future lay not in trade, but in manufacturing. Early, a few small manufacturing businesses, including a gristmill and a sawmill, gathered around a falls that was created by the diversion of a small stream on the east side of town. However, it was not until the 1840s, when the New York Central reached Buffalo from Albany, that factories took root.

The largest of these factories focused on metalwork, a not surprising circumstance given the tradition of metalworking in England, Scotland, and especially various parts of what is now Germany. In the 1840s, Germans made up a third of the city's population. Thus, ironworks were established in the 1840s, both forges, working cold or warm but not molten metal, that made small tools, and foundries casting molten metal that made products such as stoves, furnaces, saddles, harness hardware, and nails cut and formed from rolled sheet. Several of these firms specialized in the production of steam engines, both marine and stationary. The foundries used iron billets, the forges, pigs or ingots. Both products were produced and transported from elsewhere, first the Adirondacks, later Pennsylvania.

Iron works were initially located east of downtown near the Buffalo Creek, and both on the Niagara River south of Scajaquada Creek and nearby on that creek. In addition, there were several tanneries and associated boot, shoe, and harness makers, some shipbuilding, a varnish works, at least one producer of agricultural machinery and another of iceboxes, the forerunner of the modern refrigerator. By the 1850s, there were also clothing manufacturers and furniture makers. By no means were all of these products absorbed by the local economy. Modest export work had begun.

Though these factories were but a small part of an economy dominated by commerce, Buffalo was already in the process of experiencing a surprising economic change. Joseph Dart's invention for unloading grain from boats and into elevators significantly altered the grain trade. Traditionally, grain was loaded into bags that were individually transported into and out of a ship or storage facility, as well as into any mill. Dart substituted the mechanical power of the stationary steam engine for the muscle power of stevedores, and so eliminated the need to bag the grain, reduced the time necessary for loading and unloading, and increased the potential height, and so capacity, of any storage facility. All of these changes reduced the cost of shipping grain from western farms to eastern markets. Within five years, there were seven similar elevators on the Buffalo waterfront.

The development of the grain elevator did not, however, turn Buffalo into a major location for milling grain. As the West opened, flour milling moved westward. The development of the stationary steam engine meant that milling was not dependent on waterpower and local milling saved the cost of transporting grain elsewhere. Of the grain that headed to the city, most was not stored, but moved quickly out, increasingly by rail, even though in order to protect the financial viability of the Erie Canal, for a while the State of New York imposed a charge on goods that had once traveled by water, but that were now moved by rail. To make matters worse, by the early 1850s, the New York Central had secured access to Chicago through a collection of lines along the south shore of Lake Erie and across northern Indiana, eventually called the Lake Shore and Michigan Southern. A similar collection of lines eventually would be added to the Erie Railroad. Both established freight terminals along the Buffalo Creek. They also owned two of the grain elevators in the city. These railroads were successful at diverting the grain trade from the canal because they could provide service when the canal was frozen. Though water-to-water interchange of grain at the waterfront still took place, it seemed to be not so slowly dying out. The Erie Canal had begun what, in retrospect, was its long decline.

Beginnings are always overdetermined. Sensible people might have decided that it was foolish to plan a waterway that was frozen over three to five months a year, much less emptying into a lake that was often frozen just as long. New York State might have given up trying to drive the canal beyond the malarial swamps fed by the outflow of Lake Seneca into the Seneca River west of Syracuse. The Erie Canal could have ended in Black Rock. The Canadians could have harassed shipping on all of the Great Lakes except Michigan. Dunkirk might have become the eastern rail terminus for the state. But none of these things happened; nor did Buffalo build on Dart's invention and become an engineering and construction center specializing in grain elevators. What then, is one to make of the early history of Buffalo?

Such a history can no more be taken as representative of the beginnings of cities generally than Part I's history of the United States can be representative of countries generally. There needs be some other purpose. Two such come easily to mind. First, one might consider the degree to which background factors such as geography and natural resources create paths for economic growth and decline and so both enable a place's history and come to limit its possible future. Second, one might consider the degree to which the economic course of the larger political entity of which a place is a part creates paths for economic growth and decline and so both enables that place's history and comes to limit its possible future. Both questions linger beneath the surface of this Part and Parts IV and V also.

The Eighteen Seventies and Eighties: No Longer a Small Town

The years immediately following the Civil War were not good for Buffalo.[12] The city's population growth slowed to a 45 percent rate. The entrepôt economy was fading. By 1869, the combined freight leaving the city on the Erie and New York Central railroads exceeded that by canal boat. And by 1875, more grain was moving out of the city by rail than by canal boat, a proportion that continued to increase. And by the Eighties, the greatest portion of the coal coming to Buffalo was for the city's own use, not for transshipment. Even after tolls on the canal had been removed in 1882, traffic continued to decline, though for about ten years a transshipment/lumber milling trade—freighter to canal boat—based on logs from Wisconsin and Michigan and routed through Tonawanda and North Tonawanda, made up for some of the decline in the grain trade. Then, somewhat surprisingly, population growth began to increase to a more promising rate of 65 percent, though the city never caught up to Pittsburgh. With the development of larger freighters that could move grain cheaper to Buffalo than the railroads could move flour, milling started moving eastward again. Still, the geographic structure of Buffalo makes it impossible to talk about the city's economy without quickly turning to rail.

The Seventies and Eighties were a period of great growth for American railroads. Nationwide, trackage more than tripled. Buffalo's share grew enormously as well, especially in the Seventies. First came a piece of the Pennsy, a line north from western Pennsylvania that specialized in hauling bituminous coal. Then came two anthracite lines from eastern Pennsylvania, the Lehigh Valley, followed a few years later by the DLW. Thereafter, in quick succession, came the Nickel Plate, properly the New York, Chicago, and Saint Louis, a primarily freight line that connected Buffalo to Chicago and Saint Louis, and the Baltimore and Ohio, another line from the western Pennsylvania coalfields. Finally, there was the West Shore, a somewhat separable piece of the New York Central and one that also primarily carried freight; it ran between New York City and Buffalo, but regularly interchanged its freight with the Nickel Plate, an even more separable piece of the New York Central. With the expansion of railroads came an increase in railroad labor problems; Buffalo was one of the sites where, in the Great Railroad Strike of 1877, called over a 10 percent decrease in wages, the violence was such that the governor called out the militia.

Two other lines showed Buffalo's increasing commercial importance. Just before the Civil War, Canadian railroads began connecting their lines to those in the United States. Initially, this took the form of a passenger car ferry that crossed the Niagara River at where once was the village of Black Rock. Within five years, the implausibility of using a ferry to cross the Niagara in winter brought the construction of a bridge, the International Railroad Bridge, north of Scajaquada Creek, in the neighborhood still known as Black Rock. It is at this point that the Grand Trunk and Western, an eastern Canadian line, and the Michigan Central, a Canadian line owned by an American railroad affiliated with the New York Central, crossed the river and established limited yards.

The increasing complexity of Buffalo's railroad geography can be demonstrated by examining three projects aimed at a simplification of the situation. The first was undertaken in reaction to a peculiar problem: at this time, the New York Central lacked a connection between its lines from the east and that portion of its system that ran north along the Niagara River to Niagara Falls. And so, in the early 1870s the Central built a somewhat serpentine link between its mainline and yards on the east side north and then west to its Niagara Falls line. This line also connected the Central to the International Railroad Bridge. Not to be outdone, in the late 1870s the Erie, and in the mid-1880s the DLW, both built similar lines from their east side yards, though these lines went all the way to the northern boundary of the city before heading west and then south to the new bridge.

The second was the establishment of the Buffalo Creek railroad in the early 1870s. It was a switching road that extended from the New York Central's mainline, and thus the various rail yards on the city's east side, across the Buffalo River and up the strip of land between the river and the Union Ship Canal to serve the industries collecting there. Eventually, owned jointly by the Erie and

Lehigh Valley, it provided convenient interchange between dispersed parts of the local rail network.

The third came in the late 1870s with the creation of a passenger train link between the Central's terminal on the east side of downtown and its line along the Niagara River on the west. This modest link of less than a third of a mile also allowed the creation of real Belt Line passenger service with more than twenty well-placed stops around what was, at the time, the core of the city. Service was five cents, not cheap, but not all that expensive at a time when most of the working class walked to work.

Buffalo's main passenger terminals were all directly east of the downtown area, stretching north from the riverfront—the DLW, the Lehigh Valley, the New York Central, the Erie, and the Pennsy. These terminals varied in age, one dating as far back as 1855, though much altered later; not that the city had any interest in having multiple passenger terminals. In the late Eighties, it convinced the New York State Legislature to create a commission designed to consolidate them all into a Union Terminal and to eliminate the great majority of street-level railroad tracks within the city. Though a quite elegant building was proposed, no such terminal was ever built. The Erie refused to participate, pleading poverty, but demanding parity of facilities with the New York Central; the Central, always willing to kick a fella when he was down, refused to go ahead without an equal contribution from the Erie. And so, both roads staggered on with their existing, increasingly shabby facilities.

In addition to these major passenger terminals, there were smaller terminals scattered around the city—along the Belt Line in particular, but also in neighboring communities, and even in rail yards. Passengers arriving or leaving on Canadian trains used a terminal in the Black Rock neighborhood and the old Erie Street terminal of the New York Central's Niagara Falls line until it was abandoned after the completion of the Belt Line. And in addition to the major rail yards on Buffalo's east and south sides, there were smaller, often tiny yards scattered all over the city, sometimes with freight depots, sometimes with team tracks—tracks that were provided for deliveries of entire carloads of freight to be unloaded by "teamsters," for recipients that lacked rail sidings of their own. Sometimes there were both depots and team tracks.

Every major line had tracks that facilitated the transfer of cars from one line to another and sidings dedicated for major freight customers to use. And some lines also had extensive repair facilities. At different times, the Erie, the New York Central, and the Pennsy owned grain elevators on the waterfront. The Central's presence in Buffalo was so large that it had its own police force and maintained the Wagner Palace Car Company, a captive manufacturer of sleeping cars that had been part of the local rail facilities since the Seventies.

While the railroads transformed Buffalo's geography in the Seventies, its waterfront was only modestly changed. When the Lehigh Valley reached the city, it dug an extension of the City Ship Canal south into an area between the lakeshore and the many railroad tracks going south out of the city. This canal and three additional slips provided space for the transfer of bulk cargo such as coal, ore, and timber between rail cars and lake boats.

In other ways, there was a spectacular change. When the grain trade shifted back to Buffalo as the larger lake boats, now steam powered, regularly reached the city, an extraordinary number of big grain elevators were built along the Buffalo riverfront. All of these elevators were wooden. Since the machinery was powered by coal or wood-fired steam engines with their accompanying boilers, the risk of fire was constant, and some spectacular blazes resulted. But most often, fire was just an opportunity to build again with marginally newer technology. And with more grain in the city, flour mills began to appear too, for the ubiquity of steam engines meant that large-scale milling no longer needed to be located near waterfalls.

Grain was not the only industry that expanded in these years. In the Seventies, manufacturing saw significant growth. The city had a base of firms that had survived long enough to build on. The Rumsey and Schoellkopf families had built large tanneries with branches into the Midwest. But the iron foundries were most notable. Jewett & Root specialized in stoves; Farrar & Trefts in reversing engines for oil well drilling. Shepard Iron Works specialized in boilers; Eagle Ironworks in the engines that powered the machinery for grain elevators; and the Howard Ironworks and George W. Tifft, Sons & Company in steam engines more generally. Given this base, it was not surprising that the more general expansion in manufacturing after the Civil War was centered in the iron and steel industries.

There were two parts to this expansion. First, there was basic iron production. During the Civil War, the Union Furnace Company began to produce pig iron at a large site on the north side of the Buffalo River; it also had a rolling mill that produced iron sheet. When it failed ten years later, the site remained unoccupied until 1891 when it was leased to the Hanna interests from Cleveland. About the same time, Pratt & Letchworth, which also had built a blast furnace during the Civil War, first along the Niagara River and later on Scajaquada Creek near the Niagara River, produced malleable iron. It then built Buffalo's first open-hearth furnace for the production of steel for drive wheels and the frames for locomotives. This was a significant shift from the firm's earlier focus on saddlery hardware, as well as stoves and nails. Pratt & Letchworth had become important enough to the region's economy that it merited its own through track leading from the New York Central's Belt Line to its mainline to Niagara Falls. Finally, in the early Seventies, Tonawanda Iron and Steel built a small blast furnace and so began to produce pig iron along the Niagara River in North Tonawanda. The enterprise was later sold to Rogers, Brown & Company of Cincinnati, under whose auspices it also did some small-scale production of steel from this iron, apparently used for castings made by local foundries.

The second part of this expansion was an increase in more obviously manufacturing establishments. Several new firms were tied to the railroad industry. Gould Coupler, located in the east suburban Village of Depew,[13] on property between the New York Central's mainline and that of the DLW, had been doing foundry work since the Civil War and did small-scale steel production as well. Its primary product was, not surprisingly, coupling devices for rail cars. A related company, Gould Storage Battery, produced the batteries that provided the light for railroad passenger cars. The Buffalo Steam Forge works, established somewhat later, produced rail car axles. Buffalo Iron Works, another foundry, produced rail car wheels, as did East Buffalo Car Wheel, National Car Wheel, Niagara Car Wheel, and Union Car Wheel. Lake Erie Boiler and Engineering produced steam engines, mostly for maritime purposes, as did King Iron Works; Buffalo Bridge and Iron produced railroad and highway bridges, as did Union Bridge; Buffalo Cast Iron Pipe produced an obvious product; two firms in North Tonawanda produced radiators; when joined together they were known as the American Radiator Company. A surprising number of smaller firms produced steam engines; one, David Bell Engineering, a firm started in the 1840s, moved from marine engines to iron boats; Buffalo Foundry produced stationary engines, but was better known for the great variety of large castings that it could produce. The same was true of the more specialized Atlas Steel Castings. By 1900, 20 percent of the city's labor was employed in factories and machine shops such as these.

The story of metal in Buffalo in these years is, however, anything but exhausted by mentioning iron and steel production or even large castings for the railroad industry. The city was in the process of becoming a major manufacturing—metal casting and bending—town.

Most of the manufacturing plants were small, serving niche markets. Some produced small tools, others bicycles or farm equipment, one elevator frames, and as can be seen from examining any of the many industrial directories for these years, this list could go on and on. Some merit mention. The Buffalo Car

Company produced railroad cars. Buffalo Pitts Company made steam tractors and other farm machinery. Buffalo Pressed Steel Company (John R. Keim Mills Incorporated) was one of the earliest producers of thin rolled steel. Buffalo Forge, established in the late Seventies, began making what its name might be taken to indicate, small portable blacksmiths' forges. It began as a modest plant to the east of downtown, but over time, it moved in a more northeasterly direction to a much larger plant along the Belt Line. It expanded its production from forges to making and selling the small tools related to their production. It then began making blowers and pumps for the industrial air-moving market and the punches, shears, bar cutters, drills, and metal-bending equipment that it had developed for use in manufacturing these products. McKinnon Dash, a subsidiary of a Canadian company, produced adjustable dashes, the screens that protected drivers of carriages or sleighs from the mud thrown up by horses. Worthington Pump produced just what its name implied.

Another notable set of manufacturing enterprises was the breweries. During the 1870s, Buffalo had at least twenty active firms. Associated malt houses were appendages of the grain industry, which also produced animal feed. But the range of products beyond metalwork was, in some sense, a more telling example of the city's growth in these years. Atlas Oil, the city's first oil refinery, produced kerosene. By the 1870s, Buffalo Starch was the largest manufacturer of this everyday product in the country. M. H. Birge produced high quality, sometimes hand printed, wallpaper. F. N. Burt was a printer who developed a machine for the production of paper boxes, and so became a seller of such boxes. J. W. Clement was another large printer. Eastman Machine developed the first device for cutting piles of fabric for use in the clothing trade. Goodyear Lumber began a timber business in Pennsylvania that became so large that it eventually built its own railroad line to Buffalo. Knox Five and Dime was one of the early explorers of this format for slightly downscale retailing. Dr. R. V. Pierce of the World's Dispensary Medical Association built a large patent medicine enterprise.

Two firms, as different as they could be, had a long-term public profile. In 1873, Jacob F. Schoellkopf, Sr., who had been successful in the tanning business, started Schoellkopf Aniline and Dye on the upper reaches of the Buffalo River. No matter what product it tried to produce, German dye makers attacked that product by fiercely undercutting price. However, the firm kept minimally profitable and over time expanded its plant in Buffalo. Two years later, John D. Larkin started a small soap business, the Larkin Soap Company, for the wholesale trade. In the 1880s, it shifted to being a pioneer consumer products company by adding door-to-door sales.

Power is a more straightforward subject. In the mid-1870s, Jacob F. Schoelkopf, Sr., the same man who started the dye works mentioned above, bought an existing canal that began above, that is south of Niagara Falls, that provided hydropower for manufacturing companies located on the edge of the Niagara Gorge north of the falls; it relied on belt drives for delivering that power. This was an old technology mastered in New England years before. But in 1881, Schoellkopf's Hydraulic Power and Manufacturing Company constructed a small electric generation plant on the canal. Initially, this plant provided power for a grain mill owned by Schoelkopf, for a few neighboring mills, and for street lighting in the City of Niagara Falls. Not to be outdone, that same year, Buffalo boosters established a firm, Brush Electric Light Company, which used coal fired, steam-driven generators to produce power for the same purpose, and within a year, a competitor had acquired a franchise to do the same. Others followed. These plants, like Schoellkopf's, produced direct current (DC), a form of electric power that could not be transmitted over other than very short distances. One of these plants supplied electric lights to the J. N. Adam Department Store in the city.

Why all of a sudden, a welter of names? In any even modest economy, firms are established all the time. Most fail quite quickly and without notice. Some succeed, but because they are small, they are quickly forgotten. Some become large enough to be remembered by contemporaries and historians who pass by and pay attention. But most of these too disappear, at least eventually. For example, none of the railroads that reached Buffalo by the 1880s survive today. The same is true of the great steel works that were established after the turn of the century.

No historian could possibly recreate in detail the economy of any even modest size over a period of more than twenty years. Although a few of the slaughterhouses and department stores merit mention, the balance of the consumer economy, the butchers, bakeries, grocery stores, milk bottlers, dry good stores, and taverns survive in random photographs treasured by families, archived by newspapers, or donated to libraries and historical societies. For the rest of an economy, one faces a choice between ignoring names entirely or offering a few modest words for those firms that managed to survive in old histories, recognizing that they are anything but representative of the larger set of all firms. My choice has been to honor those whose meanly compensated labor helped make Buffalo's economy grow, by naming some of the workplaces they devoted their lives to. It is the least that one can do.

The Nineties and Teens: A Big City

Buffalo's growth in the Seventies and Eighties had been great enough that the city quickly left behind the economic collapse that followed the Panic of 1893. The 1890 census said Buffalo was the eleventh-largest city in the United States and the 1900 census made it the eighth-largest city in the country, larger than Cincinnati, New Orleans, and San Francisco, all of which had once been greater than it.[14] Buffalo had already exhausted one economic model—the entropôt, and had largely shifted to another focused on manufacturing. This newer economy was booming, though still based on water, rail, grain, metal, and power, though one element, water, had changed significantly.

The Erie Canal was of little economic importance anymore. Still, at the turn of the century, the state, hoping to revive the canal, began a program to improve it, rechristening it as the New York State Barge Canal. At the same time, the state filled the Hamburg Canal and all or parts of two other canals, thus recognizing that these unused appurtenances had become stagnant, fetid, and noxious. The Buffalo River was also dredged, widened, and straightened, though when it came to straightening, plans exceeded results. Separate from this effort, the area congressional delegation worked to support the revitalization of the waterfront by securing the help of the Army Corps of Engineers to build a breakwater along the lakeshore south of the river. This amenity would shelter the larger freighters coming to the new industries growing on the waterfront south of the river and so hopefully support industrial expansion into that area.

Railroads were still growing. During these years, the national rail system continued to increase, reaching its apogee in 1916. The city had become the nation's second-largest rail hub, exceeded in carload transit only by Chicago. With this distinction came the discord that accompanied the longstanding efforts of railroad employees to establish effective labor unions. Thus, the city was the site of a modestly bloody switchmen's strike in the summer of 1892. Similarly, it was not surprising that two more railroads reached Buffalo over the International Railroad Bridge from Canada. Both were American lines that had secured trackage rights—the Wabash and the Pere Marquette. And yet, in some ways, nothing had changed; while the Erie and the New York Central continued to squabble over a possible Union Terminal, the Lehigh Valley and the DLW avoided the squabble and replaced their passenger terminals with elegant new ones (1916 and 1917 respectively).

While the penetration of rail into the fabric of the city was important for its economy, the tracks remained an impediment to community life because the greatest portion of the original lines had been laid at street level. Given the degree that these lines had divided the community into many small areas, passage from one place to another was dangerous and haphazard, dependent on whether train tracks blocked one's way. To address this problem, in 1888 the city successfully petitioned the State of New York to establish a body designed to eliminate many street level grade crossings.

The Grade Crossing Commission labored and litigated for years. Eventually, it managed to secure an agreement on the part of the relevant lines to cooperate in the removal of most of the major crossings, some by raising the tracks onto embankments, others by dead ending streets at the right of way, most by building bridges over the tracks, and all by pushing some of the costs onto the city. But it took a long time. The first crossing was not eliminated until eight years after the agreements were struck, the last eight years after that. One important civic improvement did come out of the exercise, however. Though it took about ten years, the New York Central tracks that only recently had been installed across Main Street were moved into a tunnel under it and several other major streets. While the New York Central still couldn't run its freight trains directly west to Chicago from its terminal, some trains could continue on to the International Railroad Bridge or Niagara Falls.

While the commission could do little to create an effective street grid, at least it made travel over arterial streets both easier and less dangerous. Still, it was important for the city to maintain the penetration of rail transport into its fabric. While Buffalo's harbor was as bustling as ever, primarily with grain and other bulk cargo, the economic significance of the bustle had changed. Where once Buffalo's economy was based on the transfer of goods and people back and forth between land and water, with the growth of manufacturing, the economy had become more dependent on rail for the transfer of resources in and manufactured goods out.

This did not mean that the industries that grew up on the waterfront disappeared, but they had changed as Buffalo had changed. While by the late Eighties there were more than thirty grain elevators on the Buffalo River, the Panic of 1893 stopped further construction. With the rebound of the economy in the late Nineties, ever-larger elevator construction resumed, some in wood, which quite promptly burned down, and two with a new technology—steel. And not just steel, but also with mechanical equipment powered by electricity. Not surprisingly, one of the two was forever thereafter known as the Electric Elevator. These elevators and their associated mills were not fireproof; that improvement came later. But they reduced the risk of fire significantly by reducing the number of belt drives whose overheating often caused grain dust to ignite. Unfortunately, when fires did happen, they burned so hot that they could melt the steel shell.

Soon came a major technological improvement in elevator construction, the all-concrete elevator. The absence of internal timber construction minimized fire risk still more. Strangely, the first of these elevators, located along the Buffalo River right next to the Electric, was attached to a malt house, essential to the local brewing industry, and owned by the largest firm that participated in the short-lived Malt Trust. This was quickly followed by a smaller bank of elevators built to serve a local competitor located right next door.

Almost immediately, concrete elevators began to replace both wooden and steel ones, among them one for Spencer Kellogg, a local firm specializing in the production of linseed oil, an important ingredient in paint. Spencer Kellogg and its owners had moved from its origins in the Mohawk Valley to Buffalo. At first, the new concrete elevators were mostly small, no more than 500,000 bushels. Then, all of a sudden starting in 1914, three great monsters appeared in quick succession: the Connecting Terminal Elevator, 1,000,000 bushels at the mouth of the Buffalo Ship Canal; then the Superior Elevator, 1,5000,000 bushels located farther up the Buffalo River than any elevator had ever been located; and finally, the Concrete Central Elevator, 3,500,000 bushels, still farther up that river near where the New York Central rail line crossed the Buffalo River. All were built simply for the storage of grain for transportation to the east, not at a place where a grain mill was located or was later built, but always where a ready rail connection could be had. By the time the Great War was over, there were ten modern, concrete elevators lining the waterfront, eight of them whose form and bulk would entrance European architects when, in the interwar period, they continued to come to America to examine industrial design.

At the same time, hints were already apparent that water-born commerce might be less important than the existence of these great elevators suggested. Right after the turn of the century, the first major elevator and mill built away from the waterfront, served only by rail, the New York Central Belt Line, was constructed on the east side of the city. George Urban Milling Company was predominantly a rye mill; perhaps as such, it did not need great quantities of grain as might justify the cost of prime waterfront space. And then, with the great economic expansion that accompanied the outbreak of hostilities, two more sets of elevators were built away from the waterfront. One was for H-O Oats, a manufacturer of breakfast cereal that had moved from New York City; the other was for George Meyer Malt & Grain, a malting house for the brewery industry. Both were served by a New York Central connection.

The other visually spectacular portion of Buffalo's growing economy was primary metal production, an activity that lit up the nighttime sky and filled the air with particulate-laden smoke. At the turn of the century, Lackawanna Steel began constructing a mill on the lakefront, just south of the city's boundary. It was the first truly integrated steelmaker in the area. This facility was a transferred, but expanded and rationalized, plant of an existing steel producer located in Scranton, Pennsylvania on the Lackawanna River. That firm was running out of its chief local resource—a supply of anthracite coal. It also was experiencing an unwelcome amount of labor unrest at the mill and on the separately owned, but shareholder related, railroad, the DLW. Entire portions of the existing plant were moved to Buffalo, as were a surprising number of skilled workers, at least for a firm that quite obviously was fleeing its unionized workforce. Buffalo and Erie County contributed to the move by selling pieces of property they each owned at the desired site. Iron ore would come by boat from Minnesota's Mesabi Range and likewise, a particular grade of limestone from Michigan. Coal would come by train from Pennsylvania.

The plant was well designed, but full of old and new technology. Near the waterfront, on the west edge of the property, rail cars delivered coal. Moving east next came the coking ovens, then the specially dredged slip for freighters delivering ore and limestone to be deposited on docks, and thereafter, in bins farther to the east. Next to the bins were the seven blast furnaces for making pig iron still farther east were the Bessemer converters and open-hearth furnaces for making steel and finally, the various rolling mills, primarily a mill for rolling steel rails. All throughout the property, there was the trackage of a wholly owned subsidiary, the South Buffalo Railway, that did all sorts of moving of intermediate products from one part of the complex to another and also of finished product to the various railroad lines that ran near the site's eastern boundary.

Announcement of the building of the Lackawanna works served to bring other, smaller plants to the area. Local interests organized Buffalo and Susquehanna Iron and Steel and New York State Steel, while Wickwire Steel was built to provide pig iron for a wire-manufacturing firm in Cortland, NY. The first two opened early in the decade. The former was on the lakefront just north of the Lackawanna works, but inside the city's boundary; the latter, on the Buffalo River, upstream and on the other side from Union Furnace, which itself was reorganized and reopened in 1901. Wickwire, built in 1906, was located on the Niagara River, north of the city's boundary in the Town of Tonawanda, but south of Tonawanda Creek, a location made plausible by another action of the Corps of Engineers—a new, much bigger lock near where the existing lock on the canal had been located, but now in the Niagara River. When Wickwire-Spencer expanded into steel production during World War I, Semet-Solvey, a division of Buffalo-based National Aniline and Dye, soon to be part of Allied Chemical, built a coke plant nearby to supply Wickwire and Tonawanda Iron. Overall, employment opportunities as well as the local immigrant population grew significantly.

Unfortunately, several of these plants did not fare well in the brief, but intense depression that followed the famous Panic of 1907, the one where J. P. Morgan saved the day, an event that made Congress recognize that the United States could no longer survive without a central bank, and so led to the creation of the Federal Reserve System. Buffalo and Susquehanna Iron and Steel failed, and in 1910, was absorbed by Rogers & Brown, a Cincinnati firm that had earlier moved its headquarters to Buffalo when it bought Tonawanda Iron. Rogers & Brown quickly sold its new acquisition to the Hanna interests from Cleveland. At this point, it became known as Union Furnace, though eventually, Hanna Furnace. Somewhat later, New York State Steel also failed, and in 1915, was purchased by the Donner family interests from Philadelphia, and renamed Donner Steel, which then quickly bought Tonawanda Iron Works from Rogers & Brown. The Lackawanna works was badly crippled too and brought in no new technology until after World War I. Its debt load was then increased to fund both plant expansion and the purchase of coal and ore deposits; when completed it reached what was then thought of as the high debt to equity ratio—½ to 1. Nonetheless, in good years thousands of men worked in these plants and untold amounts of steel was produced.

During the Nineties and Teens, Buffalo's manufacturing sector continued to expand, adding new firms or new products from old firms. Some were in what would now be known as mass production industries. One was motor vehicles. In 1899, the E. R. Thomas Motor Car Company began producing the famous Thomas Flyer. Though famous, the enterprise was never particularly successful and closed by 1912. In 1903, two men named George entered the industry. George Atterbury started selling electric trucks, buses, delivery vans, and similar large vehicles of his own design. He then shifted to gasoline-powered autos, and by 1907, had settled on similarly powered trucks. His Atterbury Motor Car Company became well known locally and in Canada for producing fine, durable high-end trucks. It failed during the Depression.

The other George, George N. Pierce, began his career making gilded birdcages and iceboxes, then very fancy bicycles. Next came steam-powered automobiles and in 1903, he recruited a local investor, and together they began making the luxury touring car, the Pierce-Arrow. The car was an immediate hit, such a big hit that, in 1907, the factory moved from the bicycle works' location near the Buffalo River to an enormous new plant, designed by the famous industrial architect, Albert Kahn, on the mid-north side next to the Belt Line. Though Pierce soon left the business, the Pierce-Arrow was a car to be, and be seen, in. The firm continued to prosper in an elite market that was shared with Packard and Peerless.

The appearance of a fourth motor vehicle maker in the city was eventually more interesting. In 1911, Henry Ford purchased the John R. Keim Mills Incorporated, which had been one of Ford's suppliers of "pressed metal," what today would be called stampings. The plant was right next to the Erie Railroad tracks northeast of downtown. Within a year, the plant's employees went out on strike and Ford immediately shut it down. However, a year later, he reopened the facility as an assembly plant, though with new workers, of course. This action was part of Ford's move to distribute assembly plants across the country and even overseas. Apparently, Buffalo was a good place to manufacture automobiles, because in 1915, Ford built a new larger, four-story plant, this time on the Belt Line.

And there were other pieces of the transportation industry. Starting in 1912, Stewart Motor Company made light trucks and exported some of them to Europe. It survived until 1942. Harrison Radiator, in nearby Lockport, started building automobile radiators in 1911 and became a part of General Motors seven years later. Tri-Continental Corporation, known more colloquially as Trico, made windshield wipers for various auto manufacturers starting in 1917; the Fedders Manufacturing Company, once a manufacturer of milk cans, bread pans, and kerosene tanks, rather quickly shifted to making automobile radiators, initially for both Pierce-Arrow and Thomas. Buffalo Gasolene Engine Company made inboard marine engines starting in 1898, as did Sterling Engine, starting somewhat later.

More of a surprise was the appearance of an industry that had no roots in metal bending. Glenn Curtiss, a prominent aviator, had run a small airplane production plant in his hometown of Hammondsport, New York, on Keuka Lake where, believing that it would be a long time before cities had airports, he worked on developing seaplanes, then called airboats, though the planes he developed were in fact capable of landing on firm ground. With the outbreak of World War I, he found himself with large orders, not for seaplanes, but for biwinged trainers, the "Curtiss Jenny," from the British and the Canadian governments, as well expressions of interest from both the United States Army and the Navy. Unable to find enough workers in Hammondsport or nearby Bath, he chose to build a factory in north Buffalo near the Niagara Falls line of the New York Central. Then, when the United States entered the war and demand further increased, he built another plant, this time farther south on that line.

Demand was immense. In 1918, there were fifteen thousand employees just to build the airframes and assemble the planes. In Hammondsport, three thousand more built the engines.

The increase in employment at Curtiss was a result of the shift from a craftlike model to something approximating assembly-line production. This shift was accompanied by labor discord in the Buffalo factories, but still, this was the only plane of American design that was used in the war effort here and abroad. So, Buffalo was proud, and that pride was increased by knowing that other Buffalo firms participated in the run-up to American participation in the War. Pratt & Letchworth forged shell casings, Pierce-Arrow built trucks, and both Lackawanna Steel and Buffalo Copper and Brass Rolling Mills, formed in 1906 and made a part of American Brass by 1917, filled large European orders for their products as early as 1915, all skirting American neutrality policy as articulated at the time.

There were many, many other manufacturing enterprises developed in these years, enough that no particular industrial categorization system could order them and so, in alphabetical order, one might remember—Acme Shale Brick, with plants in both Hamburg and the Town of Tonawanda; American Steamship, which started in marine brokerage, but soon shifted to owning bulk cargo vessels that operated on the Great Lakes; Barcalo Manufacturing, which started as a manufacturer of beds and mattresses, began drop-forging the metal parts of bed frames, and then slowly shifted into drop forgings of other types, particularly tools such as wrenches; Beals, McCarthy & Rogers, a hardware wholesaler; the Beaverboard Company, which produced a patented variety of fiberboard building materials; Brunswick-Balke-Collander, which produced fancy billiard tables; Buffalo Break Beam, which produced parts for the New York Central passenger and freight cars; Cataract Chemical of Buffalo, which made chemicals for the leather industry; Curtis Screw, a manufacturer of threaded parts; S. M. Flickinger, a grocery wholesaler and later grocer; General Railway Signal, a most extraordinary flash-in-the-pan which, as Taylor Signal Company, developed the first successful electric semaphore railroad signal, built a big factory to manufacture these in 1902, merged with two other companies to form General Signal Company in 1904, and in 1907, shut that factory down to move production to Rochester; Goergen-Mackworth, a steel fabricator, essentially a job shop for steel construction; Hewett Rubber, a manufacturer of rubber hose and rubber conveyer belts; King Sewing Machine, which manufactured that product under its name and for Sears, Roebuck & Company at a big factory in the Riverside neighborhood; the Mentholatum Corporation, which moved from Kansas to produce that product for the treatment of aches and pains;

Molenberg-Betz, a manufacturer of commercial refrigeration systems and freezers; Niagara Machine and Tool Works, a producer of large cutting machines and forming presses; Pratt & Lambert, a national manufacturer of varnishes and later paints, which consolidated its manufacturing in Buffalo when moving its headquarters there; Seneca Iron & Steel, a producer of sheets of galvanized steel; Spaulding Fiber, a manufacturer of building materials; Spencer Lens, a manufacturer of microscopes that moved to Buffalo from Geneva, New York, and with Bausch & Lomb of Rochester, were the only manufacturers of such instruments in the United States; Vulcan Steam Forging, a producer of specialty forgings; Washburn-Crosby Company, a Minneapolis miller that opened a grain elevator and flour mill on the waterfront; Westwood Pharmaceuticals, which began as a patent medicine producer; Williams Gold Refining, a Kansas City refiner that produced gold alloys for dentistry, which moved to the city in 1912; and J. H. Williams, a Brooklyn drop forging company, which also specialized in mechanics tools, and opened its first branch plant just over the northern border of the city in Tonawanda.

Mergers continued apace. One notable merger was wholly local: David Bell Engineering joined with Buffalo Foundry to create Buffalo Foundry and Machine, manufacturers of dryers and evaporators, among other machines. And one was unusual: American Radiator merged into Standard Radiator of Chicago, creating American Standard Radiator, and promptly moved its Headquarters to a new plant in Buffalo. But most became branch plants of companies located elsewhere. Buffalo Car Manufacturing Company and Niagara Car Wheel became part of American Car and Foundry headquartered in Saint Louis; Buffalo Dry Dock, the successor to Union Dry Dock, became part of America Shipbuilding of Cleveland; F. N. Burt became a subsidiary of the Moore Companies of Canada; Howard Iron Works, a manufacturer of fire hydrants, bolt-making machinery and paper cutting presses, became the nucleus of the local manufacturing facilities of Otis Elevator of New York City; Snow Steam Pump became a part of Worthington Pump of Northern New Jersey; and Union Bridge became a part of American Bridge of Pittsburg

Existing manufacturing establishments continued to expand. Most notable was the Larkin Soap Company, which by the Nineties, had switched entirely to mail order sales, well before the start of rural free delivery of mail, much less the Postal Service's parcel post system. It soon began to package its growing product line in "combination boxes" of its products—like Harry & David or Hickory Farms today—that included "premiums" redeemable for other products, and urged the formation of local "Larkin clubs," little local cooperatives of consumers established in order to be able to take advantage of the price savings that the purchase of combination boxes allowed. Soon, the firm began to produce the premiums that it offered, most notably china patterns produced by the wholly owned Buffalo China, but also towels and furniture. It's growth after the turn of the century was dramatic.

Buffalo Forge, which had earlier expanded from the production of forges to the production of industrial fans and blowers, moved into the industrial air conditioning market. It supplied the blowers for the first major commercial air conditioning project, the Auditorium Theatre in Chicago. Unfortunately, when in the teens, one of its employees developed a viable method of air conditioning that did not require ice or industrial fans, the firm let this employee, Willis Carrier, take the invention to Syracuse where he built a famous business.

Less significant expansions were occasionally quite odd. For example, during the Nineties, Pratt & Letchworth produced very fancy cast iron toy armies that are prized by collectors today in addition to parts for the railroad industry. McKinnon Dash improbably became a major manufacturer of chain after the turn of the century. Others prospered even under new owners: For example, the Wagner Car Company continued to produce sleeper cars long after having been purchased by the Pullman Car Company. Yet, other firms completely redesigned their business models. Schoellkopf Aniline and Dye prospered enough that, by 1917, it had an office in New York City that imported chemicals for its business, primarily from English sources, and sales offices in nine other cities. The Buffalo plant had become the largest producer of dyes in the United States, and the firm was in a position to profit from the unavailability of German dyes. To better reflect its larger profile, it renamed itself as National Aniline and Chemical. The new firm controlled 75 percent of the nation's market. The city had developed the nucleus of a chemical industry.

It should not be implied from this limited listing of the city's manufacturing base that Buffalo did not produce a range of consumer products as well. Kittinger Furniture, a firm that traced its roots back to the Eighteen Sixties, began to build a serious national reputation around the turn of the Twentieth Century, but this was for very high-end reproductions of Eighteenth Century furniture, a product line more like gilded birdcages and Pierce-Arrow cars, and so not an obvious candidate for expansion. At a lower level, in the consumer products field, the grain mills in the city manufactured flour for retail consumption and animal feed. Jacob Dold Packing, a firm that traced its roots to the 1850s, was said to be the largest meat packer east of Chicago and the fifth largest in the world, though it was still not in the same league as Armour, Swift, Hormel, or

Oscar Meyer, even with its line of canned foods included and its second slaughterhouse in Wichita, Kansas. So, meat packing, of which there was a lot around the New York Central's stockyards on the city's east side, was essentially a trade for the local market, as was the case with the locally produced beer that came from the city's many breweries.

Before moving to the next piece of Buffalo's economy—power/utilities—two absences should be noted. First, Buffalo was not a center of banking. While it had had lots of banks at one time or another, by World War I it had devolved into a relatively stable set of major players. There were three commercial banks: Marine Bank, established in 1850 to serve the waterfront industries; Manufacturers and Traders Bank (M & T), established in 1856 to serve the indicated firms; and German American Bank, established in 1882 to serve that somewhat separate community, but whose name was changed to Liberty Bank in the aftermath of World War I. Three saving banks provided home mortgages exclusively: Buffalo Savings Bank, established in 1846; Western Saving Bank, established in 1851; and Erie County Savings Bank, established in 1854. Each of these banks had a law firm that was connected with it and provided services for it. Indeed, that has always been the relationship between lawyers and bankers in Buffalo. However, when serious financings were needed, they were not found in Buffalo, but in New York City, the deep-water ocean port city whose expansion, and ultimately dominance of American finance, was made possible by the very canal that aided Buffalo's history too.

Second, while the city had several insurance companies, none of them was large. Large insurance companies were concentrated either in New York City or Hartford, Connecticut.

In the Nineties Buffalo, the Brush General Electric Company and other distributors of electric power in the city formed the Buffalo General Electric Company. At the same time, a different group of investors formed the Niagara Falls Power Company. It dug a short canal upriver from Schoellkopf's and then built a generating plant on the river south of the rapids that were above the falls. That plant discharged its water through a long, deep tunnel to a spot below the falls. Generally known as the Edward Dean Adams plant, after the name of its principal developer, it opened in 1896, the same year that Schoellkopf's firm opened a second, much larger plant down in the River Gorge below the firm's canal. Both plants were augmented with an additional, on-site power station in 1904.

The Schoellkopf plant produced direct current. The Adams plant produced alternating current, power that could be delivered over long distances. Indeed, this plant was never intended to supply power directly to users, but was designed to be connected to transmission lines built by another company—Cataract Power and Conduit Company, a joint venture of Niagara Falls Power Company and the Buffalo General Electric Company—whose only purpose was to bring power from the falls to Buffalo. Oddly, its power was not the sixty-cycle power that is delivered to homes today, but twenty-five-cycle power, as a result of a mismatch between the size of the holes dug for the generators and the engineering requirements of the new AC technology. Still, power reached Buffalo late in 1896.

The industrial firms in Buffalo and those that gathered around the falls didn't care about whether the power they received was AC or DC. When their production processes required large amounts of direct current, as was the case in the falls for the refining of ore or the production of chemical compounds, they installed rectifiers to convert the AC power from the Adams plant to the DC current they needed. Niagara Falls manufacturers could use both suppliers. Among the firms there was the Pittsburg Reduction Company, later known as the Aluminum Company of America or ALCOA. It used electricity to produce heat sufficient to smelt aluminum metal from bauxite. Similarly, the Carborundum Company used electricity to produce heat sufficient to turn clay containing aluminum silicate and coke into silicon carbide, an abrasive. Both of these processes relied on the use of carbon electrodes produced in Niagara Falls by National Carbon, a branch of a Cleveland company. Castner Electrolytic Alkali, and later the Acker Process Company, used electricity to turn salt from mines in the Genesee Valley into sodium hydroxide, also known as caustic soda or lye, and chlorine gas that were combined with other compounds to produce bleaching powder. Niagara Alkali did the same thing.

Over time, other firms, also relying on direct current electric power, appeared. Acetylene Light and Power and Presto-Lite adapted the process for making carborundum by substituting calcium oxide for aluminum silicate to create calcium carbide, which it then allowed to react with water to produce acetylene gas, an unstable and thus highly dangerous byproduct used first in early automobile headlights and later in welding with the development of the oxygen-acetylene torch. Acheson Graphite produced very pure graphite by overheating the carborundum to drive off the silica. Niagara Electro-Chemical took the process of electrolyzing salt in a different direction to produce elemental sodium and sodium peroxide. Norton Emery Wheel Company mimicked the carborundum process by starting with bauxite to produce a synthetic substance that was as hard a carborundum and as tough as the naturally occurring mineral emery. Oldbury Electrochemical Company also mimicked the carborundum process by starting with phosphorus ore and coke but ending with elemental phosphorus and potassium chlorate. Niagara Falls had become an important part of the American chemical industry. One such firm chose to make its home in the Town of Tonawanda—Buffalo Electro-Chemical, a maker of hydrogen peroxide.

Hooker Chemical, which was established just after the turn of the century, soon absorbed Oldbury. Then, during World War I, Acetylene Light and Power, Presto-Lite, Acheson Graphite, National Carbon, and Linde Air Products, a firm established on the west side of the Town of Tonawanda to use a German process for the production of pure oxygen gas by the distillation of liquid air, united to form Union Carbide and Carbon, a bit belated part of the Great Merger Movement.

The prominence given to the electric power at the 1901 Pan-American Exhibition held in Buffalo served to expand usage. It soon began to outstrip capacity. Even worse, a treaty between the United States and Great Britain, the sovereign of Canada at that time, limited the amount of water that could be withdrawn out of the Niagara River for power production. As a result, in the late Teens, the Buffalo General Electric Company built a coal-fired, steam-powered generating plant, commonly known as the Huntley Generating Station, on the Niagara River, just north of Buffalo. That new plant was designed to produce the by-then more standard sixty-cycle AC power, though it produced twenty-five-cycle power as well because the electric motors already installed by existing power users were twenty-five cycle. During World War I, in order to simplify power production in the area, the federal government forced the merger of the Schoellkopf power companies into the Niagara Falls Power Company.

Electric power was important not just for industrial growth, but also for another reason. Before 1890, most of Buffalo's residents experienced life by walking and lit their houses with kerosene lamps. The relatively small upper-middle and upper classes had their own carriages or rode horse-drawn street railway cars, or after 1881, street railway cars traveling short distances using direct current, and lit their houses with manufactured natural gas delivered by the many gas companies that joined together to form National Fuel Gas in 1902. With the coming of alternating current technology, the street railroad lines shifted to it, and so increased the distances people might plausibly travel. Slowly, more homes were illuminated with electricity too.

The street railway network focused on what has, over time, come to be seen and visited as Downtown, though as in most of America, the creation of Downtown, the idea of being the place that one would go for shopping, eating, entertainment, as opposed to downtown, the location of the central business district, is a late Nineteenth Century invention. Buffalo had a central business district by the late 1820s. It was the waterfront and the area just to the northeast of the waterfront where, in the 1840s, the city's Board of Trade was located. In the 1880s, the Board of Trade moved up from the flatland along the waterfront under the name Merchant's Exchange and soon thereafter, a bit farther inland, under the name Chamber of Commerce and Manufacturers' Club. This second move meant that downtown, and Downtown, came to overlap just as was the case in most big cities. The wholesalers worked there, as did the bankers, financiers, insurance, utility and corporate executives, the lawyers, realtors, architects, engineers, and accountants, the clerks, typists, salesmen, salesgirls, and messengers, and many craftsmen and laborers. The courts, government agencies, and port and telegraph offices were located downtown, while the big department and clothing stores, most hotels, restaurants, places of popular amusement, and institutions of high culture shared the space but were Downtown.[15]

Downtown combined tall buildings and easy transport, so in Buffalo it was not possible to have a downtown until a real electric street railway system was created. The city's downtown, the place, can be fairly dated from its architectural treasures: the Erie County Savings Bank (1893); Ellicott Square Building, a Daniel Burnham building, (1895); the Dun Building, later part of Dun & Bradstreet, (1895); the Brisbane Building (1896); the Guaranty Building, a Louis Sullivan building, (1896); the Buffalo Savings Bank (1900); the Buffalo Post Office (1901); the Lafayette Hotel (1904); the first Statler Hotel (1908); the Buffalo Electric Tower (1912); and the Marine Bank building (1915).

In the same area were to be found the city's three biggest department stores: J. N. Adam; Adam, Meldrum & Anderson; and Hengerer's. All opened large stores in the 1890s, as did as an upscale men's store, Kleinhans. A bit north, three specialty upscale women's clothing stores, L. L. Berger, Flint & Kent, and Oppenheim, Collins, all opened in the 1900s. Interestingly, both J. N. Adam and Hengerer's were sold to Associated Dry Goods in the 1910s; Oppenheim, Collins was a branch of a New York City store. All were part of Downtown.

Most of the city's theaters followed the same pattern as shopping—moving slowly north. The older theaters, which had originally hosted not only vaudeville, but also drama and occasional classical performances, were closer to the waterfront. The first movie theater opened in 1896. Perhaps the first purpose-built movie theater in America was located a bit north in the basement of the Ellicott Square Building. Later, theaters were a bit north of that. However, the enormous

Buffalo Music Hall (1889), later known as the Teck Music Hall, was at the far north end of downtown. It also hosted "legitimate" theater.

If ever Buffalo's economy were in full bloom, these were the years. One need only note the list of large employers who have disappeared to see that once this was a big, important place. And the city knew it. It is hard to imagine any city ushering in a high-end motor car maker, Pierce-Arrow, a high-end truck maker, Atterbury, and a furniture maker specializing in high-end reproductions of classic furniture, Kittinger, in a place that did not see itself as fat and happy. In retrospect, however, there were at least three troubling developments in these years.

The first is most easily understood by reflecting on its meaning for Buffalo's position as the second-largest rail hub in the United States. As noted earlier, where once the city was a real entrepôt, first moving goods and people from water to water, then later moving goods and people between water and rail as well, as the city expanded its manufacturing base it increasingly became more dependent on rail for the movement of resources in and goods out. The older dependency was more of a geographic dependency than the newer one, built on the ability of the region to provide goods that were wanted elsewhere in the country or by overseas trading partners. Evidence of the decline in geographic dependency, and unfortunately, geographic advantage, was doubly apparent. A significant portion of the carloads entering and leaving the city stopped only briefly, as trains were disassembled and reassembled for their final destinations in the eastside rail yards. And some trains didn't stop at all because both the New York Central and the Lehigh Valley constructed tracks that allowed whole trains from the east or west to bypass the city completely. To some extent, the choice to center the city's economy on manufacturing recognized that geography was not as important for Buffalo's future and, at the same time, that its future hinged on a game played in a larger competitive environment.

The second is the disappearance of locally owned companies into larger companies that were either owned elsewhere or publicly owned and headquartered elsewhere. Examples of the first are Atlas Refining, which disappeared into Standard Oil; A. Rumsey and Sons, a company that dated back to 1845, which disappeared into the leather trust, United States Leather Company; and both Pierce Steam Heating and Standard Radiator, which disappeared into the American Radiator Company. The ordinariness of these transactions can be seen from the fact that Spencer Kellogg was notable for having refused to join the linseed oil trust.

What does this say about Buffalo, if anything, after all, the merger of small firms in the city had gone on for years? A good example is Union Furnace. This example and the others is a reflection of the railroads that had so effectively carved the city into pieces. Competition, at least for certain goods, was now much wider than before the national rail network had filled out. One needed either more capital to compete or needed to reduce competition by forming a trust, preferably both.

The third is the establishment of Buffalo branches of firms located elsewhere. Here, the primary example is the movement of the Lackawanna Steel Company from Pennsylvania, but equally important was the purchase of Keim Mills by Henry Ford and his subsequent choice to establish an assembly plant along the Belt Line at Main Street. But the choice of J. H. Williams of Brooklyn to establish a local drop forging plant is at least as relevant as is the choice of Rogers, Brown & Company first purchase the Tonawanda Iron Works and then later, the Buffalo and Susquehanna works. Buffalo was a good place to have a factory, just as other cities had been important for both Rumsey and Schoellkopf tanneries many years earlier.

Why was that? Some of this activity was simply the fact that even after the railroads cut transportation costs, transportation was still a part of the effective price any firm's product, at least for the customer. Having a plant near to customers was a good strategy and so, locating in a city that was the second-largest rail hub was close to a no brainer. But, at least as important was the local cost of production. Lackawanna Steel would never have moved to Buffalo had low-cost ore not been discovered in the Mesabi Range. The availability of labor mattered too. New York City may have had the largest immigrant population, but Buffalo was no slouch once the Italians joined the Polish. In a world where most manufacturing relied on large numbers of workers supplied with simple machines, the availability of lots of low-cost workers was a real advantage, especially when the resources for transportation of production were comparatively good.

The Twenties and Thirties: Moving Ahead While Lagging behind

Buffalo recovered quickly from the sharp, brief recession that followed the end of World War I. Its economy was about 40 percent metalwork, 16 percent iron and steel, 20 percent grain and flour, 6 percent motor vehicles, and 16 percent printing, an industry that is all but invisible ninety-five years later. Little was changed on the waterfront except for the slow fill of the on-land portions of the Erie Canal in the wake of the completion of the redesigned Erie Barge Canal, including the new Black Rock Lock, alterations that eliminated the usefulness of the many slips that previously dotted the waterfront. These were soon filled too.

The only significant change in the city's railroads was the building of the great New York Central Passenger Terminal in the mid-east side in the late Twenties. It was a grand building with an enormous barrel shaped roof over the concourse, twenty-five tracks serving about 140 trains a day, and a seventeen-story office tower. Adjacent buildings handled passenger baggage and the less than carload freight consigned to the Railway Express Company. The point of the move was a combination of aesthetics and convenience. The old building that the Central and the Erie had been fighting over was decrepit and the new location allowed trains to pull into the station and leave directly without having to be backed out in order to continue on. The choice was understandable, though one could already see in that choice the change in American's travel alternatives brought by the automobile. While the number of New York Central's express trains—long distance, for the most part—stopping in Buffalo was pretty much the same as ten years before, the number of its local trains was already half of what it had been ten years earlier. Both numbers would decline further in the next ten years.

The construction of larger grain elevators in the late teens recognized that bulk carriers on the Great Lakes had continued to grow in capacity and that export of grain to Europe was increasing as well. In the Twenties, many existing elevators were increased in capacity. More surprisingly, several new very large elevators were built. Two were in unusual locations. One, by the Saskatchewan Cooperative, was built on the lakefront near the Lackawanna Steel complex, and the other, just outside of the city in the Town of Tonawanda near the New York Central tracks heading to Niagara Falls, by Eastern States Milling as there was an associated feed mill there. Others were related to changes in the milling end of the grain business. While milling was declining in Minneapolis, four sets of elevators were built or altered on the Buffalo River. Washburn-Crosby, a Minneapolis miller, bought an existing elevator, built more capacity, and began to produce Gold Medal flour; International Milling from that same city, built its own large set of elevators, locally known as the Lake and Rail Elevators, and began producing Robin Hood flour; and Standard Milling, also from Minneapolis, built its own set of elevators together with a mill to produce its Ceresota flour. And then, in the Thirties, Pillsbury Company, the largest miller in Minneapolis, bought the late 1890s-era Great Northern Elevator (more than 2,500,000-bushel capacity) and built its own enormous mill nearby to produce its Pillsbury's BEST brand. Buffalo was said to have become the largest grain port in the world and the largest flour-milling center in the world as well.

The big change in the local steel industry was the purchase of Lackawanna Steel's plant by Bethlehem Steel in 1922. The years after World War I had been economically difficult for Lackawanna largely because of the added costs associated with operating a plant that had not had much of an upgrade since it had been built. Bethlehem poured money into the plant, and in the process, moved production from steel rails and pilings to sheet and plate for automotive use and eventually wartime production. Indeed, by 1940, it was the largest steel plant in the world. Unfortunately, labor relations continued to be just as troubled as they had been under Lackawanna's ownership.

Other steel plants changed ownership as well. In 1929, Hanna Furnace became a part of National Steel, headquartered in Pittsburgh, though the facility was still known locally by its earlier name. A year later, Donner Steel was sold to Republic Steel, headquartered in Cleveland. It was a site of part of the great steel strike of 1937. Hanna Furnace largely produced pig iron for the Republic plant and the two continued to share the production from the Donner-Hanna Coke Company, which had been established in 1917. In 1923, Tonawanda Iron became part of American Radiator, later known as American Standard after further mergers. In contrast, Wickwire Steel failed in 1927 and endured a receivership that continued, with only a modest interruption, until the firm was successfully reorganized in 1936. At that time, its plant was updated with a loan backed by the Reconstruction Finance Corporation.

Of steel-related manufacturing industries, automobiles began to stand out. Ford closed its assembly plant on the Belt Line in 1931 and simultaneously opened one on the waterfront just a bit north of the Bethlehem Steel plant and south of the Saskatchewan Cooperative Elevator. Apparently, Ford discovered that building cars in a multistory building was not a sensible idea. This lesson might have been learned by observing production at the single-story Chevrolet assembly plant built on the Belt Line in 1923, a bit south of the Ford plant. Whether building cars in a waterfront plant that was icebound four or so months a year with the expectation of distributing them by lake freighter was a good idea remained to be seen. General Motors clearly liked the single-story plant for it reproduced the design in a Chevrolet engine plant and associated foundry that it opened in 1938 in the Town of Tonawanda between the Niagara River and the New York Central tracks just north of the Buffalo city line. However, the Depression was hard on the locally owned auto plants. Pierce-Arrow, sold by the original owners before World War I, was closed in the mid-Thirties, as was the Atterbury Motor Car Company, builder of Atterbury trucks.

Other auto-related companies joined Harrison, Trico, and Fedders. Houde Engineering secured rights to a French design for shock absorbers that the owner had seen used on French artillery pieces during WWI and so began producing them in Buffalo. They were quickly adopted by first Lincoln Motors, then Pierce-Arrow and finally by Henry Ford for the new Model A. Dunlop Rubber, a British company, began to manufacture bicycle tires in the Town of Tonawanda, and then quickly switched to producing auto tires for the replacement parts market.

After World War I, Curtiss Aeronautical, which was the largest aircraft manufacturer in the world, saw its wartime contracts vanish in an instant. After the reorganization that allowed Glenn Curtiss to cash out his interest, the firm returned to its original activity, the design and production of airboats, one of which quickly became the first plane to cross the Atlantic Ocean. Then, in 1929, Curtiss Aeroplane merged with Wright Aeronautical of Dayton, Ohio, a manufacturer of aircraft engines and the surviving piece of the Wright brothers original company, to form Curtiss-Wright. The firm's headquarters was Buffalo, though the engine division remained in Dayton and was the crucial link to the armed forces that kept the new firm alive with orders for the production of military aircraft during the Thirties.

Meanwhile, in 1924, Consolidated Aircraft, a new company in the field, opened a plant in Buffalo, also to produce seaplanes. It opened a small field for its private use in the Town of Tonawanda just east of the New York Central tracks heading north to Niagara Falls in 1929 and was successful is securing several contracts from the U.S. Navy. However, in 1935, Consolidated left for a new factory in Southern California. It left behind a large factory and Lawrence Bell, its general manager. Bell established Bell Aircraft in the old Consolidated factory and began producing fighter planes for the U.S. Army Air Force. From 1922 to about 1928, G. Elias Brothers, Incorporated, a lumber dealer, built monoplanes, after having earlier specialized in wooden propellers. From 1927 to 1934, the Hall Aluminum Aircraft Corporation, a company most notable for developing a way to rivet aluminum plates together for a metal skin for aircraft, produced airboats for the U.S. Navy in the city before moving to Bristol, Pennsylvania, only later to become a part of Consolidated Aircraft in California. And for a few years after 1928, General Airplane produced airboats too.

A critical, but separate part of this aero complex was in a wholly different business. Near the end of World War I, the Irvin Airchute Company developed and produced the first successful parachute. While the push to develop passenger travel by air did not rely on parachutes, indeed it would have seen them as inimical to the nascent business, the major funder for the research and development of airplanes—the armed services—knew that such equipment was essential to its interests and made sure that Irvin was at least kept minimally solvent. Scott Aviation worked on producing masks, regulators, and oxygen cylinders for use by flyers.

Buffalo did its best to help these enterprises along. Its first airport, really a field for doing demonstrations of flying called Curtiss Field, opened in 1916, also in the Town of Tonawanda, but on the border with the Town of Amherst. It closed in 1926 when a municipal airport opened in the Town of Cheektowaga. By 1927, that airport offered passenger and airmail service to Cleveland, this before the New York City area even had an airport. And in 1932, the city built a marine airport on the Lake Erie portion of the waterfront.

Given that the boom years were far shorter than the bust years, the number of new manufacturing firms with a certain staying power is somewhat surprising. Buffalo Fire Appliance Company made fire engines; DuPont opened a plant in the Town of Tonawanda, generally referred to as the Yerkes plant, named after a long-time director of the lab there; Durez Plastics produced phenolic resins in a plant along the river in the Town of Tonawanda; Farrel-Birmingham, a Connecticut firm, opened a plant that produced gear-cutting machinery nearby. Fisher-Price began producing classic wooden toys at its factory in suburban East Aurora; Frontier Oil (later Ashland) built an oil refinery on River Road; Greater Buffalo Press, a printer, specialized in color work; Keystone Corporation, a chrome-plating firm, expanded its business both in terms of the metal to be plated and that on which it was being plated; Ludlum Steel built a plant for casting special alloy steels in the Town of Tonawanda; National Gypsum, a firm started by two executives who lost their jobs as a result of the bankruptcy of the Beaverboard Company, began producing drywall at a factory in the nearby Town of Clarence; and Wonder Bread, an Indiana firm, soon to be part of Continental Baking, built a large factory near the Belt Line. National Biscuit did too. Local construction companies, John W. Cowper & Sons, and Ferguson Electric began to show a certain staying power in an industry where companies had long tended to have a short life span. And more chemical and refining companies came to Niagara Falls including the Vanadium Corporation of America, a maker of steel alloys, Niacet, a maker of acetic acid and its derivatives from acetylene, and Alox, a maker of rust inhibiters.

Mergers were at least as common, however. American Brass became a part of Anaconda Brass. Gould Coupler merged with the Symington Company of

Rochester to become Symington-Gould; Gould Storage Battery joined National Battery of Minneapolis; Great Lakes Portland Cement, the local branch of a Canadian company, was acquired by Lehigh Portland Cement; McKinnon Dash merged into Columbus Chain and then returned to local control as Columbus-McKinnon Chain, located in the City of Tonawanda. Niagara Electro-Chemical became part of DuPont. Rand-Kardex and Rand-Ledger, two firms that represented a generational dispute in the Rand family of Buffalo, formed the Rand Corporation, which then merged with the Remington Typewriter firm, to form Remington Rand, a large office products company. Seneca Iron and Steel was absorbed by Bethlehem Steel, its neighbor in Lackawanna; and Spencer Lens, which had specialized in laboratory microscopes, became a part of American Optical, a Massachusetts company that had long been a producer of equipment for measuring patients for reading glasses. Washburn-Crosby became General Mills and soon began to produce cereals. While some of these mergers were clearly related to the decline of business during the Depression—Gould Storage Battery, Seneca Iron and Steel, and Spencer Lens—most were not.

Some notable changes could be found in the products of four firms. American Steamship helped to change the structure of the increasingly large Great Lake's freighters by designing them to be self-unloading thereby reducing the need for grain scoopers just as the marine leg on the grain elevator had done earlier with stevedores. King Sewing Machine had to shift its product after ownership of its sewing machine line passed from Sears, Roebuck to White Sewing Machine. Renamed King Quality Products, it began to produce radios under the Sears "Silverstone" brand. Soon ownership passed to Colonial Radio, which broadened the range of sellers for whom it produced radios. And Kittinger Furniture broadened its product line by striking an agreement to be the exclusive producer of furniture imitating that found at Colonial Williamsburg, now a growing travel destination. An outlier, Buffalo Foundry and Machine gave up on general foundry work to specialize in drying processes and so changed its name to Buflovac.

Several prominent firms failed during these years. Buffalo Pitts succumbed to its inability to adapt its technology to the gasoline engine. Atterbury and Pierce-Arrow succumbed to an inability to produce a product that suited the changing tastes of their customers during the Depression. Stewart Motors failed during the first year of World War II.[16]

None of the major banks failed in the Depression, or maybe, by not failing those banks became the major banks, but in truth, there was not much bank failure in Buffalo and as to utilities, a subject that bulked large in the years before

World War I, the only thing of interest that happened was the two expansions of the Huntley coal-fired generation station in the Thirties. What the Depression brought were all sorts of civic improvements.

Various federal agencies rehabbed one auditorium on the near-east side and built another [Memorial] near the waterfront. Also, the Buffalo Airport Terminal, the Erie County Sheriff's Office, a new federal courthouse, a [War Memorial] Stadium on the mid-north side, and a new post office were constructed with federal assistance, as was a municipal building for village of Kenmore and for the Town of Tonawanda too. New facilities were built for the Buffalo Zoo and the city's [E. J. Meyer] Hospital on the mid-northeast side with similar assistance as were repairs made to the Connecticut Street Armory and an old Cyclorama building. Federal funds improved parks in Buffalo, the Town of Tonawanda, and Village of Williamsville and built a new city water reservoir and an iconic bridge over Delaware Avenue, as well as an important new sewer line and two almost suburban public housing projects. Delaware Avenue was also repaired and widened.

Downtown had expanded earlier with the construction of an enormous new Statler Hotel that opened in 1923; the new Buffalo Athletic Club, in 1924; and the Liberty National Bank Building in 1925. In 1931, an equally massive, art deco City Hall appeared across the square from the hotel and the Buffalo Athletic Club. But the big change in downtown was the appearance of enormous new entertainment venues—the Century Theater (1921), Lafayette Theater (1922), Shea's Buffalo Theater (1926), and the Great Lakes Theater (1927) were for movies. The Erlanger Theater (1927) was the city's first structure devoted exclusively to stage plays and musicals.

That what was once Buffalo's central business district had finally grown a real Downtown, as Americans had come to know and imagine such a place, does not mean that there were no longer neighborhood centers. Remnants of many can still be seen—at three places on the west side (Grant and Ferry, Elmwood and Amherst, Tonawanda and Ontario) and one each on the Northeast corner (Bailey and Kensington), the mid-east side (Broadway and Fillmore), and the southeast side (Seneca south of the Buffalo River). But pretty near all roads still led to either Lafayette Square or Niagara Square and not just because of the city's radial street plan. By the Twenties, downtown was where the big office buildings gathered the white-collar workforce, where government facilities were similarly centered, where the big department stores set up shop, and where much entertainment was to be found. Surprisingly, Kleinhans Music Hall, the grand International Style home for the newly established Buffalo Symphony Orchestra was not even located at the edge of downtown where the orchestra had first played, but somewhat northwest at one of the gracious circles in Olmsted's great plan for the city.

Still, looking backward, it was the net of electric streetcars that had helped create downtown, and it was the automobile, particularly Ford's Model T, that sealed the development. The middle classes could now travel pretty much everywhere in private vehicles, just as the upper classes had long done. Poorer people and young people could travel comfortably on the streetcar lines.

It is somewhat odd for Buffalo in the Twenties and Thirties to think of itself, in part at least, in terms of its Downtown. Admittedly, these were the first years of an identifiable consumer economy of the kind that was symbolized by going downtown to shop, especially at Christmas time, or for dinner and a show. These were some of the things that demarked an expanded middle class, including not just automobiles, but such electric-powered household gadgets, sold as labor-saving devices, such as irons, toasters, vacuum cleaners, wooden console radios and, victrolas. Still, in terms of economic expansion, Twenties Buffalo, the area, experienced economic growth no less significant than Buffalo, the city, had in the Nineties and Teens. It was just that, if one looked carefully, it was a different growth.

But apparently, few people looked carefully. In the Twenties, a time when the grain trade had picked up, the Chamber of Commerce had already begun to worry about the possibility that the Saint Lawrence Seaway—an all-water route to Europe—would finally become a reality. In the Thirties, the chamber's worries shifted to the disreputable condition of the old waterfront along Lake Erie. Neither worry was silly. In the Twenties, construction of a fourth, expanded Welland Canal in Canada was much talked about and soon would begin. Photos of the waterfront from the Thirties show empty lots full of parked or stored cars where once there was a bustle of activity. But neither worry was centrally important to the local economy. Though the arrival of the big boats each spring and their departure just before winter swept in must have been quite a sight as they docked at the ever-larger grain elevators, the grain trade had been of declining importance to the local economy since the Eighties. It was surely not surprising that the old waterfront would decay in tandem with the shift of waterfront traffic to the river, nor that the old factories just in back of both pieces of the waterfront similarly decayed as those industries either grew, and so required more space, or shrunk, and could no longer afford upkeep.

Other people worried more about the fact that the Buffalo economy was growing more slowly than the economies in other places. In 1910, the city had slipped from the eighth-largest city in the United States to the tenth, then eleventh in 1920, thirteenth in 1930, and fourteenth in 1940. That Pittsburgh was also slowly sliding down hill in these years and Cleveland too, after it had peaked in 1920, seemed to be of no comfort, for while the city was growing more slowly, other nearby places were growing, especially Buffalo's suburbs. While the city's population grew 13 percent between 1920 and 1930, suburban growth was 40 percent. Similarly, while the city's population grew less than 1 percent between 1930 and 1940, suburban growth was almost 20 percent. Somehow it did not matter during these years that Cleveland had even lost population. Nor did it matter that, by 1940, growth within the city's boundaries had been such that the city was literally built out. There was almost no place for new housing construction other than a few blocks in the far north and a few in the far southeast. If the region were to grow, any growth had to be suburban growth. But no one seemed moved by such a realization.

It is likely that the problem was mostly psychological and thus, that positive symbols such as downtown were of great importance. The automobile had made the city more accessible to suburban dwellers than ever before, but at the same time farther away. In 1900, suburban dwellers were either tied to their little walkable neighborhoods, just as were city folk, or if really wealthy, tied to their grand isolation. By 1940, there were still the wealthy, but the balance of suburban dwellers was no longer just like city folk. They were the first local pieces of an autocentric culture and as such somehow different from city folk. It was troubling that a new center of commerce, a shopping plaza, University Plaza, was being built in suburban Amherst, though just over the city's border at the end of the Main Street streetcar line and right across from the growing undergraduate campus of the enlarged University of Buffalo. Even worse, the growth of auto ownership meant that places like Niagara Falls and East Aurora were much closer to the city economically. Ontario too was closer after the Peace Bridge was completed in 1927. That a ferry was no longer sufficient to accommodate the necessary trips to the other side of the Niagara River said more about the automobile than the regions' meager suburban development might indicate. The local economy had begun to become regional, especially as industrial Tonawanda had become a significant source of jobs and industrial Niagara Falls too.

Thus, Buffalo had reason both to be proud of its Downtown and to be worried about the decay along parts of its waterfront that the earlier central business district had moved away from.

For people who paid more careful attention to the regional economy, there was a different reason to be concerned. The Great Merger Movement from before World War I and the expansion of the Buffalo economy in the Twenties and Thirties brought plants, especially the biggest new factories, established by economic entities, most often publicly owned, and headquartered elsewhere. This expansion had worked a serious, but silent change in the structure of the local economy. Buffalo had become a branch plant town. By becoming a part of a slowly integrating national economy, an integration fostered by the continual expansion of the railroads that still dominated the city's geographic structure, Buffalo was losing some control over its economic life.

In the Seventies, Eighties, and Nineties, the liquidation of a local investment often resulted in splitting up gains among friends, or at least business acquaintances. Similarly, the formation of a new investment saw the gathering together of varying combinations of the same business elite. But by the Twenties, that was seldom the case. Exactly why, it is hard to say, but two possibilities come quickly to mind.

Perhaps the local moneyed elite knew that local investment was no longer as plausible as it once had been; after all, economic integration most often reduces transportation costs and so increases price competition. In a more isolated market, competition is lessened, and so modest control of price is easier and profitability more likely. Loss of such an advantage could easily push investment to other places, in this case perhaps, into Canada.

Another alternative, possibly attractive to the children and grandchildren of members of the turn of the century economic elite, was not to engage in economic activity at all, but to live comfortably off the return on father's or grandfather's accumulated wealth. After 1900, a slowly increasing stability of investments in corporate debt and preferred stock may have made such an alternative attractive, and the development of trust companies and trust departments in banks made management of a family fortune relatively easy. With a life anchored by a downtown club and a country club, some might live graciously, or even extravagantly.[17] They might enjoy an existence seemingly untainted by the consuming details of running a business. Their actions may have made Buffalo seem wealthier and so more economically viable than otherwise was the case.[18]

The Forties and Fifties: "These Precious Days"[19]

In the greater story of the economy of the United States, World War II is very important for the way that it shaped the postwar world economy and began the shift from an American economy focused on the Great Lakes and the Northeastern corridor toward a more national economy. For Buffalo, World War II turned out to have been more of an interlude, though, of course, the natives surely did not see it as such in the years after the war. Just as the great families made the place seem wealthy and more economically viable, so too did World War II. As the Depression slipped out of sight, though not out of mind, war in Europe became a reality after the German invasion of Poland in September 1939. In 1940, unemployment quickly disappeared with the institution of the lend-lease program of armaments for Europe and the wartime draft of young men into the armed forces. After the attack on Pearl Harbor and the American declaration of war in 1941, Buffalo almost immediately experienced a critical employee shortage. Over the following four years the area's war plants received contracts in a dollar amount that made it the fifth-largest defense contracting site in the country. Not bad for the country's fourteenth-largest city.

War work necessitated that the federal government build several new plants; among them, three stand out. Bell Aviation, which produced the P-39 Airacobra fighter, got a whole new plant and a greatly expanded and resurfaced airport in Niagara Falls. Bell's planes were primarily sent to Russia under the lend-lease program. Curtiss-Wright, which produced the P-40 Warhawk fighter, acquired a large facility right on the edge of the existing Buffalo Airport because it was impossible to fly the planes from the Curtiss-Wright facility on north Elmwood Avenue. So, partly assembled planes were moved by rail to the airport, fully assembled at the facility there, and then flown away. Spencer Lens also got a new facility when it shifted from making lab microscopes to producing bombsights and periscopes.

The most interesting thing about wartime production was all of the things that were made by local firms that were seemingly disconnected from a firm's previous products. The Buffalo Arms Division of Houdaille-Hershey, the shock absorber manufacturer, manufactured machine guns; Colonial Radio, proximity fuses for anti-aircraft warheads; Hewett Rubber, self-sealing fuel tanks; the Wurlitzer Corporation, organ makers, proximity fuses for torpedoes. But most firms did work reasonably related to their existing specialties. American Car and Foundry produced very large howitzer shells; Bethlehem Steel, the largest steel works in the country during these years, produced tanks and trucks in addition to iron and steel; Bison Shipbuilding, LST's; Buffalo Forge, ventilation equipment for navy ships; the Chevrolet engine plant, airplane engines; Central Machine Works, trucks; D-N-X Engine, an Ohio company that set up a plant in Buffalo for the sole purpose of doing war work, diesel engines for jeeps and LST's; Farrel-Birmingham and A. F. Oliver, large gears, many for the U. S. Navy; Lake Erie Engineering, large presses for the aircraft industry; Niagara Shipbuilding, tugs and lighters; Pratt & Letchworth, armor plate for tanks; Republic Steel, cannon shells and barrels; Sprecht Tool Works, bomb racks; Sterling Engine, engines for PT boats; Symington-Gould, armor plate; and J. H. Williams, forgings for planes, vehicles, and vessels. The old Schoellkopf plant of Allied Chemical became the second-largest maker of dyes in the country. Add to this list, plants that had government contracts, but to produce what is unclear, and the resulting list is very, very long, even in the secondary sources.

While few people associate the Buffalo area with the wartime Manhattan Project, Linde Air somehow ended up as the site where the uranium cores for atomic bombs were machined and National Carbon produced the carbon blocks that made up Fermi's Pile-1 at the University of Chicago that produced the first controlled chain reaction. Ashland Oil, Electromechanical Corp, Hershaw Chemical, and Houdaille-Hershey Company had smaller roles, as did Bethlehem Steel.[20]

And then it all was over. After the brief postwar recession, Buffalo enjoyed welcoming Canadians coming over the Peace Bridge to "the big city" to experience the entertainments served up Downtown. Everything seemed back to an exiting new normal. In 1951, *Fortune* magazine did a twelve-page story touting the city's industrial might. Four years later, *Holiday*, a travel magazine, did a ten-page spread. Underneath this excitement, an excitement that extended to the arts as well, change was apparent. It was just hard for some people to see.

The most obvious change had been building for a while. The adoption of the National Labor Relations Act, and particularly its enforcement during World War II, meant that collective bargaining was quite entrenched in most of the region's economy, particularly in the mass production industries that dominated its workforce. With this change had come the great growth of industrial, as opposed to construction and skilled trades, unions that had long been active in Buffalo. The industrial unions bargained nationwide, not locally. For those who wished to see, nationwide bargaining again brought home the degree that Buffalo was less an economic entity than a dependency of larger economic entities. But most people only saw that, from time to time, one could expect that Buffalo would experience the effect of nationwide strikes that were inevitably continued until local agreement on working conditions and grievance processing was reached as well. The one other topic that was regularly at issue was seniority rules, a question of both advancement to better paid, and hopefully less strenuous jobs as workers aged, and of protection against layoffs when the business cycle turned adverse. Not surprisingly, the higher than national unemployment figures in Buffalo during the recession of 1958, and the slowness of the local recovery, surely gave production workers pause.

Unionization brought higher wages and higher wages brought increased demand for housing, in particular, the cape cod style of single-family housing as well as the small cottage that was built in the Kensington-Bailey neighborhood and in parts of South Buffalo in the Twenties and Thirties. Some of these small houses appeared in North Buffalo (where, at the same time, the Buffalo two flat, a style of housing in Buffalo that can be traced back into the Eighteen Eighties, made its last stand) and in South Buffalo, but as these developments quickly filled out the available city land, most new houses were built in Kenmore and the Town of Tonawanda and in the northwest and southwest corners of Cheektowaga. Soon, fashion shifted to small ranch-style homes, often with an attached garage, and eventually to larger houses. New housing began to spring up in Amherst and West Seneca too.

Not wholly coincidentally, the geographic structure of the region began to change. The change came in two stages, both related to the internal combustion engine. In the late Thirties, toward the end of his ten years as governor, Herbert Lehman proposed building a toll road from New York City to Buffalo. The advent of war meant that the idea went nowhere, but after WWII was over, a new governor, Thomas E. Dewey, picked up the idea. The stated objective was to ease traffic congestion, and thus to encourage economic investment in New York State. Of course, the project took a long time to thread New York's complex politics, but by 1954, safely ensconced off-budget in the New York Thruway Authority, it was begun. By 1957, it was completed, and extensions were already contemplated, including one that would stretch from Buffalo to Niagara Falls, the Niagara Thruway, and another, the Niagara Extension, that would stretch along the lake from Buffalo to the Pennsylvania state line.

The Dewey administration also proposed several projects that would give the city a modern highway system, projects the state would pay for in large part, sharing only the cost of the acquisition of necessary right of way. The city seemed to welcome the plan. It included the extension of Humblodt Parkway through Delaware Park to Delaware Avenue, the Skyway Bridge over the Buffalo River, an expressway from Delevan and Fillmore to the airport (to be called) the Airline Expressway), an expressway up Oak/Elm and Michigan until it reached Main Street at Ferry, and a widened route across the north end of downtown from the Niagara Extension across Virginia, Edward, and Godell over to Michigan. The projects moved slowly because of the city's political and bureaucratic thicket, but they were welcome to a degree that even before the mainline thruway was completed, the city's Planning Commission suggested extending the Humboldt Parkway route across the Delaware Park to the Niagara Thruway and creating an expressway from the Airline Expressway northwest almost to the city's border and then west to the Niagara Thruway as well.

Not all of these projects were completed, but the point of this recitation of plans is not to measure good ideas and bad, rather to notice that, as first the Erie Canal had structured Buffalo and then the railroads had restructured Buffalo, eventually the motor vehicle would restructure Buffalo again. Truck traffic was already such a sufficient problem in the city that plans were adopted to keep trucks off the city's streets during the morning and evening rush hours and new trucking firms were building their terminals outside of the city. Indeed, the motor vehicle was going to efface some of the city's history. The Niagara branch of the thruway would run in the abandoned bed of the Erie Canal and then continue in the right of way of the Lehigh Valley railroad, which had decided to abandon its passenger and freight service into the city. Indeed, the plan for what was to be called the North Park Expressway assumed that the Erie and the DLW would similarly abandon their right of way across North Buffalo and so provide the bed for building that expressway. Serious change was to be seen by those who took the time to look for it.

It is with this understanding that we continue the order that shaped this story of the economy of what was now truly the region called Buffalo—water, rail, grain, iron/steel, metal shaping, other manufacturing, banking, utilities, and downtown.

The northerly part of the waterfront looked quite different in the Forties and Fifties, at least the Lake Erie part did. Late in the Thirties, the city decided to urban renew away the old commercial and Italian residential neighborhood, locally known as the Hooks, that was south of downtown. The plan was to begin behind City Hall and Memorial Auditorium then continue east to the spot along the river where the DLW had long had a trestle for unloading coal cars.

Doing so cleared land for building and might have marked a final recognition that the city of the 1830s had long passed. However, little else was done to this great swath of land except to build the Dante Place (now Marine Drive) Apartments, a lower-income housing project, and to use the rest of the land to begin endless disputes about planning its future.

The riverside portion of the waterfront was still quite active with big freighters, now self-unloading, delivering grain to big, sometimes modernizing elevators. Other traffic was pretty much limited to the needs of Allied Chemical, the old Standard Oil refinery, now owned by SOCONY Mobil Oil, and Republic Steel.

The outer or southern harbor still served the needs of Bethlehem Steel and Hanna Furnace for iron ore and limestone. Unfortunately, the old Ford Motor assembly plant located there was reclaimed by Ford after the war though soon closed for good when, in 1950, that firm opened a stamping plant in Hamburg. Overall, tonnage seems fairly steady, however, a careful observer would understand that grain shipments had begun to trend downward even before the opening of the long-dreaded Saint Lawrence Seaway in 1959, as exports shifted from eastern ports to Louisiana ports along the Mississippi River, a route that was fully accessible by barge from Red Wing, southeast of Minneapolis, after the completion of the lock-and-dam system built during the Depression on a stretch of the Mississippi north of Saint Louis and south of Minneapolis.

Although World War II significantly increased both freight and passenger trains coming through Buffalo, the Fifties continued the decline in railroad trackage, as well as freight and passenger service, that had followed World War I. Passenger service is the easiest to understand. Even as wartime express train service expanded to deal with both the transportation of servicemen and the gas shortage that reduced civilian travel, local, that is commuter, service had declined by half, and then by half again in the Fifties, a time when long-distance service declined only a bit more than 20 percent. Though the New York Central's station was still quite busy, this fact was only ambiguously evidence of a strong local economy.

A more obvious portent for local service was the decision of the Lehigh Valley to close its downtown passenger station in 1952 and build a new one farther east of the already inconvenient New York Central station. The DLW closed its station ten years later, after it had merged with the Erie to create the Erie Lackawanna. Its station was not replaced. Both of these lines had been created to move anthracite coal from eastern Pennsylvania mines. As those mines played out, the reason for the existence of these railroads declined.

Like all railroads, they complained that providing passenger service was a losing proposition. It probably was.[21] They and other roads complained about high local real estate taxation of their property, the slowness with which the ICC responded to problems, so-called featherbedding by the railroad unions, and outdated union work rules. There was something to all of these complaints, but they were all somewhat beside the point. There simply were too many railroads too close together in the Northeast and in the Midwest. The mainlines and especially the short, lateral or feeder lines, had been built at a density appropriate to the economy and technology of the Nineteenth Century. The internal combustion engine made many of the short lines unnecessary for anything but bulk cargo, and increasingly, long-distance cargo too.

The railroads' response to these problems made a certain amount of sense. They abandoned the short lines as fast as they could and put their faith in technology to improve their product. The last steam engine left Buffalo in 1955; diesel was just more powerful and less troublesome to operate. They upgraded signaling along their mainlines. They designed and built less complicated, more automated yards—the New York Central's Frontier yard opened in 1957 and the Erie Lackawanna's Bison yard opened in 1962—and, in an "if-you-can't-lick-them,-join-them" move, several roads created their own trucking companies to provide local delivery, and all brought out so-called piggy-back service designed to move truck trailers on flat cars. None of these ideas were stupid and over time, all but trucking lines spread nationwide, but they did not address the major problem—the density of mainlines with their embedded costs and balance sheets that showed values that could not be supported with existing revenues and that guaranteed accounting insolvency if any of these lines were abandoned.

Compared to rails, grain looked fairly good and steel, really good. Some of that grain was placed in winter storage, indeed whole boats were laid up in winter to augment the storage capacity of the elevators. Some of this grain delivered to Buffalo was there for transshipment by rail, but an increasing amount was not, as it was not just milled into flour, but also turned into consumer products. General Mills had begun producing cereal there even before WWII and Pillsbury, cake mixes, after.

Still, two grain-related plants transformed themselves in strange ways. Spencer Kellogg closed its plant on the river in 1948 and soon thereafter that plant went through many hands, including as a malt house, until in the Eighties, it was bought and refurbished by Saint Mary's Cement, a Canadian firm, that also needed regular freighter resupply. And then in the Fifties, when the George Urban mill along the Belt Line on the east side was shut down, it was bought by Nabisco, which retrofitted the plant for the production of Milk-Bone dog biscuits, previously produced in New York City, starting in 1908.

During the war, all the major iron and steel firms worked flat out and while production declined after the armistice, it picked up again during the Korean War and held fairly steady thereafter. Some new investments were even made. A major problem was labor unrest as there were five strikes between 1946 and 1959, some lasting, and so disrupting production, for more than three months. Modest changes could be noted. In 1945, one firm, Wickwire-Spencer, was bought by Colorado Fuel and Iron, an independent steel company, located in Pueblo, Colorado. But no other significant change happened until 1962 when the region gained another steel plant, Shenango Ingot Molds. Shenango built a plant that used Donner-Hanna pig iron to create molds primarily for Republic Steel, but also for Donner-Hanna. Also in 1962, Bethlehem opened a new, continuous, zinc bath, galvanizing mill across the street from the main mill property. It could process the widest coils, the ones favored by the auto industry, and used the best technology available to the industry.

Auto manufacture was significantly reshaped. As noted above, Ford closed its assembly plant when it opened a stamping plant that produced body panels, in part to supply Ford's Canadian assembly plants. Similarly, the Chevrolet assembly plant was shifted to producing axles. Only the engine plant, including a forge and foundry, on River Road returned to its old product line when the war was over. Harrison Radiator continued in its line of work as did Trico, Houdaille (which moved its headquarters from Detroit to Buffalo in 1955), and Fedders. Parts manufacturing for export to assembly plants located elsewhere seemed to be Buffalo's niche.

Buffalo's aircraft industry was not a source of unbridled optimism. Immediately after the end of its wartime production run, Curtiss-Wright left Buffalo to return to Columbus, Ohio. It left behind a research lab across from its assembly plant at the airport that included a large wind tunnel. The lab was donated to Cornell University and continued its work, a significant part of which was for the U.S. Defense Department, under the name Cornell Aeronautical Laboratory. Engineers from the lab established two very successful local companies—Moog Industries (1951), a manufacturer of servo-mechanisms, initially for aircraft, soon for missiles, and Servotronics (1959), a manufacturer of a broad range of control mechanisms for aviation and defense purposes.

Bell Aviation also shut down its production facilities after the armistice, but it too kept its large research laboratory in Niagara Falls. This lab produced the X-1 rocket plane that in 1947, was the first airplane to fly faster than the speed of sound, and the X-2 that in 1956, managed to fly three times faster than the speed of sound and to an altitude of more than twenty-two miles. However, the firm never managed to design an effective fighter jet. Its most effective product, the Bell 47 helicopter, which was based on research that started in 1941, began production in 1946. Unfortunately for Buffalo, but not for Bell, production (ultimately 5,600 units) was moved to Fort Worth, Texas, in 1951. Still, Bell had a lot of contracts for defense work related to missiles and continued the pattern of its founding. Several engineers from the firm created Sierra Research Corporation, initially producers of military radar for the U.S. Navy.

Still, one can see why a certain optimism was in order. The Buffalo Airport was expanded in 1955 to accommodate increasing traffic and by then had regular service from American, Capital, and Mohawk Airlines. Three major firms opened branch plants in Buffalo about the time the war was over. Western Electric, the manufacturing arm of the then telephone monopoly, AT&T, took over Curtiss-Wright's plant on the Buffalo-Tonawanda border where it manufactured telephone equipment, insulated wire and switchboard cable. Westinghouse took over Curtis-Wright's plant at the airport where it manufactured large electric motors for industrial purposes. Sylvania bought Colonial Radio after the war and turned it into the firm's radio and television division that produced televisions for Sears in 1948 and a full line of televisions under Sylvania's name by 1949. Then, in 1954, it closed the old King facility and opened an enormous new television factory in Batavia, but at the same time built a new factory near the Buffalo Airport in which it consolidated its work in military electronics. American Machine and Foundry built an entire plant that perfected, and then produced, automatic pin-spotters for bowling alleys and also began producing parts for missiles.

Other firms developed larger defense contracting business. Cornell Aeronautical Labs secured diverse design projects—flight simulators and anti-missile defense systems and built new wind tunnels for testing models of hypersonic missiles.[22] Worthington Compressor built compressors and diesel engines for work in defense facilities and on naval ships. And, Wurlitzer expanded into electronic pianos and organs, as it continued the production of proximity fuses and added missile components, link jet trainers and miscellaneous defense-related parts.

New firms with some staying power are an interesting bunch. American Precision Industries produced motion-control mechanisms and heat-transfer products; Cannon Design was an architectural firm; Delaware North, managed and provided food and beverage concessions, premium dining, entertainment, lodging, and retail in large venues; Freezer Queen, manufactured branded frozen entrees; Goia Macaroni, a firm with roots in Fredonia, moved its production facilities from Rochester; Graphic Controls, the product of a merger of several producers of precision charts and marking systems for recording instruments, moved its production facilities from Long Island to Buffalo; Niagara Frontier Services was a grocery wholesaler that became Tops Markets; and Rich Products produced a soybean oil-based dairy creamer. No one seems to have noticed that none of these firms had anything to do with metal bending. Rigidized Metals, a manufacturer of steel panels embossed for both strength and beauty, was a notable exception.

An odd collection of firms was sold during these years. Bell Aircraft was bought by Textron, an early conglomerate. Buflovac was bought by Blaw-Knox and Durez, by Hooker Chemicals. Symington Gould purchased the Wayne Corporation that produced pumps and became Symington-Wayne, and at the same time began to shift its focus to oil field products. Jewett Refrigerator was sold to Ruslander & Sons, a local Buffalo firm that specialized in refrigeration for food service and hospitals. Founded in 1916, O-Cell-O, the inventor of the synthetic sponge, was unaccountably bought by General Mills in 1952, a move that was held together only by both products being sold in grocery stores. And Wildroot, "a little dab will do ya," whose hair tonic was essential to a cut of teen American males for a generation, was sold to Colgate, who then closed the factory and manufactured the product elsewhere.

Other plants expanded the range of their products. For example, Linde designed and built liquid oxygen plants worldwide, especially in connection with the use of the new basic oxygen process for steel making. But others just disappeared. The Niagara Falls plant of the Aluminum Company of America closed in 1949; American Car and Foundry closed after WWII, only to reopen for Korean War work, but with the armistice, closed for good; Farrell-Birmingham closed its foundry in 1962; Irvin Airchute moved its production first to North Carolina and then to Southern California; and New York Car Wheel shut its foundry in 1958. Barcalo Manufacturing did both. In 1940, it developed a lounge chair, the Barcalounger, a precursor to the La-Z-Boy. After World War II was over, it began making this product in greater and greater numbers, soon sold off its other business, moved its manufacturing to North Carolina, and by 1960, the headquarters had left too.

Buffalo banks prospered during these years, and affiliated lawyers with them; utilities was another matter. In 1956, a large portion of the Schoellkopf Power Station located in the Niagara Gorge below the falls was destroyed when the wall of the gorge in back of the plant collapsed upon it. The site was rendered unusable and so a new plant needed to be built. The site chosen was upriver and the plant, a pumped storage facility built behind an enormous dam and earthen retention wall, was constructed, not by any Schoellkopf entity, but by the New York Power Authority. This new plant was placed in service by 1961; it left the Huntley Plant as the only remnant of the electric power production that began in Niagara Falls.

Downtown was still lively at night, with several first-class hotels,[23] four or five big movie theaters, and two first-rate nightclubs—Chez Ami and the Town Casino. However, the downtown business and political community was still worried; to them, downtown was in distress. Their evidence was both thin—a modest decline in office occupancy—and obvious. After the opening of University Plaza in Amherst, the war intervened, but when it was over, suburban shopping centers appeared quite quickly: Delaware-Sheridan in the Town of Tonawanda in 1950, Northtown Plaza on the Amherst/Tonawanda border and Thruway Mall in Cheektowaga in 1952, Southgate Plaza in West Seneca in 1954, and a standalone Hengerer's in Amherst in 1958. It seemed as if the city were being surrounded at a time when one of its venerable downtown stores, J. N. Adam, was being shut down, though its handsome remodeled building was going to house A., M. & A., whose own building was being torn down for the new downtown mall.[24] There were fewer movie theaters than there once were and yet another one was going to disappear, the Lafayette, across from where the new public library was built. And the Erlanger Theater had been torn down for a parking lot.

The language of the downtown movers and shakers was multifarious: Not as beautiful as we would like, deplorable parking, semi-slum, marginal retail establishments, unsightly appearance, a segregated slum of the worst kind, and blighted areas. All evoked the proposition that downtown was not like the suburban malls. It was old and shabby. It was not a place where someone might proudly say, to steal from Rodgers and Hammerstein, "everything's up to date" in Buffalo. Up to date meant the 1939 New York World's Fair, the streamliner, the airliner, the United Nations Complex on the East River, the Lever House, Philip Johnson's Barcelona chair and, of course, television. It was speedy expressways, not leisurely parkways. Up to date was not dark or deteriorated; old or small or raggedy. And it was international, not ethic.

What the city did first was to hire lots of experts to do lots of studies. In the mid-Fifties, it also tore down various office and retail buildings to create a thousand new parking spaces—curiously only 40 percent of what the experts had suggested. Soon after, the city began urban renewal projects on the edges of downtown. The first, an idea broached as early as 1952, was begun in earnest in 1958; it wiped out the largely Black, near eastside, Ellicott District neighborhood. The second, begun soon after, wiped out the largely Italian, near westside neighborhood, known only as the Lower West Side. However, not much building was taking place; the only really new office building was the International Style Tishman Building on Lafayette Square opened in 1959.

I suppose that being up to date was particularly important for a city that had been falling behind in the great cities' population race for forty or more years and for the first time had serious local competition for population from suburbs. By 1950, Buffalo had slipped another notch to the fifteenth largest; it was no more than two-thirds of the metropolitan population. By 1960, it was the twentieth largest, had lost a bit of population, and was no more than one-half of the metropolitan population because the suburban population had grown by a surprising 60 percent. Given these figures, being up to date addressed the anxiety that was pervasive underneath Chamber of Commerce braggadocio that filled public announcements of public and private works. And, to the extent that downtown was a shopping destination, there was perhaps reason to worry. Downtown had been encircled with shopping alternatives.

The great plan to demolish old buildings and build parking lots during the mid-Fifties was a perfectly plausible response, if one was right that people from the suburbs were not willing to come downtown because it was a hassle to park. Similarly, plans to build expressways and widen arterial streets fit with a perception that people found it a hassle to shop downtown unless having already driven there to work. Of course, there were other ways to see the downtown problem; after all, there were many regional shopping centers in the early Twentieth Century as enumerated above. Perhaps there is a maximum distance that people will travel for what was Downtown shopping, in which case all of the destruction was irrelevant.

However, anxiety is only in the strangest sense relevant to the other great decision made in the name of reviving downtown—the use of urban renewal funds to tear down the neighborhoods on both the east and west, after having previously leveled the neighborhood to the south. Perhaps there were some people who were afraid of being near Italians; there were, of course, significantly more people who were afraid of being near Blacks. But the really interesting thing about both projects is that a large roadway was envisioned between downtown and each neighborhood—the Oak-Elm Arterial, the Niagara Thruway, the

Skyway and Niagara Street. It was as if each neighborhood was an embarrassment, something that made it visibly clear that Buffalo was not as "up to date" as was Kansas City in "Oklahoma!" The root notion seems to be that people would come Downtown only if downtown was visually sanitized.

We do know that, in these terms, "the operation was successful;" the great difficulty is understanding whether the other half of the ironic joke is true, whether "the patient died." Maybe downtown was in the process of moving, as it had once before when it moved from the waterfront north to Lafayette Square. Or maybe it was simply disappearing; after all, Downtown is a recent social/cultural invention. But what is clear is that the source of most of the funds for housing and urban renewal in these years did not come from the budget of the City of Buffalo, but from the state and federal governments. By 1950, Buffalo, the city that in 1931 was able to build and pay for a striking art deco City Hall, was simply too poor to pay for all of this work. That this is true may well have been the real reason that downtown people were afraid.

At the same time, there is something a bit strange about embracing the new/the up to date and simultaneously, an old economy. This embrace of the old is still apparent in two stories that are regularly told about the remnants of the city's first economy, the entrepôt economy of trade. The stories about the decline of water and rail transportation in Buffalo in the Forties and Fifties are interesting, but misleading. The story about the decline of water transport says that the opening of the Saint Lawrence Seaway in 1959 killed the transshipment trade in Buffalo by allowing ocean freighters to bypass the port. In one sense, the story is true. Shipments of grain through the port of Buffalo declined quite radically. However, the problem with this story is that in the Nineteenth and Twentieth Centuries, the transshipment trade had peaked and declined at least twice before that as rail freight rates for the relevant grains and the products of their milling changed. Thus, the decline of the grain transshipment and waterfront life in general was not just a result of the opening of the seaway.

What happened in the Fifties was the accumulating impact of two changes. First, the slow return to prosperity in Europe after the end of World War II meant that European markets for grain were slowly declining at the same time that the markets in South America and the Pacific basin were increasing. The completion of the lock-and-dam system on the Upper Mississippi River permitted the development of a very economical all-barge route down that river to a revived port in Louisiana, a port that could easily serve South America as well as the Pacific basin through the Panama Canal. The cost of the transshipment in Buffalo, and thereafter the rail leg to Atlantic ports, made the Great Lakes route significantly more expensive than the all-water route on the Mississippi, except for grain destined for manufacturing in Buffalo. Noticeably, this shift in the grain trade began before the seaway even opened.

Second, the viability of the transshipment trade depended on the relationship between the cost of lake shipment to Montreal and beyond, as against the cost of lake shipment to Buffalo and then rail shipment to equivalent East Coast ports. The former route was not regulated, but still was subject to changes in the three bottlenecks in the lake route—the locks at Sault Saint Marie, the locks at Montreal, and the size of bulk grain ships; the latter was subject to the ICC approved rates for two possible commodities—grain and flour. It was at least possible that the cost of the rail segment could have been altered to meet the cost of the all-water route. However, the railroads seemed uninterested in doing such; they saw little reason to reduce costs solely to benefit Buffalo; after all, they were already losing volume and so income to trucking. Moreover, what they really wanted was the income from the whole trip and in the Sixties, they would seek to secure just that by filing for a unit train rate from Minnesota to the East Coast, a route that did not have to go through Buffalo. In truth, the transshipment trade with respect to both people and things that built Buffalo in the 1830s had been at risk since the 1870s when the railroads reached, and made more economically plausible as points of origin, the grain growing regions of the Midwest and Great Plains.

The story about the decline in rail transport says that the interstate highway system killed the railroads. The problem with this story is that the decline in railroad trackage antedates World War I. As noted earlier, passenger travel declined in the interwar years. Initially, the reason seems to have been the growing use of automobiles for regional transportation. The truck seems to have had the same result with respect to less than carload freight, even that sent through freight forwarders such as Railway Express. But trucking was still relatively local. It couldn't be much otherwise given that an army convoy Dwight D. Eisenhower commanded by driving from Washington, D.C. to Oakland, California in 1919 took about twenty-four days.

Roads improved slowly. After the passage of the Federal Aid Road Act of 1916, state and local funds began to be devoted to highway reconstruction that these political entities saw as important enough to shoulder the 50 percent of funding not supplied by the federal government based on an approved plan the state had produced identifying such highways. Quickly, the country had the numbered system of U.S. highways. During the Twenties and Thirties, as roads improved, so did trucks, this before much public attention was paid to a postulated need for an interstate highway system. Thus, the interstate highway system simply continued a process of long standing that recognized the greater flexibility of truck transit: It could get to locations where it was implausible for railroads to extend tracks because less than carload freight was involved, or even if freight was of carload size, goods were so light as to make the cost of rail service implausible.[25]

At the same time, these stories provide a modest insight into how Buffaloons[26] thought and still think about their place. For them, it was other people, and particularly, the governments that other people have harnessed for their own interests, that had brought the demise of what Verlyn Klinkenborg aptly, but just slightly ironically, called *The Last Fine Time*.[27] Blaming others is a useful way of avoiding the pain of looking carefully at the activities of one's friends and neighbors, what they did or did not do, or even what they could not do or could not have done. After all, forty to sixty years of relative economic decline is unlikely to have been brought on mostly by the thoughtlessness or malevolence of others.

Sixties and Seventies: The Centre Did Not Hold[28]

With the transshipment trade winding down, the city's first economy, the waterfront, became quieter, though hardly silent. Clearly worried by this development, the city struggled to revitalize the waterfront in a classic example of attempting to salvage sunk costs. In an unusual example of planning ahead for disaster, 1955 Buffalo gave the revitalization job to a newly established public corporation, the Niagara Frontier Port Authority. Unfortunately, this new entity had no source of funds, but was supposed to acquire such by tapping the American share of the tolls from the jointly owned Canadian and American Peace Bridge. The Canadians quickly put a stop to that idea. One year later the Port Authority was given ownership of the Buffalo Airport, which had recently been refurbished by the city, perhaps with the idea that the rental payments from the airlines for the use of the building's gates were going to support the Port Authority's work.[29] This was not a good idea either, so in 1967, the Port Authority's name was changed to the Niagara Frontier Transportation Authority and with this change it accepted responsibility for the city's bus lines as well. There still was no money other than rentals and fares to support the enterprise and so waterfront revitalization was all but guaranteed to languish as it had only a small constituency to push for it.

Changes in the region's railroads were less a result of a narrow combination of law and geographic possibilities than of the legacy of such. The Northeast simply came to have too much railroad trackage for the economic activity that needed railroad service. First, the Erie and the DLW merged to form the

Erie-Lackawanna. Next, the DLW's grand station by the river at the foot of Main Street was closed and soon thereafter, that line's great coal trestle where the river met Lake Erie was demolished. Then, a southern railroad, the Norfolk & Western, bought the Nickel Plate and the Wabash.

By the mid-Sixties, Buffalo's local passenger service was down to two trains a day on the Erie; the New York Central had abandoned all local service and cut its through trains by another 25 percent. Then, in quick succession, the Pennsy and the New York Central merged to form the PennCentral, which quickly went into bankruptcy; Amtrak, a government corporation, took over passenger service nationwide; Hurricane Agnes destroyed crucial trackage on the old Erie mainline that sent the Erie-Lackawanna into bankruptcy; the oil crisis that followed the Yom Kippur War sent the price of diesel fuel soaring; the Lehigh Valley, largely under the control of the Pennsy part of the Penn Central, went into bankruptcy; and Conrail, another government corporation, took over the greatest portion of the northeastern rail lines. It took only eight years for the structure of railroads that had shaped the region, and particularly the City of Buffalo, to be transformed. All that was left was Amtrak; Conrail; Norfolk and Western; the C & O/B & O affiliation called the Chessie System, which controlled an old line called the Buffalo, Rochester, and Pittsburg, and the Pere Marquette; plus two purely local enterprises—the Buffalo Creek, the terminal railroad and the South Buffalo, which served the Bethlehem Steel Plant. Buffalo's days as a major rail hub were over, as abandoned tracks and empty yards now testified.

In the Sixties, grain still came for the flour mills, which still were a significant part of the milling industry nationwide. There were, however, far fewer grain elevators engaged in the transshipment trade after an increase in the cost of rail transport from Buffalo to eastern ports and a more competitive rate for unit trains (trains consisting of cars all of the same kind for one destination) from the Midwest to those ports. Among the elevators closing were the Electric, Concrete Central, Connecting Terminal, Superior, and the Saskatchewan Pool.

Though Colorado Fuel and Iron shut down the Wickwire-Spencer Plant early in the Sixties, war was generally good for the steel industry. As the Vietnam War heated up deliveries of iron ore, coal, and limestone to the mills picked up and so did steel production. But as American participation in that war wound down, steel production began to decline as well. Even more troubling, during that war Bethlehem chose to build a wholly new plant on Lake Michigan at Burns Ditch, Indiana. Initially, the plant was just a collection of finishing mills supplied with billets made in Buffalo. Still, it was troublesome for the Lackawanna plant. And the increasing cost advantage of foreign steel makers with their wholly new plants built with the best new technology was not helpful either. Although two new mills had been built—a bar mill and a galvanizing mill, and some basic oxygen furnaces too—employment at the plant lurched down. The plant simply had too many old parts. Perhaps it was even located in the wrong place. Meanwhile, the smaller, more focused Republic plant seemed to be doing better, though it too was seeing ominous signs as other Republic Steel plants were being closed during the Seventies.

The auto industry followed the same path as steel with growth in the Sixties and trouble with both quality and imports in the Seventies as federal regulation of auto emissions and auto safety began to bite. Still, there was no appreciable impact on local firms or branch plants supplying the industry.

With respect to manufacturing more generally, in the early Seventies, the new history of Erie County, the first such history in fifty years, spent a lot of effort to show that Buffalo firms have long been, and still were, devoting much effort to research into new or improved products and processes.[30] Most of the firms it showcased are found earlier in this book and most of the ones that were not were engaged in metal bending of one kind or another or in electro chemical processes. The exceptions were a producer of pharmaceuticals, a custom manufacturer of wooden tanks and a manufacturer of plastic disposable medical supplies. The overall impression suggested that a diversified industrial base meant that the city's economic future was bright. The future turned out to be a bit different.

When Bell Aircraft closed in 1976, the sixty plus years of an aircraft industry had run its course, though remnants still survived. Moog had acquired an international reputation, Servotronics prospered, and the Cornell Aeronautical Laboratory had been separated from university control and became a public company named Calspan Corporation that engaged in all sorts of activities including auto-safety testing, accident recreation, and defense-related research. The company even developed the prototype for the FBI's fingerprint identification technology. The public company was soon sold to Arvin Industries.

Sale to outsiders by families or groups of investors is also a common story for these years. American Steamship, the owner of self-unloading boats on the Great Lakes, was sold to GATX; Anaconda sold the Buffalo Brass plant to Atlantic-Richfield in 1977; J. W. Clement, the printing company, expanded into California and was then sold to Arcata Graphics; Fisher Price, the toy company, was sold to Quaker Oats, as was Goia, the pasta company; Graphic Controls was sold to Times Mirror; Kittinger Furniture was sold serially to General Interiors and then to General Mills; Westwood Pharmaceuticals was sold to Bristol Myers and Worthington Compressor was sold first to Studebaker and then to McGraw

Edison. The reverse also happened. The Semet-Solvay coke plant was sold to a local investor, as Tonawanda Coke, and Allied Chemical spun off Buffalo Color as a public company.

More ambiguously, Houdaille Industries moved its headquarters to Florida; National Gypsum, to Texas; and US Rubber Reclaiming, to Mississippi. All eventually closed their plants in the area. Buffalo China was reorganized in an attempt to stay viable. Less ambiguously, Allegheny Ludlum (once Ludlum Steel) shut its steel-casting plant; Farrell Foundry shut down its second plant; Tonawanda Iron shut down completely and Western Electric did so as well.

Some interesting firms started in these years. Multisorb Technologies developed a range of products that protected goods from the damaging effects of moisture and Wilson Greatbatch developed and then produced the batteries that made pacemakers for cardiac patients possible. Four engineers at Calspan went out on their own to form Ecology and Environment, an engineering and consulting firm that has acquired an international presence. The Lidke family bought two small steel products makers near the Bethlehem Steel plant. At first it produced parts out of steel sheet for the auto industry, but eventually, built Gibraltar Steel, a national firm that primarily produces steel products for the building industries. And Dan Roblin created Roblin Steel out of the remnants of Buffalo Bolt in North Tonawanda, Wickwire-Spencer in the Town of Tonawanda, and American Locomotive in Dunkirk.

To think of higher education as an industry in Buffalo would have been silly any time before the Sixties. The relevant schools reflected the religious differences that bulked large in the city. The oldest entity, the private University of Buffalo, was little more than a collection of small professional schools from its founding in 1846 until 1913, when it finally opened a College of Arts and Sciences at the site of what once was the Erie County Poor Farm at the city's northeastern border. The next school created was Canisius College, a Catholic school for men established in 1870 by Jesuits. Quickly there followed the public Buffalo Normal School (eventually Buffalo State College) established in 1871. D'Youville College, a school for women, established by the Gray Nuns of the Sacred Heart, opened in 1908. Much later, Rosary Hill College (eventually Daemen), a school for women, was established by the Sisters of Saint Francis of Penance and Christian Charity in 1947. Then came Villa Maria College, a school for women, established by the Felician Sisters of the Immaculate Heart of Mary in 1960; Immaculata College (eventually Hilbert), a school for women, established by the Franciscan Sisters of Saint Joseph in 1964; Troicare College, a school for women, once Sancta Maria College, established by the Sisters of Mercy in 1965;

and then in 1968, Medaille College, a coed school, once Mount Saint Joseph College, established by the Sisters of Saint Joseph in 1965. Four of these schools earlier served to educate members of their founding religious orders.

All eight of these schools largely served Western New York students, as was the case with the similarly raucous collection of local hospitals. Meanwhile, in 1962, as part of the political attempt to repair the embarrassment that the State of New York did not have a proper state university, the University of Buffalo became one of the four university centers within the State University of New York system. Estimates of enrollments by 1970 centered on twenty thousand and eventual enrollment targets were offered at forty thousand and more. Such an entity might become an economic engine for the area if a large proportion of these students were from outside the local region, but for the next few years, copious amounts of time were spent deciding that the new campus should be located out in Amherst and in exploring architectural plans for that campus. In the meantime, though enrollment increased enough to necessitate building temporary classrooms on the existing campus and at three other locations, no classes were held on the new campus until 1973; a core of buildings slowly followed.

These years were good for banking as a construction boom made clear. Western New York Savings opened its new building on Lafayette Square in 1964; two years later, M & T opened its glorious white tower right across from where the hulking old red sandstone Erie County Savings Bank building had been. That bank replaced its old building with a new gleaming glass tower home attached to the new Main Place Mall. Finally, Marine Midland (the old Marine Bank) opened a hulking brick-faced tower bridging Main Street that established a southern boundary to the area in 1972.

To talk about downtown in these years is, to a significant extent, to talk of governments and banks. The completion of a shortened Oak-Elm arterial, which connected what became known as the Kensington Expressway, built in what once was the Humboldt Parkway, to one end of the proposed Airline Expressway, was finished thus isolating the Ellicott District redevelopment project from downtown. However, community opposition finally killed the Virginia/Edward/Goodell project for an inner-ring expressway. Most of the private development that all of the urban renewal was supposed to bring to the city center came from the new bank buildings and from the Buffalo News Building (1973), located across Main Street from the War Memorial Auditorium, with an orientation that betrayed the hope that any reconfiguration of the waterfront would bring Lake Erie closer to its doorstep.

Downtown saw other major building projects; most were public including the William J. Donovan State Office Building (1962), built on the site of the old Lehigh Valley station; the new Buffalo and Erie County main library on Lafayette Square (1964); the Dulski Federal Office Building (1971) on Delaware Avenue; and the Buffalo Niagara Convention Center (1978) on Franklin Street, in back of the Statler Hotel which, by then, was a "boutique hotel" *avant la lettre*, inside an office building. If one understood the dependency of banks on government regulation, it is clear that very little private investment was brought by all that urban renewal.

As for reasons for more people to come downtown, all of the old department stores still survived and after 1969, Downtown had its own Main Place Mall, this despite the fact that the Boulevard Mall on the Amherst/Tonawanda border had opened in 1962, the Thruway Plaza had been enclosed and renamed the Thruway Mall in 1968, the Seneca Mall had opened in 1969, the Eastern Hills Mall had opened on the Amherst/Clarence border in 1971, and Hengerer's added a second standalone store, this one at Delaware and Sheridan in 1965. On the other hand, there was increasingly little reason to go downtown at night, as over these years all of the movie theaters had closed, though a movement was underway to save the Shea's Wurlitzer organ and then the whole theater as a performing arts center. The remaining real attraction was the Studio Arena Theater, which was located in the old Town Casino in 1965.

It is often said that there is nothing like a war to improve the economy of a metal-bending town. Such was true in Buffalo with the onset of the Korean War as well as Vietnam. Few seem to speak of what happens after the war is over. However, new eyes could see. By the fall 1973, a slow drive from the city line to downtown on Buffalo's seemingly misnamed Main Street, left one bewildered that there could be that much traffic on a street that screamed out how little commerce was transacted on either side. Similarly, in 1974, when taking the New York Central to New York City one started from the glorious, but empty terminal on Padrewski Drive. Hearing ones' shoes echo when walking through the concourse because almost no one else was at a place having twenty-five gates, but using only two, and with only one of nine ticket windows open, made it clear that the city possessed any specialness only in its mind's eye. And if one could read architecture, one could no longer see specialness in any neighborhood's business district and often only speculate whatever industry had been—"mass production" was the synonym most offered by people who lamented its passing, "Rust Belt," by others who did not—located nearby.[31] Unfortunately, things were still going to get worse.

Eighties and Nineties: Bottoming Out

By 1980, the idea that waterborne commerce was important to the area called Buffalo was clearly quite silly. It probably was no longer true fifty years earlier. It also was no longer true that sixty years after the peak of rail trackage in America, once having been the second-largest railhead after Chicago, made the railroads important to the region. It was good to have both modes of transport available, if otherwise needed, but it was unlikely that most branches of industry would locate in the area because of their existence. Indeed, whatever industry had once been, it was not clear what "industry" was likely to refer to going forward. To understand all of this it is best to follow the order water, rail, grain, iron/steel, metal shaping, other manufacturing, banking, utilities, and downtown that has provided the modest framework for this story.

By the late-Eighties the waterfront had become quite quiet. General Mills still received grain for its needs at its Frontier Elevator, as did Pillsbury at the Great Northern. The Standard Elevator and the Lake and Rail were largely used for storage, but that was it for the grain trade. And by the turn of the century, Pillsbury had called it quits and the Lake and Rail would soon be abandoned. Most remaining deliveries were of sand, road salt, cement, and asphalt for local use, each chronicled lovingly by the newsletter of Lower Lakes Marine Historical Society, now known as the Buffalo Harbor Museum. Its doing so only provided more evidence that a time had passed.

Slowly, other activity appeared. Waterfront housing began to be built starting from the north. With city development aid, a Hilton Hotel was built just north of the Niagara Thruway, southwest of City Hall. The Buffalo and Erie County Naval and Serviceman's Park opened near the mouth of the Buffalo River. It had several decommissioned navy ships that visitors could tour.

Railroading took a strange u-turn. After the federal government's decision to sell Conrail and the enormous tsouris that accompanied the event, it turned out that Buffalo was pretty much back in the 1850s, for it was again served by two railroads. CSX ended up owning the old New York Central's tracks and that line's Frontier classification yard and the Norfolk and Southern ended up owning the old Erie Railroad's tracks and that line's Bison classification yard. These two railroads did not get along any better than their predecessors did.

In 1982 Bethlehem Steel, which had slowly been reducing production and so employment, shut down, all but for good—one bar mill was left behind and the galvanizing mill too. Republic Steel, which had continued making investments in its plant along the river, shut down the next year, as did Shenango Ingot Molds. Roblin Steel closed in 1986. All that was left was Gibraltar Steel, which eventually would own a surprising number of plants, but only one small one in Buffalo.

Autos did better, but not well. The Chevy Tonawanda foundry that cast the engine blocks, axels, and other steel parts for GM plants shut down in 1983. In 1987, Trico began the twenty-year long process of moving all production to plants in South Texas and Northern Mexico that were paired so as to take advantage of a tax provision that made it inexpensive to use large amounts of low-cost Mexican labor to assemble parts made in the United States and then ship the finished goods back home. Then, in 1994, the Chevy Axel plant was sloughed off by General Motors into American Axel, which was told to go it alone. A year later, General Motors did the same thing with the Harrison Radiator plant, which became a part of Delphi Automotive Systems; it too was told to go it alone. At least the Chevy Engine plant and the Ford Stamping plant in Hamburg were still within the comforting corporate umbrella, though total employment slowly ratcheted down.

Other bits of local manufacturing followed. Mobil Oil shut down its refinery on the Buffalo River in 1981. Ashland started the shutdown of its Tonawanda refinery on the Niagara River one year later. Acheson Graphite closed in 1982; Dresser Industries (the final parent of Gould Coupler), in 1986; Spaulding Fiber, in 1992; and Westinghouse, in 1985. The best result in many cases was shifting a plant to another owner. O-Cell-O sponge moved from General Mills to 3M. Atlantic-Richfield sold the Buffalo Brass plant to a group of local investors in 1985. They, in turn, sold the plant to a Finnish firm, Outokumpu Oyl in 1990. What was clear was that industry was dying out in Buffalo and quite quickly.

After years of fiddling, construction of Buffalo's light rail line began in 1979. During the years the city's population plummeted, the Great Inflation devoured a good portion of the value of the federal grant that was going to pay for the system and a decision was made to switch the subway part of the system from the short downtown section to the longer, more northerly section. As a result, the available funds could only support a line from the Waterfront to the University at Buffalo's Main Street Campus, not all the way out to the new campus in Amherst. While this construction was in progress apparent change had taken place in downtown.

For a while banking seemed to continue to do well. Three new buildings, all gathered around the second-most northerly downtown station on the light rail, created a significant new business area—a big steel and glass addition was added to the Buffalo Savings Bank (by then, known as Goldome, a tribute to the dome on the bank's main office), across the street, two new towers located in a new plaza bore the name of Key Bank, a new bank in town, and just to the south of the towers, a new building for Liberty Bank, soon known as Norstar, when it and a Rochester bank merged under that name, and thereafter became Fleet Bank, after further merger into that New England institution. Unfortunately, that was not really the case. Marine Midland Bank, the city's largest bank was sold to the British bank that became known as HSBC. About the same time, the Savings and Loan Crisis of the early Eighties quickly claimed two of Buffalo's oldest banks. The Western New York Savings Bank closed in 1982 and was merged into Goldome. The Erie County Saving Bank, whose tower anchored the Main Place Mall, closed the same year. Its assets were split between Key Bank and M & T. Eventually, Goldome too was closed. Again, assets were split between M & T, which acquired the original bank building and the new addition, and Key Bank. Buffalo was effectively down to three banks.[32]

Other downtown events were equally mixed. The Genesee Building, a wonderful old office building, was turned into a Hyatt Hotel. However, during these same years the Hens & Kelly Department Store chain closed down all of its stores, both city and suburb, leaving downtown with one less reason for people to shop there. Then, in 1987, Hengerer's closed its downtown store when it was absorbed into the Sibley's chain from Rochester. Next, in 1991, L. L. Berger's closed all of its stores. Finally, in 1993, the last shoe dropped when A, M & A's closed its downtown store, as Bon-Ton, a Pennsylvania firm, took over most of A, M & A's suburban leases. There was then little reason to be downtown except on government or banking business, to go to the downtown branch library that still had a magnificent collection, though not for long, or to attend a play at the Studio Arena Theater or some other entertainment at the rehabbed Shea's Theater, repackaged as Shea's Performing Art Center. This all was very sad, especially when one noted that, in 1987, the McKinley Mall opened in Hamburg and in 1989, the Galleria Mall, the largest in the area, opened in Cheektowaga, both intentionally sited, not with respect to the extension of city streets into the suburbs, but with respect to the New York State Thruway, the de facto main artery around which the area was reorganizing itself.

Though city partisans refused to accept the fact that by the Nineties, Buffalo was a region, a region in which the city, now fiftieth in size, was clearly a modest part—about a third of the population. Indeed, though as a matter of political amity the region was referred to as either Buffalo-Niagara Falls or Western New York, in truth, except for badly polluted industrial sites and decimated urban residential neighborhoods, there soon would be little empty land between the north side of Niagara Falls and the south side of Hamburg and Orchard Park. Some would of course cite this fact as evidence of that great urban demon—sprawl. Most of those people had never seen real sprawl as in places like Phoenix and Tucson, Denver, Albuquerque, Chicago, and Minneapolis. Indeed, it was clear that an impediment to city prosperity was the fact that the multitude of political entities in the region left it so fragmented that it was almost impossible to create or execute, regionwide planning initiatives, much less to mount effective programs of city aid. Indeed, Erie County has been unable to recreate a county planning board, an entity with no actual power to do anything but to produce more "shelf art," after petty electoral politics brought the old board's defunding.

Why put the question of economic entity first in this set of observations? Why slowly give up on the thread of community that began this Part, that was promised in this book's title, and stressed in the introduction? There is a point, a simple point here that is important to remember. Buffalo never was a community. It had communities. The combination of Joseph Ellicott's radial street plan; the fragmentation of the city that the railroads brought; and an ethnic immigrant population that, on one hand, wanted to live together as a defense against those people it could not trust because they spoke a language barely understood, and on the other, because, to the people they could not trust, immigrants were dumb, dirty, and worshiped in the wrong church, was a variety of racism that made it impossible for Buffalo to be a community and that survives today. Fragmentation only increased as later immigrant populations, especially Blacks, but also Hispanics, found this to be a better place to live than the one before.

The only community that the city, and eventually the area, had was the economic community of class. There were identifiable ethnic neighborhoods that tried and failed to keep together when moving to the suburbs became a real possibility and whose destruction is properly lamented, but the greater destruction was that of the hourly middle class, that completely implausible, but in retrospect obvious, product of American ascendency after World War I that began to collapse by the end of the Vietnam War. Later, in the attempt to stave off the results of that collapse, came the destruction of the salaried middle class of white-collar middle management, of the people who had used education to escape from a background that was often hourly working class. For both groups, what may have mattered was the local community of schools and youth baseball leagues, local churches, and the wider community of friendships formed at work or in shared recreational activities in the suburbs or in portions of the city with suburban densities or housing styles. This community is mostly gone, shattered by the rise of the two wage-earner, middle-class families that, in the region called Buffalo, was built a bit on transportation, on chemical processes, on banking, and a lot on metal bending.[33]

It is important to remember that this story of Buffalo is not in any way special beyond the specialness of any place people call home. New York City lost its manufacturing base at the same time that Buffalo did. Albuquerque and Tucson had their downtowns destroyed at the same time as Buffalo's, and in no way did they have metal-bending economies. Suburban growth is the dominant form of the towns to which, it is said, Buffalo jobs left. In the largest measure, housing follows a combination of human desires, transportation alternatives, and individual economic resources. When the only possibility was walking, housing was built near jobs. As the availability of public transportation grew, housing grew where public transportation made it easy for jobs to be accessed. To a large extent, the auto made it possible to significantly loosen the link between where one lived and where one worked. Of course, wealthy people always had more options; they rode in carriages when most people walked or took public transit; they were driven when others rode. Still, the notion that within available economic means most Americans chose to live where they did because of governmental regulation or advertising baloney is likely to be true only at the margins. Most Americans who wished to live in the suburbs did so because this alternative was economically available to them, and they liked it.

Some Americans for whom the suburban alternative was economically available experienced it as socially treacherous. That their experience is abhorrent or even a denial of their rights is unsurprising. However, any confusion of a democratic with an egalitarian society is a great mistake. What is important is that in many democratic societies, though by no means all, arguments for greater equality are possible and, after a lot of work, occasionally successful.

The Twenty-First Century: Maybe . . . Hard to Tell

The early part of the Twenty-First Century in the United States is easy to write about because something happened. Its economy came apart. In contrast, in Buffalo, almost nothing obvious happened during the Great Recession other than earning the dubious distinction of having housing prices there fall much less than in the rest of the country by previously having them risen much less. For that reason, the recession was less steep in Buffalo too. It is not that nothing happened in the region called Buffalo, but that it is not clear what all that happened amounted to.

The most surprising thing in these years is that for some not obvious reason, all of sudden, there was money sloshing around in the consumer economy. It could be seen in the revival of the center section of a north Buffalo arterial (Hertel Avenue); in the modest increase in the number of restaurants that people with money to spare go to; in the ability to quickly fill new, hardly luxurious, luxury lofts that appeared in old industrial buildings near downtown, and increasingly, farther north near the river; and in the rapid run up of housing prices in first in the great central northerly trending area of the city, then the more northerly areas and finally in parts of the long-dilapidated west side. All of this would be reason for optimism if one could figure out where the money was coming from. But nobody knew, and upon reflection, the answer is not obvious.

It is not that, all of a sudden, the dominant employers in the metropolitan area have shifted from government to some part of the private sector. Examination of the categories that have regularly been used to examine the city's economy make that clear by running down the list starting with water. From time to time, one or more of the surviving grain elevators is used for storage, but employment on the waterfront has barely budged. Indeed, the real economic possibility in that area is a new hockey arena, an amateur sports facility called Buffalo Riverworks on Ganson Street, an arts destination called Silo City off Ohio Street, the completion of a modest tourist attraction related to the Erie Canal terminus, and more housing. This new residential development is slowly closing the gap between the initial housing on the urban renewed lower west side and the old Dante Place Apartments.

Nothing has happened with respect to railroad transportation or with grain. As for steel, one steel warehouse/fabricator, Ryerson, left the city in 2006 after ninety-two years and consolidated its local facilities in suburban Lancaster. The old American Brass plant shifted from Finnish to Swedish ownership in 2005 and then to German ownership in 2011. American Axel closed in 2007. Harrison

Radiator was repurchased by General Motors in 2009; it seems modestly prosperous. The Chevy Tonawanda Engine factory has been continuously updated for new engine lines while employment has continued to decline.

The miscellaneous industrial group shows no clearer pattern. American Precision Industries was sold to Danaher Corporation in 2000; Buffalo Color was shut down in 2003; Calspan, which had been successively owned by Arvin Industries, Space Industries International, Veridian and General Dynamics, was finally returned to local ownership in 2005; Freezer Queen closed 2004; after sixty-three years of growth from its beginning as a neighborhood bakery, Kaufman's Bakery was sold to Stroehmann Bakeries in 2000 and closed four years later; and Ruslander closed in 2004. Still, showing that it can be done, after more than 125 years, Eastman Machine still makes cutting technology for clothing manufacturers worldwide, even after that business has largely left the United States.

Retail has been battered. The Seneca and Thruway Malls were demolished and the latter limps along as a modest power center. Delaware-Sheridan Plaza seems always on its last leg, Eastern Hills Mall at best dodders on, McKinley Mall is showing its age and so is the even older Boulevard Mall. Northtown Plaza hopes to survive with the aid of new, ambitious ownership and a Whole Foods Market.

The less ambiguous change in the local economy is in white-collar employment. In 2003, Geico built a large call center that continues to expand at the Cross Point Business Park in the far northern reaches of Amherst and two years later, Citibank opened an equally large office in the same place, this time for people doing the back-office processing of banking transactions entered into elsewhere. Bank of America opened a similar facility after Fleet Bank was merged into it in 2005. Another large call center, Ingram Micro, also expands, as did a group of debt collection agencies in the aftermath of the Great Recession.

Meanwhile, starting in 2007, the Lockport Savings Bank, an institution that dated back to 1870, began to grow by buying small bank networks in New York, Pennsylvania, and Connecticut and the renamed itself as First Niagara Bank. In 2011, it took over the retail banking business of HSBC when that firm, still reeling from the banking crisis, abandoned its U.S. retail business. Two years later, HSBC closed its local headquarters, but left behind its existing back-office facility located in downtown Buffalo. By this time, First Niagara had its headquarters in the old Larkin Soap Company warehouse a bit east of downtown. It soon was large enough to be bought by Key Bank.

A hint that the region was growing a new industry could be identified by recognizing that when Bank of America closed its back-office facility in 2014, all of the employees there were quickly absorbed into the local economy, apparently in similar jobs. The choice of Blue Cross of Western New York to build a new headquarters near the waterfront in the lower west side region and of Fidelis Care, the renamed Catholic Health Care System, to centralize facilities at the other end of downtown, might together suggest that downtown was also growing in white-collar employment, except that the departure of HSBC left its tower building at the south end of Main Street, the city's largest office building, almost empty until M& T relocated scattered technological facilities there.

Equally ambiguous, but much more publicly touted, is the growth of the High Street Medical Corridor. It is surely not a bad idea to move Women's and Children's Hospital to High Street and to relocate the city facilities of Millard Fillmore Hospital there also. Both are parts of Kaleida Health, as is the Buffalo General Hospital. Constructing a new building for the University at Buffalo's Medical School there too is surely an improvement on the possibility of refurbishing the school's existing facilities while educating a class in those facilities. But none of these decisions does more than move economic activity from one place to another within the urban matrix. They do nothing in the direction of increasing employment in healthcare, though in the short run, construction industry employment is increased.

The claim that such co-location will result in growth is much like the claim that corporate mergers will bring growth from "synergies." This latter claim is untrue at least as often as it is true and, when true, usually means that jobs will be cut. The local track record for such combinations is hardly reassuring. The attempt to bring the Erie County Medical Center, the region's best trauma center, together with Kaleida, was an abject failure papered over with the creation of an empty coordinating body called the Great Lakes Health System, an entity that doesn't even include the other major hospital in the High Street corridor, the somewhat state-funded, but increasingly privatized, Roswell Park Cancer Institute. And the failure to figure out a way to paper over problems with respect to abortion and contraception has made securing the assistance of Fidelis Care with the education of medical students and residents is an indication of the difficulties of making claimed synergies anything other than a naked hope.

Also helpful are the lessons to be drawn from several recent projects that involved governmental participation. In the mid-1990s, the Buffalo Sabers needed a new hockey arena to replace the existing old, but charmingly shabby,

War Memorial Auditorium. The idea was to place the new building on the waterfront. Money was quickly found. Recently, the need for a new stadium for the Buffalo Bills, who now play in suburban Orchard Park, started a community ruckus because the project did not require that the new facility be located within the city on some place near both downtown and the waterfront. After a big study, the project is going forward just as the ownership wanted—in Orchard Park. Earlier, there was the "choice," largely dictated by the State of New York, to use part of a set of state grants, colloquially called the "Buffalo Billion," to build a large fabricating facility for Elon Musk's Solar City firm to manufacture solar panels on the site of the old Republic Steel plant. The shell was quickly finished, though not without certain claims of corrupt bidding, but the product changed to solar roofing materials and Panasonic seems to be an additional occupant for the short run.

All three of these projects might be contrasted with an effort in the 1990s when the bi-national authority that owns the Peace Bridge decided that it needed to double the capacity of the existing bridge in order speed traffic, especially truck traffic, that was said to be increasingly diverted to the crossing between Detroit and Windsor. It was also said that the long wait time for truck traffic to clear customs contributed to a high local incidence of asthma and bronchial problems. The authority planned to build a second span directly south of the existing one. A part of the Buffalo community objected to this plan on the ground that Buffalo would be better served by building a more distinctive, "signature" span, a good idea for local morale, but not closely related to the idea of quickly recapturing traffic that might be diverted elsewhere. Litigation ensued and by the time that it was resolved, the chance to capture the traffic was passed and no bridge of any kind was built.

It is hard to offer a reasoned opinion on any of these projects. At least some people do not care where Bills or Sabers play their games or what gets manufactured in a state-funded building. The idea that wait times significantly influences the allocation of truck traffic between the two border crossing points seemed then, and now seems, implausible, though as an asthmatic, it seems a good idea to get diesel trucks out of any neighborhood as fast as possible. But it is not the substance of these decisions that is important for the Buffalo economy. What is important is that a significant portion of the populace is unwilling to recognize that Buffalo is a region and thus it is from a regional perspective that economic decisions must be made. Equally important, is the fact that it is normal for people in the area to resort to litigation to stop development plans that do not meet their personal preferences. Neither circumstance makes this region an attractive one for locating economic activity.

Recap: of Buffalo's Economic Decline

What brings about local economic decline? The answer is not the same for all cities but depends on the kind of economy that a particular city was built upon. For an entrepôt, a change in transportation patterns is key; for a manufacturing economy, it is changes in technology, transportation costs, or what people want. In either case, it is an alteration in the underlying competitive position that a particular locality possesses. But decline is not inevitable. In a wonderful story about Boston's economy, Edward Glaeser does a good job of showing how that city recovered from several declines by reinventing itself on the basis of its local resources, primarily on the skill sets of its residents.[34] Decline is never thus simply caused; it is also a failure to draw on possible local skill sets, or an absence of relevant skill sets that allows decline to continue.

Buffalo's economy peaked somewhere between 1900 and 1920 when the city had slid from the nation's eighth- to its eleventh-most populous city. One might date this decline to 1916, the year that America's railroad system began its decline by registering the first decrease in active trackage since 1830.[35] Another possibility is 1900 because the census numbers show that by then the city was no longer growing as fast as before. In either case, sometime between 1900 and 1916, Buffalo had made the shift from an economy based on its being an entrepôt, to a manufacturing economy. It had reinvented itself just as Glaeser's Boston had done earlier. Still, this newer economy was tied to transportation as much as was the old, particularly to the railroad.

Two World Wars masked the decline of the railroads, as did the Depression. However, even in the Depression years, the shift to truck transport had already become noticeable enough that in 1939, a federal commission proposed building what would become the Eisenhower Interstate Highway system some eighteen years later on the ground that truck traffic was already clogging the nation's roads. As the highway system grew, less-than-carload traffic fled the railroads, then full-carload business too. Oil and chemicals increasingly moved by pipeline and truck respectively, and grain by barge. Perishables moved from iced boxcars to air-conditioned tractor trailers. And, of course, personal cars and airplanes eventually moved almost all passengers who once moved by rail.

In Buffalo, the design of the city's trackage created its own problems, even before these nationwide changes were felt. By choosing to deadhead the various railroads' mainlines from the east near the end of the Erie Canal or at the waterfront, both passenger and freight trains not beginning or ending at the city had to pull into the terminals there and then be backed or pulled out in order to continue on their way. Deadheading was annoying. And the great freight yards on the east side, sized and built for an earlier era, had become significantly congested by the late Nineteenth Century. It was this congestion that brought the New York Central and the Lehigh Valley to open lines with modest yards to the southeast around the city. Indeed, it was the necessity to pull into and then back or be pulled out of the downtown yards, together with the crowding at the old station, that caused the move of the New York Central's passenger terminal from downtown to the east side in 1929. With a bypass track and a new station, there was no reason for that line's trains to stop in Buffalo, except to pick up and drop off passengers, supply local industry, or change crews.

Local industry too had its problems. Start first with steel. The decline of the American steel industry dates back to the Depression, but again was masked by World War II, the Korean War, and to a lesser extent, Vietnam. Capacity increased for a while during the 1940s, but most of it was built using the by then quite old, open-hearth furnace process. After the Korean War, no investment was made in basic steel making, except for the building of a few new facilities. In contrast, European and Asian steel makers who rebuilt after WWII, rebuilt with the latest technology. As installed American capacity wore out, the industry simply contracted. Eventually, mills closed, and if not, were modified as little as possible to accommodate newer processes—the version of the basic oxygen furnace, called the oxygen lance, and continuous casting machines are the best example—but only occasionally to maintain, or make up for lost capacity.

The decline of Buffalo's steel-making business followed the general pattern of the industry. Though in the early Fifties, Republic Steel bought land—Tifft Farm, once the Lehigh Valley's waterfront yards—for purposes of expansion, the site was never used, except as a dump. And Bethlehem Steel built a new galvanizing mill that lasted for more than fifty years, a good run for any technology that survived into the new century proving that investments in the best new technology might have paid off. But in general, from an employment peak at the end of WWII, the local industry slowly contracted in tandem with the national one so that it was gone by the early Eighties. It didn't matter that coal was nearby and iron ore deliverable by lake freighter. Lower cost production abroad, combined with lower cost ocean transportation, made it unprofitable to continue production in Buffalo, just as in Baltimore, Chicago, Cleveland, Pittsburgh, and Youngstown.

Steel-based manufacturing is a more mixed story. The foundries that predated the mills and lived off its products have slowly disappeared. So did some storied names—American Standard (plumbing), Remington Rand (steel furniture), Buffalo Forge (industrial fans), Fedders (air conditioners), Gould Coupler (railroad couplers), and the Pullman Car Company. But some firms remain. Ford has a stamping plant, though it did not replace its big assembly facility on the waterfront, the second plant that Henry Ford built in Buffalo after he chose the city for his first plant outside the Detroit area. General Motors still has an engine plant; a radiator/air conditioner plant has recently returned to the mother hen's protection from different ownership. American Brass limps along under new, serial ownership. But no one would identify Buffalo with metallurgical products anymore. There are not very many American cities against which one might unfavorably compare Buffalo's position.

Then there is grain. The American grain industry has anything but declined in size or importance. It still produces and exports enormous agricultural surpluses after processing all that Americans need. However, milling has again moved from the East to the Midwest, as changes in freight rates for flour made the cost of electricity a less significant consideration. Equally important, the completion of a system of locks and dams on the Mississippi, and the dredging of a deep-water channel to New Orleans, has meant that the Atlantic grain export trade has moved from the East Coast to the Gulf.

Buffalo's position as the largest-grain port in the world declined in tandem with this national change. Thus, the completion of the Saint Lawrence Seaway did not ruin the grain trade, an ancient Buffalo canard, but accelerated it. And so, it was the choice of milling companies to build new plants closer to the farms and the diversion of the export trade down the Mississippi (and later by rail to Seattle) that doomed the elevators and mills. Thereafter, the loss of favorable rail rates for grain to and from Buffalo added insult to injury. Yet here good management-union relations slowed the decline and indeed sustains the continuing presence of General Mills on Ganson Street and the Chevrolet Engine factory just north of the city boundary along the Niagara River, in contrast to the poor labor relations in the steel mills may have contributed to their demise in Buffalo, and nationally.

Two near misses for the Buffalo economy should also be noted. Buffalo was once a center of aircraft manufacture. Curtiss-Wright had opened a factory here before WWI and so did Consolidated, the progenitor of Bell Aviation. As a result, Buffalo had a municipal airport before New York City. There even were seaplanes built here, and a seaplane port and assembly hanger at the foot of La-Salle Park. This enterprise foundered after an incident when, one March, a new model was triumphantly pushed into the Niagara River ready to be flown to its purchaser the next day. Unfortunately, overnight the wind shifted, and in the morning, the officials gathered for the great event found that the plane was trapped by lake ice.

During WWII, both Curtiss and Bell had enormous workforces and produced large numbers of fighter planes. But after the war, Curtiss shut its plant and moved its limited production of airplane engines to Ohio, and Bell, though it did some great engineering, lost out on jet plane production contracts, and built its helicopter plant in Texas where it could test completed planes all year round. Unfortunately, neither firm built bombers during the war, the planes that in civilian garb created the commercial aviation industry we know today, and Bell never had any luck with its designs for jet fighters.

The other near miss was electrical equipment. After the war, Western Electric and Westinghouse moved into empty war production facilities; Sylvania built a research facility and even manufactured television sets in Batavia. Little of this manufacturing activity lasted past the Seventies as production of electrical equipment moved both South and overseas. Here, in contrast to the grain trade, truly poisonous labor relations at Westinghouse, where the more left wing, United Electrical Workers, and the more right wing, International Union of Electrical Workers, battled for shop floor control. Thus, local conditions did not help the industry grow.

Still, it is puzzling that during the war all sorts of Buffalo companies could manufacture all sort of things that were way beyond their narrow expertise, and after the war was over big companies could quickly repurpose large custom-built wartime manufacturing buildings. Why did these local firms, having proven that they could do different kinds of things, seem to have settled back into their own familiar industrial grooves rather than begin attempting to bring forth new and different products?[36] But to ask that question is to forget the character of the region's economy before war began—mostly branch plants of major national firms and smaller local plants, many of which had been engaged in the same kind of work for a generation or more. Neither kind of firm was likely to be naturally "entrepreneurial," to use a word that was not common in those years.

Why not? First, remember that much of the wartime work, though done with patriotic fervor, was not done by choice; after all the federal government could have seized the plant and directed what work was to be done there. Next, remember that much, maybe most, of the work was done in branch plants of larger national companies. It was the national entity that agreed to do the work. Branch managers had no say. Some might have passed had they been given the choice, for branch managers are risk adverse. New product innovation is a very risky activity; failure can destroy careers.

But branch managers also do what they are told, and so, during the war they did what they were told: build new products as part of the war effort. They try to do what they are told very well. Make or exceed branch production targets and make, or better come in under, branch cost expectations; that is how to become divisional managers. When the war was over, innovation, beyond simple brand extension, was not on the corporate agenda. Branch managers were probably happy that it was not. Remember: new product innovation is a very risky activity. Failure can destroy careers; and so, risk adverseness took over again.

Finally, in those circumstances where wartime production plants were locally owned, much of the risk of trying to do something new was eliminated by there being but one purchaser, and one that had a rather deep pocket. No one had to guess whether there would be a market for a new product and then send out sales personnel to hustle up buyers. Experimentation is a high-risk strategy. Most adult owners of even locally large businesses are notoriously careful about new products; they are anything but embracing of risk when it comes to family wealth. All of which is not to say there are no serial entrepreneurs. Locally, the Rich and Jacobs families are notable examples; but the fact that such people are notable suggests how uncommon they are.

Given this depressing tale, it might be asked why Buffalo has a sense of recent greatness, of the oft-told tale that at one (unspecified) time people from Toronto came to Buffalo to experience life in the big city. Though the City of Buffalo had dropped from the eighth-to the fifteenth-largest city in this country in fifty years, the postwar years were kind to Buffalo and cities like it in the Northeast. As the last man standing in the graveyard, at the end of the war the United States was the only viable economy in the Northern Hemisphere. It had decided on an Associationalist economic model structured to provide high wages supported by high prices, an economy that brought tremendous middle-class growth.

The ability to fill the abandoned war plants, when combined with federal support for home ownership, meant that the area saw significant growth as the returning veterans established families. This growth was destined to be in suburban areas, since for all practical purposes, the city was effectively built out. Growth outside the city limits, together with an otherwise buoyant local economy at a time when it was accompanied by a national sense of wellbeing, hid the fact that the city's decline had been of long standing. It was only later, when the Vietnam War did not provide a lift to Buffalo's economy beyond the reduction of potential unemployment provided by the military draft, that collapse was felt as the containerization of ocean transport and trade policy began to undermine the high-wage, high-price economy. Cheaper imported goods began to displace domestic production. It is a story all Americans know far too well, one in which Buffalo stands out only by being part of the first wave of victims.

If economic decline cannot be entirely a matter of economic entities alone, what else might it be? It depends on where and how one looks. The City of Buffalo has lost half of its population; the Region of Buffalo has almost held its own, though given the growth of the United States, it has significantly fallen behind. A good local economist suggests that to catch up, the region would have to lose another 10 percent of its population—all poor people, which is likely true and equally implausible given the degree to which Buffalo is like Stockton in the Sixties—"Fat City," a good place to live because living there is cheap, at least for some people.

At the same time, the upper-middle class, the people whose money is sloshing around, seems to have grown proportionally larger while the middle-middle class and the lower-middle class (the hourly middle class) have clearly diminished both proportionally and absolutely. No one in his or her right mind would say that such diminution is a good thing. From a fiscal perspective, in the good years before the Great Inflation these two segments of the larger community were where the money was, where a small marginal tax rate increase would fill coffers to overflowing because proportionally, these were by far the biggest segments numerically.

From a humane perspective, the same thing is true. The "evisceration," a word carefully chosen, of the lower (unionized) middle class broke a political promise made in the Great Depression and redeemed in blood by service in World War II, Korea, and Vietnam, of a better life for the working class. Similarly, the shrinking of the middle-middle class of white-collar middle management destroyed the lives of at least two generations of Americans.

Often it is said that labor brought this about itself and that American corporations could no longer afford broad middle-management ranks. There is a modest amount of truth in both statements. Labor intransigence over both wages and working conditions was helpful only for the last men (and they were men) standing, but management resistance to joint problem solving, offered in the guise of protecting management prerogatives, meant that in negotiations held both faraway and nearby, management was an even partner in the eventual destruction of unionized labor, as well as many of those companies trying to protect their bottom line. And the decimation of middle management makes this point clear. Capital is clearly mobile; Buffalo surely suffered from this mobility when local capital chose to sell and not reinvest locally. But the return on capital is also socially determined. It does not have to be 14 percent or 40 percent or any particular number between say five and infinity. By saturating the financial markets with ideas that pushed for returns to be ever higher, academics may have been allowed to retire, should they ever choose to do so, and comfortably,[37] but the cost of their comfort has come out of the hides of the middle classes below us.

It is important to particularize the cost of a possible retirement. The capital recovery period for the employment of all but the most lavishly compensated humans is substantially longer than that of invested capital, at the very least, three times longer. For communities, perhaps double that. A working life truncated by as small an amount as possible—labor's preference and management sort of agreed—is less painful than one terminated earlier, it is true. But for a community, the failure to maintain a future that would accommodate such working lives for longer than even a generation is more than painful, it is disastrous as the story of the gradual demise of the Buffalo economies of transshipment and metal bending ought to make clear. Social acceptance of a longer recovery period for capital or a lower expected return (they are mathematically equivalent) might render any possible retirement less comfortable, but it surely would have improved the lives of many of Buffalo's no longer former residents and either their parents or their children or both.

Whether the loss of geographic or industrial advantage is more difficult for a community to recover from is not clear, but in Buffalo at least, geographical seems to be the case. The city sold its spatial organization to the railroads in the Nineteenth Century. Whether doing so was a good idea or not, it was surely an easy choice given the way that metal bending, its industrial advantage, depended on rail for export beyond the distance plausible by wagon or the limited number of markets for lake or canal freight. At least one hundred years ago, that advantage was in decline. If ever there were a late wake-up call, it was the choice of Ford Motors to put an assembly plant in Loraine, Ohio, not Buffalo, in 1958. Loraine was close to what were going to be two interstate highways, I-90 and I-80, had a modest harbor, good rail connections, a still-viable steel mill, and even a suburb named Amherst. What could be wrong with the choice? And yet, not so many years later, Buffalo frittered away the chance to possibly rescue the last bit of its transshipment advantage by fighting over the need for a signature bridge, an argument that ignored the underlying insanity of a related argument over whether truck inspection (that the Canadians were willing to provide space for and that would have partially addressed the health concerns of Buffalo residents near the bridge) had to be done by armed customs personnel (essentially a federal labor issue) that the Canadians did not see the need for when their citizens' lives were the ones at stake.

This kind of tenacious myopia about the role of change in urban life is best seen in the endless discussions about saving a downtown that urban renewal almost killed. Two things are routinely lost in this discussion. Downtown died in cities that never bent much metal and had limited geographic advantage, essentially wide places in the road by some train tracks. Consider Albuquerque and Tucson. Neither city was close to reaching its political boundaries in the Fifties, both had big public universities and one, Albuquerque, was constrained to the north and south by Native American reservations and on the east by a mountain range. Both developed large suburbs (Albuquerque, one on the other side of that mountain range) and saw their downtown die when it became too far to drive there except to interact with the business of government. And in Albuquerque, which in the Sixties began to benefit from being a place where two interstate highways crossed, growth never brought back downtown. It was simply irrelevant to the region's economy.

The demise of Buffalo's downtown was thus not notable, but banal. As any careful reader of Jane Jacobs's *The Death and Life of Great American Cities*[38] would understand, the densities that Americans wanted for their homes turns out to be difficult to turn into secure communities without segregating by income so as to know who doesn't belong on the street. Developers did not push Americans into these densities either. If suburban densities were not wanted by Americans and at the same time were not within their budget, they would not have bought them. And, given the small sizes of suburban homes after World War II, returning GIs surely weren't being pushed into buying more house than they could afford because it was glamourous. Lot size, and so density, pretty much guaranteed suburban-style development, even when raw land was available within political boundaries of a city. The existence of the automobile made living in these places possible and easy once the expansion of commercial facilities followed housing expansion, and even easier when such development preceded housing.

Racism also played a part, but in cities like Buffalo, so did ethnicism, the movement of whole old ethnic neighborhoods into a given suburban area, into which other ethnicities were not welcomed, especially if religious divisions were also present, a process that in certain eastern suburbs of Buffalo had been going on before the Depression. None of this was a good idea, except for providing some people, but never all people, with the housing choices they wished. Unfortunately, the New York State constitution makes it all but impossible to annex territory. It requires a favorable vote from both the annexor and the annexee, a provision put in its constitution by an anxious Westchester County seeing New York City creeping toward its borders, and at a time when the Bronx was still a really nice place to live. That requirement guaranteed that Buffalo was never going to annex any of the suburban towns.

This inability made the death of the regional economy also the death of a way of life, that of the hourly middle class and its equivalent in the Black community. As jobs for the hourly middle class disappeared the remnants of that class either left the city for the suburbs or more often for the American South and Southwest. This left the city with a Black population of varying class fragments, including the poorest of the poor, a similarly poor White population, and a White population of middle-middle and upper-middle classes whose remaining in the city, a city that they loved quite deeply, depended on the quality of the education offered to their children by a school district that was increasingly impoverished and under integration orders of various and recently increasing disruptiveness, a growing charter school movement, and a public school teacher's union that had grown up on tit-for-tat bargaining just as had all of the unions in the area, but in a circumstance where, by law, any negotiated contract stayed in force until a new one was agreed to by both parties. One party, the schools, had nothing to give.[39]

Unfortunately, a political entity cannot shut down like a failed hedge fund. All the municipal bankruptcy process does is to trim expenses that are not contractually guaranteed and return the parties to the bargaining table. Even if such a process were likely to be successful, filing bankruptcy was clearly not an acceptable alternative in a city where its Black residents finally had achieved the control denied them for many years, and where it was reasonable to believe that White residents would use the occasion to subtly, or not so subtly, suggest that the action of doing so was an admission that the long-time denial of control was not racist, but principled. And so the city was left with no alternative but to continue to be a mendicant carrying its begging bowl between a county government whose voters felt themselves to be already too economically squeezed by the same collapse of the local economy, whatever the reality might be; a state government that had starved its public universities and was forcing a similar starvation diet on its public schools, all in the name of a fragile, probably erroneous, belief that lower taxes would bring economic growth; and a federal government that was being similarly starved, and for the same reason.

The political problem of having the promises made to the hourly middle class come undone was, to put it short and anything but sweet, a bitch. It required either the continuation of an old economy or the appearance of a new one. When the two previous economies failed, there was but one choice, the appearance of a new one. As an old Valley girl would say, "As if . . . ."

What were the possibilities? In the late 1990s and for the following years before the Great Recession, there was much chatter about the "New Economy," a reference to internet sales and, in a broader sense, anything internet. Richard Florida captured the era with his talk of the importance of the "creative class" and his index of bohemian and gay friendly places whose existence exemplified that class.[40] There is a sad little story about the unwillingness of Buffalo movers and shakers to sign on to a planning document that noted that the city needed to become more friendly toward gays and bohemians. That non-event says important things about the still-deep Roman Catholic heritage of the place and the growing Evangelical Protestant churches. But, in truth, Buffalo was never going to be a part of the creative class of internet people. That boat had already sailed to California and Utah, Boston and New York City and besides, the New Economy was skewed to the needs and wants of most of the hourly middle class. Buffalo families had long internalized the idea that kids of either gender who spent long hours alone in the basement or in their bedroom were creepy and likely up to no good, though why it was better for these kids to be out on the street with their friends drinking beer, smoking dope, and dreaming up implausible get-rich-quick schemes, is a puzzlement.

However, the New Economy was anything but the only one around in these years and later. Sampling from these ideas in no apparent order is, in its own ways, instructive. Start with the economy of localism. For generations, economists have lampooned the notion that a community could grow by each of its families doing the laundry of another such family and charging for it. Only by exporting goods the production of which a community has a comparative advantage could a city grow. Neither idea is wholly nutty. Exports make sense, except where the export is a diminishing natural resource. Local service economies are to be found most anywhere. Even into the early Seventies, aging downtown Buffalo office buildings with modest rents had small sales and service businesses—for example, watch sale and repair, jewelers, fountain pen and office equipment sales and repair, leather goods sales and repair, printers—that subsisted on trade that congregated mostly before work, during lunch hours, and after work. Though most have been destroyed as these buildings are demolished or repurposed for single employer or residential use, some remnants still subsist in small suburban strip plazas, though they are often opened by franchisees who remit some of their profits to companies that are anything but local. Unfortunately, sharing the profits with a franchisor pretty much undermines the reason for economic localism—keeping the benefits, including profits from enterprise locally.

In Buffalo, ideas about economic localism that regularly emanate from the west side and nearby areas generally center on urban food production—bakeries, urban farmers' markets, restaurants, community kitchen facilities for small-batch manufacturing—and always stress walkable neighborhoods, and most recently, urban farming and food trucks. The pictures are all of sunny days, not winter snowstorms and, implicitly, trade on the word "healthful" in an attempt to avoid speaking about "more expensive." They all ignore the high failure rates and the necessity for start-up capital, which tends to be lacking in neighborhoods filled with refugees after the demolition of the hourly working class or even more vicious wars.[41]

Less spoken of, but in some sense more plausible, is the economy of location. Buffalo is at one end of an area, sometimes called the Golden Horseshoe, which starts in Toronto's eastern suburbs and swings around the western end of Lake Ontario, maybe as far as Rochester. A significant number of Canadian firms have offices in the Buffalo Region and a few lawyers have made a nice living facilitating such transactions and managing the tax implications. Some local logistics providers assist as well. Traffic the other way is much more unusual, but not unknown. Why the region does not try harder to exploit this possible locational advantage is unclear. Though it might provide hoped-for jobs for the hourly middle class, maybe it is just a planner's fantasy. One hopes that the reason is not an unwillingness to admit that the fabled dependency relationship of Toronto on Buffalo has turned out to be in the other direction. People may be nostalgic; economies seldom may.[42]

More often one hears of a so-called eds and meds strategy, usually rendered as building a regional medical center and capitalizing on our many institutions of higher education. This idea has a certain attractiveness, if only because of the success of places like Boston and Palo Alto, Atlanta, and Houston, that have succeeded in building somewhat synergistic economies out of these pieces. It is also a good idea because healthcare and higher education teem with good middle-class jobs. Pulled apart, it has certain obvious problems.

Start with healthcare. Though the University at Buffalo's Medical School is remarkably old, Buffalo has anything but a first-mover advantage in the field. Cleveland, Pittsburg, and Rochester have been building their regional medical centers for many years. Maybe it is possible to siphon back some of the patients from those communities, but one has to doubt the likelihood. Which is not to say that building good local healthcare facilities is a bad idea. It is anything but. If the Medical School were to fold, and hospital care with it, that would pretty much signal the real death of the local economy. After all, it is already difficult for our hospitals to fill the ranks of all the specialists that they desire; in a more marginal healthcare system, "difficult" might well turn into "impossible." Moreover, until quite recently, the Medical School's residency programs were too weak to prop up the existing weaknesses of the hospitals and vice versa. But a modest regional healthcare center—really two modest healthcare centers, given that one of them proudly wears the label "Roman Catholic" and seems determined to remain separate—is not going to provide an anchor on which to build this economy, especially since the one thing that healthcare systems lack is jobs for the hourly middle class that filled the area's factories for years.

Education is not a much better bet though for somewhat different reasons. The Claremont Colleges are often cited as a successful example of small schools prospering by sharing resources to build a brand that nevertheless allows each school to maintain its distinctive identity. Such cooperation is unlikely here in Buffalo. First, the Catholic, or once Catholic, colleges seem to have not even been able to negotiate a joint purchasing agreement, much less to discard their separate identities based on the religious orders that sponsored each school. The inability to avoid offering similar programs also undermines any likelihood of working together,[43] though a recently announced joint program in a health healthcare specialty is a welcome counterexample.

Over on the public side, one finds deep city/suburban animosities. The endless complaints from city partisans about the failure of SUNY to locate its new campus downtown are still heard nearly fifty years later. Even though one no longer hears the University referred to as the "State University of Jew York," one still hears complaints that all of the economic development that has accompanied the establishment of the University has benefitted Amherst, a town that did not need it. This claim is surprising because the limited amount of economic development that the new campus has brought to the area is more of an embarrassment to the University than a benefit to Amherst, as the most visible development has been the recent explosion of rather shoddy student housing that the Amherst Police and local volunteer Fire Departments sometimes quietly, sometimes not, suggest is a drag on their resources.

The antagonism between the University and the much older State College is best symbolized by a long ago suggestion that the State College transfer its undergraduate social work program to the University and the University should transfer its Graduate School of Education to the State College so that each would have a complete program in one of these fields.[44] The Graduate School of Education based its objection to such a swap on the proposition that the state colleges were not authorized to offer doctoral programs, even though most of the school's students were masters' candidates. The College's objection was that that swap would deprive it of a signature program and force its students to travel far for their education, similarly makeweight objections.

And the notion that, considered alone, the University could anchor an eds and meds strategy ignores that most of the Engineering School's departments,while not Johnny-come-latelies to the engineering world, until recently were remarkably small, only recently have been close to adequately funded, even for their size, and are heavily dependent on foreign students enrolling in their programs, students who, because of their immigration status, find it difficult to remain in the area, even if they wanted to.

All of these considerations suggest that those who are pushing an eds and meds strategy do not understand the real benefit that educational programs provide to an area. Higher education is a good clean export business. Students come; take some classes; students go. In between, they spend money locally and by coming and going in great numbers create good middle-class jobs, though very few of them are jobs for the hourly middle class. Middle-class jobs provide a basis for a local retail economy. They provide the cash in pockets, and they pay local taxes because their jobs are tied locally. But to create such an export business, one must have programs that draw students from outside the region who can be educated and returned to their home area or are so taken with the area that they choose to stay. Neither the State College nor the University has demonstrated the long-term ability to do much export business. Indeed, the ability to draw students from outside the Western New York area has been declining since the euphoria that accompanied the creation of the old state university system.

Moreover, the decline of the use of that anti-Semitic epithet, suggests what ought to be obvious—there is no indication that the local community wants an export business. It objects to the export of its children elsewhere and is at best, lukewarm to the import of other people's children, even if they dutifully leave.

Two more small points need to be made. First, it is important to notice that none of these ideas for economic development in this area focused directly on replacing the jobs for the hourly working class and the middle-management jobs that supported a good portion of the rest of the middle class. One exception is the attempt to exploit the possible remaining locational advantage of our proximity to Canada though growth in logistics. A possibly more direct route would be an emphasis on "advanced manufacturing," the production of small batches of complex, limited tolerance goods through the use of computer-driven machines. Both strategies have a certain problem. Despair over limited alternatives seems to lead to criminal activity, especially drug use. The willingness of firms in both industries to hire persons with a criminal record and especially a drug problem, even one in the past, is small. This is a "Catch" numbered somewhere up in the fifties.

Second, there is the problem of local financing of new businesses, a problem that has existed for probably one hundred years now. Banks can seldom do such financings, and their ability is even less now. Public financing is pretty close to impossible because of the political risk of failure in an activity where failure should be the expectation, not the exception. The area has no surplus of angel investors; indeed its economic situation suggests that no one should expect otherwise.

This story and the accompanying analysis leaves the region with the problem identified by the title of this book. What might one do while waiting for rain? What might make it possible for individuals with ideas to choose Buffalo, the region, as the place to realize their dreams? Part III attempts to provide a good answer to that question; and based on that answer, Part IV will attempt to apply it to Buffalo, an attempt that will require confrontation with the troubling distinction between economic development and community development and in particular, the question of what community is the appropriate one to pay attention to. But first, a modest example of how all the above-mentioned dysfunction works together is in order.

Understanding Economic Change in Buffalo: A Coda

In 1906, when Frank Lloyd Wright's Larkin Administration Building was opened, it was the most modern office building in the United States, perhaps in the world. It was of steel frame construction and had a large central atrium that, together with long stripes of floor-to-ceiling windows down all four sides, allowed natural light to penetrate all floors, each of which was completely without barriers except for supporting piers. It was air conditioned throughout and had double-pane windows to minimize heat loss in winter and cooling loss in summer. Though to a Twenty-First Century eye it seems rather strangely massed and looks quite a bit like an Egyptian temple, it is generally recognized as a masterpiece of design.

During the Depression, the Larkin Companies had fallen on hard times and so by 1943, they sold the Administration Building. After the buyer's plans to build a truck terminal on the site fell through, the city took possession in a tax sale. Though the property was extensively advertised, no bid was received for more than $26,000. Apparently, such a bid was beneath notice and was rejected. The city also rejected the idea that the building be outfitted for use as a community center and instead suggested that the Erie County's Welfare Department be located in the building or that New York State use it for emergency housing or for storage of Selective Service records. Neither entity showed any interest. Several private parties took options on the building, but later declined to purchase. Meanwhile, the structure was left to rot as vandals stripped it. Once its demolition was announced, a large amount of hullabaloo was raised by architects and newspapers across the country, and even in the *Buffalo Evening News*, but in the end, in 1950 it was torn down, ultimately to build a parking lot.

Why focus on this obscure episode in Buffalo's decline? Though books and articles have been written about the Larkin Administration Building and its demise is always part of the call to action of local historic preservationists, a focus on preservation or architectural heritage is not important here. What is important is the implications that might be derived from the juxtaposition of two things: the city's finding a small offer for the building beneath notice, while making no significant effort to save it, and the absence of great citizen efforts to save the building. Admittedly, in the late Forties, there was no great historic preservation movement to tap into. Still, no group of citizens apparently gave a thought to trying to stop the demolition by chaining themselves to the fence; no great candlelight vigils were held. In a place that regularly tells itself that the Fifties were a great time in Buffalo, the combination of pride and indifference in this story is quite astonishing, as well as revealing of the position that the city was left in as the history of its economy played out then and still today.

So, if the city did not want to own the building, why turn down a small offer? My best guess combines two considerations. First is political: any mayor would be faulted, perhaps pilloried would be more accurate, in the next election for accepting less than the assessed valuation. The cry "sweetheart deal" would be heard throughout this tiny fractious land. Second is economic: Wright's buildings were famous for their leaky roofs and by 1950 the building had been empty for seven years. During a good bit of that time, rain and snow came in through holes in the windows that had been made by various local miscreants and the interior had been extensively stripped of valuable materials. It would likely have cost a small fortune to rehab the building and the city had been having trouble funding capital expenditures since the beginning of the Depression. It had every reason to see that the building was not saved. This was easy to do: just delay and let local politics do the rest.

In some places, delay infuriates the citizenry. It is a way of life in Buffalo where politics has been described as a contact sport founded in the ethnic neighborhoods created by railroad tracks and exacerbated by religious rivalry, where all entities practice as the basic rule for agreeing to any action, "You don't get something unless we get something too." Might any of the parts of the citizenry have been willing to buck the basic rule and fight to preserve the Larkin Administration Building?

Consider first the local neighborhood. The building was nestled among warehouses on the edge of a small, classic, Buffalo hourly middle-class neighborhood surrounded by railroad tracks on all four sides. Its ties to the city at large were two public transportation routes out of the district. One was Clinton Street, west toward downtown and east to a large pocket of factories, and the other, Fillmore, north and south to other factory belts. Both streets surely had neighborhood grocery stores, butchers and bakers, barber and beauty shops, hardware stores and, of course, taverns, as was the case in other working-class neighborhoods in Buffalo. The neighborhood had a Roman Catholic church, a Ukrainian Orthodox church, and at least one Protestant church, not at all unusual in Buffalo, but also not a recipe for neighborhood harmony. Not surprisingly, few people in the neighborhood seem to have identified with the city at large. Perhaps more surprisingly, the people who lived in the wealthier parts of town, people who probably never passed through the Larkin neighborhood, since the axes of travel for such people were northerly, not easterly from downtown, did not identify much with the city at large either.

The neighborhoods in the wealthier part of town were no less insular, even though railroad tracks did not demark them. Since they were originally suburban neighborhoods within the political city, they were demarked, as would any new suburb today, by house size, club memberships, shopping, schools, leisure activities, and of course, churches. The wealthiest predominantly lived just north of downtown between Elmwood and Linwood, and west or southwest of Delaware Park. They were predominantly, though by no means exclusively, Protestant; their children often went to private schools, sometimes residential; they had city clubs and country clubs, the latter at various times focused on sailing, yachting, golf, tennis, and driving—in earlier years of horses, later automobiles. The less wealthy lived on the fringes of these neighborhoods in smaller houses. They were less thoroughly Protestant; their children went to public schools, their entertainments tended to be public and to a certain extent church related.

What held the two groups together was their relationship to the Buffalo economy. The wealthier tended to be owners of, or descendants of owners of, major local businesses. In the Eighteen-Nineties and later, most sold their business to larger entities and put the proceeds into continuing their lifestyle based on returns from portfolio investments. The less wealthy tended to be middle management in major local businesses, and after sale, in the now branch plants of national businesses, owners of lesser local businesses, or professionals, especially in law, medicine, securities, real estate, insurance, and banking. Middle management tended to identify with their firms and professionals with their clients. Only the owners of the lesser local businesses tended to identify with their city.

Why was it that these disparate groups identified so little with their city and in particular, with its needs going forward? Start with the residents of the Larkin Building's neighborhood. Residents of the neighborhood remembered that there had once been plenty of jobs in what is now called the Warehouse District and in the small factories along the railroad tracks and in the rail yards themselves, but they also had vivid memories of the Depression, the war, and its aftermath. Perhaps some were optimistic about the future, but most were happy to hunker down in the neighborhood. They had learned to expect little to nothing from their efforts, often including their efforts to protect their families. A long history of factory and yard labor led to an acceptance of dependency on the vagaries of their bosses, of the economy, of industrial accidents, and many had experienced multiple changes in the ownership of their employer. They had not only learned to be dependent; they had also learned to be passive in the fact of dependence. Moreover, like most working-class neighborhoods in Buffalo, a long history of geographic isolation led to a narrowness of vision. Together dependency, passivity, and narrowness of vision made it hard to see the possibility of reaching out to the surrounding community for assistance, especially after the Depression had made it quite clear the truly limited power that accompanies chronic dependency.

This is not to say that Buffalo's workers were incapable of organizing—city directories list an amazing number of unions in all sorts of trades and industries—but working-class life was then, and is now, primarily defensive, mutual support in the recognition of mutual dependency. Unionization was not a push outward of the forward looking, but defensive, especially in the "trades" of which my favorite is the ticket takers, an offshoot of the various theatrical unions. Dependency leads to the politics of, "I better get something too," of comparative impoverishment, that is endemic still today in Buffalo. Had the neighborhood understood the value of the Larkin Administration Building and sought help from other neighborhoods, it is highly unlikely that such help would have been forthcoming. Most of such neighborhoods were pretty much like this one.

As for the wealthier people who probably didn't even know of the neighborhood, most of the wealthiest probably didn't care enough to do anything, but for a quite different reason. As the city became a branch plant town during and following the Great Merger Movement, family fortunes that once were tied to the wellbeing of the city were shifted to portfolio investments, which was to say, to nowhere. The position of the individuals who benefitted from these portfolios in the small world that was Buffalo was mostly established by what the family once had been, not what it was now. Thus, they too had no reason to look forward and every reason not to do so as change threatened their social position. In the Fifties the markets were up and there were three other Wright-designed buildings in the city. In what sense were the city's problems with the Larkin Administration Building their own? Of course, this indifference was not true of all. The most notable exception was Seymour H. Knox, Jr. whose passion for, and donations of, modern art changed the somewhat stolid Albright Art Gallery to such an extent that it became the Albright-Knox Gallery. But for this group, looking backward at family achievements was easier than looking forward. Years of comfortable living limited local concerns.

For the less wealthy, a certain present-mindedness directed at the wants and needs of the faraway corporate masters or at the current needs of clients was the order of the day. Life could be comfortable, if not lush, if it all worked out. For some, a promotion and a move elsewhere would make life a bit better; for others, it was the retirement of one's seniors that would bring orderly advance. But, except for the owners of the lesser local businesses, the major forward to be considered was retirement. And for these owners, forward most often meant incomes, taxes, union contracts, the need for capital investment, savings for their kid's education, and ultimately, one's own retirement. None of these people had much time to pay attention to what the preservation of the Larkin Administration Building would mean for Buffalo.

The fate of the Larkin Building is not particularly important in itself, but as an example of what has been the region's economic history, it is. The region had a great run for a while in the Nineteenth Century and then had enough accumulated capital to delude itself about its continuing prosperity. But through the Fifties, it was slowly working down most of those capital assets to salvage value. Its story is not of the winner's curse, but of the "also ran." By the Eighties, after pretty much every asset that had reached salvage value had been salvaged, the region was left with nothing to build on except people with long-honed skills who still looked backward and who still played, "I get some too," year after year after year. Of course, by then there were suburbs against which the city could play the card of a stolen population, an argument that supplied both political parties with excuses for doing the same old things we always have done, but amplified by the growth, and thus concentration, of the Black population in the city. That growth allowed overt and covert disputes about racism to hide the fact that no one had any idea how to get the local economy, thought of, as one would have expected, as my political unit's economy, going again.

Well, not quite "no one." Here and there surprising things were happening well outside the political fray. The Town of Amherst built a fairly large economy of office jobs and a bit of light manufacturing for which success it is always blamed. The Chevrolet Engine factory managed to figure out that if management and union gathered together under the banner of joint problem solving, they could keep the plant alive, though at reduced headcount, and even prosper while General Motors was falling apart. Sterilite Manufacturing built business manufacturing plastic items for the medical profession at a very unpromising location along Bailey Avenue in the city. Multisorb-Technologies developed and packaged all sorts of drying agents in a plant in West Seneca near the much-derided expressways that city partisans always claimed had ruined the area. Derrick Corporation in Cheektowaga developed a large business producing industrial screening technology for both wet and dry applications without anyone even noticing, just by keeping quiet. The only thing holding these odd developments together was avoiding passivity, resolutely looking forward, and ignoring the, "I get mine too" mantra. Doing so was possible, though only by ignoring what was going on everywhere else.

PART III

Thinking about Economic Development

AT THIS POINT A patient reader will have completed a long story about the American economy since the Civil War and an equally long story about the Buffalo economy during the same years. Such a patient person—the only kind of person who will have gotten this far—is thus entitled to a review of the path taken, of the path going forward, and of some of the reasons for the shape of that path.

The topic is "Community, Economy, and Law in a Time of Change." Understanding this topic requires that one first understand the history of an economy and so, of economic change. Part I started with this topic from a national perspective. Part II continued with this topic but shifted to Buffalo's economy. This shift was made not because Buffalo provides a good case study—to be such, it would need to be representative and representativeness with respect to the American economy over so many years would require examination of many more cities than one. Rather, it shifted to a narrower area for understanding simply to provide an example on the basis of which a more concrete discussion of economic change could be had. It was also an easy way to begin to introduce community into the discussion.

Some readers might wonder if it makes sense to devote so many words to economic change since everyone knows that economies change. Such wondering readers surely also know that what is most often taken to be more important, what regularly gets argued about, is why economies change. Admittedly, while both parts suggest a possible understanding of how both the national and the Buffalo economies have changed, they have hesitated to supply answers to the why question. This hesitancy comes from a mixture of two reasons.

The first reason is simple. Until one understands *how* an economy has changed it is impossible to understand *why* it has changed, since change is often a matter of growth here and decline elsewhere—decreasing and occasionally stopping, not just growth, but also economic activity *simpliciter*—somewhere else, as well as the reverse. Growth or decline everywhere tells no one anything.

The second is less intuitive. After years of listening to discussions about why an economy has changed, it has become apparent that this why question is in fact a proxy for a different set of questions. How can change be stopped? How can things be made to change back? How can growth be restarted, preferably in the way I want it to occur? Or in desperation, how can growth be restarted, any growth?

It is doubtful that these questions are answerable, for they all seem to presume that some set of governmental policies—law, in its various forms, as defined in Part I—can answer them. While, from time to time, law may help or hinder change, it is most likely that, as a causal factor, all sorts of other changes in the economic and social surround most often overwhelm law. Thus, it is not that law is irrelevant or ineffective or even detrimental to economic change, but rather that its salience is so completely embedded with other pieces of life that to conceive of law as an engine of growth, or even as a set of train tracks along which growth happens or doesn't, is a category mistake. Law's role is more modest, but not irrelevant, in ways that patient readers hopefully will come to understand as this book continues along its way. However, before examining the role of law, it is important to explore the question of why economies change—the matter of how an economy comes to grow in some place and decline somewhere else. Part III starts with an understanding of economic growth and so establishes a framework for a discussion of the why of economic change.[1]

The literature on growth is vast within the discipline of economics. Much of it has been directed at understanding how less developed countries might become more developed. Since the 1950s, most of this literature has been a statistical enterprise based on simple models through which great gobs of data are run looking for significant correlations. This literature is impossible to read in detail, interesting in summary, yet largely unhelpful in concrete cases. The cognate work in economic history or economic geography is much the same, though the narrative tradition in these fields makes it more readable.

The more recent stream of work, often spoken of as the "Washington Consensus," emphasizes the rule of law, reduction in barriers to trade and investment, and the privatization of state enterprises. This literature is simplistic in its emphasis on dismantling the remnants of state socialism, as if the Cold War distinction between socialism and the free market made any sense in the Twenty-First Century. The economic structures that we call markets are infinitely more complicated than can be encompassed by the simple, ideological distinction between socialism and capitalism.[2] The same is true of the bludgeon called the rule of law, a similar remnant of ideological warfare, as shown by the late inclusion of the protection of private property within its otherwise procedural compass.

A more helpful body of work on economic growth is by Jane Jacobs, an urbanist best known for her book *The Death and Life of Great American Cities.*[3] That book is not irrelevant to the question of economic growth, and so will be discussed later, but more directly relevant are two other books of hers that might be characterized as economic understanding: *The Economy of Cities* and *Cities and the Wealth of Nations.*[4] The latter book is the more accessible one.

Jacobs's work is helpful for three reasons. First, it is written in the English prose favored by readers of histories, and not in the more internationally understood mathematics so beloved by contemporary economists. Second, it seems to fit this country's history quite well. Third, this book does not attempt to offer a universal theory of anything. America is a big enough problem taken on its own. So Part III will explicate Jacobs's understanding of economic growth and then ruminate on several crucial parts of that understanding with the object of fashioning a version of Jacobs's thought that might be useful for understanding the why of change and hopefully growth.

Cities and the Wealth of Nations Recounted

In her first sentence Jacobs identifies what "we all want: instructions for getting or keeping prosperity."[5] In chapter 1, she delivers a thorough excoriation of the work of economic theory for failing to deliver what "we all want," and then she sets to work herself to produce what academic economics has not done. She roots her work in three assertions. The first is that cities are the basic units of economic life and the source of economic growth. This assertion is hardly surprising to anyone who has read *The Death and Life of Great American Cities.* She is correctly understood as a devoted partisan of urban life. (That she is erroneously known as an opponent of suburban or rural life is, for present purposes, irrelevant.) For Jacobs, urban life in Great Cities is by nature economically vibrant and the only real problems with city life are the economic or political actions that sap its vitality, perhaps unintentionally, but always balefully.

Her second assertion is more important. Cities grow as they do two things. Initially, local entrepreneurs learn how to produce goods that the city has regularly imported. In Jacobs's words they "add new work to old work."[6] These goods both replace the previous imports and can be used as exports in trade with other, similarly situated cities. The funds freed by the substitution of lower cost, locally produced goods for higher cost imports and those earned from the newly created exports can then together be used to purchase new, more sophisticated, imports. Again, local entrepreneurs learn how to produce these new goods that the city now imports. These new goods both replace the previous imports and can be used as exports in trade with other, similarly situated cities. The funds freed by this round of import substitution and earned from the newly created exports can then be used to purchase additional, possibly more sophisticated imports, and the cycle repeats itself again and again.[7]

The third assertion builds on the second. As part of the import substitution process, groups of producers, working in competition and with one another, begin to improve on production processes; out of these improvements they create both better versions of old products and new and different products. Both create additional streams of exports on the basis of which further income is earned, which too can be used to purchase additional, still more sophisticated, imports, thus further feeding the import substitution process.

Yet, this rendering of Jacobs's descriptive theory of economic development fails to explain how/why the process of economic development starts, or for that matter, stops. There are two reasons for this absence. The first is that Jacobs believes that the process of economic development is "natural." This belief is implicitly founded on her earlier book, *The Economy of Cities,*[8] which begins with the anthropological speculation that concludes cities preceded agricultural settlements. For Jacobs, the archetypical city is initially an exporter of some natural resource. Trading centers, entrepôts of all kinds, have no place in her analysis, one that is heavily based on her vision of an ideal industrial manufacturing economy. Tinkerers in these natural resource exporting cities take it upon themselves to start making things that replace the imports earned by supplying natural resource exports to others in need of them.

Jacobs's second answer for the absence of an explanation of how/why the process of economic development starts sounds even more odd to contemporary ears. She puts it bluntly, if gnomically; "Economic life develops by grace of innovating; it expands by grace of import-replacing."[9]

Such a reason, partaking of a thing unknowable, unbidden, and undeserved, has been as unsatisfactory to economists as was her assertion that cities preceded agricultural settlements was to anthropologists. Even Nobel Memorial Prize economist, Robert E. Lucas, who asserted that *The Economy of Cities* crucially influenced his second career as a theorist of economic development,[10] felt a need to name that which Jacobs left unexplained. He called it "human capital." Thereafter, Paul Romer took that idea, generally referred to as "exogenous growth theory," and ran with it.[11]

Not surprisingly, Jacobs's answer to the question of why/how the innovation/import substitution process stops is no more expansive than her answer to why/how it starts. "A city that loses export work without compensating for the losses is doomed to decline."[12] And so, rather than expand on either observation, Jacobs focuses on two seemingly tangential questions: What happens to the regions surrounding an import-replacing/export-creating innovative city and what might be done to halt or reverse its decline?

On the first question, that of the regional impact of growth, she identifies "the five great economic forces of expansion":[13]

1. City growth provides expanded opportunities within the city for new and different imports from its region.
2. The technology developed in the city makes for increasing agricultural productivity.
3. While such increased productivity usually leads to diminished job opportunities in agricultural areas, city growth opens jobs for those so displaced.
4. As cities become congested, it becomes cost effective to move city industrial facilities to nearby areas in the region.
5. Doing so increases the stock of capital in those areas, both from the increase of land values and from the profits earned from the goods and services provided by local residents to the transplanted facilities.

If these five things happen simultaneously and in a reasonable balance, then city regions will prosper, even develop small subregions of activity that begin to develop their own subregional import replacing/export creating economies.

Unfortunately, if these five forces are not kept in equilibrium, cities will shape "stunted and bizarre economies in distant regions,"[14] each corresponding to one of these forces:

1. When distant regions without a thriving city are developed only in response to the markets that cities provide for new and different products, those regions become supply regions, always vulnerable to economic decline should demand shift. They become "colonial economies,"[15] even if they are not located in foreign countries.
2. When such distant regions are recipients of technological development, especially of agricultural technology, the local residents able to take

advantage of that technology are better off, but the lot of those citizens no longer needed for local production processes is usually worse.

3. Conversely, when the need for workers in a city draws employees from distant regions, the lot of the individuals who leave is improved, but that of those who stay behind is not.
4. When industrial facilities are transplanted to distant regions, those regions are improved in the short run, but like colonial economies, become vulnerable to market shifts that render such facilities redundant. They become what Jacobs calls "transplant or industrial supply regions."
5. When capital is directed to distant regions, it may produce an improvement in the life of that region's citizens, but that is all. Unearned capital is a gift, not a catalyst.

Here, as part of a discussion of the impact of outside capital investment on a distant region, Jacobs offers one of her strongest statements about the process of economic development:

> But how did it happen that no import-replacing city was catalyzed in . . . [a] region so bountifully benefited by the capital goods that loans, grants and subsidies can buy? For an answer we must understand that whenever and wherever import-replacing cities do rise and flourish, imported goods and services play three different roles in their economies. For one, cities put their imports to use, consume them, just as any settlement does.
>
> But as far as development of their economies is concerned, that is the least of the roles imports play in cities. They also represent 'things earned by city export work.' This is basic. The very process of earning imports requires versatility at production and improvisation. That is to say, the earning process itself promotes and supports the symbiotic nests of suppliers and producers that are important in a city's economy. As the export work that a city casts up ramifies and diversifies, so do these local producers ramify and diversify, and so do the imports that the city is earning automatically diversify in service to diversifying production. The process of earning imports is thus crucial for bringing a vigorous city to birth and life and remains crucial for continued development. Development cannot be given. It has to be done. It is a process, not a collection of capital goods.[16]

The third role imports play is, of course, to serve as candidates for replacements with local production.[17] Thus, for Jacobs, local "versatility at production and improvisation," in short, the innovation that Lucas and Romer fastened onto, is crucial to the process of earning the imports on which local economic growth depends, innovation that results in the replacement of those imports and the creation of new exports.[18]

Highlighting all of these risks for distant regions, and thus the importance of innovation, replacing imports and creating exports, raises the question of how any nascent economy avoids the fate of becoming a supply region, of endlessly being part of what Jacobs derisively calls "backward/advanced trade."[19] After all, advanced economies are not likely to want the products of import replacement in backward regions for, in all likelihood, such products are less sophisticated than the imports replaced. Jacobs's answer to this dilemma is that backward regions can trade replaced imports among themselves and so earn exports among themselves, trading as relative equals until such a point as innovation allows trade with more advanced regions on a similarly equal basis.

On the second question, that of halting or reversing decline, Jacobs implicitly sticks to her emphasis on nature and grace as the sources of economic growth, for she talks only of three things that governments regularly do to address such decline, things that she labels as "transactions of decline."[20] Governments attempt to use "prolonged and unremitting" military procurement to prop up stagnant local economies, develop similar direct subsidies to poor regions, and promote trade between advanced and backward regions.

According to Jacobs, all three of these strategies only make the economic situation of a declining region worse. First, production for military purposes is not production that makes possible the process of innovation/import substitution that builds economies through export earnings. Exports there may be, but only exports as part of backward/advanced trade. Such innovation as may result from military procurement practices is unlikely to be transferred to export creation that might lead to earning imports unless the cycle of procurement is intermittent, a politically difficult condition once local economies become dependent on military expenditures. Second, direct subsidies paid to backward regions (just as the funds directed toward military procurement) will by definition come disproportionately from economically strong regions, reducing the ability of such regions to redeploy the gains earned from exports in pursuit of new innovation/import substitution/export creation. Such transfer payments thus have the potential to sap the strength of the advanced region. And last, backward/advanced trade does not benefit the exporting region, for such trade does not earn new imports that might provide the base for import substitution and so for the purchase of different imports.

The presence of transactions of decline might be used to identify declining regions,[21] but Jacobs does not use them for such purposes or even as cautionary tales directed at the proposition, "Avoid doing these things at all cost." Instead, she offers them as support for the process of "open-ended drift."

> Earlier, I defined economic development as a process of continually improvising in a context that makes injecting improvisations into everyday life feasible. We might amplify this by calling development an improvisational drift into unprecedented problems, then drifting into improvised solutions, which carry further unprecedented work carrying unprecedented problems . . .
>
> "Industrial strategies" to meet "targets" using "resolute purpose," "long-range planning" and "determined will" express a military kind of thinking. Behind that thinking lies a conscious or unconscious assumption that economic life can be conquered, mobilized, bullied, as indeed it can be when directed toward warfare, but not when it directs itself to development and expansion.[22]

A passage this steely-eyed reminds one of Jacobs's battles with Robert Moses and his city planners over the possible construction of a Lower Manhattan Expressway or the extension of Fifth Avenue through Washington Square Park. One might also be reminded of Auden's observation that, "Law like Love" is something that, "we don't know where or why," just as it is something that "we can't compel or fly."[23] Notably, it provided an occasion for two serious reviewers to express displeasure at her denigration of the potential for public policy to improve the life of cities.

Thomas Bender, an intellectual and cultural historian whose work has focused on New York City, wrote an interesting review of *Cities and the Wealth of Nations* for *The Nation*.[24] After identifying Jacobs's "extraordinarily insightful discussions of the way street life works" in *The Death and Life of Great American Cities*, and implicitly her later books, Bender observed:

> [T]here has been a tendency in intellectual, and particularly academic, life of late to devalue this sort of observation. However right Jacobs may be, her detractors imply, her intellectual mode lacks the universalizing power of the work she so tellingly criticizes. This response to her work has interesting implications: it reveals a division in American culture, and makes manifest the current hegemony of the academic mind with its commitment to science, formalism and abstraction.[25]

He noted that in the "life of the mind in America" Jacobs's work was thus "a necessary complement and counterweight to academic discourse."[26] And yet, while praising her work, he enacted his own explanation by pointedly criticizing Jacobs for treating the city as a natural, rather than a politically, constructed object and observed that by doing so, and thus allowing "drift" to determine the city's future, she supported "potent structures of private power that have foreclosed opportunity and undermined justice."[27]

A similar, though more generally hostile, criticism was offered by Robert F. Wagner III, once deputy mayor and chair of the City Planning Commission of New York City and son of Robert F. Wagner, Jr., who was mayor of New York City during the years when Jacobs fought with Robert Moses over the possible construction of the Lower Manhattan Expressway. Wagner complained about Jacobs's denigration of planning, commenting that "when approached flexibly and with some modesty, long-range planning does work, even in the area of economic development." And, comparing her with the famous economist, Adam Smith, Wagner concluded:

> [I]n her own way Jacobs is . . . a believer in the "invisible hand." In her vision, cities, freed from national interference, planning and welfare programs, would prosper. Adam Smith's "invisible hand" did not work [in] the past; there is even less reason to believe that Jane Jacobs' would work in the future.[28]

For Wagner, it was thus "appropriate" that Jacobs had incorporated the title of Smith's great work into the title of her book.

I suppose that some may be bewildered to discover that an author who still proudly lists the Conference on Critical Legal Studies on his resume would write a book about law and economic change in a time of significant economic dislocation, if not destruction, finds instructive a theory of economic development that leaves crucial questions of causation to nature and grace, much less has good things to say about drift and the invisible hand. Perverse or deeply postmodern—should they be different—might also come to mind. Moreover, import substitution is pretty much agreed to be a failed economic development strategy, or so it would seem. And leaving economic development to the so-called private sector has recently turned out quite awfully.

Perhaps all of this is true. At the very least, there are all sorts of things to object to in *Cities and the Wealth of Nations.* One of Jacobs's ideas that was omitted in this recounting is that cities would be more effective economic units were nations split up into city-states. While perhaps theoretically defensible on the limited grounds that Jacobs offers—the function of convertible currencies and the ability to foster innovation through the imposition of tariff barriers—this idea can nevertheless be aptly described as loony, given the cost of currency transactions and the obvious political problems. Likewise, her understanding, implicit throughout the book, that economic growth means growth in industrial manufacturing, while understandable in 1961 when Jacobs published *The Death and Life of Great American Cities*, and maybe even in 1969 when *The Economy of Cities* appeared, by 1984, when *Cities and the Wealth of Nations* came out, can only be described as cranky perversity.

Still, Buffalo is a place that once long ago had a vibrant economy, but now just limps along. All of the failed strategies for economic development that Jacobs identifies as such, indeed derive, to her satisfaction at least, from her theory, are failed strategies advocated by planners and tried in Buffalo's own economic history. This fact suggests that Jacobs is onto something. And so, it is important to try to separate the intelligent parts of her book from crankiness in the hope that doing so will be help in understanding economic development in a time of decline. So, nature and grace will be explored first, then the work of the invisible hand, and finally drift.

Of Nature

Of the two most difficult concepts to understand in *Cities and the Wealth of Nations*—nature and grace—nature is the easier one. Jacobs's treatment of an economy as a natural object is not an invocation of the Aristotelian notion of nature as a natural order, a world comprised of entities with innate properties, gathered in appropriate categories. Her understanding is probably closer to Adam Smith's understanding of the nature of man as one with "the propensity to truck, barter and exchange one thing for another,"[29] or as Veblen's "engineer"[30] who seems to tinker out of curiosity alone, though unaccountably Veblen cannot be found in the index to either book on economic development. Still, for usage in the Twentieth Century, it is best to begin analysis with the Romantic understanding of nature as something fundamental in all the world, natural being, that is tamed in man by his association with the institutions of human life, with material and immaterial ways of living. Nature is that which is outside of man. A dispute that followed from the Romantic idea of nature was over whether it is good or bad for man to dominate nature. This dispute was played out in questions about the development of modes of transportation—first the canals, then the railroads—and of various industries—mining, smelting, brick making, and all kinds of factories that relied on steam engines for power, and thus coal-fired boilers. Another parallel dispute can be identified in arguments over the attempts of county landlords to "improve" on nature in the name of creating "picturesque" views on their estates.

By the late Twentieth Century, the Romantic understanding of "nature," "natural," and their relatives, such as "native," had devolved into a collection of normative signifiers—good things, except when they were not. Thus, "native" plant species are good things while "non-native" or "invasive," are words that make the moral valence even clearer, species are bad and should be extirpated. Animals in their "native" habitats are good, but those same animals in zoos are not, or at least may not be.[31] "Natural childbirth" is good; drug-assisted, or for some even doctor-assisted, childbirth is bad, as is the case with natural sources for vitamins, whole grains, and home remedies. "Organic" works pretty much the same way. These usages imply that human intervention into nature is undesirable, apparently because humans are in some way an alien species, not a part of nature.

Of course, this set of usages does little more than replicate the perhaps more fundamental distinction between nature and culture. Culture somehow distorts nature, makes life artificial and thus bad or unnatural, or so it is regularly implied, if not forcefully said. Still, it is hard to see the valorization of the "natural" as anything else than an example of a cultural practice, and so an expression of a preference for one set of cultural practices rather than another. Preference in this sense does not imply arbitrariness. Most preferences are reasoned, not whimsical, at least unless one equates taste with unreason, and so has a narrow notion of what might count as a reason. So, an objection to Jacobs's treatment of the city or its economy as a natural object is really an objection to a certain set of cultural practices, in Bender's case, the notion of "markets" as natural things and in Wagner's, the notion of the "invisible hand."

Both men's points are well taken for markets (and so economies) are anything but natural, whatever the "free marketeers" may say, at least if what they mean by "free" is free from law. Markets are intensely constructed by law starting with property, crime and contract, and working out from there. There are thus multifarious possibilities for structuring any economy and the results of any such structuring will be no more or no less natural than the previous structuring. "Deregulation" is thus close to an oxymoron, for this program is simply the substitution of one set of structures for another. Thus, when Bender worries about "drift" and Wagner about reliance on the invisible hand, each is expressing a preference for a legal structure that he believes will better deal with a problem in a legal structure current in a time and place. Bender's use of "natural" is thus a rhetorical strategy designed to signal a preference without having to specify and defend the structure he prefers. Wagner's argument works the same way.

There is, in principle, nothing wrong with their shared rhetorical strategy. However, they may be deeply misguided where, as here, law is concerned. When it comes to legal change, cause and effect are anything but tightly knit. Consider only the New Deal economic structure described in Part I. Had World War II been fought to an uneasy draw or had the Allies won, but with the United States economy left as prostrate as the British economy in fact was, it is anything but obvious of what use these New Deal reforms might have been. After all, as soon as the United States was no longer the last man standing in the graveyard, the Associationalist economy began its slow decline in effectiveness. So, exactly which set of legal relations will best fit with a given distribution of resource endowments among a set of potential economic actors at a particular time is anything but easily knowable. The random fact of having the law appropriate to the time and circumstances and an appropriate distribution of resource endowments as well, may play a bigger role here than reason.

The key word here, of course, is reason. It would be silly to assert that Jacobs's understanding of economic development is the product of unreason, whatever one might think of the conclusions that she reaches from her exercise of reason. She firmly believes that the conclusions she derives from her observation of the American economy demonstrate that the academic branch of reason called economic development theory, the bunch of theory that she so thoroughly excoriates in the first chapter of *Cities and the Wealth of Nations*, is completely wrongheaded, both in its understanding of economic development and in its prescriptions for governmental action. So, as Pierre Schlag makes clear, "when reason runs out," when the application of the standard academic learning seems not to work, or worse, seems to lead to perverse results, it is a mistake to double down.[32] Try something else, and if nothing else comes to mind, at least stop doing harmful things, seems a better course of action.

To some, such a plan of action may sound like letting nature take its course, for example, letting the invisible hand do the work. Yet, it is doubtful that this is what Jacobs's work implies. Consider *The Death and Life of Great American Cities*. There she was equally derisive of the academic learning about urban planning, and so argued that doing nothing to declining neighborhoods was better than the then-current urban renewal programs. But in other circumstances, for example, when preserving a stock of buildings of various ages or a variety of uses, she was quite explicit about the role that law might play, as was the case with respect to her loopy advocacy in *Cities and the Wealth of Nations* of creating small city-states in order to allow for the creation of tariff barriers to protect nascent industries, as classic a use for law in economic development as there could be. There is a difference between a directive to governments to stop doing harm and one to leave markets alone.

Of Grace

What then of "grace?" Why is the place of grace in economic development so difficult to understand that twenty out of the twenty-one reviews of *Cities and the Wealth of Nations* never mentioned it and the one that did quoted the relevant passage and then dropped it immediately?[33] Ignore the pervasive secularism in intellectual life in America. In this context, it is uninteresting. Consider instead that the most astonishing thing about Jacobs's statement, "Economic life develops by grace of innovating; it expands by grace of export-replacing," is the way that it yokes one of the most secular of subjects—economic life—one of the things of Caesar, with one of the most sacred of subjects—the mystery of grace—one of the things of God. Since Christians have had two thousand years to puzzle about this mystery without getting much beyond a formal definition of grace—a gift or blessing that is unknowable, unbidden, and undeserved—there is some reason for intellectual hesitancy. Still, it is important to try to understand why Jacobs might have done something as strange as yoking these two things. After all, grace is not a word chosen for no reason.

The key to understanding the place of grace in economic development is to note Jacobs's lack of interest in the question of what actions bring economic development. She says that development is a process not a product. "Development cannot be given. It has to be done." Thus, communities can neither will development (it is unbidden), nor by hard work make it appear (it is undeserved.) And prosperity standing alone is not evidence of development (it is unknowable). Prosperity might only result from the transient transfers of wealth by a governmental entity. Moreover, development stops when exports are no longer saleable and are not replaced through the process of creating new exports as part of the process of creating innovative substitutions for imports, a failure that Jacobs can no more explain than she can explain the beginning of that process. The structural parallelism between her understanding of economic development and the mystery of grace is clear.

The attempt to explain the seeming mystery inherent in economic life starts with Aristotle who asserted that a fair economic exchange had to be of proportional equivalents. If the things exchanged were not thus equal, then one of the parties to the exchange was taking advantage of the other. What he meant is still debated, but a thousand years later, scholastic philosophers came to understand that in some exchanges both parties might receive more than was exchanged without the exchange being unfair. Unburdened with the notion of utility, these philosophers saw the excess received as a "gift." It was not a great analogical stretch to see the abundance beyond exchange value as an example of that grace that was God's gift to mankind. "Gift" was the standard category for the receipt of more than one deserved; it was an easy alternative to "grace."[34]

One of the odd benefits of modern economic theory is that this problem, which was difficult for the scholastics, is now quite easy. We know, or at least believe we know, that different people can value the same goods differently. It is said that people may see utility differently, though one should be careful about the simplicity of this common answer. It is just as easy to pose the why/how question with respect to utility as it is with respect to economic development. Moreover, the only measure of utility that economics has available is price, but the relationship between price and value is no easier to identify than that between development and antecedent cause. Value is unknowable and so unknown, approximated only by price. Whether it may be bidden and if secured, deserved, is not an easy question to answer.

The choice to substitute the unknown for the, at best, poorly understood is not uncommon in human culture. On the science side, consider phlogiston and ether; on the law side, consider *quasi in rem* and sovereignty. The space between the unknown and unknowable may not be all that great and the choice to substitute the unknowable for the unknown does make a certain sense, at least if one suspects that efforts to reduce the unknown to known things are part of a destructive snipe hunt. Jacobs may have been concerned that such destruction might be in the offing, given the extraordinarily foul review of the literature on macroeconomics and economic development that she offers in the first chapter of *Cities and the Wealth of Nations*. In such a circumstance, the substitution of grace for the obligatory call of further research is not hard to understand.

Jacobs's identification of economic development with grace also makes a certain historical sense. Fernand Braudel's grand narrative of European economic development gains much of its coherence from its relative geographic linearity as the center of economic life takes four centuries to move northwest from Venice to London.[35] At each stage, good reasons can be found for the rise of one city and the decline of another. However, these are but sufficient conditions for the change. No necessity can be uncovered. Similarly, Meinig's great story of the geographic dispersal of the American economy westward comes to lose even that linearity after World War II.[36] Sufficiency in this story is plentiful. Necessity is not to be found.

In such circumstances, identifying economic development as a matter of grace affirms an important thing: I do not know; the necessary and sufficient conditions cannot be specified. This theoretical position, of relative ignorance, has its own virtue, for ignorance tends to dampen, if only a bit, arrogant single mindedness in policy prescription, and support a certain humility on the part of experts. And where others' lives or sacred fortunes are at risk, humility is probably a good thing. Set aside grace for a while and turn back to the substance of Jacobs's argument about how economic development works—the complex of innovation/import substitution/export creation. This piece of Jacobs's argument talks more directly of economics, which is to say, of markets, which inevitably leads to concerns about the invisible hand.

Of the Invisible Hand

In certain, generally left-leaning intellectual traditions, support for the work of the invisible hand and the implicit disavowal of government management of the economy, is the equivalent of the sign of the devil. Jane Jacobs's reliance on the motive force of both nature and grace could be read as an affirmation of relative ignorance about the creation and destruction of economic lives and things, and thus an embrace of the ideology of the invisible hand. Her list of actions that are to be avoided, actions that either seem like economic development or are inimical to economic development, could be taken as support of such a reading as well, since most require government action or encouragement. And her focus on trade could be read similarly. Such a reading—the comments of Bender and Wagner would be examples—seems off the mark. However, Jane Jacobs does not stand aside from the problems of creation and destruction when speaking of economic change, but rather opposes governmental action that purports to aid economic development when it manifestly does nothing of the sort. Attention needs to be paid to false growth—transactions of decline, before examining real growth—matters of innovation and trade.

The topics on Jacobs's lists of don'ts are essentially all the same. A community should not become dependent on others to provide the basis for its economy. Thus, she cautions about becoming a natural resources or agricultural supply region or depending on the transfer of manufacturing capacity or technology or capital for investment from elsewhere, or on remittances from absent family members, as well as state or national governments, and especially on defense expenditures. The reason for all of these don'ts is the same. Domestic economies/governments change. These sources of funds may disappear and leave the community with no economy at all. Indeed, for Jacobs, seemingly prosperity, economic activity stimulated by transactions of decline, hides the economic rot underneath. Thus, communities that wish to experience economic growth need to avoid reliance on the kindness of friends, as well as strangers, because real prosperity is locally earned.

Prosperity is earned by innovation that fuels export trade. But export markets change just as domestic economies/governments change. Why prefer trade to transactions of decline? For Jacobs it is because earnings from exports can be used to import additional products or services that might encourage the development of other products or services for export, the earnings from which can be used to import additional products or services that might supply the occasions for developing other products or services for export, the earnings from which can be used to import additional products or services *ad infinitum*. It is not exactly that simple, since the key word here is innovation. But, before turning to innovation, it would be best to restate Jacobs's understanding of economic growth, which consists of a series of four seemingly orderly steps.

Step one: Local people—artisans, tinkerers, engineers, entrepreneurs—decide to produce a product previously imported from more advanced economies. The savings derived from such production are then used to import other goods from those more advanced economies, thus improving the overall life of the community. Step two: The now locally produced product is also exported to similar and less developed communities within a region. The earnings from these exports are also used to import other goods from more advanced economies, again improving the overall life of the local community. Step three: The new imports purchased as a result of steps one and two provide occasions for local artisans, tinkerers, engineers, and entrepreneurs to devise methods for their local production, and thus, the process of import replacement/export earning potentially starts again. Step four: Sometimes the actions of the local artisans, tinkerers, engineers, and entrepreneurs result in the development of a product that is so "new" that it can be sold locally as well as exported to more advanced economies. In such circumstances, the overall life of the local community is directly improved as in step one, and the earnings from these exports are once again used to import other goods from more advanced economies that provide occasions for local artisans, tinkerers, engineers, and entrepreneurs to devise methods for local production, and so, the process of import replacement/export earning potentially starts again.

It is important to understand that although Jacobs calls this process a "reciprocating engine," there is absolutely no necessity, no reciprocation to any of these steps. At best, nature or grace tie the steps together. Even the savings in step one and the earnings in steps two and four need not secure new imports. They may be invested abroad or simply squandered. Still, the proposition that economies grow through trade seems a sound, if not a simple one, at least until one wonders about what brings local people—artisans, tinkerers, engineers, entrepreneurs—to decide to produce locally a product previously imported from more advanced economies. This is the problem of innovation. It is here that Jacobs's discussion of urban life in *The Death and Life of Great American Cities* becomes significant. For her the important element in economic development is the complexity of city economic life, full of the small, diverse enterprises, that makes for Great Cities.

It takes about two hundred pages for Jacobs to make this argument in *Death and Life*. She begins by showing that successful city neighborhoods need to address the problem of personal safety in the presence of strangers. Dealing with the problem of personal safety requires that, among other things, there be people on the street at all hours and that for people to be on the street at all hours the neighborhood must encompass mixed uses—residential, commercial, and industrial, as well as buildings of various ages. But, by mixed use, Jacobs most often speaks of the mix, not of residential with commercial, but of commercial with industrial, since for her residential neighborhoods are too small to support vibrant commercial life beyond a few necessities such as groceries and meats, hardware and candies, and dry cleaning, uses that are typically most active in the morning and evening. Thus, in one case she speaks of "the workers from the laboratories, meat-packing plants, warehouses, plus those from the bewildering variety of small manufacturers, printers and other little industries and offices, [who] give all the eating places and much of the other commerce support at midday."[37] A similar list notes, "The floor of the building in which this book is being written is occupied also by a health club with a gym, a firm of ecclesiastical decorators, an insurgent Democratic party reform club, a Liberal party political club, a music society, an accordionists' association, a retired importer who sells maté, a man who sells paper and who takes care of shipping the maté, a dental laboratory, a studio for watercolor lessons and a maker of jewelry,"[38] a list heavy with afternoon and evening uses.

In lists such as these there is a hint, though no more than a hint, of how an economy might work, though Jacobs speaks not of economic strength, but of urban liveliness. In explaining the conditions for such liveliness, she starts with a distinction between primary and secondary uses, the former "which, in themselves, bring people to a specific place," such as offices, factories and dwellings,[39] and the latter, "enterprises that grow in response to the presence of primary uses, to serve the people the primary uses draw."[40] She then observes, "When a primary use is combined . . . with another that puts people on the street at different times, then the effect can be economically stimulating: a fertile environment for secondary diversity."[41] Thus, mixed use might be seen to be essential to effective, economic functioning.

By the time Jacobs writes *Cities and the Wealth of Nations* she has transformed these observations into the proposition that a lack of diversity of uses makes impossible the aggregation of producers who can support innovative import replacement and export creation. This understanding conveniently fits with the distortions produced when the "five great economic forces of expansion" do not act in a balanced way and with the "three transactions of decline," both wonderfully Maoist locutions. Still, a collection of negations does little to explain how innovation occurs from a diversity of use.

Occasionally, Jacobs attempts to provide a description of what innovation amounts to. She starts with "the addition of new work to old."[42] And to explain what she means she provides a simple example—a firm that electroplates tableware then moves to electroplate metal chairs and table legs. She also draws from the work of Charles F. Sable on northern Italian manufacturing: a manufacturer of tractor transmissions modifies that product for seeders; a manufacturer of packing machines redesigns them to fit in a smaller space; the manufacturer of injection molding machines modifies them to use a different feedstock. At still other times, Jacobs calls attention to the development of postwar bicycle manufacture in Japan from repair, based on scavenged parts, through parts production for replacement, to completely new production or to a chemist at 3M looking for a better adhesive, finding a worse one, and using that worse one to create the sticky note.

It is not clear that Jacobs's examples of innovation are all the same and none are Bill Hewlett and David Packard in a garage or Steve Jobs and Steve Wozniak assembling the first Apple prototype, though, at the start, both projects relied on various small manufacturers for parts and so fit with a city of small manufacturers helping one another with work—exactly the economy that Jacobs identifies in *Death and Life*. Perhaps she does not care whether these examples are the same, for she seems to tie them all together by observing, "[S]uccessful import-replacing often entails adaptations in design, materials or methods of production, and these require innovating and improvising, especially of producers' goods and services."[43] This is more of a sweep of the hand than a specification of anything

What she does care about is made clear by the locution that she uses in the first of her books about cities. It is "Death and Life" not "Life and Death." In that book she fought those practices that she felt destroyed the diversity that created the liveliness of cities. In *Cities and the World Economy*, she fought those things that she felt destroyed the diversity that created the possibility of a growing economy. Indeed, all of the don'ts that she identifies in this book similarly minimize the possibility of diverse economic uses because there is no need for such uses in supply regions or in places where the technology or investment are supplied by others, rather than earned. And in any places that such economic liveliness may appear, it is a false liveliness that will disappear when supply runs out or is no longer necessary, when technology is no longer given, or when capital ceases its flow.

It is doubtful that Jacobs believed that diversity guaranteed replacement of imports and the new creation of new exports, else she would not have talked about grace or nature. And it is similarly doubtful that she could have believed that engaging in transactions of decline might not be part of a sensible strategy for keeping a community's body and soul together. But, for her, that community would need to recognize that maintaining body and soul is not the same thing as building community wealth with the accompanying real economic liveliness that does more than maintain, but makes possible growth in, body and soul. For this reason, such decisions to engage in transactions of decline were to be avoided, just as is the case in cities that find that their export markets are in decline and do not replace those declining exports with other possible exports. They too are on the road to economic destruction.

It is important at this point to note that while *Cities and the Wealth of Nations* may identify a necessary precondition to innovative import replacement/export creation, it does not explain why or how such innovation takes place. There is no reason to hold this deficiency against Jacobs's understanding of economic development, for at least four better-known understandings arguably do no better—John Maynard Keynes, Robert Lucas and Paul Romer, Richard Florida, and Michael Porter.[44]

Start with Keynes. One might rely on Keynesian "animal spirits," said to reside in humans in an economy, as the driving force of economic development. Many writers on economic development seem to believe that it is humans who make a difference in the growth of economies. But Keynes's idea, famous as it is, is still just a way of saying, "I don't know. Something is going on here that is not explained by the usual three factors of production—land, labor, and capital, beloved by economists." It is no more than a secular version of grace, at best a modest specification of nature.

Next consider Robert Lucas, who gives *The Economy of Cities* credit for drawing his attention to innovation, though he can no longer remember how he found the book, and Paul Romer. They called the unexplained residuum after regression analysis accounted for by the traditional three factors of production in economic development theory as "human capital." This nice mediating concept has often been identified with education, and work on human capital has become an important topic for economists, many of whom don't cite or probably don't even approve of Jacobs and who may well mistake statistically significant relations for causal ones.[45]

Identifying human capital with education is an interesting idea. For example, economic historians have argued that the relative swiftness of the growth in manufacturing in America in the Nineteenth Century can be accounted for by the fact that our population was better educated than that of England, Germany, and France. However, that one can identify a measurable surrogate for an abstract concept does not mean that measuring that surrogate is a good idea. Using education as a measure of human capital might seem plausible, except that if it were plausible, then the economic center of our economy would be Midwestern university towns, places such as Bloomington or West Lafayette, Indiana, Iowa City, or Champaign-Urbana, Illinois. And manifestly, that this has never been the case.

Substituting patents, seen as more direct evidence of innovation, for education, as some scholars do, is not much better. Historically, most patents lead nowhere and, under the current patent regime in the United States, most patents are either an example of Kuhnian normal science—valuable, but hardly innovative—or of ideas so far ahead of industrial practice as to be anything but an example of new work growing out of old work. This is especially true since to obtain or maintain a patent, one does not need to use it.

That both educational attainment and patent filings provide dubious measures of human capital does not mean that Lucas and Romer's concept lack explanatory power. But it is possible that other understandings of the concept might do better. For example, Richard Florida argued that it was not a generally well-educated populace that brought economic development, but a particular subset of that populace, the "Creative Class," who were drawn to places that were already full of people like themselves, open to lively, authentic urban environments.[46] He identified such environments with the aid of an index of the existence of, and support for, bohemian and gay subcultures. It was an interesting idea, though it seemed to explain neither the decline of manufacturing, nor the later concentration of finance in greater New York City, a notable center of bohemian and gay life. Apparently, some of these subcultures drew more human capital than others.

Florida's understanding of human capital ties Lucas and Romer's idea loosely to place. Michael Porter's earlier work on industry clusters does so even more strongly.[47] For Porter, it is always best to have large numbers of people in a given location engaged in related enterprises. Having more mutually dependent participants engaged in an enterprise makes it more likely that one of them will come up with the crucial innovation that makes a big industrial difference. Thereafter, competition among such enterprises will quickly drive any new product forward: see early Silicon Valley or the Route 219 corridor in eastern Massachusetts.[48]

Economic development officials and economic planners call Porter's work "cluster" theory. It has two problems, the first of which is quite practical. While a cluster can be really helpful, indeed exciting on the up cycle of any local economy, on the down cycle it is awful, even disastrous. The collapse of a cluster, like the collapse of any monoculture, is what happened in Buffalo and all throughout the Rust Belt. Edward Glaeser's work on the history of the Boston economy[49] suggests that such a result is not a necessary one, though his explanation for why that city avoided decline is not particularly generalizable and his writing on Buffalo asserts that it won't happen in Buffalo.[50] So, it is at least possible that a local community might be willing to trade less of an upside for less of a downside.

The second problem with Porter's idea is more theoretical: confirmation bias. How work on industry clusters might identify clusters that never developed any significant innovations is not a trivial matter. Nor is it obvious whether the network that is an existing cluster grew around an isolated innovation that made it convenient for other, supporting firms to co-locate around the innovative firm or whether such supporting firms were adventitiously available when needed.[51] In support of subsequent co-location, one might note that though it takes human capital to recognize the possibility of innovation and then act on it, human capital, at least young human capital, is famously mobile and thus will quickly migrate to wherever lightning strikes.

If human capital is likely to aggregate after successful innovation, then it may be that innovation is more likely to be successful where such capital is diversified, not concentrated, as Porter would have it, and so provides the multiple competencies that many stories that entrepreneurs seem to find crucial to their achievements. From there it is but a step to the recognition that the chain of ideas just reviewed has returned this discussion to where it began, with Jane Jacobs's argument in *Death and Life* about the importance of local diversity for economic development. Jacobs supports her argument with the example of the differing fates of Nineteenth Century Manchester and Birmingham, the former highly concentrated in cloth making, a specialty that eventually died out, and the latter quite diversified and in the mid-Twentieth Century quite vibrant. Edward Glaeser has a famous paper that uses data about economic diversity to argue that Jacobs's ideas about cities and their role in spawning ideas best explain economic growth.[52] Still, it is possible that this dispute between conceptions of diversity is pointless. If innovation is driven by tinkerers, called "engineers" by Veblen,[53] and often called "geeks," or more charitably, the "Creative Class," then having groups of these people located together (Porter) probably helps, just as having any needed resource close at hand (Jacobs) helps too.

More important, in the end, the great diversity of views about innovation, suggests that it may not matter much that *Cities and the Wealth of Nations* does not explain why or how innovative import replacement/export creation takes place. After all, such knowledge, if it could be had, would likely make a difference in any given place only at the margin, only at the fuzzy border where the explanatory force of land, labor, and capital run out. While it would be a mistake to follow the practice of medieval cartographers and mark this border with the warning, "Here Be Sea Monsters," it would also be a mistake not to remember that, at any given place, neither diversity of economic activities nor their clustering can be summoned into being. Likewise, human capital cannot be forced to come or remain. The best a given place may do is to make itself attractive to those who might bring use or talent, as well as to welcome the bearers of either should they arrive so that they feel newly at home and may choose to stay.

Having spent all this time and reader's patience exploring step one of Jacobs's understanding of economic development, it is time to look at other steps. Step two—trade with similarly and less developed communities within a region—raises different questions. The plausibility of the suggestion that trade, and so economic development, begins within a region, made in *The Economy of Cities*, is strongly supported by the discussion of the shift in the Early Republic from a commercial-centered economy to one based in manufacturing on the East Coast as found in Ratner, Solow, and Sylla, *The Evolution of the American Economy*.[54] These authors' discussion begins with the observation that, in each of the four main Northeastern port cities—Boston, New York, Philadelphia, and Baltimore—manufacturing grew as a result of trade swapping natural resources and finished goods between these cities and their nearby hinterlands, as *The Economy of Cities* suggests would be the case. Indeed, the initial railroads in each of these areas of the country were laid out to connect each with its nearby regions. It was only later, after railroads connected these four separate economic islands, that they began to trade widely with one another. Earlier, the costs of littoral transportation limited such trade.

This example suggests that the market for replaced imports, and thus possible new exports, is likely to be heavily influenced by transportation costs, since trade expanded directly in response to a reduction in such costs. Thus, in order to understand the export potential of what Jacobs sees as an undifferentiated process of new work being added to old work, one needs to take transportation costs into account not once, but twice.

This is because for import substitution to work, the substitute product only needs to be cheaper than the combined cost of the import and its associated transport costs. To turn such a substituted product into an export, its value must be greater than its cost plus the cost of transportation; in effect, its cost must be less than it would need to be to qualify as an import substitute by an amount equal to the cost of further transportation. Such a level of required cost reduction has the potential to be nontrivial and so the effective area within which trade in such replaced imports is likely to be limited, as was the case in the Early Republic and later in frontier Buffalo where gristmills but five miles apart could survive in separate markets.

Where the required cost reduction is nontrivial for import replacement goods, Jacobs's assertion that goods produced in the process of import replacement are good only for trade with similar economies will initially seem to make a certain amount of sense. Transport cost constraints there still will be, but they will bite least in economies located in an area delimited by transportation cost savings where value is similarly understood. However, here as is often the case, Jacobs neglects class/wealth distinctions, the recognition of which complicates matters.[55] Import replacement goods are likely to be tradable in limited amounts with both backward economies and advanced ones, at least within the region where transport costs are low. In backward economies there will be a few middle-class people who may find even modestly improved goods to be affordable luxuries and in advanced economies there will be many relatively poor people who may find these same goods to be a budget extender.

In a very important sense, step four is little more than a funhouse mirror image of step two, even though in this case, the economy has broken free of the import replacement model of innovation. Goods produced for export to more advanced economies can also find a fair number of buyers in similar economies and even a few relatively wealthy buyers in less advanced economies. But such a quibble, while relevant for filling out Jacobs's understanding of economic development, only reinforces the seeming problem with her asserted attachment to the invisible hand that supposedly clears the market at the appropriate price and produces an amount of innovation sufficient for economic development to occur. If the invisible hand is the actor behind Jacobs's curtain, why does the process of earning imports only sometimes lead to significant economic growth?

Consider the many industrialization strategies based on import substitution that were tried in the developing, less developed and war-ravaged economies in the years after World War II. Import replacement on the mercantilist model worked spectacularly in postwar Japan and Korea, though significantly less well in Brazil and India, and horribly in many other places. While Jacobs regularly argues that a mixture of economic uses brings economic liveliness, she has no more idea of how to bring about such a mixture than she has of how it is that innovation drives import substitution. This is because her ideas are all about how to avoid replacing what she sees as an expected liveliness of the diversity in a Great American City with a likewise expected dullness of uniformity, the stagnation of a rural economy, or the false prosperity of a natural resource or transplant economy. Thus, it is not surprising that for her grace carries much causal weight. This is a problem for her understanding of economic development, not because grace is incapable of carrying such weight—it clearly can, but because the explicit point to Jacobs's model is the provision of "instructions for getting or keeping prosperity."

If *The Death and Life of Great American Cities* doesn't work to explain the mystery of why the process of earning imports through trade based on the creation of innovative exports only sometimes leads to significant economic growth, the problem with hers, as with all of these suppositions about alternative causes of economic development, is partly one of evidence. The evidence that might support an understanding about human capital—aggregated or dispersed, geographically concentrated or not—and economic growth is subject to a serious selection bias, as was noted earlier with respect to Porter's emphasis on clusters as a source of growth. It is reasonably easy, *after the fact*, to identify circumstances where an aggregation of people doing what seems to have been similar, or at least related, things, work together, and later competitively, to bring into being a major change in the details of an economy. Unfortunately, it is very difficult to identify similar aggregations that went nowhere. And it is even harder still to identify the aggregation of people doing different things that developed no innovations, except in the sense that they are obviously everywhere, as the world surely has seen far more failed attempts at innovation than successful ones. So, reliance on economic theory, the theory that describes the implicit reason that is the invisible hand, may in the end, be a dubious idea. If so, grace may not be too far from the mark, and if such is the case, it seems now time to explore Jacobs's preference for drift.

Of Drift

What makes an espousal of drift so difficult for a modern reader? Consider again the point of Jacobs's inquiry in *Cities and the Wealth of Nations*: "[I]nstructions for getting or keeping prosperity." This is a classic rational intellectual and political enterprise, though oddly of the kind that, in other places, Jacobs derides. Given what else she says about economic development, to what extent does Jacobs's objective make any sense?

To speak of grace, as Jacobs does—"Economic life develops by grace of innovating; it expands by grace of import-replacing"—is to speak of an experience beyond reason. If a topic is beyond reason, then it is beyond disciplinary understanding, a knowledge that is not properly a part of academic life. Thus, it is hardly surprising that Lucas would read Jacobs's work, ignore grace, and instead pursue the study of human capital. Even more difficult, such a topic is beyond political life, a place where a looser variety of understanding attempts to build structures designed to ensure that reason may restrain passion. It is such beyondness that both Thomas Bender and Robert F. Wagner, Jr., seem to object.

When a society experiences economic hardship, it turns to authority for relief, as is plain from the stories in Parts I and II. Peasants may petition majesty and citizens may demand that elected officials respond to their constituents. In the latter case, relief always is accompanied with plans, with reason, some narrative understanding of what went wrong, and what "we" will do to make it right, preferably before I need to stand for reelection. The reelection constraint is a quite important one. "God will provide . . . in due course" is not much of a campaign slogan and not since the imaginary, if not the real, Herbert Hoover have even the partisans of free-market ideology run on a platform of wait and see. Rather, their story regularly looks to some change—further deregulation, lower or different taxes, alterations in fiscal or monetary policy, or even a return to the gold standard—that will bring renewed growth. Reason is thus deployed in the service of faith in a mysterious thing, the invisible hand of the market.

Jacobs was neither an academic nor a politician. Still, what is both interesting and strange about her understanding of her project of "getting or keeping prosperity" is the way that it misses a rather obvious inference to be drawn from the actual discussion in *Cities and the World Economy* and *Death and Life*. Both books focus less on getting prosperity, than on avoiding false prosperity and keeping the real thing from being destroyed.

In *Death and Life*, Jacobs sees the vibrancy of street life in her neighborhood, identifies it quite correctly with mixed use and then, forgetting the lower East Side of Manhattan in the Late Nineteenth Century, another place with vibrant street life and mixed use, treats both as an indicator of economic prosperity. She therefore attacks anything that she believes might detract from mixed use, as if such is inimical to prosperity. She will thus forever be understood (unfairly, as noted above) as having provided a critique of suburban residential housing patterns that often are, in fact, evidence of prosperity. But, as for the actual relationship between mixed use and prosperity, she leaves it all quite mysterious.

Similarly, in *Cities and the Wealth of Nations*, Jacobs sees growing, vibrant cities, identifies them quite correctly with innovation as part of the import substitution process, and then, forgetting all of the cities in which either import substitution did not occur or did not lead to innovation, treats import substitution as a process that will yield prosperity. She therefore attacks anything that might detract from the process, as well as anything she sees as masquerading for the prosperity earned through import substitution. To the extent that she will be remembered for this work, she will also be remembered for inspiring Lucas and then Romer to investigate human capital. But, as for understanding what brings innovative import substitution, she leaves it all quite mysterious. As in her earlier book, seeing the need for a ladder, Jacobs assumed a ladder, an intellectual maneuver that, given her demolition job on economic theory in her book's chapter 1, is not as far as she might wish to situate herself from the economist of disciplinary humor who, seeing a burned-out light bulb, declined to replace it, because "the market" will fix it. What should one make of this paradox?

Start again with Jacobs's statement of objective: to supply "instructions for getting or keeping prosperity." For Jacobs, getting prosperity is a matter of innovation/import replacement/export creation plus nature/grace and keeping prosperity, a matter of not doing things that might kill innovation/import replacement/export creation plus nature/grace or create a false sense of prosperity by relying on one or more of the transactions of decline. Note that, given the role that Jacobs assigns to nature/grace, there is little room for governmental action to move the economic development process along. Remember that she called development "improvisational drift into unprecedented problems, then drifting into improvised solutions, which carry further unprecedented work carrying unprecedented problems," and that she rejected the "'Industrial strategies' to meet 'targets' using 'resolute purpose,' 'long-range planning' and 'determined will'" because they "express a military kind of thinking" inappropriate to "development and expansion."[56] In such circumstances, "open-ended drift" is about all that is left for Jacobs to advocate, especially given the degree to which she had criticized the existing economic literature on economic development.

It is thus rather easy to understand why governmental officials would be happy to act on the basis of the best, or at least the most politically attractive, available academic economic theory, for academic learning provides useful cover when such theory prescribes action and so produces photo-ops, the staple of political life. It is just such actions that Jacobs would strongly resist for they are likely to be costly and unhelpful, even if to do so she needed to mimic the structure of the theories she opposed. It is equally easy to understand why critics such as Bender and Wagner, but also other of her reviewers, would object to her reliance on drift as part of an economic development policy. In support, these critics might have called upon the work of the great American legal historian, Willard Hurst, who put it nicely when he criticized Nineteenth Century legislatures for engaging in the "bastard pragmatism" of "drift and default."[57]

American pragmatism is mostly of the "try something" variety. It is directed toward action. For such pragmatists, theory is only good if it can be made operational as a program of action. This is particularly true of the social sciences, but it underlies common criticisms of research in the hard sciences and writing in the arts and humanities. One ought also to note that in economics, even the partisans of the invisible hand pitch their theory in the direction of governmental agencies doing something—repeal regulation, change regulations, lower costs, lower taxes—just as do the partisans of the governmental hand—raise minimum wages, raise governmental benefits, regulate more closely, forbid this behavior.

Still, it is a mistake to argue that, in advocating for drift as an economic process, Jacobs is taking sides in the endless fight among economists about the structure of markets. Jacobs's fight was with what, to her were unwarranted, and often destructive claims of expertise. In *The Death and Life of Great American Cities*, her fight was with the planners who claimed special, professional insight into how cities best worked and sold their vision to governmental elites. In *Cities and the Wealth of Nations*, her fight was with the economists who claimed special, professional insight of how economies best worked and sold their vision to governmental elites. That the actual actors in both instances were the same governmental elites should not be taken to imply that Jacobs opposed governmental action. She offered prescriptions for positive governmental action in both books: in the former, to spur diversity of use and in the latter, to help nascent industries. What she opposed in both books was what she saw as bad governmental action that interfered with the economic and social creativity of ordinary American citizens as they improvised solutions to problems they encountered. That Jacobs might support the citizens who opposed the conclusions of expert thought transgresses only the line that expertise erects to maintain its privileged specialness. In such circumstances, it is perhaps sensible to embrace "open-ended drift."

Saving Pieces

So now it is time to attempt to fashion an understanding of economic change that is useful for thinking about the United States over the past 150 or so years from the scraps left after examining Jacobs's work. First comes trade because, despite all the well-intentioned efforts of the buy-local advocates these days, the economists are right—no community has ever grown by taking in one another's laundry. Which is not to say that doing one another's laundry is not important. Most professionals, the backbone of the upper-middle class, both take in the local laundry and rely on local laundry services. Though the subject is far more complicated than Jacobs took it to be, trade is still crucial to economic development.

Second, Jacobs two lists of things that a community may do in pursuit of economic development that do not lead to economic development are eminently sensible. All are variations on the proposition that economic development must be earned; it cannot be given. Monetary transfers from governmental entities may improve the circumstances of current residents of a place, just as is the case with the location of branch operations of businesses located elsewhere. Both fulfill the need of politicians to be seen to be able to deliver jobs for local constituents. However, both additions to the local economy can as easily disappear as they appeared. Only locally developed innovative exports are likely to bring sustainable economic development, and even these run the risk of being replaced by more innovative products developed elsewhere, not to mention sale to others with different interests.

So third, what then about sustainable innovation, about the workings of the invisible hand and the problem it implies in terms of drift (and default)? Jacobs's understanding of economic development in terms of import replacement/innovation/export creation is not so much wrong—indeed, on the surface, it seems quite right—but rather it is an understanding that analysis demonstrates is far too simple for the phenomenon it purports to illuminate. More complicated than standard economic theory of comparative advantage, it is still not complicated enough. Moreover, in linking innovation with economic diversity, it raises more problems, especially with contemporary economic explanations of innovation than it purports to solve.

All this said, taken loosely, by putting trade and innovation front and center, Jacobs's understanding of economic development has the possibility of moving contemporary discussion away from jobs and tax base, away from political boundaries and past glories, away from public works and tax subsidies and instead toward understanding the conditions that might make our communities attractive to people whose presence might lead to innovative economic activity and, equally importantly, encourage them (and current residents) to stay, if such activity were to ensue.

The use of the subjunctive in the previous sentence suggests that finally it is time to return to nature and grace. Nature seems to be a completely unhelpful concept for discussing economic development. Its usage has too clearly devolved into an epithet for designating value (or its absence) to be taken seriously. Moreover, when applied to markets, nature is silly. Markets are not natural things. They are created by the rules that the players in them observe as constrained by their entitlements and governmental actions. Change, even intentional change, is always possible, though not always a good thing, and never a good thing for everyone. But change always comes because someone dislikes the outcomes of a given structure of entitlements and rules, not because of there being any natural market. However, there is no linear relationship between governmental action and change; the space between can be far larger than that between cup and lip. Grace is another matter.

There is nothing wrong with Jacobs seeing the process of economic development through innovation as a matter of the workings of grace. She was clearly not centrally interested in it. Instead, once she saw a threat to her beloved Hudson Street neighborhood, she tried to figure out what made it tick and to attack what would destroy its vibrant life. This concern led to *The Death and Life of*

Great American Cities. And in doing so she taught us a great deal about urban residential life. Later, she saw an economy collapse around her and tried to figure out what made economies tick and what might destroy them or create a false sense of their growth. This concern led to *The Economy of Cities* as clarified in *Cities and the World Economy*. And in doing so she taught us a great deal about economic life. That her work is reactive should not be allowed to denigrate the insights that she developed defending what she loved, one of which was the idea that economic development was like the mystery of grace.

This idea seems particularly important. The winners in economic history need to understand that their triumph is unknowable, except in retrospect, and both unbidden and undeserved, especially undeserved. Such knowledge is important because of the recurrent narrative of God's bestowal of grace on a people. A Protestant Christian like Jacobs would be deeply bothered by that language, undermining, as it does, the importance of unknowable, perhaps unbidden, and surely undeserved. In the post-Reformation North Atlantic, it is quite easy to shift from grace, a humbling concept for the undeserved, to the triumph of desert. Such a shift has accompanied the justification of recurrent episodes of the destruction of countries, economies, and peoples. An affirmation of the importance of grace in episodes of economic development may possibly chasten a few from the easy identification of grace with our special merit.

And so, it would be good to join with Jacobs and rely on grace as the most appropriate term for the source of economic development were such a usage not unfashionable, were not downright off-putting, in the Academy. If one were not to follow Jacobs and rely on grace for understanding why/how economic development happens, what word might be a good substitute? Other words might describe a space where cause is unclear, but wonder is not absent. "Serendipity" would have had a lighthearted, positive connotation; "randomness," an invocation of statistics that might be taken as an echo of ghost towns as well as archeological digs at once urban spaces; "luck" or "Fortuna," a sense of gambling and thus odds; "happenstance," the sense of something more mundane, such as finding a coin in a parking lot that might be quite valuable, but just is worth face value.

However, none of these terms seems quite right, if used to supply the missing causal element in Jacobs's understanding. Economic growth and development is not a mundane happening, and trying to calculate the odds of it happening is a foolish activity. Statistical probability is not likely to be much easier to determine and, though a positive connotation is clearly apt, lightheartedness is somehow inappropriate. All of these terms seem to imply that economic development is a perfectly natural thing to expect. But it is not. It doesn't happen very often, and it seldom lasts for a long time either. It is the inappropriateness of words such as serendipity, randomness, luck, and happenstance, all of which connote natural processes in the Aristotelian sense, that seem to lie behind Jacobs's choice to speak of economic development in terms of grace in the sense of gift—undeserved and unbidden from an unknowable giver. Each of these suggested substitutes fails to identify something strange, mysterious, miraculous even.

"Magic" is a term that connotes strangeness, mystery, miracle, even wonder—the tiger suspended in midair, the coin plucked from behind a child's ear, might seem to be a good substitute for grace, as a way to explain what causes economic development. It affirms the same thing: "I do not know," the necessary and sufficient conditions cannot be specified. Except that, as colleagues here at Buffalo reminded me, magic really is a human contrivance. There is always a trick behind magic, as the phrase "magic trick" makes clear. There is no trick behind grace and, in any case, that word and Jacobs's discussion affirm that there is no human contrivance that can explain, nor trick that can bring about, economic development.

Which is not to say that there cannot be stories of economic development that are not simply strange, perhaps mysterious, even miraculous, where in the narrowest sense, causation is clear—the existence of A made possible B—but where at any greater scale, causation is hard to identify. Throughout *Cities and the Wealth of Nations* there are such stories. A good one is Jacobs's presentation of the growth of the bicycle industry in postwar Japan, a movement from scavenging for parts to producing parts to producing complete bikes. Scavenging in postwar rubble is easy to understand. However, machining parts requires the existence of cutting and grinding machines and of a ready supply of metals to be formed. Then there is the need for both the machinery for tire molding and rubber supplies. Though it is perhaps possible that low-wage labor will make these goods saleable where they are made, to succeed as an export strategy, one needs a large export market where high wages make the imported product competitive, low import barriers help maintain the low-wage advantage, and a local culture that is open to accepting foreign-sourced goods. This concatenation of circumstances is simply too implausible to predict.

Then there is Jacobs's recounting of the famous story about the discovery of the post-it note. It needs a company large enough to have a research department with an adhesives chemist who brews up an adhesive that fails at its task of attaching grit to paper. This chemist has to be open enough to the world to recognize a possible use for this adhesive that is completely outside of the corporation's product line. Simultaneously, the firm has to be open to commercializing products outside of its product line, able to see the potential of the product, and also wealthy enough to mass produce and market it. This is getting us close, not to monkeys and typewriters, but to one monkey with one typewriter.

It is not clear that Jacobs understands that she may be writing about such strange concatenations of events, but if she does, she has a ready answer. Her understanding of economic life assumes a lively, diverse metropolis where pretty much anything any innovator might need or want is close at hand. There is a problem with her assumption for it makes her understanding of economic development tautological. Given her assumption, could there possibly be a diverse metropolis that was not economically vibrant?

Michael Porter ran into the same problem when, reasoning backward, he noticed that economic development seemed to take place where there were groups of firms, both competitors and suppliers, roughly engaged in the same trade or industry. The examples of this phenomenon that are usually given, and Jacobs mentions them too, are Silicon Valley in California and the group engaged in the fashion clothing industry around Milan, Italy. Today we might add the Napa-Sonoma vintners group, the Central New Jersey pharmaceuticals group, and the North Carolina medical devices group. Still, there is probably no way to know how often it is the case a group of firms roughly engaged in the same industry tried hard but failed to form a viable cluster. Such is a likely outcome, and a circumstance that may make any local community that had such a cluster feel worse about its lot than if that community had none. Might there be more such communities than fewer? Surely. In both cases the choice by Jacobs and Porter to assume a ladder when it is necessary to climb makes thinking easy, but not therefore plausible, even though it is probably the case that the observations of both are correct. Both seem to have mistaken cause for effect in a circumstance where admitting that something strange, mysterious, or miraculous has taken place would open one up to certain intellectual criticism.

It is wrong to be afraid of such criticism. So, this book has settled on "rain."[58] The word seems apt for a boy from the Fifties Midwest, where the image of a farmer studying the sky looking for rain to preserve parched crops is iconic. Pictures of the Dust Bowl of the Thirties reinforce the lesson about what happens when rain does not come. At times, farmers in the Buffalo region look at the sky in much the same way. Gerard Manley Hopkins noted that "the sots and thralls of lust/Do in spare hours more thrive than I that spend,/Sir, life upon thy cause," and so implores "O thou lord of life, send my roots rain."[59] Citizens of Buffalo have uttered similar thoughts, both about its climate and about its economy.

The need to act while waiting for rain also seems more honest an understanding of the position that city economies find themselves in than one based on the importance of Keynesian animal spirits or human capital or the Creative Class, or clustering, or even the vibrant economies in great cities. All these alternatives come awfully close to saying, "I do not know," without quite admitting it. All play into the need of economists and others to specify the determinants of economic growth, to the inability to leave well enough alone, while treating market solutions as naturally the best, a dubious proposition.

Whatever might be the case with academic economists, for others there is no reason to be offended by the need to act while waiting for rain. Though Jacobs suggests certain things that will either not allow a community to grow or give it a false sense of growing, her entire book implicitly recognizes that one cannot specify those things that are likely to make an economy grow. Indeed, it assumes that growth is unlikely to follow from the intentional structuring of law or any other part of life, a point she makes abundantly clear. Affirming the existence and importance of rain, allows communities to focus on those things that might make the humans now living in the community to be pleased to live there and hopefully live better, rather than worse, while waiting.

Doing so also seems to fit best with the real impetus of Jane Jacobs's works. She cared intensely about what made life better or worse for humans, whether they lived in her beloved Greenwich Village or not. And she particularly hated those things that made these lives worse—expressways that cut through neighborhoods, faceless high rises that made people less safe, vast expanses of parkland that were only a magnet for illegal activities, government largess that drove people who had helped a community by making an honest living in it, out of that community. And so, it is to questions about the lived experience of communities that Part IV turns to by looking at Buffalo, not as a micro version of America, not as representative in any sense, but as a particular place where growth happened, and then it didn't. Buffalo is also a place where law responded, as it often does, to the human unhappiness and sense of loss that accompanies the stoppage of growth. However, that is a topic that must be partly postponed until Part V.

PART IV

Consider Buffalo

Some Perspectives

For a resident of Buffalo, chapter 12 of *Cities and the Wealth of Nations*, ought to make it clear that Jane Jacobs is onto something, that her understanding of economic life should be taken seriously. Reading about "Transactions of Decline" ought to cause such a person to keep silently saying, "Yeah, we tried that too and it didn't work." It is as if Jacobs had taken the region called Buffalo as her example for the chapter.

Jacobs speaks of three types of transactions that are both evidence of decline and contributing causes. The first is "prolonged and unremitting military production." The next is "prolonged and unremitting subsidies." And finally, heavy promotion of trade between "advanced and backward economies."[1] All three are to be found in the story about the region called Buffalo offered in Part II. The first is the most limited—the story of the aftermath of two wars and, most notably, the decline of Bell Aircraft. Also relevant are the problems at Bethlehem Steel and many other manufacturers in finding new markets after wartime contracts were terminated. The next is the endless story of the political city's, and to a lesser extent, the whole region's, constant search for federal, state, and county money for urban renewal; roadway, subway, sewer, and stadium construction; schools; and waterfront revival; not to mention various tax breaks offered to businesses enlarging, or newly establishing, local facilities. And the third, which starts as early as the great Lackawanna Steel Company, is the proud recruitment of branch plants, producing goods whose profits flow elsewhere, an endless list, most notable for the occasional exception—Eastman Machine, Pratt & Lambert, Pierce Arrow, Kittinger Furniture, and Spencer Kellogg.

Jacobs believes all three kinds of transactions are examples of the same economic relationship—dependency. In the first case, while exports are sometimes produced and paid for from profits earned elsewhere, only rarely does this work lead to innovations that might result in new work. In the second case, no exports are even created; tax funds raised from the profits earned elsewhere, but also locally, are directed to benefit local life. In the third case, exports are produced, sometimes in great quantities, but the profits of those exports do not flow back to the community in a way that would permit the community to use those profits to purchase more and different imports. Instead, they flow elsewhere. Branch plants allow the residents of a community to earn a living and so support local commercial activity, but only as long as others find it profitable for them to do so.

Still, Jacobs's views explain only part of the Buffalo region's economic life and offers no clue about what that region might do while waiting for rain, while waiting for import replacing and export producing processes to begin. To understand both matters, we might first examine a city that seemingly and successfully reinvented its economy four times—Boston.

Edward Glaeser wrote a very good piece summarizing Boston's economic history since 1603.[2] He argued that Boston's economy experienced four periods of growth and three of decline and attempted to explain each. The first period of growth was between about 1640 and 1740 when the city sold "food and other basic goods" to the colonists of Maryland and Virginia who were busy growing tobacco for export to England.[3] Boston eventually lost this market with the growth of ports nearer to those colonies, namely Philadelphia and New York City, for whom transport costs were lower. The second period of growth came between 1790 and 1840 when independence from England expanded the potential scope of international trade. Boston came to dominate this trade because the boats that engaged in it "were to a large extent owned and operated by New Englanders, often Bostonians."[4] The city's dominance of this trade disappeared when the growth of steam-powered ships made irrelevant the skills of building and crewing the wooden clipper ships on which such trade had previously depended.

The third period of growth was between, perhaps 1860[5] and 1920, when " low-wage Irish labor and Yankee capital and factory technologies" allowed Boston to become a manufacturing economy centered in shoes and textiles.[6] This manufacturing economy declined, as did the rest of the Rust Belt, though seemingly faster than Buffalo's version of that economy did, as better weather and hostility to unionization beckoned entrepreneurs South and West once changes in transportation made such movement possible. The fourth period of growth started by 1980 when the region became "dominated by four export industries: professional services, education, finance and healthcare."[7]

The arguments in support of this reading of Boston's history are largely ad hoced, buttressed with the modest math of the economic historian and a modest overlay of conservative economic politics. The destructive forces tend to be technology, primarily of transportation, and geography; the constructive forces tend to be education and skill transfer.[8] Complaints about Glaeser's method are clearly foreclosed by the fact that all of Parts I and II are similarly ad hoced: It is impossible to explain why a given rose bush grew by a given fence post except with ad hoc explanations. Also, it would be foolish to deny that history reflects the historian's political valence or to be surprised that Glaeser would focus on human capital given all his work on that topic both before this study and since. But what is surprising is one short line near the end of the introduction: "Boston's mid-twentieth century decline was pretty inevitable."[9] It is quite difficult to see how the ad hoc can be inevitable.

It is rather doubtful that the growth of a port in Philadelphia was in any way inevitable, nor was the American Revolution (much less the winner of the ensuing war). The explosion on the Great Eastern could have led to abandoning steam technology and a return to sail for a generation, and had World War II ended differently, the centrality of manufacturing in American life could have well resulted in a quite different economy today. And yet there is something remarkable in the fact that the growth of the transshipment trade in Buffalo was relatively coterminous with the great days of Boston's clipper ships; the turns toward and away from manufacturing as well. It seems implausible that the difference in the two region's current circumstances can be some difference between Irish and Polish immigration; at least both groups reacted pretty much the same to Black migration into their home turf. And though there is a significant difference between shoes and textiles in Boston and metal and metal bending in Buffalo, the relatively synchronous timing of both economic collapses makes one stop and think about inevitability

There is, of course, at least one significant difference. By 1980, Boston had recovered from the demise of its manufacturing economy, while Buffalo had not yet bottomed out. Glaeser does not mention Jane Jacobs, whose work he knows, and who credits post-World War II investments in Boston firms by American Research and Development, an early venture capital firm, as being partially responsible for Boston's revival. The lack of a financial sector beyond basic banking in Buffalo is not a trivial matter, and one of long standing. And of course, Boston had more than a two-hundred-year lead in terms of undergraduate education, a topic Glaeser emphasizes in his explanation of Boston's revival. Playing catch up is always hard, but significantly, when Buffalo began to try to catch up, its schools faced inward and for men, Catholic, at a time when the Protestant elite seemed comfortable sending their male children away to college. To get at such longstanding problems, it is best to fit the history of Buffalo's economy from back in Part II, with Glaeser's brief narrative.

Buffalo, like Boston from the mid-Seventeenth to the mid-Eighteenth Centuries, began as an entrepôt. Jacobs does not discuss such places, but Fernand Braudel does. He sees not manufacturing, but trade, as central to the growth of capitalism from the Fourteenth to the Eighteenth Centuries. In American frontier communities, trade remained central well into the Nineteenth Century. Initially, trade in Buffalo was not as grandiose as that of a major seaport; indeed in 1800, Buffalo was barely a place. But it became a significant trading place, and so the area grew enormously in the years after the Erie Canal had been opened and then again twenty years later when the New York Central reached the city.[10] By 1860, it was the tenth-largest city in the country, though less than an eighth, the size of Philadelphia, half the size of Boston, and two-thirds the size of Chicago, a city that hadn't yet experienced its Great Fire. This growth was largely based on the lake/canal and later lake/rail transshipment activity. From the West came grain, then logs; to the West went manufactured goods, then coal after the Pennsylvania railroads—DLW, Lehigh Valley, and Pennsy—reached Buffalo, and most important, people. The centrality of the grain trade, even though already experienced as intermittent, can be seen in the name of the first major organization for the business community. It was the Board of Trade, not the Chamber of Commerce.

Like Boston, Buffalo developed some manufacturing capacity while specializing in trade. Initially, Buffalo's capacity was in three areas—hides, timber, and metal work. Tanning survived even after the exhaustion of local supplies of hemlock bark by importing bark from Pennsylvania and only disappeared after the tanneries were sold to U.S. Leather, the Leather Trust, which soon shut them down. Lumbering began to die out about the same time. As logging moved inland from the coastal areas of the Great Lakes, the prime mode for the transport of tree trunks changed from ship to rail and so the center of the trade moved west to Chicago. Metalworking, brought by German immigrants, survived much longer. It comprised both foundry work—the casting, then sanding and polishing, of large items such as boilers, engine cylinders, tie rods, couplers, and wheels—and forge work, the shaping metal bars and slabs into agricultural and other tools.

The region held its own compared with other growing regions of the country all the way through 1900. The Civil War had been good to the city, as most wars are for strategically located regions, especially those far away from the fighting. In the aftermath of peace, the grain trade declined as more milling was done in the Midwest, especially Minneapolis. Grain thus reached the East as flour shipped by rail. Later, a shift in rail freight rates increased the relative cost of moving flour as against grain and so brought the grain storage business back to the city; transshipment moved from lake to rail. During these years manufacturing grew and soon began to challenge the predominant place of trade in the local economy as is evidenced by the establishment of a separate Board of Manufacturers in the city, an event that, in a few years, led to the merger of the two interests in a more neutral sounding Chamber of Commerce.

Manufacturing was now more completely centered in metal work, though pig iron production increased and even some steel was produced. Products tended to be directed toward agriculture—threshers, steam tractors, or railroad transportation—car wheels, drive wheels, couplers, undercarriages, sleeping cars, and oddly bridges. But there was some milling, some refining—petroleum for kerosene, linseed oil for paints and varnish, coal by-products for dyestuffs, corn for starch, wheat for flour and animal feed, and animal fats for soap; and some marine work, especially engines. Surprisingly, though Buffalo was the second-largest railhead in the country after Chicago, it never developed a locomotive works, as did Dunkirk, though some freight cars and many sleeper cars were built there.

While it is clear that Buffalo did much import replacement in these years, and much new work was spun out of old work, it is not clear how much significant innovation took place. The only major innovation that can be identified as having originated in Buffalo came not out of manufacturing, but out of the transshipment trade, Dart's mechanism for unloading grain boats. Yet, no industry grew up to manufacture the device or improve it. Although the city's waterfront later became known for its grain elevators, Buffalo developed no particular expertise in designing such, much less developed a core of construction firms to build them. So, if innovation did not create and sustain the eighth-largest city in America, a city that could hold a Pan-American Exposition though it had no ready access to any other part of Pan-America than Canada, what did?

There are at least three, though possibly more, answers to this question. The first is the most direct and most dispiriting to the natives[11]—Nothing. As an accident of transportation geography, the region's reason for being was dependent on transportation technologies. Growth began as a transshipment point between lake-born commerce and, first the Erie Canal, then later, the railroads. In the beginning, at least, such manufacturing in Buffalo was either primarily for local consumption—brewing is the most obvious example given that the lack of refrigeration or an effective bottling process until after World War II limited an export trade—or for trade within a regional area delimited by transportation. By 1901, this transportation-based economy was in full bloom. True, there had been some disquieting developments, most obviously, the New York Central's construction of an east-west bypass route that avoided the congestion in that line's yards, themselves designed at an earlier time to accommodate the city's position as a transshipment point. And, for all of the advantage that Niagara Falls offered for AC electric service, it was surely notable that the first great demonstration of the potential of that technology was at the World's Columbian Exposition held in Chicago in 1893. Still, in 1901, there was no reason to believe that the existing transportation patterns were going to change. Except they did.

As transportation patterns changed, both away from rail and toward truck and, later away from tramp steamer and toward container—the city's reason for being more than a local market town ceased and so the area slowly began to decline. After the national railroad grid was completed, the City of Buffalo kept on growing, but at a lesser rate than similar cities. So, it slowly drifted down the census's table of the country's largest places as the growth of truck traffic began to limit the importance of transshipment business tied either to the port or the railroads. As transshipment declined, rail declined too.

With the growth of truck travel tied to a grid of interstate highways, economic growth shifted toward transportation-critical cities, those located where north-south and east-west routes crossed—places like Columbus, Indianapolis, and Nashville—not places such a Buffalo on the edge of the grid. As this new grid system matured, the last of the city's transportation advantage disappeared, and so the region began to lose population.

That this process of decline has taken about one hundred years is hardly surprising. That span of time is hardly long in city life. Consider Bruges, once a thriving seaport. It declined starting in the early Sixteenth Century as its access to the sea slowly disappeared, yet held on until the beginning of the Twentieth Century, a full four hundred years, when changes in shipping technology allowed it to benefit from the construction of a new port nearby. Similarly, New Bedford, a city that peaked fifty years before Buffalo, still hangs on.

However, it is best to leave open the possibility that Buffalo had nothing underpinning its economy in 1901 and move on. It may be simply too early to decide whether that is the case. Instead, consider a somewhat opposed understanding of Buffalo's economy that explicitly builds on Jacobs's understanding of the mechanism of economic growth, affirms that such an innovative economy existed in Buffalo before 1900, but asks why innovation might have tailed off in the years thereafter.

This second understanding of what might have created and sustained the eighth-largest city in America begins by noticing that Jacobs is a champion of the small—the city, the neighborhood, the small business, but not the nation, even the state, or the large corporation, much less the multinational corporation. If Jacobs's recipe for a healthy city economy is to be measured not by the number of Kodak, IBM, Xerox, Microsoft, Hewlett-Packard, or Intels in the area, but by the number of diverse small firms, then it is at least possible that Buffalo had an economy that was truly thriving during the last part of the Nineteenth Century. Unfortunately, for historians at least, most small firms leave behind few traces of their business. So, rough numbers are about all that one can use to get a sense of what kind of an economy Buffalo might have had.

Here, the careful work on Buffalo's economy by Mark J. Stern, a demographer, is of modest help.[12] His data suggests that in 1870 commercial and manufacturing establishments employed about nine workers on average. This number increased to twelve to fifteen workers over the next thirty years. While the data for 1909 suggest an implausible jump to thirty-eight workers on average in but nine years, it is clear that some period starting in the late 1880s, 1890s, or early 1900s, local business establishments began to increase in size. Which is not to say there were a large number of these average-size firms. Though the number of workers per firm seemingly had dropped to thirty-three by 1914, about a quarter of the workforce then labored in establishments of fewer than fifty workers and about the same number worked in establishments with more than five hundred employees. So, Buffalo established this average by waffling wildly around it, just as the city establishes its average temperature.

In the earlier years it is likely that there would have been more small establishments. Were they diverse? Stern asserts that they were, though his data is not very convincing: it reports only participation in the ten-largest industries in the United States. And Buffalo boosters have long trumpeted the diversity of its economy, though of course, based on no data here either. Though it is always difficult to infer backward, much less backward more than fifty years, two interesting bits of information suggest that such may have been the case. Studies measuring industrial diversification find that Buffalo's was among the most diverse economies in the United States. One, looking at data from 1950 found it to be seventeenth out of ninety-three areas;[13] the other from 1970, found it to be thirteenth out of 106.[14] If one takes Jacobs's ideas seriously, then one might cautiously infer from these modest findings that a large amount of, if not nationally, at least regionally significant innovative manufacturing probably was going on.

The story of the growth of what became the Pierce Arrow Auto Company is instructive. That firm changed from the production of refrigerators and birdcages to bicycles to motorcars. Such wild shifts suggest that there were at least some examples of old work giving rise to new work. So too with the Pratt & Letchworth Ironworks that moved from producing hardware for saddles and harnesses, to nails, then railroad drive wheels, and undercarriages and even to high-end toy soldiers. The Buffalo Forge Company, famous, or perhaps infamous, for having allowed Willis Carrier, one of its engineers, to go off on his own to manufacture home air conditioning systems while it continued to work on large commercial and industrial systems, also supports this understanding. It started making what its name implies—forges, soon added to its product line the tools it used to produce the forges, as well as the blowers that supplied air, and thus oxygen, to the forges it produced. It then shifted to producing industrial blowers more generally, which led to commercial air conditioning. Other examples might be supplied.

What then led to the petering out of this modestly innovative economy? A good guess can be built by recognizing first that, during the Great Merger Movement in the years before pre-World War I, many Buffalo firms got included, but Buffalo never became the headquarters of any of the new entities—indeed, the fact that Spencer Kellogg Refining fought inclusion in the Linseed Oil Trust is notable local lore. At the same time, after 1900, when Buffalo entrepreneurs built a sizeable business, they were often bought out by larger, more national companies. Second, for reasons speculated about in Part II, the families whose investments were bought out seem not to have invested their newly realized wealth in new local businesses in the area as they had in the 1880s. A kind of local disinvestment took place. And of course, the remaining large, locally focused entities—banks—could not be relied upon to pick up the slack. These banks were sensibly risk adverse, banking being a very scary business, with at best a bit more than a one percent return on assets.

Meanwhile, the region was still a good place to make things, so the no longer locally owned plants of American Brass, National Aniline, Republic Steel, and SOCONY-Mobil Oil stayed, but effectively became transplants, just like the pieces of Ford, General Motors, Bethlehem Steel, and Westinghouse that were intentionally located here. When no longer locally owned manufacturing facilities and true transplants provided a great portion of the region's employment, Buffalo turned into a great middle-class town. Everything seemed just fine. But it wasn't, for such facilities don't lead when it comes to continual innovation, as the story of the DuPont Plant on River Road pointedly demonstrates. Though improvements to the process for manufacturing both cellophane and rayon were invented there, most production was placed elsewhere. And such plants don't stay when times get tough. Thus, the decline of the Buffalo economy is nothing but a textbook example of what Jacobs's theory says will happen when small becomes large and not local. Again, however, it is best to set aside this explanation and explore another before choosing among these possibilities.[15]

This third understanding of what might have created and sustained Buffalo starts with the observation that, in a very real sense, Buffalo's economy was anything but diversified. Yes, the city had a good deal of milling, some petroleum refining, some dyestuffs manufacturing, and other odds and ends, but it was mostly a metal-making and metal-bending town, and of a particular kind, one that relied on mass-production methods. Buffalo had some one-of-a-kind manufacturing specialists—Lake Erie Engineering, which still makes large metal-forming presses and ships them all over the world, is a good example—and a nice collection of independent foundries and machine shops, however most of the metal-making and metal-bending enterprises in the area starting in the 1880s threw labor, at most semiskilled labor, not capital, at mass production manufacturing tasks, because labor, especially immigrant labor, was cheap and to the extent that much capital was required, long product runs reduced the per unit cost of capital significantly.

Such a choice, if it was a choice and not a default, was not stupid; or at least dozens of other communities from Wisconsin east to lower New England—the so-called Rust Belt—made the same choice. The grain elevators on the riverfront may have captured the attention of European visitors, but it was the mills along the miles of railroad tracks that provided employment to the immigrants who streamed into Buffalo in ethnic waves, the people who defined the social life and religious life of the community, as well as its politics. And it was a modestly prosperous community. After 1880, the average wage rate in Buffalo was, and for a long time remained, above the national average.

Thus, it is important to remember that what the city had developed was the equivalent of a natural resources-based economy. As Jacobs makes clear, in such an economy, if the resource runs out or the market shifts, the local economy has nothing to fall back on. An economy based on locational advantage or transplants is exposed to the same risk. Buffalo, and all of the Rust Belt cities, experienced the same shift away from both mass-production manufacturing and metal bending and toward more capital-intensive production processes, lighter materials—both metal and plastic—and overseas production—divisional, contract, and competitive. The reasons for this shift are, for present purposes at least, uninteresting. But the fact of this shift is important, as can be seen by adding two neighbors—Cleveland and Pittsburgh—to the mix of Buffalo and Boston.

In 1820, when Buffalo and Cleveland were essentially nothing, Pittsburgh was already a midsize city. In the 1820s, Pittsburgh saw great growth, so that by 1840, it had settled into a position as around the tenth-largest city in the country, at least if one included its poorer, eventual merger partner across the Allegany River, imaginatively called, Allegany. By this time, Buffalo was already a midsize city while Cleveland was still a quite small one. By 1860, Buffalo, benefiting from the canal and lake and rail commerce, was about the same size as the continuously growing Pittsburgh. By then, Cleveland was a midsize city.

For a while thereafter, Cleveland grew faster than either Buffalo or Pittsburgh and so caught the other two in 1880. Each city grew significantly in the 1890s so that all three were close to being tied for the seventh-largest city in the country, though both Cleveland and Pittsburgh were slightly larger than Buffalo. Of course, neither Pittsburgh nor Buffalo understood that, from this point on, they would grow more slowly than the rest of the county and so would fall in the league tables of big cites. Meanwhile, Cleveland continued to grow, eventually becoming the fifth-largest city in the United States in 1920, before it too began to grow more slowly than the rest of the county. By 1940, Cleveland was the sixth-, Pittsburgh was tenth-, and Buffalo was fourteenth-largest city. Thereafter, each city drifted and then lurched down the table of cities by size.

Of course, after World War II, the great period of suburban growth made city population essentially irrelevant for understanding urban areas. At this point, a better measure of economic advance is not growth in city population, but instead the SMA (the Standard, later Statistical, Metropolitan Area). These figures tell a surprisingly complementary story. During the 1950s and 1960s, the three SMAs known as Buffalo, Cleveland, and Pittsburgh continued to grow, but after

1970, the population of the central city anchoring each area dropped like a rock and growth in the suburbs failed to make up for the loss. The economy of each area slowly, but seemingly coordinately, fell behind its peers and so each continued to fall in ranking among the country's largest metropolitan areas.

If one begins to compare Buffalo with Cleveland and Pittsburgh, the most obvious similarity is that the latter two also had significant nonmetal-making and bending assets. Pittsburgh even had major nonmetal corporations headquartered in the city and both it and Cleveland had significantly stronger, locally anchored financial sectors than Buffalo. These differences are worth mentioning, not because they suggest differences from Buffalo's economic situation, but rather because they suggest the banality of the situation in all three places. In the 1970s, places with a significant focus on metal making and metal bending all experienced significant economic stress leading to population decline. The cities may have suffered from White flight, but the areas suffered from the abrupt decline of a local manufacturing economy that provided significant export earnings. And perhaps more important, each economy had produced very little innovation, very little new work growing out of old work, which might augment the regional economy when the old work was no longer a source of export earnings. In Boston, though the industries are different, the story is pretty much the same, except temporally and in terms of eventual recovery.

Seeing that different local economies can experience identical shocks and remembering that Buffalo experienced the last shock too, ought to remind one that Jane Jacobs never says that the processes she identifies cannot be combined. A city might have both a vibrant sector that is regularly innovating, replacing imports, and creating new exports, and a sector that is functionally natural resource dependent/transplant dependent, that is doing little or no innovation, replacing no imports and creating no exports, and so is prone to losing its economic vibrancy all at once. If this is so, and it is important to remember that Jacobs presents an understanding of economic development, not a fully fleshed out typology of possible economies, then it makes sense to return to all three explanations of the decline of the Buffalo economy and piece them together.

Start with the first explanation for what created the Buffalo economy—nothing. Buffalo is clearly an accident of geography and because of that accident, the Erie

Canal ended there. That meant that from the beginning, it was an entrepôt, a place that was important for the transshipment of goods. And its importance as such is shown by the fact that in 1860, it was served by two railroads—the New York Central and the Erie—and was the tenth-largest metropolitan area in the nation. That Chicago's extraordinary growth—it more than tripled in size between 1850 and 1860 and then more than doubled in the next ten years—helped to push Buffalo down in the league tables for size should not be taken to suggest that the city's geographical advantage had disappeared. Good evidence to the contrary can be found; in the years after the Civil War, three more railroads—the DLW, the Lehigh Valley, and the Pennsy—extended dead end lines to the city's waterfront just to participate in the transshipment trade, by then both coal and grain.

It was during the years between the Civil War and the Pan-American Exposition that one might argue that Buffalo built a diverse manufacturing economy, one that replaced imports and innovated to create new exports. This is part of the second explanation for what created the Buffalo economy. While experiencing no episodes of explosive growth, the region held its own against other regions that had begun to fade, such as Albany and New Orleans, though not against areas that were growing rapidly, such as Minneapolis and San Francisco. It would not have been stupid to say that, in 1900, Buffalo's manufacturing economy was reasonably balanced between brewing, chemicals and dyestuffs, grain, railroading, metal and metal-bending products, supported with an adequate rail and water-transport network, and blessed with an abundance of electric power. It was a typical Midwestern city, and located on the far side of the Appalachians, Buffalo was by definition, a Midwestern place similar to other nearby cities such as Cleveland and Pittsburgh.

It was also apparent during these years that there was both a strength and a weakness to Buffalo's tie to the geography of transportation. The tie to the railroads led both to supplying goods to the railroads—wheels, brakes, trucks, sleeper cars, and bridges—as well as the jobs required by the rail yards all over the area. However, as the bypass tracks built in the 1880s mutely suggested, there already was, in the rapid re-centering westward of the Midwestern economy, a hint that the region's locational advantage was an ephemeral thing. Changes in freight rates, relative production costs, and technology could quite quickly shift advantage to disadvantage. If change were adverse to locational advantage, what in the economy would take up the slack?

Here then, it is important to recognize the third explanation for what created the Buffalo economy. In hindsight, the event that all Buffalo histories take to be evidence of the great strength of the region—the moving of the Lackawanna Steel Company from Scranton to the Lake Erie shoreline, a mill designed to produce steel rails—was not an unalloyed benefit. The coming of what ultimately became a branch of Bethlehem Steel after Lackawanna Steel failed in the aftermath of the Panic of 1907 seems to be *not* evidence of the region's strength but rather a portent of the relative decline that was already shown in the 1910 Census, when the Detroit region became larger than the Buffalo centered one. The mill was effectively a transplant, sited for its locational advantage. As little more than a branch plant, its future was tied to executives headquartered elsewhere. Similar branch plants followed quickly, primarily in autos. Indeed, they were still coming to Buffalo in the 1950s. Such diversity as the region possessed was in the process of declining, while that local control of large enterprises was being transferred elsewhere and, for reasons that still escape me, local innovation was declining as well.

The decline of innovation is hard to explain, for it is not the case that there was no innovation or local growth. Jacobs argues that large companies are less innovative than small ones and transplants still less yet. Perhaps she is right. That Pittsburgh (1920) and Cleveland (1930) began their relative declines right after Buffalo's might supply some support for her proposition. Still, it is not as if all of a sudden, relatively small businesses magically disappeared after the turn of the century. Trico windshield wipers were innovative for that time; Harrison radiators, perhaps, as well. And new businesses were being created, most notably, the Pierce Arrow Motor Car Company, the Sterling Engine works that specialized in small marine engines, and the Kittinger Furniture Company, though admittedly these were all high-end specialty enterprises at a time when mass production for a middle-class market was the growing economic model. In contrast, one could see that much of Buffalo's innovation is reactive to the big ideas that originated elsewhere. The most obvious example is auto parts, but the best example is an absence that can identified by noticing that in the Part II history of Buffalo's economy there is no equivalent to Rochester's Kodak or Xerox, a technology that transforms an economic activity that stimulates others to try to improve on that technology, to innovate in return. The great exception is Dart's grain elevator where no one in Buffalo seems to have given a thought to centering elaboration of that technology in the city.

Innovation has continued. Engineers at what once was called Harrison Radiator designed the cooling system for the Apple iMac flat-panel personal computers, Eastman Machine continues to improve its products for the simultaneous cutting of the great stacks of fabric that are central to mass manufacture of clothing throughout the world, and Moog Industries and Servotronics, remnants of a briefly bustling aircraft industry, are doing quite, quite well. But the singularity of such innovative activity provides evidence of its larger absence.

Perhaps the decline of innovation was due to a failure to recycle local capital locally when firms were bought out, to keep reinvesting in the Buffalo region. The early Twentieth Century growth of securities markets, especially in corporate debt and preferred stock, made it easier to turn gain on the sale of a family business into income-producing investments that allowed owners who were tired of, and children who had no interest in, the grubby details of business life to live comfortably. Or perhaps decline was just bad luck. After all, most everywhere, regions are trying to grow, indeed growth has been the mantra of the United States since 1750, before there was any such thing as united colonies, much less states. Not all places seem to have been equally successful; bad luck might have something to do with it, or the absence of grace or rain. And yet, it is hard not to believe that available venture capital and deeper financial networks make a difference, if only in making good luck, grace, or rain effective.

Whatever brought the early Twentieth Century decline of innovation, looking backward, one can easily summarize the economic story of Buffalo in terms that Jacobs uses. The area started as a natural resources economy—after all a geographic locational advantage is not any less natural than a mineral deposit that would be useless were it impossible to reach the site or to move the ore to market. Then Buffalo seemed to build a diversified import replacing/export creating economy, only to slide, through no particular fault of its own, into being a transplant/branch plant region. Buffalo stopped being a hotbed of innovation and yet hid that fact by remaining an industrial monolith that provided good, if dirty and at times dangerous, jobs for large numbers and several generations of immigrants and their families.

Just how this happened seems easy to describe. With a base of foundries and forges, a large immigrant population, and a good transportation network, especially railroads and their suppliers, Buffalo was an obvious place to put a steel plant, especially one that specialized in the production of rails. And with one plant there already, it is hardly surprising that others thought the idea was a good one too. The same logic applies to auto assembly plants and their suppliers, especially since the immigrants kept piling into the region until the end of World War I. To the extent that the cliché that these immigrants were former farmers is true, they provided a supply of unskilled (at least with respect to industrial processes) labor. Given that supply, it was again hardly surprising that large industrial plants, especially those in the automobile end of metal bending, came to Buffalo too, given that immigrant families tended to be big and so a ready supply of labor was going to be available even after most immigration was shut off. And of course, the political City of Buffalo was perfectly happy with any such large enterprise that created a demand for the existing supply. Employed workers are happy voters and happy voters usually vote for incumbents.

Since economically, World War II was a war based on steel production and the gasoline engine, it was at least forty-five years before anyone might have noticed that, despite what the experts might have said, a once diversified economy had become significantly less diverse. Already well-greased wheels simply rolled down hill until the economic engine crashed into a wall and burned, at which point the political city said over and over, "We know we need jobs, and we are trying hard to secure them," a mantra that avoided admitting that we failed to notice that over these years the region had become less economically resilient.

Before we move on, it is important to briefly return to the question of inevitability that Glaeser raised. In no sense can it be seen as inevitable that the city located where Lake Erie drained into the Niagara River was going to be a metal-bending town, nor that once it became a metal-bending town, metal bending would become so dominant that the economy would slowly roll into a wall where it would crash and burn. DuPont could have begun production of cellophane and rayon in Buffalo, and along with Allied Chemical's dye plants, created a growing chemical industry. After all, Kodak just sixty miles away, was essentially a chemicals company based on a transparent substrate and dyes. It was also a mass manufacturer and to the extent that it was an optics firm, Buffalo had one of those too. At the same time, it is not surprising that a metal-bending town crashed and burned; dozens of them across the Midwest and the Northeast did so too. And so, this is where Buffalo is now: a sense of loss and a political imperative to act, but still no reason to admit accumulated errors over a period of about one hundred years of relative prosperity, since it is not clear that political Buffalo could have done anything to cause the region's economy to increase its diversity.

So, it is time to review the regularly cited strengths, on the basis of which plans for the resuscitation of Buffalo's regional economy might be built, as well as the equally regularly ignored problems with those strengths, and then the political context within which work on such possible plans would need to be carried out.

Strengths, Problems, and Political Context

Let us start where most such analyses start—location and resources. "What does the region called Buffalo have that someone might want?" Well, traditional locational advantages clearly have been exhausted. The export/import trade left long ago and whether the truck traffic to and from Canada crosses at Buffalo, Detroit, or Lewiston, there still will be a negligible impact on the region's economy. Cross-border trucks just don't stop except to pay tolls and get customs clearance. Indeed, having to stop here more than briefly is a barrier to using Buffalo as a crossing. As for newer locational advantages, the area is still a great place to live. While it cannot compete with the southern claim to endless summer, the area is warmer than most of the Midwest in winter and cooler in summer. That is not a bad advantage for middle-class people who are in the region for some other reason.

Questions of resources are more difficult. Clearly, at present, Buffalo possesses no important natural resources, at least until access to freshwater becomes such in fifty to one hundred years. The other, sort-of natural resource is our waterfront, but as is shown by San Diego's continued growth after it chose to cut off access to half of its waterfront by building a convention center there, waterfront development is nice, but not all that it is cracked up to be. Chicago has a much more spectacular waterfront (also separated from the city's residents by a very busy highway). Tourists who are there may enjoy driving along it, primarily in summer, but mostly it is an amenity for the region's residents, just as is Buffalo's waterfront, which is more like what Baltimore's Inner Harbor has become.

Still less of a natural resource, but one regularly cited as a basis for the revival of the region's economy, are the regions' tourist attractions. These assets are real. Buffalo has one special art museum—the Albright-Knox, soon to be "AKG" as a result of a large donation for its expansion, another very good one—the Burchfield-Penney, and a surprising number of good galleries, as well as some wonderful surviving architecture—residential, commercial, and industrial, but realistically, Buffalo has no French Quarter, no Old Town, and no Greenwich Village around which to hang these classic middle-class amenities. Sports teams probably draw more visitors to the area.

Regularly added to these assets are a convention center, a casino and, again of course, the waterfront. The difficulty with this package[16] is that tourism, as Niagara Falls demonstrates, is a lousy basis for an economy and gambling may have succeeded as the economic basis of Las Vegas, but everywhere else, even in Atlantic City, it has not been a big success. The reason is simple. An economy builds a vibrant area to the extent that it provides decent, middle-class jobs. Tourism, conventions, and gambling do anything but that. They provide lots of low-wage employment. There is very little return to the community as a whole from such jobs. Visitors leave money behind, but by the time it is split up, community residents don't get much.

A set of four, more directly "economic" resources usually begin with the region's hospitals, UB's Medical School and the words "biomedical" or "life sciences." This idea is bewildering. Buffalo sits in between two regional medical centers—Rochester and Cleveland. What Buffalo might offer that these two cities can't is largely a mystery. About the only thing is the lack of a comprehensive cancer treatment center such as Roswell Park in Rochester. More significant, healthcare in the United States is a perpetual disaster. It is difficult to fathom why anyone would bet that whenever the national system settles down so that healthcare is profitable and so throws off a continuous stream of good middle-class jobs, Buffalo will have generated the right mix of services at the right price.

Now, none of this is to say that it is a bad idea for the University at Buffalo to throw all sorts of money into a new medical campus next to both Roswell and Kaleida Health's Buffalo General Hospital and the new building for its Women's and Children's Hospital. After all, for some time it has been an open secret the school was going to risk its accreditation if it didn't get new facilities and a tighter relationship with its clinical and residency programs. If the region lost its medical school, regional healthcare would all but collapse and any chance of economic revival would become vanishingly small.

But when thinking about the potential for things medically related to spark development in Buffalo, it still must be remembered that such development likely would require a rather tightly integrated set of entities. The local line up is not all that promising. The region has two hospital systems—Catholic and Protestant—that at best, get along somewhat difficultly and one of which has all but severed its ties to the medical school; a public hospital that is continuously on the ropes; and a cancer treatment center that is being pushed off state support into an unclear future as neither public nor private. All have an excess of hospital beds, a resource during the Covid-19 pandemic, but otherwise a dubious one. It is unlikely that healthcare is going to provide a base for spurring economic development.

Three other possible resources get less public attention than they get from the economic development community. The first is so-called advanced manufacturing—small-batch, heavily computerized, custom-made parts, often metallic, and using very expensive machines; think Twenty-First Century version of the Twentieth Century machinist's job shop. Every so often there is a newspaper story about such a firm with its new machine, so there really is some of this economic activity going on locally. How advanced manufacturing scales up to a larger portion of the economy is, however, obscure. The same is true of logistics, the job of arranging transportation for stuff all the way from seeing to it that one large piece of machinery gets from point A to point B up to managing an international firm's entire supply chain. One of the larger of such companies is headquartered locally and this field must be lucrative because one often sees ads from common and private carriers willing to do this work too. Perhaps here there is a location-specific advantage related to the Canadian border. Back office/professional support work is quite visible in the community. It includes local and out-of-state banking, insurance and computer hard and software firms, and generally employs college educated, if not always graduated, individuals. The region's locational advantage has been described as having a well-educated, fast-speaking workforce, without regional accent. Given the initial spurt of activity in this field it is surprising that it has not seen more growth of late. All three areas show modest potential with some possibilities for spillover of employees from firm to firm, thus diffusing skills, and at least the first two, for fissuring into separate firms and so increasing the overall size of the economic activity in the field.

Another economic activity probably contributes as much to the existing economy of the region as any other, has more export potential than most and yet, is so deeply troubled as to never feature in a list of economic development possibilities—higher education.[17] Historically, areas with a large concentration of higher educational alternatives seem to have thrived because such institutions generate a lot of middle-class, faculty, and administrative jobs. Buffalo has a substantial excess of this resource. And students from all over the world come here for education, albeit not in great numbers. More importantly, they leave, hopefully better prepared for employment than they might have been elsewhere. Thus, higher education could be seen as a classic import/add value/export business. And focusing our institutions of higher education on that business would have the added advantage that imported students do not need local jobs after finishing their education.

Unfortunately, as in the case with healthcare, higher education has a religious problem and city/suburb problem to boot. For reasons that seem to go back to the religious orders that founded the various Catholic schools and that a necessary treatment of each other as equals seems impossible, these colleges cannot even form a modestly integrated system, much less the equivalent of the Claremont Colleges. And the fact that the older public school, a state college, is in the City of Buffalo and the newer school, a University Center, is in suburban Amherst seems too to make it impossible for the two schools to cooperate as equals. At the same time, the fact that suburban students at the three campus Erie County Community College would prefer to attend programs in other counties than go into the city campus and city students find it difficult to attend programs in the suburbs only adds to the dysfunction that comes from the dumbfounding, but embarrassingly intense, competition for a dwindling local population base that all schools, except the University Center, engage in. 'Tis a pity too, because were the various institutions to shift their attitude from covert and overt feuding to one of mutual support, the region might have an unusual advantage by marketing itself as a place for any student to come to because it has so many, different schools to choose from, surely more than any applicant might need.

If, for an instant, one were to ignore the inability of our institutions of higher education to cooperate, one might notice that the region has an unspoken resource, its children. Though making this statement brings forth thoughts of Jonathan Swift's famous essay, "A Modest Proposal," this is a serious possibility. Buffalo is a third world country, as the urge of some of its citizens for it to develop an island economy indicates. Like such countries, we must export or die. The ability to export our children could be an unacknowledged resource. To build an economy based on higher education, an import/export business, requires the willingness of first-rate scholars and teachers to live in the Buffalo area and to stay when fancier schools call. Here we might have a comparative advantage. As noted above, the region has a more plausible climate to offer than in our perverse machismo we usually admit. And Buffalo is a great place to raise children, large enough to allow them a sense of freedom and small enough to keep parents from an overwhelming sense of panic. Academics most often form classic middle-class families.

The value of a good primary and secondary education system to such families cannot be underestimated. Here, the state of our public, K-12 schools is a troubling problem. Were we to attack that problem—the notion that we, or anyone, will solve it is implausible—we would have an additional resource for securing and retaining the quality of scholars and teachers essential to a higher education import/export business. These individuals will raise more children than the area can absorb, even if higher education becomes a growth industry. Their perception of the quality of the potential exports that would be their children will influence their willingness to come and stay. That willingness, in turn, will influence the quality and volume of the potential imports that will be their students, the rock on which any such business will be built.

While there is no particularly strong basis from which one might build a regional economy, several weaker bases taken together might provide a substitute, and so it is best to continue by examining the other critical aspect of competitive advantage—a viable political unit with a viable political culture that could provide support for any chosen advantage. Unfortunately, here one looks in vain. First, it is clear that the City of Buffalo is not such an entity. It limps from fiscal crisis to fiscal crisis looking for others to help it survive and praying that no one will suggest that the city completely take over the even weaker Buffalo Public School System. Maybe Erie County could become a better choice, though obviously, it is not now, separated as it is into twenty-six towns, the basic unit of local government in New York State, three cities, and twelve villages and riven as it seems to be by petty political infighting that largely mimics its long-dominant city/suburb divide. Joining Erie and Niagara Counties would only increase the number of implausible local economic units. Joining Buffalo and Rochester, and so focusing on the eight Western New York counties, might provide a more diversified economic base, but does so at the cost of creating an entity that is probably too large to think of as a local government. So, it is best to stick to Erie County and the governments within it.

However, doing so leads to a second impediment to the development of a competitive advantage in the area—its local politics. Here one might be reminded of a timeless Black metaphor from tidewater Maryland and Virginia—"Like crabs in a barrel; when one tries to crawl out the others pull it back down." Local political life in Western New York is a matter of, "Me too, or you get nothing," of multiple participants who have veto power over anything that is proposed to be done and who will run to law at the least provocation to stop something that is in the least bit distasteful or even benefits someone else and not them.

This attitude is not just found where actions require the cooperation of the many units of local government. Admittedly, such cooperation is made difficult by a legal rule, enshrined by a 1927 amendment to the New York State Constitution, that makes it effectively impossible for larger local units to expand by annexation, a grotesque limit on sensible local governmental growth, done in response to the fear of Westchester County residents that New York City would annex part or all of it. But "Me too, or you get nothing," is also the mantra all of local public authorities, each of which has its own mission and constituency, led by political appointees, and offering patronage jobs. The same is true of individual departments within any local governmental unit. And one should not forget all the neighborhood associations and civic betterment groups, unions, and varying religious organizations who want, and often have, a veto too. As a result, we have multiple small units each fighting for the last scrap of meat from the bones of a very scrawny chicken and yelling about graft and corruption on the part of everyone else, a joke to a boy who grew up in Chicago, where from birth, one was taught what real graft and corruption was.

Were there an effective political machine to impose an answer to pressing problems, there might be some way to move forward, but instead we have four political parties, some containing several factions. Each piece of our panoply of interested parties, indeed each elected official, has a standard answer to all questions, "What do I get out of this?" And so, the dribbling away of Buffalo's Community Development Block Grant funds into tiny local projects supporting each council member's local political base was an open scandal, *as* is each county legislator's similar use of member items. In both institutions, the fight for personal staff is unseemly, at best, more likely unconscionable. So, in a deeply troubled area, every player on the team fights for individualized credit with respect to a gain of inches when that team is on its own eight-yard line, to use a particularly apt Buffalo sports metaphor. And this behavior is not just a matter of city or even county politics. One or another of the various town governments is from time to time an embarrassment.

And then there is the region's difficult politics of race, ethnicity, class, and religion, fueled by the willingness all of our media outlets to treat any two-bit press conference or release as if it were news, rather than "same old, same old."

The first two—race and ethnicity—are the rock on which the culture of "I want mine too" has been built, of envy fueled by distrust fueled by residual hatred. The third—class—often manifests itself as support for unionized labor, since unionized labor still is an important part of the local political class. This is an unfortunate focus, given that today, the nonunion workforce is the base of the working class. Here again, the politics of envy and of delivering for one's constituency does not engender an accommodating force in the community. The fourth—religion—is simply sad, the conversion of ancient doctrinal disputes and ethnic rivalries into principled objections designed to see that things are done "my way."

The behavior of the allegedly private sector and well-meaning, public citizens is no better, drenched as it is in nostalgia and cries of, "Not In My Back Yard!" There is no shortage of examples. The Peace Bridge debacle had good, public-spirited citizens joining together to slow a public project down, but unable to agree about anything and so, ending up with nothing. There is also the great Commercial Slip restoration project, a piece of real estate so valuable, of such grand historical significance, that in 1936, it was an auto dealer's storage lot for new cars. Restoring the slip cost a fortune to create a modest amenity that was followed by construction of an infinitely cheaper, ground-level recreation of the old canal and slip system that seemingly satisfies the public, at least in the winter when it is used for skating.

A particularly egregious example of dubious behavior was a long-ago fight over a possible expansion of the Buffalo Zoo into Delaware Park as a solution to its endless problems with maintaining its accreditation. Here, as well-meaning a group of opponents as one could find, though one that seemed unable to understand that the use of parkland has changed significantly between Olmstead's day and our own, stopped the creation of an attraction that might have become more than a footnote in travel magazines. Thereafter, two different, but similarly shortsighted groups blocked the zoo's move from the park to a larger space elsewhere in the community. And, even earlier, there was the endless dispute over the location and structure of the subway, a dispute that dragged out so long that the project never reached its intended destination because inflation ate up a large portion of the grant. All of these disputes are examples of the two great forces for getting nothing done in the community—nostalgia and NIMBY.

More private fights have the same complexion. There is the unseemly discord over relocating Children's Hospital to a more central, less disruptive location. It took ten years of silence after that fight to a draw to bring it to a sensible conclusion. Or the legislative understanding that keeps the Buffalo Philharmonic from offering a concert series other than at the admittedly breathtakingly beautiful Kleinhans Music Hall, a location that screams of the lost past of an effective public transportation system and of a gentility that has long departed from our scene. But the granddaddy of them all is the Outer Harbor. The number of grand plans for that area must occupy a shelf or two in both city and county halls. As explained in Part II, in 1955, the redevelopment of the waterfront was given over to the Niagara Frontier Port Authority, the immediate ancestor of the Niagara Frontier Transportation Authority. For nearly fifty years, the public achievements of this effort at redeveloping a plot of abandoned railroad tracks and failed commercial ventures consisted mostly of grandiose ideas, opposed by this or that scrap of the active public community, including, especially, our now only newspaper, and the construction of a small boat harbor. Eventually, a political squeeze that transferred the property to a different entity secured for the region the modestly attractive waterfront park, parts of which its citizens might have enjoyed while waiting for the perfect plan and for possible residential development whose appropriateness provides another occasion of public squabbling, currently about a concert venue.

Though it would be implausible to assert that the region called Buffalo has an obvious economic strength and equally implausible to assert that it is possessed of a viable political unit or culture that might act to take advantage of any existing economic strength were there such, it cannot be said that there have been no attempts on the part of government/law in the region to support development. There have been many such attempts. It is just that, at best, none of them have been more than modestly successful. In order to understand why this is so, one must return to Jane Jacobs on transactions of decline.

The Difficulty of Avoiding Transactions of Decline

Why is it so difficult for communities to avoid transactions of decline? After all, no one likes dependency, contrary to recurrent statements about welfare mothers and recipients of disability benefits. It is spirit crushing to be robbed of one's independent dignity, that is, if the spirit of the dependent has not already been crushed by the circumstances leading to dependency. Thus, public officials do not like to go begging any more than poor people do, but such is what dependents must do. To maintain dignity, public officials always recharacterize the task of begging. We are selling the community or the university or the charity, they say, or bringing administrators, legislators, graduates up to date on what we have been doing or keeping in touch with our constituencies. These are just some of the euphemisms for a task that no sensible person wishes to have to do.

For units of government, begging by officials is impossible to avoid once decline sets in, for with decline the need for revenue increases at the same time that receipts from the usual sources of revenue—property taxes, sales taxes, even income taxes—decrease and the needs of constituents—voters—increase, generally disproportionately. In the City of Buffalo, for example, the cuts in staffing at the Police and Fire Departments are a not particularly open scandal, but a scandal nonetheless. So, in some sense, begging is part of the job description. However, "begging for what" and "begging for whom" are crucial questions often elided (or worse, conflated) by advocacy directed at government/law. Let us start with the fractious question of "begging for whom," a question about economic class.

The devolution of cries for economic development from, "Make this place just like it once was," through, "Provide jobs that will keep our children here," on to "Provide jobs that will keep current adults here," to "Bring us any jobs, good jobs!" finally landing on the plaintive, "Bring jobs . . . please," is both heartrending and evidence of failure to understand the significance of ghost towns. Jobs don't come because one wants them. They may come even though one doesn't want them. They do not necessarily come to neighborhoods that need them. They often come to neighborhoods that don't need them. Economies are thus mysterious and unpredictable. The best one can do is to prepare the ground for their arrival and hope. Unfortunately, in Buffalo (and possibly similar places) thinking about and doing economic development suffers from separate objects of attention: the poor, the working classes seen as an undifferentiated whole, and the middle classes. Start with the easiest of these objects—the poor.

It is a mistake to believe that economic development will alleviate poverty to a significant extent. The mixture of social deficits, language deficits, and various incapacities, addictions, and discriminations that abound in poor communities are so complicated that a job, even a better job with a "living wage," is unlikely to "lift," an odd spatial metaphor, someone out of poverty. Which is not to say that money, whether coming through grants or wages, will not make the lives of poor people better. The lack of money aggravates these debilitating conditions. Economic development may make it easier for poor people to secure the necessary money to do the "lifting" by one's own bootstraps without the aid of tax-funded transfer payments. Still, it is important to remember that contrary to what the economists tell us over and over, the economic tide rarely, if ever, raises all boats, much less all boats equally. It is a mistake either to focus on or confuse economic development with solving the problem of poverty, other than in the sense of making money a bit easier for poor people to secure, for much of the problem that is poverty has little to do with the economy.

Why is it important to remember this? Poor people do vote, even if not in large numbers. And poor people are geographically segregated in this, and many other areas of this country into political entities such as the City of Buffalo. They thus get their own representatives who need to get reelected. To do so, they just as much as every other representative, need to deliver services to their constituents—help with the bureaucracy and an occasional job within and without that bureaucracy. In particular, they also need occasions to call attention to the things that they have done for their district. Generally, this means photo-ops, getting one's picture on television, or at least in the paper, hopefully standing in the front row, always crowded together with others who are responding to the same imperative. Down a tier is a picture on an official website in business attire or with a hard hat and shovel breaking ground or with a big scissors opening something or delivering an oversized check to a local organization, while trying not to look too silly. Still lower is standing behind a podium announcing a program. Lowest is the common press release touting some more intangible achievement. To garner such occasions, local representatives will try to drive what are commonly, but most-often wrongly, treated as if they were economic development funds into the area such elected officials represent.

Securing economic development projects, and so campaign publicity materials, will however, do close to nothing for local or area economic development in districts full of the poor. Poor people need better neighborhoods. They need supermarkets, dry cleaners, drugstores, gas stations, restaurants, and childcare providers, and similar privately supplied "public facilities." They need safe, secure, airy, affordable housing. They need clean, well-lit, and well-maintained streets and parks, libraries, good public transportation, good sewers, good schools, good police protection, and even baskets of flowers in summer. However, in their case, these things are matters of simple humanity. Provision of such, or even of facilities like community centers, are probably better seen as community development projects and should not be confused with, or undertaken as exercises in, economic development.

Perhaps elected officials know that commercial revitalization efforts, housing development, even streets and parks and libraries, are really community development projects, but feel that part of getting reelected, especially of remaining part of a majority party, requires that some nod, however ineffective, be made in the direction of delivering on economic development goals. And most often, such projects, under whatever rubric they are undertaken, are an unalloyed improvement in poor neighborhoods. They may also provide good photo-ops and something to crow about at election time. However, as economic development projects, they will fail. Retail sales is a small-margin business with a remarkably large requirement for working capital. Poor people in poor neighborhoods lack such working capital and so are not good candidates for bank loans either. Thus, capital will have to come from other neighborhoods and so profits will flow back into those neighborhoods. Thus, commercial revitalization will at best, create a few service jobs—cashiers, stockers—for local residents. A few jobs do not remake a poor neighborhood.

The same is true of residential development and the provision of absolutely essential public amenities. New construction, or even rehabilitation of existing structures, may create a few jobs in the local community, but most of the employment will benefit other areas because these are places where the people who already have the needed skills choose to live. Indeed, if there were a significant number of people in the local area with the needed skills, that area would, by definition, not be poor. Some local residents might learn or improve skills on such projects, but such growth in skills does not generally lead to founding a flourishing construction company, much less a construction materials supply company, the kinds of businesses that might actually be part of an economic development effort. Thus, talked of as economic development, commercial revitalization, housing, or community facility construction will eventually be judged a failure and, as such make life worse, for failed expectations make life grayer.

Of course, economic development in an area may mean that some poor people will have more money, though of course, in some cases, more money will be undermined by the gentrification of their neighborhoods. But seeing that poor people have more money, even so-called earned income, as if just living isn't an entitlement to some income, will not bring economic development to a poor area. Thus, however attractive as a matter of election and reelection politics, even to speak of, much less to focus economic development on the problems of poor people, especially in the central cities where poor people are concentrated, is a serious mistake, a category mistake, and an embarrassment as such.

Problems of the working classes, groups of individuals who hold, or wish to hold factory jobs, construction jobs, transportation jobs and service jobs of the kind that, in America, were or might have been, unionized in the 1950s, are quite clearly problems of economic development. The difficulty with such a statement is that it is very difficult to decide whether, at this time and in regions such as Buffalo, economic development is likely to be able to address these problems.

The story of the transformation of the great mass of subsistence farmers, native or immigrant, into factory hands and thus into the working class, and the simultaneous fight of middle-class artisans determined not to be reduced to working-class status by the displacement of traditional artisanal methods of production with newer factory methods, has often been told and just as often forgotten. More well known, but less remarked on, is the transformation of a part of the working class into the lower-middle class during the 1950's. This transformation, best identified with the ability to purchase a small, newly constructed suburban house, came largely through the unionization of great swaths of the factory labor force at a time when the United States economy was significantly protected from international competition because European and Pacific industry had been devastated by World War II. It marked the creation of the contemporary structure of most Northeastern and Midwestern cities. Lower-middle class incomes allowed otherwise working-class individuals to migrate from central cities to suburban locations, leaving behind an unstable mix of poor people, minorities of various economic levels, and upper-middle, and sometimes upper-class families devoted to urban living, but dependent on private alternatives to increasingly decrepit public schools.

As ought to be perfectly clear to anyone who has not been living in a hermetically sealed environment over the past thirty-five to forty-five years, for all practical purposes, the economy that made such a transformation possible disappeared in the late 1970's and early 1980s. This new portion of the middle class initially coped by shifting to a two-wage earner model of family life. Such a model is, at best, precariously stable; the loss of one job immediately tosses a family into first, increasing debt, then relative poverty. Adding insult to this ever-present possibility of devastating injury is the transformation of norms in the upper reaches of the middle class, where the gradual acceptance of college-educated women in the workforce at professional or near professional, if not necessarily equal salaries, accompanied by a further extension of the model of the two-wage earner family, has created a great gulf between the income of blue-collar middle class and that of the white-collar middle classes.

The decline of mass factory employment and its replacement with a model, called "advanced manufacturing," closer to that of the traditional machinist's job shop, together with the explosion of computerized manufacturing processes, means that individuals who are comfortable in securing some postsecondary education and simultaneously are willing to adjust to irregular, but necessary, changes in highly specialized employment that do not generally offer an obvious path for advancement, are at a premium in the workforce. This change indirectly, but seriously, raises the question of whether the now largely vanished, unionized lower-middle class of mass production factory employees sought their factory jobs, so-called grunt work, because they were easily available, if deadening, and fit a certain macho image of what a "proper" working man might do for a living. An alternative understanding might be that such jobs were at the limit of these workers' abilities, sometimes intellectually but probably more often in terms of a preference for learning and working with one's hands, as opposed to the butts in seats method of education and the employment opportunities that flow from such a preference.

These alternatives are of course, not really an either/or but partly a cultural question and partly a question of learning style and a lot in between, as Mike Rose's work has shown.[18] Unfortunately, it is a question that few people engaged in economic development are paying attention to. The mantra of jobs, jobs, jobs that fits a political need when it comes to constituent service and reelection, assumes that jobs are fungible, except with respect to salary. This is surely not true. If the flood of young men and old into factories was mostly a question of culture and availability, then perhaps any well-paying job will do, though one should remember that: culture eats structure for breakfast. If, however, this flood was a result of hard-wired intellectual preferences for learning and working hands-on, then there are real problems hidden in the notion that pretty much any economic development will bring jobs that will revitalize an area for the benefit of the working classes.[19]

The fabled "New Economy," is not friendly toward hands-on learning and working. Look at some of the sectors touted as part of that economy. Advanced manufacturing is not hands on; lab bench medical technology is hands on in part. Logistics, a small, retail part of a just-in-time economy, is still pedal to the metal, except when it requires computerized recordkeeping above the level of the local FedEx delivery person and increasingly, this is what long-distance trucking has become. Back office/professional support is all butts-in-seats learning and work. Computer-geek jobs seem to be butts-in-seats work, except possibly for system maintenance. If great swaths of the working classes share a preference for hands-on learning and working, then there are real problems that all the efforts in the world directed toward economic development will have trouble dealing with, at least as part of, the New Economy.

This potential mismatch between preferences for learning and possibilities for employment is made more serious by another mismatch. The period for returning an investment in capital goods is significantly shorter than a working life. For individual workers, skills do not accumulate over the years in the way that invested capital is supposed to accumulate. Redeploying capital after ten to fifteen years is far easier than redeploying labor after the same number of years. In the no-more-than-five-year horizon of the private equity crowd, or the three years of the high-tech entrepreneurs, redeployment of labor is impossible, except for the most flexible of recent college grads in low-level administrative jobs and for computer geeks, once the love of the venture capital crowd, both groups of whom share an even shorter attention span. This is not a matter of old dogs and new tricks, but of sunk costs that have created a life that, though fragile to the cosmos, is solid to the humans in question. For these humans, the long run of capital recovery may never come. This is a serious political problem.

From time to time, it is suggested that those members of the working class who cannot make it as part of the New Economy have a future in a remnant of the old one, as home maintenance, repair and remodeling craftsmen, or maybe as local store owners. Small businesses of these kinds are likely to be more of a curse than a blessing. First, small businesses require working capital, and while the working classes have more of such than the poor, it is unlikely to be true that there is enough in most such households. Even if there were, given the failure rates of small businesses, it would be quite foolhardy for a business advisor to suggest that putting the available cash into a small business was a good investment. Better a CD or no-load mutual fund, preferably an index fund.

Second, suggestions such as these ignore the importance of unionized work in the transformation of portions of the working class into the middle class. Small businesses, even relatively successful ones, have lumpy income streams. A middle-class lifestyle is built on more secure income streams, on salary not on wages. What unionized factory employment provided was the reasonable assurance of a regular paycheck. It turned wages into something a good bit like salaries. With an income stream that showed some resemblance to a salary, it was possible that wages could be made to support mortgage payments, as well as car payments, and boat payments, and furniture payments, and pool payments. Indeed, as a result of this transformation, the working class had available to it the entire panoply of middle-class schemes for financing capital expenditures that once were relatively merchant specific extensions of credit, but that now, except for houses and cars, are mostly credit card debt. A return to lumpy income streams, even with ownership, or maybe especially with ownership, is not obviously anything other than an example of second best, foisted on the working classes in the name of acting in their best interests.

The lack of good alternatives to traditional working-class jobs is a serious problem. The working classes vote, more than do the poor. They are less spatially segregated than the poor, spread over city and suburbs and, when searching for inexpensive housing, semirural areas as well. Still, those who represent them, just as those who represent the poor, need photo-ops. Representatives in predominantly working-class areas favor public investment in new and improved parks, boat ramps, and stadia, whether high school or vaguely professional, seemingly on the assumption that the children of the working classes need healthy outdoor activities and their parents, family diversions. These are, of course, community development projects again spoken of as if they were something else, usually sold with the only modestly true mantra that extensive community amenities attract jobs. These representatives also regularly express significant support for expenditures that improve educational opportunities for both children and young adults.

While educational expenditures surely benefit some portion of the working classes, the difficulty with other public facilities such as those identified above is that they assume the existence of surplus income that, in many cases, perhaps most, is not there. They are investments for the higher parts of the middle classes. That said, some sympathy ought to be offered to the officials in predominantly working-class areas needing reelection. It is not clear exactly what public expenditures other than in education might possibly help their constituents. While no such representative would pass up the chance to stand proudly in front of a new, or reopened, factory in locales that need such, those chances are few. Pictures taken in front of a site where adding a new product line means buying one big machine and hiring three additional workers are not likely to bring forth great public acclaim. Likewise, pictures taken in front of a school announcing that school taxes are being raised to lengthen the school day so that children get a more complete education, or in front of a community college where those taxes would go toward expanded retraining of individuals who have lost their jobs, are little better. None of these events will have much political traction even with those individuals for whom factory work was mostly a question of culture and availability. For those who have a more hard-wired intellectual preference for learning and working hands on, such events are mostly irrelevant, possibly a sham.

For both groups, infrastructure is probably a better investment, though seldom does one see a local representative standing proudly in front of a big hole in which a new storm drain is being sunk, or in front of a street torn up for resurfacing, for while the project is going on, the lives of these voters are being seriously disrupted. And brownfields being remediated seldom gather photo-ops either, being work done based on hope without reason. And so again, it is not clear that if such public economic development activities are undertaken, they are going to be of much use to those for whose lives are intended to be benefited.

What then of the middle classes,[20] often described as the backbone of stable government and society? Two things are odd when considering their problems, problems that are more like hangnails than are the problems of the poor and working classes. First, it is at least possible, perhaps likely, that the economic health of an area can be correlated with the relative size of the middle classes in that area. The larger the middle classes, the healthier the local economy. "Correlation" needs to be used carefully. It is very difficult, indeed probably impossible, to decide causation—whether it is the existence of relatively large middle classes that cause economic growth or whether economic growth brings about the development of relatively large middle classes. And it may make no difference.

Second, the middle classes' fears about the insecurity of their own position and that of their children make them particularly ungracious with respect to anything that they believe, however rightly or implausibly, might result in a diminution of their comfort—read here home value, or their children's schooling—read here college admission prospects. They will NIMBY to death any change in their settled ways, even when they benefited from similar changes at an earlier point in time. As they have the time and other resources that enable them to become politically active at the drop of a hat, they most often get their way in matters of public dispute, even when doing so undermines their own obvious economic interests.

To work in reverse order, why fear? The middle classes cover a great range of social position in the United States. Mostly white collar, though surviving pockets of well-paid, unionized, blue-collar employment still exist, in general, the middle classes are demarked by the possession of varying amounts of postsecondary education ranging from the two years now required of new recruits to the City of Buffalo's police force, to the post-professional degree residencies/fellowships that have proliferated in medicine and the sciences. The real hallmark of middle-class social position is a certain amount of income available for discretionary spending—while one can be a spendthrift at any level of income, one has to be at least middle class before qualifying as a miser—and yet, the absence of significant inherited wealth. The fear is, of course, that somehow that income will run out.

And such fear is easy to understand. In the years between 1962 and 1980 (to choose arbitrarily, but carefully), the Fifties economy of high wages and secure employment collapsed. It was in that economy, an economy insulated from significant international competition and surprisingly free from significant technological change, that the middle classes expanded in scope and number. Their expansion instantiated the New Deal's Associationalist understanding of a well-run economy; creating such an economy was the point of the New Deal reforms.

The impact of that economy's collapse can be seen in at least two ways. First is the experience, common to individuals born in the Fifties, of being able to deliver to their children a relatively lush lifestyle but realizing that these children are finding it difficult to earn current income equivalent to that of their parents at the same point in their careers. Second is the disappearance of the New Deal's basic impulse to spread the society's wealth because there would be, and then magically there was, more to go around. As that possibility became less and less the case, Lyndon Johnson's Great Society programs turned into the more middle-class environmental programs of the Nixon administration and then sputtered out entirely. Tax cutting, the withdrawal of marginal dollars gathered for the purpose of spreading the wealth, and the redirection of those dollars into maintaining social position, became the cause of choice. This cause is best illustrated by one of its earliest manifestations, California's Proposition 13, which protected homeowners who had seen the value of their investment in housing—the rock-bottom, middle-class asset—soar faster than their income and thus found their middle-class status threatened because greater real estate taxes on the increased value of their property were eating into the disposable income that measured their social status. Afraid, and perhaps rightly so given economic trends, the middle classes became defensively stingy. They remain so today.[21]

Fear reduction through economic development is a possible strategy, though it is doubtful that it could be a successful one. Still, the modest correlation between the relative size of the middle classes and the economic strength of an area suggests that it might be sensible to focus economic development on the presumed needs of the middle classes, while keeping in mind that the correlation might, in the end, turn out to be spurious. If this suggestion were to be followed, one might reason in two ways from the somewhat obvious proposition that, to be middle class is to be able to undertake a significant amount of discretionary spending.

First, if ever there were a case of demand creating supply, this is it. If there is potential money sloshing around, eventually people will come to provide occasions for spending it. And once such opportunities appear in a given locale, others will come to try those opportunities, bringing, thereafter, other suppliers. Soon it will be said that the area is a "happenin' place." While it would be a clear mistake to refer to such a process as a virtuous circle, it is not inappropriate to notice that this is what has happened on Hertle Avenue in Buffalo once the street and its scape were rebuilt. A middle-middle class neighborhood began to put discretionary spending into businesses that somehow seemed to be newly attractive and soon, suburbanites started following.

Second, consider the possibility that with more places to spend, more people might be attracted to an area were jobs are available. And if there were more people who might be willing to come, more people able to create jobs might be willing to try to do so. If more people were to try to create jobs and some succeeded, then there would be more places to spend discretionary income and so more people who might be willing to come bringing more people able to create jobs who might be willing to try to do so. This is closer to a virtuous circle. It is surely the assumption upon which Richard Florida's work on the "Creative Class" is built.[22] It may be the assumption on the basis of which much contemporary economic planning proceeds.

It is important to recognize that, however sensible, a choice to focus on the middle classes, their needs, and desires, as those who are most likely to bring economic development to the region called Buffalo presents a real political problem, not to mention a possible moral failure. These are the people least in need of help from government/law in its pursuit of economic development. The working classes pay taxes, and the poor as well, at least to the extent that their purchases are subject to sales tax and their rent contributes to the payment of property taxes. Surely tax expenditures, broadly defined, that take from the poor and working classes to benefit the middles classes are suspect public activities. Such a plan would require a serious justification that might well be hard to supply.

Having pondered the question of "begging for whom," it is time to turn attention to the other question, that of "begging for what," and so to return to Jane Jacobs and speak of what it is best not to beg for. Here is where politics and economic development meet with difficult consequences. Jane starts her list of transactions of decline with "prolonged and unremitting military production."[23] Although the combination of Bell, Moog, Cornell Labs, the steel plants, and various unnamed government contractors up through the Vietnam War years might be seen as enough to qualify Buffalo, there has been precious little of such military production in the region for the past twenty-five to forty years and in decreasingly fewer places nationwide. Whether the current economic situation shows the effect of the withdrawal of such production is unclear, though doubtful. The region's addiction to protecting the tiny little airbase in Niagara Falls from the relentless Pentagon budget cutters counts for something, but it is surely not a big contribution to the regional economy, though it may be so with respect to the local economy of Niagara Falls and the adjoining town Wheatfield.

The second item on Jacobs's list, "prolonged and unremitting subsidies to poor regions,"[24] is another matter entirely. For the past forty plus years, it appears as if the only activity that the region's congressional and state legislative delegations engage in is helping local politicos (yes, this is not just a matter of the City of Buffalo) secure funding from the state and federal governments. The most constant beneficiary of these efforts is the state subvention required to keep the Buffalo Public School system from completely imploding; but bridges, highways, ports, airports, rivers, streams, building repairs, environmental remediation and our funny little subway with its related bus system are all the beneficiaries of the state and federal, and even occasionally county, largess. Items such as historic preservation and affordable housing tax credits should not be forgotten either.

Now, obviously the region does reap benefits for these efforts of our various legislators and executives. But the question comes, at what cost? In one sense, the answer is at no cost. Except for the sham of the special school aid for the state's biggest cities, most of these funds are supplied out of state and federal programs of general availability, or at least they were much more such until the revival of legislative earmarking at the federal level, a practice that often was, and surely will again become, an open embarrassment. Unfortunately, of course, that the existence of such funds for capital projects perpetuates, because it partially makes up for, a system of local taxation based on existing political units that often makes little or no economic sense. All these units are limited in their ability to incur debt by legislation or constitutional provisions that together pretty much guarantee that local political units will remain dependent on state and federal governmental largess. The standard mechanism for avoiding these limitations, the establishment of a public authority that has a continuing stream of income that could be used to pay off its debt, radically limits capital investment for other than a very narrow range of infrastructure needs. Enforced dependency does little in the direction of developing a modest amount of economic self-sufficiency.

Jacobs's third item on her list of transactions of decline is "heavy promotion of trade between advanced and backward economies."[25] Here is where Buffalo has put its small amount of money, not that Buffalo is unusual in its choice. Still, one would think that with the region's—here today, gone tomorrow—experience as a branch plant town in industries such as steel (Bethlehem, Hanna Furnace, Republic, Wickwire), autos (Chevrolet, Fedders, Ford, Harrison, Trico), electrical equipment (Western Electric, Westinghouse), chemicals (Allied Chemical and Dye, Hooker Chemical, Union Carbide), and banking (Norstar/Fleet, HSBC), the region would have avoided, *at all costs*, branch plants of national or international corporations. But that is not the case.

The reason is simple. The desperate plaint noted above, "Bring jobs . . . please," is hard for any politician to resist, and not senselessly. After all, there are some short-term problems that, if left to fester, preclude long-term solutions. Community survival is one of them. Without jobs, a community becomes a retirement home and soon thereafter, a ghost town. Ghost towns don't hold elections and so don't need politicians.

The political response to this need for jobs of any kind has been to create local, regional, or statewide industrial development agencies/authorities or IDAs. Originally, they were designed to help firms from outside the local area build new facilities by offering lower cost financing through a clever manipulation of legal form. As the IDA was a public entity, it could borrow at a cheaper rate than the private firm. And so, the public entity would borrow the money necessary to purchase the real property and to build the desired facility on that property, then lease the completed project to the firm that wanted to move into the area at a cost that would pay off the public entity's debt. The cost saving was the difference between the cost of borrowing by the IDA and that of the potential employer plus the avoidance of some income tax by turning not deductible mortgage repayments into deductible rental payments.

Lots of these deals were done until the mid-Eighties when federal tax law was changed to make them impossible to do for other than nonprofit entities. At this point what local IDAs could then and still offer is the elimination of local taxes and occasionally state taxes, generally sales taxes on the materials used in construction, and the reduction of real estate taxes on the resulting structure for a given, negotiable number of years to an amount established by contract in a PILOT (payment in lieu of taxes) agreement.

The shift from reducing taxes owed to the federal government to taxes owed to local governments immediately turned these programs into local political issues but did not change the idea—create incentives for locating new, or expanding old, plants in a community. Although there is much disagreement about the effectiveness of the programs undertaken by IDAs, the real problem that they highlight is that there is no certainty what their name, "industrial," means any more, as evidenced by the fact that sometimes the older ones have changed the first word in their name from "industrial" to "economic" and the newer ones mostly have used "economic" from the beginning.

Arguments over what counts as "industrial," apparently a narrower category than "economic," are difficult. The reality in the Buffalo region is that most economic development programs produce white-collar jobs, many going to college graduates, or various versions of advanced manufacturing that assume some community college education. These are unlikely to count as replacements for the industrial jobs whose disappearance so decimated the hourly middle class in Buffalo, or if they are such replacements, suggest that the cultural understanding of the preference for factory work is the correct one, despite the fact that a good deal of popular culture that goes under the name of "country music" suggests to the contrary.

And so, the "for whom" question quickly returns, even after having been intentionally set aside. This reappearance is easy to understand because, when tied together with Jacobs's observation about backward-advanced trade, for that is what we are talking about whenever these programs are used to bring new plants to the area, the "for whom" question is far more significant than most of the petty complaints about these programs raised in the local community—questions such as: Should the rehab of an aging hotel count as redevelopment; Might it be sensible to rehab gray fields such as abandoned malls or strip plazas, even though they are going to create more traffic and so rile the neighbors; Will the firm actually deliver the number of jobs promised; Should we help hotels as against medical offices as against retail as against entertainment; Will these be living-wage jobs; Should the expansion of local firms be supported; Might projects be limited to circumstances where "but for" the assistance, the project would not be done; et cetera, et cetera, and so forth?

All of these subjects of dispute are really about the appropriateness of a project to the needs of the neighborhood in which the project will be erected, for in the case of new facilities sought by national corporations, the national norm from which the bidding starts is to provide such incentives. For more local projects, a neighborhood without a grocery store or pharmacy or a bank, all cry out for support. In a neighborhood with plenty of these, and many other things, support may be unnecessary.

If a community engaging in backward-advanced trade is only staving off inevitable decline, then who is benefitted by governmental support for such trade, who is likely to secure the kind of jobs that will be newly available, is a damn important question? If the answer is kids with college degrees who could just as easily emigrate to some other part of the United States where jobs for such graduates are readily available, then maybe a second or third thought ought to be given to the appropriateness of governmental support, however much parents may wish to have their children live nearby.

Think back to cluster theory discussed in Part III. What does one do if one may have the makings of a cluster of firms in a particular economic sector that essentially requires postsecondary education of potential employees? Consider higher education; Buffalo might have such a cluster if its institutions of higher learning could get their acts together. As noted, higher education is a good export industry. Kids come; kids go. Meanwhile the administrators and faculty—nationwide there are more of the former than the latter, so the order is correct—supply a solid cohort of middle-class incomes in the community. Is it therefore a good idea to try to keep more of these students from exporting themselves? Boston seems to have kept lots of the graduates of its institutions of higher education. Is doing so therefore a good idea?

This appears to be a hard question. It is both tangential to the activities of IDAs and important for understanding contemporary society. If hourly working-class jobs are not to be found in great numbers, then the failure to secure employers who are able to provide such jobs can hardly be lain at the door of IDAs. At the same time, the impoverishment of a whole segment of the American work force is hardly a trivial matter to be laid off on a failure to secure necessary postsecondary education skills, as is indirectly suggested from time to time. The problem we have here is not like that of children being sent to bed because they ate too much candy and couldn't finish their dinner. Again, it might be argued that an expansion of middle-class jobs might lead to an expansion of working-class jobs, but the mechanism of such an expansion is by no means clear, and if the assumption is that the necessary jobs will come from construction, home remodeling, and maintenance work, there is a real problem with that assumption too.

The hourly middle class thrived because it had secured something close to a salary, the rock on which a middle-class existence is built. Construction, remodeling, and maintenance are anything but salary-like employment. Employment in these fields is highly correlated with the cycle of economic activity and with warm weather. Yes, there were layoffs in the mills and factories during recessions, but at least under unionized conditions, seniority protected those who would have found relocation most difficult and for the rest, unemployment insurance supplied a bit of a cushion. Intermittent employment has never fared well in any domestic unemployment insurance scheme because such schemes try to tie compensation to contributions from employers. Only after a significant number of years of continuous employment do the employer contributions begin to cover even the modest benefits provided. Thus, providing such benefits to individuals who work intermittently is an economic problem for the funder of such benefits that either militates against providing them or leads to complaints from employers that provide more continuous streams of employment.

Perhaps construction, remodeling, and maintenance jobs are the best that can be provided for the once hourly middle class with a preference for "working with ones' hands" if that this preference is cultural, but not therefore any less real. In some sense it is more real, for it is a deep understanding of the self. One can understand the fury of a class of people whose social status has been diminished by economic change and who, at the same time, is regularly told not only that there is nothing to be done, but also shown that society will work hard and invest money to expand jobs for people who have a far different understanding of the self, of white-collar, college-educated people who look down on people working with their hands. If the preference is somehow a more hardwired preference for how to learn, at best, it is likely that fury will be replaced by despair. Hardly a net gain. In such circumstances, subsidies designed to secure more jobs for white-collar, college-educated people seem to be a rather cruel political choice that would require much deep thought and an extraordinarily strong belief that an increase in middle-class jobs will necessarily be followed by an increase in working-class jobs.

When one puts Jacobs's reasons for avoiding the dependency that comes with backward-advanced trade as explored in Part III, together with the limited range of jobs in which such trade is possible, and the segment of the population that is perforce excluded from the limited economic assistance that we, as a society provide, it is difficult not to conclude that a certain caution ought to be exhibited before entering into transactions that are not specifically directed at the original objects of our concern for industrial economic life. Not that there should be no such transactions undertaken, but that agreements that foster backward-advanced trade need to be entered into cautiously. It may be very sensible to attempt to build a large middle class. But action directed at doing so may not be the best idea. This is especially true given that it is hard to know when, much less if, rain will come to improve a local economy. Perhaps it would be better to undertake projects that would allow a middle class to be happy to bring ideas that have a possibility of bringing economic growth to the area and happy to stay if these ideas do bring rain. It is this possibility that needs to be addressed next.

Making Buffalo Attractive to the Middle Classes[26]

In a democracy of the middle classes, the central questions are and should be about the middle classes, about what makes for a strong set of middle classes. What will bring the upper classes to part with their money, is an important question, but not central to this question. As concerns investments, they will part with their money on such terms as they choose and, as to supporting government, they will have to be content to part with their money as others may choose. For this reason, the upper classes might best choose good works over family dynasties. And, as for the poor, it is important to remember that moral obligations are often slighted when money is scarce. In a world where rain is both infrequent and unpredictable, the middle classes, who no more than the upper classes deserve their position, however much they may think they have earned it, should remember that generosity is a virtue and there but for the grace that is rain, might each of us walk.

What might bring the middle classes to a city, to the region called Buffalo even, and if rain came, cause them to stay, is not the precise question that needs to be asked. Cheap land, labor, and capital, and nearby necessary resources would answer that question, however, at the cost of continuing to drive the hourly middle class out of its social position and ignoring the poor. Such would not be a good thing. So, the precise question that needs to be answered is: What might bring the middle classes to come to a city and if rain came, cause them to stay, that at the same time, would benefit the hourly middle classes and hopefully ameliorate the lot of the poor? On one sunny afternoon my friend Les Foschio and I came up with slogan that has long seemed to me to is a good place to start. The middle classes want their communities to be safe, clean, and beautiful.

Start with safe. Jane Jacobs defined safe as having plenty of people on the street all day and most of the night. However, she was talking about Manhattan and, as it has turned out, most cities are not like Manhattan. So, one needs to understand safety in more place-specific terms. A good example for refocusing Jacobs's discussion is suburban life. Why are suburban enclaves safe? It is not because there is nothing to steal or because they have lively streets, but because they are socially homogeneous. The homogeneity helps distinguish strangers who may be up to no good from the people who belong there. Can this be racist? Classist? Snooty? Of course. But it is also why, in such neighborhoods, the best disguise for a would-be thief is an appropriate car or a truck that labels the occupant as a person likely to have been hired to do some job like home repair or gardening or utility meter reading or appliance delivery.

In less socially homogeneous neighborhoods, a frequent, but irregular police presence is often a necessary substitute, in apartment buildings, a concierge or doorman. The lack of both is part of what made high-rise public housing such a disaster. But the important thing to remember is that safety is neighborhood specific. A low-income neighborhood where most of the residents are homeowners is more likely to be safe with less need for police attention than one where most of the residents are renters. A neighborhood in transition from the former to the latter is probably in need of the most police presence.[27]

Why start with this topic? Police and doormen are expensive. Being the former is also dangerous and requires an enormous infrastructure to be effective. Being the latter assumes that an effective police force will provide necessary backup. Without a reasonable (and maybe unreasonable) guarantee of safety, the middle classes will avoid a city, or at best come in, and quickly leave, only to the limited areas where safety seems adequate. Money spent on safety is always money well spent. It says to residents that we want you to stay and to visitors that we want you to come. It is welcoming just as is a generously staffed fire department.

Next, clean. Clean, obviously refers to garbage and litter, and in Buffalo, snow plowing. Still, it might better be understood more widely. First, there is the issue of storm and sanitary sewers. If there is some alternative, no one will want to live in a place where streets regularly flood, and nothing is done about it. The same is true of places where sanitary sewers overflow, even if only into drainage ditches of local waterways. Second, there is the issue of roads. Clean streets that are regularly striped; regularly, but quickly and thriftily, repaved, preferably a bit at a time and on days and at hours when traffic is least interrupted; and are repaired without delay, also make a place attractive. Anything less is annoying in fact and in effect, since it indicates that a place is not welcoming to either its residents or possible visitors.

Beautiful is an obvious reference to parks and street trees and planters and vistas and architecture, the kind of things that fill Buffalo booster videos, all of which somehow believe that six months of good weather make up for the snow, as well as the gray, the mud, and the debris that appear after the snow disappears.[28] But there are lots of other details that count. New Mexico and Arizona decorate the overpasses that cross their interstate highways. Doing so says, we're happy to have you here; you might want to stop. In contrast the route from Buffalo's airport to downtown goes under many utilitarian street bridges, one modestly decorated foot bridge that looks like it is a cage for zoo lions passing through and a rusty railroad bridge that looks like it hasn't been painted since Calvin Coolidge was president. Farther down, the physically depressed section of that road, along what was once Humboldt Parkway, looks like retaining walls on rivers that routinely flood and yet, all over this country, there are noise barriers that might create the same effect, but are significantly less plain, sometimes even visually lively. Why would anyone feel welcomed to the City of Buffalo when driving downtown from the airport?

Embarrassingly, the big thing that the middle classes want but that is missing from this slogan is something that an economic development program can't supply—choice. Cars, houses, jobs, clothing, good grocery stores, restaurants are important, though, in the case of cars, as any large suburban parking lot will indicate, the choices the middle classes may make turn out to be rather narrower than those available. With respect to housing, some like suburban single-family homes, others urban apartments; some urban single-family houses, others suburban apartments. The list of possibilities could be longer and for many, the choice changes with age, family size, and station. For some sprawl is great, for others, anathema; for some old houses offer unparalleled possibilities, for others, only new construction will do. Walkable neighborhoods and small, hip shops; easily drivable neighborhoods and big chain stores. Shopping often; shopping seldom. Big gym, small gym, no gym, pool; public transportation, easy parking—preferably right near the door. But whatever the set of preferences at a time and place, the middle classes deeply dislike criticism of the choices they make, even if and for some especially if, such criticism comes from what objectively might be called "people like us." So, to best welcome middle-class people with middle-class income and hopefully marketable ideas, a community needs to have lots of choices available.

Admittedly, doing so is not made easy by the middle classes themselves, for the middle classes are deeply opinionated and not just on divisive social issues, but on the topics that taken as a whole, they want to be able to exercise choice about. As noted before, they will NIMBY any project that they feel will "change the neighborhood," that is, bring a possible decline in the value of "my house," with a ferocity that would make mother bears defending cubs seem negligent even, or maybe especially, if the change is directed at allowing other people the degree of choice that in principle is desirable. Almost all agree wholeheartedly with Senator Russell Long's adage, "Don't tax you; don't tax me; tax that fellow behind the tree!" And the self-righteousness that may be expressed on topics such as bike riding, eating organic, going green, staying fit, GMOs, mindfulness, pesticides, recycling, synthetic fabrics, or yoga can make one wish for the conversation to return to such weightless topics as the precise notes in a cabernet, the best barrels for maturing a single malt scotch, and the Bills' prospects for next season. Loving, and so welcoming, the middle classes can thus be hard. Satisfying them even harder.

There are, however, some things that the middle classes want that governments can supply that are less expensive than good streets and sewers, but still that would be experienced as welcoming to people who might possibly bring economic development to a community and keep it there—efficient government, not in the sense of low taxes, but in the sense of quick acting. Though potential and actual entrepreneurs almost always express their concerns about government in terms of too much regulation, that objection is generally, though not always, silly. Still, local and state regulation could be much better. Permitting and licensing could be, indeed should be, a one-stop, one-day, cafeteria-style enterprise, and the same is true of inspections. Whether the question is zoning, building, remodeling, health, signage, patio, parking, curb cuts, business licenses, tax identification numbers, or any of the dozens of topics relevant to starting a new, or improving an existing business, the purpose of regulation might best be that any citizen, but especially any entrepreneur, would need only to comply with regulations written in such a way as to minimize the need for time-consuming, formal, discretionary administrative action such as the endless variances needed under most zoning ordinances and planning as a community debate about aesthetics. This is what business friendly means, or anyway should mean. In supplying quick answers to straightforward questions, government would show that it understands that delay is costly. That would be welcoming, more welcoming than, for example, a process like that in the town of Amherst where the Planning Board first approves a site plan for a development and only afterward the Building Department starts over with work on the building permit, both increasing cost for developers and giving them the ability to change the concept for the development at a later point in time. Even better would be a process that would understand that regulations designed for new construction are likely inappropriate when applied to the rehab of older buildings, much less of seriously dilapidated buildings, at least in a city that has a surplus of such. Better still, would be the exercise of discretion in a way that recognizes that the actual circumstances of rule application are more important than the formal rule, and a willingness to defend that discretion in public. Such administration is the difference between sensible and senseless bureaucracy.

Unfortunately, the City of Buffalo or even the region that bears its name is not wealthy enough to tackle many of these things, and the political structure makes doing so impossible. Targeted investments in infrastructure are literally not made because that political structure is based on two principles. The first is, "If I don't get mine, nobody gets nothing." This principle makes it all but impossible to undertake legislative actions in circumstances where historic circumstances create problems only for some portion of a political unit's districts. It is also why the Community Development Block Grant program in the city amounted to nothing; the money had to be spread equally and equally was too thin.

The second principle is, "People, which is to say jobs, before things." This principle is why the area is thick with public employees, many of them on federal, or occasionally state, grants, none of whom make much money, and all of whom must have something to do. The result is that most any department is over supervised and understaffed. In such a world, any task must be taken very seriously, because if it were not, then the people doing and supervising that task might be in danger of losing their jobs. Very serious jobs take a lot of time, care, and concern to get them right, so delay becomes evidence of the importance of the task. This is the essence of bad bureaucracy.

However, it would be a mistake to place the blame for the inability to address problems in both city and suburbs on legislative and executive process alone. There is plenty of blame to go around. Principles of equality would require one also to include the willingness of the judiciary to jump in on zoning, siting, environmental, procedural, and jurisdictional fights in a community at the behest of any citizen who dislikes any decision and then to allow delay to do its subtle work.[29] That the Delaware courts can manage to dispose quickly and firmly of corporate litigation with many more zeroes on the tab than anything seen in local courtrooms in years, suggests that the courts in New York, like so much of the law everywhere, put formal equality ahead of substantive timeliness, lest judgment be criticized without the ability to mount a processual defense. Such behavior is anything but welcoming.

Indeed, delay is not only evidence of a community that is not welcoming, but also of one that is essentially hostile to change. In Buffalo newcomers who bring ideas and money are welcome, but only if existing hierarchies are respected, with the modest exception of investors who save local professional sports franchises, and even here, the objective stinks of resistance to change. Still, a much better, if less amusing, example of grudging acceptance of change can be found in the relationship between housing and economic development. The pleas for jobs and better housing for the poor and discriminated against are regularly accompanied with seemingly well-intentioned resistance to gentrification and sprawl, likely accompaniments to the desired objects.

Two things that are guaranteed to accompany increased economic activity, indeed, among the best evidence of its occurrence, are gentrification and sprawl. Some middle-class people will want to live in oversized houses on either oversized lots or undersized lots, but seldom on lots that gracefully blend with the size of the house. These homes need to be far enough away from employment as to provide the basis for complaints about the length of the daily commute, as if the complaint alone provided evidence of the importance of the job. Others will avoid sprawl with one of two gentrification strategies—either the tear down and build more grandly strategy or the find a place with "good bones," buy it cheap, and spend lots of money to recreate its glory strategy. The former upends an upper-middle class neighborhood; the latter, poor neighborhoods. Each gentrifies in its own way. Each is as ineluctable as B following A in the English alphabet.

In Buffalo's case, all who wish to see economic development, but neither sprawl nor gentrification should reconnect with the City of Buffalo's social history and recognize that after 1825, economic development brought sprawl and some gentrification in several directions for more than one hundred years. The recurrent objections to Irish and German and Polish and Black immigration over these same years was both an objection to religion, ethnicity or race, and to the disruption of settled relations among the city's peoples, and so was about resistance to change.

Hopefully, these observations make it clear that an economic development strategy that tries to make a community welcoming to the middle classes that might bring development possibilities and preferably not take such with them should they leave is neither an unalloyed good nor an unalloyed bad idea, for neither the new nor the old people in a community are without merit or fault. At the same time, hopefully these observations also have shown what kind of changes would be necessary to improve the chances that Buffalo, both the city and the region, and other similar places might have a chance of growing should rain come. However, the real plausibility of recognizing the indicated priorities depends less on such actions, standing alone, than on whether they will improve the lives of the people who once were, still are, or hope to be a part of the hourly middle class whose settled lives have been so totally disrupted over the past forty to fifty years.

The answer to this question seems to be determined in the same way as the minimum wage/living wage question. The relevant consideration is not how close to zero the obvious impact of the inevitable increase in prices on total employment is, but whether such an increase in prices will be greater than the benefit provided to the intended beneficiaries of the increase. After all, the rest of us can probably afford the higher prices. So too, here the relevant consideration is whether the cost in taxes of focusing governmental action on capital spending for infrastructure and reducing the time cost of administrative regulation (and perhaps the small civic improvement programs that would be foregone) is greater for the hourly working class than the value of better safety, cleanliness, beauty, possible time-savings in dealings with government and maybe eventually choice to these beneficiaries. The answer—that these benefits exceed the costs—seems clear, else spending twenty years working on this project would have been foolish. Others may, of course, come to a different conclusion.

And Well-Schooled

Embarrassingly, the slogan just now parsed didn't include "well-schooled" in what middle-class families look for in a community. Public K-12 education in America is a disaster area. While the disaster is not improved by not being thought about, or not being talked about, it is clear that most writers about economic development have nothing useful to contribute. Nonetheless, appended here are a few observations, all of which will solve nothing.

What is fairly agreed upon is that a large proportion of middle-class families see, and routinely enact, the proposition that education is key to maintaining social standing and hopefully advance. At the same time, it also could be fairly agreed that there is a proportion of the population that does not agree with this proposition, or is not able to, or at least seemingly enacts such disagreement. However, there is absolutely no agreement about why the latter group does not share the former's belief in the value of education and no amount of discussion is likely to reach agreement on this latter question. It also seems fair to state that the middle-class believers feel that their children's education, and so life chances, are threatened by the inclusion of children from families that do not share their belief in the value of education or at least the kind of education offered. They act on this belief by seeking out school districts that have as few children as possible from families whom they believed do not share their belief.

The Buffalo region has far more school districts than it needs, but the persistence of such fragmentation is relatively easily understood by the fact that most, or at least most of the schools within each, are relatively homogenous, as reflects the pattern of economic segregation in suburban neighborhoods. For that reason, most school boards are relatively functional and significant school board/teachers' union warfare is unusual, that is, except for the City of Buffalo. The Buffalo School Board has often been terminally fractured and its relationship with its teachers' union hasn't been even vaguely peaceful for at least thirty years. A recent Federal Civil Rights Division investigation of the magnet school program has only brought more discord.

Add to this the continued emptying out of the Catholic School system in both the city and much of the county and the similar effect of the charter school movement on the Buffalo Public Schools.[30] Thus, no one in their right mind would suggest that, in the city at least, there is any reason for middle-class parents to consider moving to Buffalo unless the cost of private schooling options, which are not very many, but are fairly good, are financially possible. None of this mess helps make the region attractive to middle-class parents. If one adds this problem to the lack of an obvious foundation on which to build an economic development strategy, the political attractiveness of backward-advanced trade, and the terrible political structure, the region's lack of growth seems fairly understandable.

Et Cetera

Occasionally, persons interested in the region called Buffalo today ask questions that might translate as, "What are the residents of Buffalo thinking that they are waiting for when they are in fact waiting for rain?" At times, when in their fragmented, fractious isolation, their dependent passivity and their hostility to outsiders and to change, they play the, "I get some too" game, it is easy to get the feeling that they really seem to believe that when rain comes it will bring back the Fifties of their imagination, one that was not heading for a disaster, but instead was heading for long-term growth that would leave most everyone safe and secure in their social and economic roles. And that is when it is appropriate to shout. That past is past! It will never reappear! Hopefully, Americans will again see an economy in which most everyone will be safe and secure in their social and economic roles, but it will be a different economy and it will be a different social and economic security. Tom Wolfe said it best, "You can't go home again."

Technologies change, social roles change, the economies of other places and nations change, understandings of the good change. History may rhyme, but it does not repeat itself, much less go in reverse. When rain comes, if it comes, it will be the rain of different technologies, different jobs, different roles, and a different understanding of economic and social security. Security is obviously the most important question for individuals at any point in time and economic security is different for different portions of the populace.

Right now, for the relatively wealthy, security is getting the most cash out of any job or investment as fast as possible for opportunities are often quite fleeting. For the upper-middle and lower-upper classes for whom security once was the likelihood that any job held for more than a few years would continue until retirement, security is harder to come by but is the ability to continually update skills and carefully save in tax-protected investment vehicles. For the rest of the middle classes, including the hourly middle class, tenuous security is provided by a combination of such things as government employment, a two-wage earner family, government-benefit programs, and knowing lots of people in lots of employment niches who might know of possible jobs when a current one disappears. What has disappeared for most of this group is the onetime security of the hourly middle class that came from unionized employment or its modest equivalent of generally shared expectations. This latter form of security is highly unlikely to reappear very soon.

The point of being open to a changed world and to the middle classes is that, with such openness, Buffalo can possibly take advantages of those different technologies, jobs, roles, and understandings to create a vibrant local economy, one that might deliver more economic and social security to it residents. Without such openness, the best we in Buffalo can hope for—after all, there are ghost towns throughout the American West and Nineveh completely disappeared—is to become a modest tourist attraction where people come to learn about a past that is dim to them, places like Salem, New Bedford, Saint Augustine, Leadville, Bisbee, Silverton, or New Harmony.

It would not be surprising if at this point readers expect to hear the suggestion that the residents of the region called Buffalo ought to draw a nice warm bath, slide into its comfort, and slit their collective wrists. Such a suggestion is, however, beyond imagination, because one can only be this angry about a place one loves. Sometimes it takes a four-by-four straight to the temple to get the mule's attention and that is what this Part is meant to be. In these unpromising circumstances there is no place for either nostalgia over, "The way we were," or for anger kept alive by picking at the scabs. So review once more, this time with feeling.

In a relative democracy, best understood as a middle-class or bourgeois democracy, private economic actors are, by definition, and can behave as part of, that democracy. Government actors, from time to time, can behave that way as well. One might expect that such actors would jump at a strategy based on the interests of the middle classes. Unfortunately, this region has an ossified, inbred private and public culture still locked in the Fifties and Sixties when it may have been born, littered with more interests that might block change than there are elected officials. Grudges often survive unto the biblical third or fourth generation, a survival aided and abetted by the fragmented local political structure and magnified by the concentration of the poor and African Americans within the city's boundaries, boundaries that can be traced back to the mid-Nineteenth Century and that are completely dysfunctional in the Twenty-First.

If one cannot gather together to look forward, back is easy, easier than it might seem. After all, when it comes to economy, law, the major tool of government, works best to slow the pace of economic change. Such is, of course, what local elites want so that they may work their existing capital investments down closer to zero and then move to Florida or Arizona, griping as they go about the passing of the good times.

Government can provide pleasant, often necessary, civic improvements. But, regularly, the creation of urban amenities, always a good thing best understood as community development, is confused with support for economic development. To be blunt, these projects generally offer little in the way of economic development other than a short-term boost in construction industry employment, often shamelessly supporting private actors who turn out to have been lucky in the investments they have made. Here too one regularly hears complaints from other successful actors: "Why don't I get some too?"

In contrast, government does quite poorly when it works to accelerate the pace of change. See, for example Ralph Wilson Stadium, which has brought exactly zero economic development to Orchard Park despite earlier assertions to the contrary that are currently being duplicated with little chance of change in the result, or the University at Buffalo Center in Amherst, which has taken years to bring ugly student housing and a few motels.[31] Neither project would have done any better had it been located on the waterfront, contrary to what decades of downtown Buffalo boosters have argued.[32]

Government decisions about public expenditures may advance development; still, caution is in order. Governmental actions taken in the name of advancing economic development objectives can easily impede economic development. Lack of water, sewers, roads, and transportation facilities can be a significant detriment, just as can poor investment in such facilities—the Buffalo subway comes immediately to mind.

Still, where economic development, however that might be understood, is concerned, looking forward is difficult since it may well be that the primary effective strategies will help the middle classes, those in the community that need such help the least, and so provide the least payoff for many elected officials and probably are threatening to existing elites. In such circumstances, it may be that looking backward is not the worst possibility. Still, one might hope for something better. Waiting until the old people die off and the poor and working class move away is not likely to be an effective economic development strategy. And Buffalo surely needs one.

Academics who publish observations related to current events are always asked, "Well, then, what should we do?" As if an education brings wisdom and not just perspective. It is in this circumstance and with this past that the relevant question needs to be remembered: If economic development is something a community can no more command than a farmer can command rain, what might be sensible advice to that community to occupy its time while waiting for possible rain? Three suggestions come to mind, none of them likely to be popular.

First, "Grow up!" For at least the 130 years, Buffalo's regional political culture has most obviously reflected the distribution snacks at a rather rowdy afterschool program. Mike Royko, the patron saint of comedic political commentary in this country and fixture in Chicago, made this point in a column of his that every person who claims to participate in the political life of the Buffalo region ought to remember when it comes time to respond to someone else's policy proposal. Slats Grobnick, the personal Everyman of Royko's muse, was a loyal foot soldier of the Chicago Democratic Party. After hearing the stirring words of Jack Kennedy at his inauguration—"Ask not what your country can do for you, ask what you can do for your county"—Slats repaired to the local ward committee meeting. Enthused by Kennedy's noble thought, Slats spoke at length at that meeting urging the Party to act on this uplifting credo. After he finished, the ward committeeman uttered equally stirring words—"What's in it for me?" It is time for us to stop being a community of ward committeemen from Chicago.

Second, the governmental action that is most likely to be a catalyst to economic development is a welcoming openness to it and no more than the tiniest amount of delay and public acrimony over the process.[33] A communitywide understanding that all economic development is going to displace existing commercial and social relations in any community would likely aid development as well. It is important to remember that it is only by displacing existing economic forces that capitalism earns its hoped-for returns on investment. In this region at least, the wish that economic development would come without capital destruction is a fantasy of English and German democratic socialism. Would that it were true.

Third, it is time for the middle classes to stop policing "my back yard" as if the value of that sacred piece of property was the be all and end all against which civilization is to be measured, and to stop the endless complaining about property taxes. Property taxes support the public schools and community colleges that make our children exportable. And, in any case, if any lesson can be gleaned from the history of democracy, the point of government is providing jobs for some of its citizens. Do not begrudge governmental employment; begrudge the low value of the uses to which it is put . . . moving paper slowly, writing useless reports, holding news conferences touting projects that amount to erasing a pimple on the elephant's behind, adding to the list of things that public education needs to be "very concerned" about and fighting on non-existent principle with other people who genuinely wish to be helping too.

PART V

What Then about America?

IT MUST SEEM MORE than a little incongruous that an author who bases a crucial argument on *Cities and the Wealth of Nations* should wish to speak about a national economy. After all, one of the rocks on which that book is built is Jacobs's assertion that there is no such thing as a national economy, only a collection of economies of cities and their regions. Unfortunately, this is a patently loopy assertion. However much that Jacobs's thought can help one to understand the economic history of a city/region such as Buffalo, it does not therefore follow that all of her ideas need be taken seriously. National economies exist. They are of course, significantly more complicated than city/region economies, if only because of the special problem of managing a national currency.[1] However, as a city's economy consists in trade among its citizens, so too, much of the American economy consists in trade among its citizens who, for local purposes, nevertheless correctly see some of that trade as part of import substitution and export creation. This is not a surprise in an economy as large as ours. Still, for analytical purposes, nations may prosper within the effectively larger market that is a great portion of the world, more or less in the same way that cities do within the nation. They grow through import substitution and export creation brought forth through the mysterious process sometimes called "innovation." And as is the case in city/regions, when national economies are not growing, the citizenry acts as if governmental action can and should bring forth rain. So, the real question for discussion at the national level is the same one that should be asked at the city level: What is plausible to be done while waiting for rain? We will get to that question soon.

Some Perspectives

To address the question of what to do while waiting for rain it is best to start first by remembering the subtitle of this book: Community, Economy, and Law in a Time of Change. I defined those terms in Part I. First, "economy" is *a persistent market structure that is the fusion of an understanding of economic life with the patterns of behavior within the economic, political, and social institutions that enact that understanding.* And second, "law" is *the many and variable actions undertaken by lawyers and other governmental officials, the formal and effective norms originating from the practices of these individuals, and the systematic presuppositions shared among them.* There were plenty of examples of change in the pieces that might make up an economy in Part I and an increasing amount of law. However, in that Part, little attention was paid to community and where community appeared it was mostly in terms of the sociological sense of class. In contrast, Part II also had many examples of change of the pieces that might make up an economy, but not much law. Community played a much greater role in that Part as the more general concept of class fissured along the lines of race, ethnicity, religion, and eventually political entity; each changed in salience over time. Part IV was much like Part II in its exploration of the topics set forth in the subtitle and this Part V will likewise be much like Part I in the topics discussed.[2]

Change is almost constant in a story of the American economy. The only time when change does not bulk large is in the Fifties and Sixties, and even then, change bulks large, only not in America. Change engulfed both Europe and Asia. In the past 150 years, Americans have seen changes in transportation—railroads, steamships, autos and trucks, great oil and natural gas tankers and the containerization of less than freighter-loads of goods. There have been changes in manufacturing—small factories replaced artisanal production, larger factories replaced smaller ones as interchangeable parts became the norm, then electric motors allowed factories to move away from hydropower and steam engines, while manufacturing moved from local to national to international with changes in transportation. Higher education expanded downward in the social hierarchy and this expansion was accompanied by the development of electronic technologies, pharmaceuticals, and medical devices that were the stuff of fantasy even in the Fifties and Sixties. Finance morphed from a distant utility serving mostly the well off, into a fearsome, because hard to manage, necessity for almost everyone. And as Robert J. Gordon made clear,[3] at least up until the Seventies there was an enormous, largely unmeasured, change in the American standard of living.

Law, other than the law of mine and thine, is not a constant in this story; it bubbles up from time to time until, in the Thirties and early Forties, it takes center stage, then all but disappears until the Seventies, after which it returns from time to time. Such appearances are the most important piece of the story, for when some citizens are hurt by economic change, they often go to law for relief. If these citizens are important enough, law tries to do something to address the hurt. This is the story of the memorable legislation before World War I as mentioned in Part I—the Sherman Act and the Clayton Act; the Interstate Commerce Act, the Elkins Act, and the Hepburn Act, and the Federal Reserve Act; as well as other legislation less directly related to competition, such as the Pure Food and Drug Act of 1906 that forbade interstate trade in mislabeled or adulterated foodstuffs or drugs and the Federal Trade Commission Act of 1914 that gave this commission the power to prevent unfair methods of competition and unfair or deceptive acts or practices; and the many attempts at labor legislation. So too of all the New Deal legislation and of deregulation and reregulation in transportation, communication, and finance starting in the Great Inflation and continuing even after the Great Recession. What is surprising, though, is that with all these examples, which together show that going to law is an ambiguous activity—sometimes law acts and sometimes it does not; sometimes, when it acts the citizens who hurt get what they want and sometimes they do not; and sometimes, when these citizens get what they want, law actually solves the problem, and sometimes it does not—still, citizens continue to go to law with a modest amount of optimism.

Starting before our un-Civil War, the United States was an archipelago of agricultural/trading economies where such manufactured goods as were available were either imported or artisanally produced. These economies extended inland from port cities but were only modestly connected by coastal trade. The advent of steamships, canals, railroads, and the telegraph began to alter this economy by extending its reach both inland and coastwise, but the advent of factory methods of production in both cloth and armaments did not significantly displace artisanal production elsewhere. The 1870s and 1880s were a time marked by price deflation and an enormous economic expansion lead by growth in railroad trackage and by an increase in manufacturing, both of consumer and producer goods. Equally important were the expansion of manufacturing into the Midwest, the enormous increase in European immigration, and the growth of farmer and factory worker objections to these economic changes.

The 1890s through the Teens signaled the greatest extent of railroad growth, continued growth in manufacturing and immigration, and the development of nationwide competition. The 1880s had seen attempts by local manufacturers to combine in order to maintain some local control over output and so price, but in later years, this movement toward combination took on a national scope, as the business trust and then the holding company structure permitted combination on a much larger scale. Eventually, enforcement of the Sherman Anti-Trust Act called a halt to this movement and instead, the manufacturing economy settled into an oligopolistic form, as did transportation under the Interstate Commerce Commission. Local electric power networks formed themselves. Concern that the economy had reached a sufficient size to need a better financial system brought the establishment of the Federal Reserve Board. New products were all the rage, including moving pictures and especially the automobile, which didn't amount to much until Henry Ford began production of his Model T, and the airplane, which didn't amount to much at all.

The Twenties and Thirties saw an expansion of the entire economy, then a complete collapse and thereafter, painfully slow growth, all while that economy was largely insulated from European competition by high tariffs. Growth continued in the production of consumer electric appliances and entertainment, as well as the aircraft industry and consumer financial services, though only a limited portion of the population experienced the results. More troubling was the unwillingness of stable oligopolistic industries to invest in plant and equipment. In contrast, smaller more competitive businesses seemed to support the Associationalist economic ideas for a high-wage, high-price economy structured to some degree by federal power that was the Roosevelt New Deal.

After World War II finally pulled the Depression economy out of its doldrums, the postwar economy of the Forties and Fifties, still protected from foreign competition, this time by the lingering effects of the war's economic devastation, sailed along as if the Depression and that war had been but an unfortunate interlude. Notable were the great suburban real estate expansion, the coming of television and home air conditioning, and the fatter paychecks that increasingly came with health and pension benefits for a unionized workforce in mass manufacturing industries. The start of the interstate highway system promised that it would soon be easier for the wealthier hourly middle-class families to go farther in their bigger cars.

If one ignored that pesky war in Vietnam and the ructions associated with it, the Sixties and Seventies started out as if they were a continuation of the Fifties. Suburban expansion was accompanied by the malling of America and the growth of suburban employment in service industries and light manufacturing. But, as the years passed, more headlines reported the closures of northeastern, then Midwestern manufacturing plants occasioned by an increase in lower priced imports, economic growth in the South and West, and the continuing decline of rural population nationwide. More psychologically disturbing was the abandonment of the gold standard and the, at first slow, and then faster, growth in inflation that economists could neither explain nor contain, except by referring to the growth of the OPEC oil cartel and the great increase in oil prices that followed the two Arab-Israeli wars. This was the Great Inflation.

Luckily, no war followed; unluckily, during the late Seventies and early Eighties, nothing pulled the economy out of its muddle. The supposed cure was deregulation, though little was tried, other than airplane deregulation under Carter, until Ronald Reagan became president, when railroads, trucking, and water transport got similar treatment. Almost immediately the supposed cure began to backfire. The carnage in airlines was immense, less so in railroads because much of that carnage had taken place already, but in both cases, the industry settled into a rather stable oligopoly. The same is true of telecommunications, which saw less complete deregulation. But the real disaster was banking where, quickly, deregulation destroyed the savings and loan industry and cost taxpayers a fortune to clean up the mess. As that disaster wound down the computer and telecommunications revolution gained speed. That revolution brought a one-time improvement in business productivity and an explosion called the internet that quickly triggered a boom in dot.com stocks. When, right after the turn of the century, that boom crashed, it set the economy for such a loop that the Fed drove interest rates surprisingly low and for a surprisingly long time. All the while the Northeastern and Midwestern economies continued to lose jobs and population while the South and West gained both.

The Twenty-First Century started off with a combination of low interest rates, new financial products, an unusual amount of money sloshing around all looking for yield, and adventitious, if not old-fashioned fraudulent, behavior in the deregulated financial system. This combination almost collapsed the entire banking system and did collapse the housing market. The carnage was unbelievable, and the ten years of remedial action still hadn't ended the Great Recession.

Just exactly what does this long—even in summary—story add up to? Where is the American economy? Part I argued that it was at best, in the middle of a story and that, in such circumstances, it is difficult to see how the story would work out. A large number of pages later, this still seems true. However, it is important to attend to the opinions of others: those who see these years as a long period of great growth of one kind or another, and those who see these years as a long period of economic decline. For the first group a currently obvious referent is the fantastic growth in the electronic media for communication and production—computers of one kind or another, cell phones of one kind or other, and cable and now wireless communication technology and devices. The so-called New Economy. Another referent is often the equally fantastic growth of finance as an industry that has largely replaced staid old banking.

Assertions such as these are examples of serious part/whole mistakes. Have some segments of American economic life changed significantly? Without a doubt. Electronic media for communication and production and the growth of finance as an industry are the two best examples. Nevertheless, growth here and decline or stasis there does not make an economy, though they might describe an economic present. An economy is a relatively stable, structural whole something we have not had for the past fifty years. Even the trumpeted growth segments have not reached relative stasis. Electronic media have reconfigured themselves every five or so years since the era of the punch card back in the Fifties and finance, a much newer bit of the economy, has crashed first in the late Eighties, then again in the late Nineties, and finally, it nearly brought down the entire economy in 2007–2008. It would be wrong to characterize these years as a period of great growth.

Those in the second group who see these years as a period of great decline emphasize the disappearance of the great manufacturing establishments teeming with unionized labor that produced both consumer and producer industrial goods. And the losses here are just as obvious as the gains elsewhere. Buffalo provides as good an example as any other place—three steel plants, two oil refineries, three electrical manufacturers, one dyestuff manufacturer, two airplane plants, numerous abandoned grain elevators, steel foundries or fabricators and rail yards. Different lists could be made for different places—Buffalo lacked smelters, glass works, textiles and footwear. It had but one clothing manufacturer, but still, the picture would be much the same. These absences are easy to see.

However, this litany too represents a serious part/whole mistake. While the decline in manufacturing in the Northeast and Midwest is real, so is the growth in the South and West. Again, growth here and decline or stasis (which is what recently has been reached in many of these places) there does not make an economy; they just describe an economic present. They omit as much of the story as does the endless trumpeting of electronic media and finance. And there is a central story, a long-term constant around which that story can be centered, though not a particularly joyful one.

Although its roots can be found all the way back around the turn of the Twentieth Century, since the Fifties and Sixties the American economy has been, and still is, a consumer economy. Consumer economies are middle-class economies, for it is the middle classes that have the discretionary income necessary to support them. Up until the Fifties and Sixties consumer goods were primarily domestically sourced; now they are internationally sourced.[4] This shift was the result of an openness to international trade partially borne of ideological considerations and partially of an attempt to maintain the standard of living of the middle and lower-middle classes. It has had the result of largely eliminating the domestic capacity for the production of consumer goods through the use of large quantities of semiskilled labor, an elimination of capacity that in part contributed to the need for cheaper international goods to provide support for those class segments, a vicious circle if there ever were one.

Here, it is important to understand that this shift has had greater social than economic consequences. America still manufactures an enormous amount of stuff, some for domestic consumption and some for export. However, the elimination of domestic capacity for production of consumer goods through the use of large quantities of labor has caused an absolute decrease in the number of middle-class incomes earned by employees who are semiskilled. The decrease in a particular kind of job has been especially destructive because these jobs have traditionally been held by individuals, predominantly, but hardly exclusively, male individuals, who like to learn/work with their hands, as against learn/work with their butts in seats. The resulting downshifting of incomes for middle to lower-middle or even lower-class individuals has had the effect of exacerbating the downward shift in the percentage of the population who can comfortably live in a one wage-earner (with some help from a spouse) household and so toward a mandatory two wage-earner household.

The shift to a mandatory two wager-earner household has had enormous social implications, in part because the dominant narrative about American life expects economic change to be a one-way ratchet. By definition, middle-class life implied the likelihood that a comfortable life could be built on a single wager-earner with no more than a high school education. With the decline of the number of semiskilled jobs in the manufacturing sector of the economy, whatever may be the case with that sector's importance in the economy,[5] there has been a decline in those jobs that both drew high school graduates and paid well because they were unionized. The remaining sectors where employment has been growing either required no more than a high school education but paid less than a middle-class wage or paid a middle-class wage (or greater), but required some college education, a college degree, or even a graduate degree. Even more troubling for those who once might have been employed in the manufacturing sector was one of the results of the modest increase in gender equality: the two-wage-earner dual college degree (or more) household. Such a development seemed to expand the upper-middle class at a time when establishing even a lower-middle class household had become a stretch for many who had grown up in a single wage-earner, lower-middle or even a middle-middle class household.

The forgoing recital of the accumulated results of economic change, even if limited to the Great Inflation and the following years, when offered at a time when many people are still alive who can recall the relative stasis of the Fifties and early Sixties, should point up the problem for a government when change impacts the lives of its citizens. Machiavelli addressed that problem when he observed, with respect to a change in rulers, that if a ruler "refrains from laying hands on the property of his citizens and subjects, and on their womenfolk," that ruler may not be loved, but will not be hated.[6] These citizens and subjects "will live contentedly, and [the ruler] will have to deal only with the ambition of a few men, which can easily be restrained in various ways."[7] This observation is relevant to changes in economic life as well.

The great silent work of law, of mine and thine, of property and contract, of tort and crime, instantiates one aspect of Machiavelli's observation about the importance of contentment, for it is this body of law that most people initially rely on in times of change. However, when the great silent work of law is insufficient to cabin change, Machiavelli is less helpful, for he offers no clues about managing people's expectations of using their property or acquiring more in the future, other than his reference to ambitions and the implied threat of "restraint." Unfortunately, managing expectations and ambitions has become an increasingly important object for the work of American law as change has become more insistent over time. Why is that so?

The primary reason why economic change tends to undermine the contentment of citizens is that many, perhaps most, participants in an economy simply value stability. For families it is hard enough to navigate the vagaries of life and health together without having to contend with the stress of employment coming and going, of schools closing, district boundaries changing, inflation eating into paychecks and savings, or deflation making the repayment of debt more difficult. Communities build their ability to deliver services based on stability as well. Changes in population, the needs of residents, the cost of maintaining or replacing roads, park equipment, police cars or fire trucks can quickly throw budgets out of whack and so turn politics testy.

Capital and labor are not very different when it comes to change. Capital does not like to operate in a relentlessly competitive market; the place where marginal cost equals marginal revenue is just too scary, for any upward change in costs or downward change in sales threatens loss and perhaps a slide into bankruptcy. Unsurprisingly, this story shows multiple attempts to create understandings of the conditions for proper competition—the union company in a more local economy, the trust, the holding company, the business association as first instantiated by Herbert Hoover as Secretary of Commerce and then later by the NRA, resale price maintenance, and the recurrent drive for the establishment of effective oligopolies. Labor does not like to operate in competitive markets either; the stability of employment is the base upon which lives are built. Even when employment is consistent, changes in ownership or even of supervision are unwelcome reminders of the potential frailty of a settled family life.[8]

This is not to say that change is equally hard on capital and labor; such is surely not the case, for there are differences in the capital recovery periods for investments and lives. The recovery period for capital investments is generally thought of as seven to ten years. After that period, change is pretty much water under the bridge and toward the end of the period, it is fairly easy to accept the economists' adage that sunk costs are sunk and move on, though in the case of industries where oligopolistic competition has made for comfort, the matter may be otherwise. In contrast, the recovery period on a life, or even the lives of a narrow community, is incommensurably longer than that of economic assets. A way of life, a settled way, is an asset class for which diversification is impossible, except possibly by having many children as a hedge for the costs associated with old age. Alternative investments are costly, and always are wrenching, if for no one else than for individual families. Here, sunk costs are not sunk, but a way of life, and the capital recovery period for a way of life may be fifty, even seventy-five years. For communities, the appropriate capital recovery period may even be that of the Rule Against Perpetuities—life, or lives, in being plus twenty-one years. The torque from this mismatch in capital recovery periods negatively impacts the more numerous, if not therefore the most loudly heard, group of citizens.

The secondary reason why economic change tends to undermine the contentment of citizens derives from the choice of citizens to seek advantage, or restrain others from doing so, by going to law. Governments regularly face citizens who see possible economic advantage by going to law for help in securing that advantage, just as those who experience disadvantage seek to repair that damage by going to law. The former variety of the task of managing expectations and ambitions does not bulk large in this story, but examples are remarkably common—water rights in both the rainy east and the arid west; construction of ports, canals, railroads, and airports; cattle pasturage or drilling or mining on public lands; liability for disasters at atomic power plants; and copyright protection of computer programs, come easily to mind. The latter, more numerous, cases are usually part of stories about the People and the Interests—farmers and railroads; farmers and elevator operators; employees, unions, and employers; investors and securities sellers; depositors and banks; potential borrowers and banks; policyholders and insurance companies; customers and utilities; minorities and employers or landlords or places of public accommodation; consumers and purveyors of pharmaceuticals or foodstuffs or other manufactured products; humans and air or water polluters. All bulk large in Part I.

Both types of responses to change may act to undermine the great silent work of law in maintaining the contentment of citizens, and so peace, in the realm. Unfortunately, going to law is not as simple as it might initially seem for, while law may respond, indeed often does, the space between what is asked of law and what law returns can be quite large, as the many and varying politics of law work their contradictory ways out. And so, the results of going to law can be uncertain, even if one ignores the limited overall efficacy of law, whether seen as a matter of deterrence or of channeling behavior.[9] No one got what was wanted in the aftermath of either the dot.com bust or the 2008 financial crash. Gains can be reversed in the continuously contentious atmosphere of legal conflict, as labor learned in the Teens and Twenties. Or one may get what one wants and find that it is not helpful, as was the case with the savings and loan industry or find that the effect of what was thought to be an important change is only effective at the margins, as was the case with wage and hour legislation. Then there is the problem of the effectiveness of intent in a changing world, of a future different from that expected and so of the irrelevance of hard-won success, such has been the case with the deregulation of the aircraft industry and of banking and finance more recently. Going to law is thus an unruly, unpredictable activity. As such, it may do less to quiet citizens who seek advantage, or restrain others from doing so, than a Machiavellian might have hoped. At the same time, the kind of restraint that Machiavelli implies would be an effective alternative is not popular in a relative democracy. Other means of securing even the grudging commitment of citizens to a government are not particularly obvious.

Strengths, Problems, and Political Context

Despite what was said earlier, Jane Jacobs was not wholly wrong when she argued that the city is the proper unit of economic analysis, as is obvious when considering the strengths of the American economy. In general, the larger the unit the more difficult it is to analyze an economy, at least unless the area is relatively large and the population relatively small. Lichtenstein is easier to analyze than Switzerland, which is easier to analyze than Germany, which is easier to analyze than the United States because the larger the economy, the more the details smear out as in an increasingly out-of-focus picture. This holds true unless, perchance, the relevant unit of analysis has a pretty homogenous geography, geology, history, and topography, like, say, Iowa. The United States with a large land mass, a large population, a complicated geography, geology and topography, and a tangled history, is particularly difficult to analyze without smearing out almost anything. Still, one might highlight the following

The country has little in the way of natural resources except coal, natural gas, oil, and incredibly rich, well-watered soil in the Midwest. It is self-sufficient in food and is a large exporter of several crops. Its best resource is probably its general openness to commerce with the world; most of its occasional bouts of buy American, military or otherwise, are understandable, if not therefore good, efforts to protect small, geographically concentrated, dying industries.

Its next best resource is its educational system, however troubled that may be. At the PreK-12 level, the great international standards, testing fad will hopefully fade. The system's problem is primarily that it is pressured to do too much with too little in too uniform a way for a rather highly diverse student body, even among the White population, rather than to do fewer tasks for all, individually better. Higher education seems most to suffer from the reverse problem, of doing too little with too many, providing what is, for many, a basic education at an exorbitant cost, but stratified in a way PreK-12 is not, so that for some it delivers an extraordinary education, but for many, maybe most, little more than a ticket evidencing attendance and a deferral of the necessity to grow up. Were this education less stratified by income, the stratification would be less troubling, though not necessarily any less troubling than that of the elite schools in Europe and Asia.

Below this level of generality, it is hard to see, but these strengths also seem apparent. It does not hurt that ours is a reserve currency; such does provide our economy a bit more maneuvering room. And it really helps that we have cobbled together a good transportation network for goods and, for many people. Its consumer goods sector—groceries, drugstores, clothes, and home goods/décor—is innovative, if trivially so, and its chemical and pharmaceuticals sector is innovatively quite similar and often not trivially so. Other pieces of manufacturing, especially metals and plastic, do extraordinary things with machines that it often has to import.

The FIRE (Financial, Insurance, and Real Estate) industries and others that keep the paper moving within businesses are good at keeping the paper moving, though they are less good at creating innovative products. Real Estate is good at producing commercial and industrial space. Innovative insurance products are few and far between, and that is probably a good thing, as delivering the traditional ones well is far more essential to any economy. Finance is far less of a disaster than it is usually seen to be. Below the largest, most banks deliver good services at modest cost, and provide an essential utility for commerce nationwide. Innovation in this sector is almost always a disaster for anyone other than the well-compensated.

Three modest notes are in order. First, the telecom sector is rife with innovation; the significant question is of what value. Second, the illegal drug industry is probably the most innovative sector of the economy. Unfortunately, it would likely be less innovative were it legalized. Third, it is not obvious whether any of the sectors discussed earlier provide a basis for rebuilding the American economy, at least if one understands the difficulty of finding good middle-class jobs for those humans who wish to learn through, and work with, their hands. Now for problems.

The greatest problem in our economy is surely the persistence of oligopolistic structures that protect themselves by defensively accreting possible new competitors while buttressing existing product lines with relatively trivial patents or "new and improved" products, as if they were old nationalist or socialist state enterprises. Union structures, where they still exist, tend to match oligopolistic management structures, and so provide an understandable, if anything but self-reflective, reason for management to oppose unionization. The recurrent choice of government to avoid absorbing social costs—health insurance, unemployment insurance, and workers' compensation insurance, are good examples—makes it difficult for unions to act differently and piles costs on growing businesses at a time when they can least absorb them.

Some oddnesses. Natural resources, even the abundant ones, tend to create more social discord than most economic activities. Such discord is not good for any economy. The weakness in the education we provide for workers who prefer to work with their hands leaves this part of the workforce significantly unprepared for such jobs as actually are available. Wildly overpriced healthcare could not possibly be tolerated were it not for the fact that the cost is partially passed off to both management and labor. The large market of inexpensive, but not new, things raises quite directly whether an economy based on the provision of consumer goods is viable over a long term. The taking of one another's laundry has long been thought not to be such.

There are four important weaknesses in the FIRE sector—three simple in concept. The real estate industry is simply incapable of producing good housing at a moderate price. The part of finance that consists of the largest banks is still a disaster zone. However, it remains such because neither the federal government nor the relevant banks wish to admit that the problem is not regulatory, but structural. Even worse, all possible answers directly raise questions of embedded capital, which is to say value. The problem of embedded human and other capital is also at the root of the health insurance disaster.

Much more complicated is a problem in that branch of finance that is not banking. Modern portfolio theory's assertion that one cannot beat the (stock) market over some "long" run, seems to have been interpreted by money managers as, "I can get paid well for beating the market if the long run never comes." And pretty much everyone with a large amount of money wants to beat the market—insurance companies, pension plans, university endowments or other trust funds, investment funds, hedge funds, large banks, and a whole bunch of entities readers probably have never heard of, and would disapprove of, if they had. The strategy seems to be to harvest gains regularly and sell on the least hint of problems. And it seems to work fairly well; at least a lot of people use it in all sorts of other markets. However, it does not interact terribly well with corporate management, much less other corporate employees.[10]

Management is generally compensated based on a metric of steadily increasing net income, so-called increasing stockholder value, or increase in stock price and/or on total return—the combination of stock appreciation, cash dividends, and other cash distributions, generally a matter of share buybacks that strip companies of retained earnings, or worse are funded with debt. Missing forecasts of increasing earnings, much less actual losses, are ruthlessly punished with declines in stock price and can lead to demands for a change in management or the sale of the company from so-called activist shareholders.

The result of this dynamic between management, the stock market, and activist stockholders is that much money is tied up in corporations that are regularly receiving the message that innovation needs to pay off very quickly . . . or else. Perhaps such is okay; some people argue that public companies aren't very innovative anyway. But there is a possible problem deciding which way the cause-and-effect arrow points and in either case, it is clear that there is far, far more money to be found in the part of the investment sector that is busy owning and trading already funded investments in products and processes and surprisingly little money in possibly successful products and services that struggle for funding, not obviously a good state of affairs in an economy that is regularly said to be short on innovation.

And then there is the new Gilded Age. The first one was trouble, but at least people could see what industries these men built. The current group, now growing for at least forty years running, would be in real trouble since they "toil not, nor do they spin," if it were not for the fact that their efforts have fattened the retirement accounts of the upper-middle class and the endowments of the fanciest universities and family foundations/offices. In time though, dismantling these empires will occupy far more productive energy in our economy than had the fat cats chosen not to prosper so much.

And then there is the political context, an occasion where many people would talk about our Gilded Age and party politics. There is no question that some of the new Robber Barons of finance and their well-paid associates lavish funds on the party of their choice, usually, but not always Republican. However, there is no particular reason to believe that these people are buying elections in the old-fashioned way. And it is really unlikely that they could fool that large a part of the electorate with advertising alone. So in all likelihood, one party really has to be selling something that many people want to buy. Since a lot of voters are not buying what the Democrats at the local level are selling, the new Gilded Age may be a truly abhorrent aspect of the political universe, but it is unlikely to be a significant force in partisan politics. Its impact on society is far more significant in the pervasiveness of the surely erroneous notion that it always pays to buy the absolute best talent, as if the second best could not possibly be a quite astonishingly good bargain, or that merit and luck are quite easily distinguished.

Far more important is the upper-middle class, college-educated professionals, an important part of the Democratic Party. This part of the party believes in the importance of doing well by the large parts of the American populace who are seen as poor, downtrodden, and discriminated against, as well as for environmental causes of all kinds, refugees, women's issues, healthcare issues, and schooling issues. This is a group that is politically active but does not have a lot of money for any one cause, and surely not enough to bankroll the party, and so must always secure some group of people or some governmental entity to support its good ideas. And these are quite often very good ideas. Unfortunately, this group fails to understand that just because an idea is a really good one does not mean that any other part of the effective body politic will be willing to fund it. It also tends to think that the serious moral questions on which it is often correct about, are not questions for debate. This belief leads to much anger because it is often untrue.

A section of the Republican Party is less professionally narrowed and a bit broader in social spectrum: The middle-middle class to lower-upper class is mostly college educated. However, it is also mostly, in some sense, entrepreneurial. It includes lots of small businessmen—franchisees, manufacturers, contractors, auto dealers, repair shops, and of course restaurant owners—and some larger ones as well. Once this group of people was known as petit bourgeois, but the context of being "in trade" has been lost, though not the sense of being the bedrock of the economy. Most of these people feel that their enterprise is always at the edge of bankruptcy where every tax or new regulatory regime threatens not just solvency, but family welfare too. They are also politically active, though without the means to spend large sums in support of political causes either.

Strangely, these individuals do not understand the economy very well for they regularly confuse their personal economic survival with the health of the economy. It is not unusual to find such people directing complaints toward the more professional class in terms of, "You don't know what it means to meet a payroll," who regularly reply with something like, "You would do better if you treated your customers/workers more fairly." Both groups fail to recognize that the prosperity of individuals says very little about the state of an economy. A prosperous economy might treat its customers/workers well or poorly, just as might a weak economy; similarly, a prosperous economy might support lots of small businesses or decimate their ranks, just as might a weak one.

And then there is the broad portion of the middle class that stretches from the middle-middle with middle-management jobs, through the lower-middle, struggling to maintain such jobs, as well as well-paid unionized labor, and into the upper reaches of the lower class—what in this book often has been called the hourly middle class. Starting in the Tea Party days, the chattering class began to notice these people and, of late more and more chatterers have done so. It's about time.

The reason why it has taken time is that the Robber Barons and their financial associates live in their own world; the upper-middle class of college-educated professionals are offended by the broad middle class because it identifies the group as essentially racist, socially conservative, Fundamentalist Christians who always support economically conservative Republicans; and the entrepreneurial middle class believes that because the broad middle class is socially conservative and Fundamentalist Christian, it has to be made up of economically conservative Republicans. All three groups are confused. The broader middle class is not uniformly socially conservative, Fundamentalist Christian, or economically conservative. None of these concerns hold the group together. Rather, the group feels itself to be economically deprived, not necessarily in the sense of poor, though there is some of that, but in the sense of being socially and economically dumped upon, treated by one and all without understanding its way of life, much less according it respect.

Its members remember, or their parents or grandparents remember, when it was honorable to serve in your country's armed forces, not a default choice for lack of other economic opportunities; when working with your hands was equally honorable after service had been completed; when hunting and fishing (and baseball in some places, football in others) were sports you taught your kids, not soccer or lacrosse or field hockey or ultimate frisbee. Some of this broad class still thinks of itself as countryfolk, but many are not. They are from urban or suburban areas or middle-sized towns. Some of them think of themselves as farmers or miners or lumberjacks or oil hands or construction workers or just factory hands, but all think of themselves as having lost economic purchase on their lives. And they see themselves as having lost their social place too, especially this.[11]

Some might be seen as libertarians, angry at all governmental regulation; some in the Midwest are from union families, angry with American firms moving jobs to Mexico and China. Others want immigration stopped to preserve jobs for Americans; still, others want lower taxes and fewer government employees. Almost all want workers compensation, unemployment compensation, social security, and healthcare benefits protected, if not increased. Their list of possible scapegoats is long: Blacks, Jews, immigrants, feminists, atheists, the LGBTQIA+, Muslims, Catholics, and surely the Tri-Lateral Commission fits somewhere in there too. But the more time one spends listening, and the more that the shrillest cries get filtered out, the more it becomes clear that what one hears is anger at change that has left "real Americans" behind, that and a desire for a time when there was more economic space between them and the truly poor.

It would be stupid to purport to predict the longer-term interaction of these four factions of the political structure in America. This is especially true because of the uncertain relationship between the factions and the anything but congruent interactions between them and various social concerns about race, religion, gender roles, gender identity, sexual preference, sectional identity/urbanization, foreigners, international /military role, environmentalism, species conservation, science, etc., etc, and so forth. However, it is important to understand the relationship between the economic strategies each seems to favor and the likely outcome of those strategies.

The Robber Barons and their financial hangers on always focus on government support for capital formation. From one perspective, this is a sensible idea. Without capital, innovation is likely to be stillborn. The difficulty with the ideas pushed as supporting capital formation—limited taxation of incomes, both personal and entity—are however obvious. Start with individual taxes. At some point, individual capital accumulation is of necessity going to have to be used for portfolio investment. There simply aren't enough good small ideas with real potential floating around and, more importantly, even if there were, it is very hard to tie such ideas to equity investors. The faddishness of venture capital and the short time frame for investment and end point—IPO or SPAC—rather limit such funding. Angel investors are even harder to match with good funding opportunities. And increased portfolio investment, like increased real estate investment, so often results in price inflation rather than in economic growth, that it is probably not a good target for support. And with corporate entities, the pressure to return capital to owners suggests that little innovative activity will be catalyzed. One might postulate that modest tax rate increases would make little difference in the rate of capital formation and that the only likely loss from such rate increases would be to the endowment funds of nonprofits that usually get funneled into portfolio investment in most, though clearly not all, cases.

The upper-middle class, college-educated professionals who provide one of the core parts of the Democratic Party are often confused when they offer ideas for economic development. Their confusion is basic. The transfer of funds, either directly through government programs or indirectly, through regulatory regimes, for the benefit of the less well off, increases wealth, but does not therefore bring overall economic development, except highly indirectly through such feedback as may happen—not large, but not negligible—from retailers, through wholesalers and producers, to the innovative uses for such funds by producers. The result is the delivery of a quite thin sliver of funds moved toward any economic development objective.

Now, none of this is to suggest that such redistribution is a bad idea; it is a really good idea. But is it also a category mistake? Increasing the income of those with a significant shortage of such helps those people, but only modestly affects the economy as a whole. Increasing such income probably does more to allow those who worry about the existence of relative poverty to sleep more easily at night than it does to improve the overall economy, just as it clearly increases the opportunities and dignity of those in relative poverty more than it limits the opportunities and dignity of those from whom such funds are procured.

The entrepreneurial portion of the Republican Party regularly makes an astonishingly parallel argument and mistake, as does the upper-middle class, college-educated professionals of the Democratic Party. The argument is that economic development would increase if taxes and regulation were reduced, and for many people, that argument is honestly made. The mistake is to conflate an increase in personal resources with economic development. Assume that all of the tax reduction and the savings from regulation reduction were to be devoted to increasing employment and decreasing prices. Whether the enterprise is retail, manufacturing, or service, for such tax or other cost reduction to result in economic development, the increased employment or increased sales will first have to work their way up through the retail, wholesale, and producer chain, or first through increased purchasing elsewhere and then up through that chain, for it to support even a narrow sliver of innovative activity that brings economic development, again, an awfully expensive way to improve the economy.

Again, none of this is to suggest that either tax or regulation reduction is therefore a bad thing. They may be well warranted. But they are warranted on grounds other than improving the economy and so here, a caution should be offered. The category mistake that the upper-middle class, higher-educated professions are making is at least significantly designed for the benefit of others (one cannot forget that increased employment opportunities for this class often follow from government programs), while among the most likely beneficiaries of tax and regulatory reduction are the entrepreneurs themselves. Self-interest counsels caution when evaluating arguments such as these.

The broader middle class has not yet really disclosed a more or less fully formed understanding of economic development, beyond a certain xenophobia that wishes immigration halted, if not rolled back, on the proposition that better-paying jobs would be available if fewer people were seeking the available jobs. Interestingly, this group seems not to have focused on establishing regulatory barriers as a possible strategy for raising wages or on removing regulatory barriers as a strategy for opening possibilities for employment and, except in the Northeast and metal-bending Midwest, there is little interest in unionization as a strategy for raising wages.

An obvious addition to this line of thought would be explicit advocacy for strengthening, and perhaps expanding, existing welfare benefits programs, especially unemployment insurance and workers' compensation insurance, but also the various social security and health programs. Here though, for the broad middle class a certain anti-tax bias that can easily be understood from the marginal value of tax dollars in maintaining class status, might push the other way.

Though the possible prescriptions for economic development commonly offered by these four parts of the American social matrix are quite different, there is one thing that unites them. Each sees actions that might be taken in its interest, or the interest it has chosen to represent, as addressing problems of economic development. These actions are anything but. No one should be surprised that even in the third person, self-interest turns up in the body politic. Still, the fact that except when engaging in estimating the likely results based on a calculation of political strength, these suggestions ought not to be taken wholly seriously, does not bode well for the body politic.

Transactions of Decline

Much of the discussion in Part V has made a comparison of city/region economies and the American economy. This is not because the similarities between the two are overwhelming, but because the differences are often instructive. As noted above, at the national level, economic activity is so large and diverse, both geographically and commercially, that most all of the detail smears out. Similarly, no one could possibly expect to see the details of Buffalo politics in the previous discussion of the American politics of its economy; the relevant questions are different and their scale as well.

Yet recurrently, one hears the American economy has collapsed, fallen apart, fallen behind, self-destructed, endured siege, and many other locutions, all of which sound remarkably like what can be heard as descriptions of Buffalo's economy. Does the similarity of these assertions suggest that the country has already begun to regularly enter into transactions of decline as a way to prop up its economy? Such an assertion is doubtful, but the topic still merits some discussion.

Jane Jacobs described the three types of transactions of decline as "prolonged and unremitting military production," "prolonged and unremitting subsidies," and heavy promotion of trade between "advanced and backward economies."[12] In the Vietnam War years she may have thought it sensible to separate military production from subsidies, but that is no longer sensible. At the national level, the difference between military and other subsidy is politically insubstantial; only the images evoked to support the values alleged to be served by the subsidies differs. Military procurement and base maintenance images are red, white, and blue, those associated with agriculture are of rural fields or orchards, and those associated with trade protection are of families gathered around its breadwinner.[13]

Trade protection is the easiest to understand. As Part I makes clear, trade protection is usually a cover for the modestly orderly shrinking of an industry. Doing so may be a waste of money, but it is not prolonged and unremitting. Military procurement and base maintenance are a slightly different circumstance. The endless attempt of the military to close bases and cut back procurement of expensive hardware makes it clear that this is a fight internal to the national government between two of its branches, one of which serves a local constituency and the other of which does not. This situation is like the situation in cases of trade protection and should be addressed similarly, but slowly and unfortunately somewhat less rationally than that model.

Farm subsidies are a very difficult question. They are an example of the continuation of the Associationalist model of an economy that dates to the early New Deal. The deregulation fetish that started in the late Seventies erased some of these expenditures, a portion of which has not been supplied by the federal government, but rather, by individual users of the "subsidized" goods through the price mechanism. The unfortunate problem is that no one has yet figured out how to deregulate agriculture in an even modestly orderly way because these subsidies not only underpin the prices of farm products, but as such, these prices also underpin farm values and farm values support farm banks' lending practices and so the greatest portion of America's surviving rural communities, each of which is represented by two senators. Also important to understand is that agricultural subsidies are significantly common worldwide, only differing as to the extent of the crops they cover. Though such subsidies are clearly prolonged and unremitting, there is something else going on here than decline simpliciter.

Backward-advanced trade is an entirely different question. The difference here is that, in some of this trade, America is the advanced economy and in others, the backward economy. Consider three examples: clothing from Vietnam, Komatsu heavy equipment from Japan, and iPhones from China. With clothing, Vietnam is obviously the backward economy in the transaction. So, what about all the jobs lost in America? Such is the classic result of backwards-advanced trade in the advanced economy. From the perspective of the backward economy it gains jobs that will likely leave as soon as a more backwards economy becomes a viable competitor. From the perspective of the more advanced economy, it is exporting jobs elsewhere; all domestic consumers are advantaged while some domestic producers and their employees are disadvantaged. If there is a loss domestically, it can be attributed to the unwillingness of consumers to subsidize the wages of others because of a lack of community fellow feeling.

Komatsu heavy equipment from Japan is a different matter. There is no backward economy in this transaction. Caterpillar produces equivalent goods. There may be an unwillingness of Japanese buyers to buy the American product either because of trade barriers or because of community fellow feeling, but this is not a transaction of decline on either side. What then of iPhones from China? The trade of American design technology for Chinese manufacturing technology completely mangles Jacobs's categories, as the design all but assumes the existence of the manufacturing capacity as part of the design/manufacture/price package that went into the development of the product. Though the deal in one sense turns on relatively low labor costs in China and so seems much like the manufacture of clothing in Vietnam, the availability of Taiwanese manufacturing technology in China was a necessary part.

In the American case, the only real backward-advanced trade where America is the backward party is in the natural resources area: coal once, natural gas more recently, and in various agricultural commodities at various times, most recently alfalfa. There would be probably more of such trade had farm support programs died out after World War II. But neither variety is truly part of an advanced-backward trade. At least for the past seventy years, they have been more of a side business to the primary business of first metal bending, and more recently finance, retailing consumer products and services (including housing), and exporting culture.

Why then discuss transactions of decline other than to maintain a parallelism designed to help the reader not get lost? It is important to understand that there is an important difference between city and national economies. Jacobs's categories don't transfer directly from one to the other. Her idea that economies grow from innovation that takes place as a matter of grace, or as used here, rain, transfers well. Transactions of decline, on the other hand, suggest a caution at the national level. It could only transfer directly from modest-sized cities such as Buffalo to small nations—Lichtenstein, Bhutan, Guinea-Bissau. This is because the political economy of even modestly large nations—Hungary, Kenya, Peru—is too complicated for Jacobs's model.

In large, long-developed nations, the political economy of the place becomes almost impossible to keep in outline on even a few coherent pages, as should be evident here. In such nations, the shift of a part of the economy (clothing, for instance) into an advanced-backward structure that would surely qualify as a transaction of decline in Vietnam and so couldn't be turned down there, any more than, in Buffalo could a large back-office transplant, is anything but in an economy as big as America's. At the same time, it can create havoc in the political economy of the country for which it is a sensible economic transfer of local work to another place. The two-factor model of international trade is just too simple, not for any economy, but for any modestly large polity. Hopefully, readers will understand this.

Making America Attractive to the Middle Classes

What then should a national government do when faced with change? Associationalist remedies did not end the Depression of the Thirties. Deregulation was no more helpful in the Nineties or the Twenty-First Century. Keynesian remedies worked well in the Forties and the Eighties at a time when such thought was not highly valued and quite poorly in the late Sixties and Seventies when it was in vogue. Moreover, academic judgment is seldom univocal, whatever one may make of the claim to universalizable knowledge on which economics as a discipline is based. And so, a certain serious caution is probably appropriate on the subject of academic views about economic development. This body of learning is often offered as determinative when change has worked adversely or been insufficient to right an economy, especially in places in the midst of a long period of economic decline such as Buffalo or, according to some, America. Still, a review of certain common policy prescriptions is in order, if only to have reason to set them aside.

These days, the views of academic economists fall into two camps. One is an urge to "do something" based on a set of observations relating to human capital.

In the Fifties, Robert Solow and others developed models of economic growth as part of a drive to understand how to help less developed countries become more developed. Solow's model postulated that growth proceeded from increasing inputs of capital and labor and treated all of what could not be explained by the model, what was exogenous to it, as inexplicable technological progress. In the Eighties, Robert Lucas and Paul Romer altered the Solow model by bringing the unknowable technological progress into the model.[14] The point was to try to reduce what could not be explained by a model of economic growth, in effect explaining technological progress, making it an endogenous part of the model, and so developing the "New Growth" theory. Lucas and Romer argued that technological progress was a result of the deployment of "human capital," which they attributed to a combination of investment in education and research and development, factors that might be increased through the exercise of governmental policy.

In the hands of economic planners, Lucas and Romer's work lead to an economic development strategy called "eds and meds." It is based on a plausible observation that regions that have strong investments in the delivery of higher education and simultaneously have strong investments in the delivery of health care services regularly prosper. This observation has a strong intuitive appeal. Both education and healthcare generate large numbers of clean middle-to upper-middle class jobs. Such jobs generate a modest amount of disposable income. The existence of a modest slosh of discretionary income makes a place attractive for people who make money by supplying the amenities—ethnic and other restaurants, wines, olive oils, fresh breads, fresh fruits and vegetables, clothes, fancier cars, larger housing alternatives—that satisfy the tastes of middle-and upper-middle class people. Having such amenities makes living in such a place attractive to those same people and a region with a relatively large proportion of such people is likely to be prosperous.

Of course, hidden in these observations is a thorny question of the direction of causation—does the underlying prosperity of the region make investments in eds and meds profitable or do the investments in eds and meds make the region prosperous? But set that question aside and focus on a different one. How many eds and meds centers can a country, even one as large as America, support? There are about 140 schools of medicine, though fewer regions with one since several regions have several such schools. Most medical schools have their own university hospital and most of these hospitals lose money. Most medical school/hospital complexes are part of a university and so, in one sense, the strategy is already in place to some extent. So, if eds and meds is a route to economic development, what is being talked about is in some way a desire to expand both parts of the local economy as well as to attract other such people.

Ignore the matter of how that growth is supposed to work. Instead, consider the question of first mover advantage. Exactly who is going to go to the nineth cardiovascular center other than the people already in the region? For example, Buffalo. Perhaps a few of the people who now go to Cleveland, Pittsburgh, Rochester, Boston, or New York City will stay in Buffalo for their surgery. It is highly unlikely that people from any of these other places will come to Buffalo, so all that can be expected is that some people in rural areas who might have gone to already existing centers such as Cleveland, Pittsburgh, or Rochester will move their treatment here. Medical referral networks are surely more stable than preferences, as between Applebee's and Chili's. So, such movement is thus not likely to be large.

Consider next the mechanics of actually making such a project work. What would be required in the absence of a single, dominating institution in higher education and a single, integrated hospital system for the delivery of medical services? In higher education, one would need a cooperatively competitive set of relations among the various institutions. At the very least, cooperative marketing efforts would be called for. Ideally, consolidation of duplicate programs would be desirable. At the very least, the medical school would have to have really good relationships with the existing hospitals/hospital systems in the region. Here again consolidation of duplicate facilities would be desirable. Again, consider Buffalo. The publicly supported schools of higher education cannot get along and the private, most often religious, institutions do not play well together either. The medical school only works with one of the region's hospital systems and that one is a jerry-rigged combination of public and private hospitals. Success is not likely.

Now, none of this should suggest that investments in either higher education or medicine should be forgone. The one thing that is reasonably clear is that a region in which healthcare falls apart is a region that is doomed, as any rural area with a small hospital bravely fighting to stay open knows and knows well. And institutions of higher education are real assets in any community. It is just that the number of cases nationwide where eds and meds did not turn into a real economic winner must surely far outnumber the real winners. Thus, the economic observation that leads to an eds and meds strategy is probably leading most communities down the road to disappointment. If doing something is a good idea, something other needs to be thought up. Before discussing what that something might be it is best to look at the other regularly discussed economic development strategy.

Directly opposed to the "do something" school of economic thought about economic development is the other, contrasting school of "do nothing." This notion, often identified with some variant of the efficient market hypothesis, believes that left to its own devices, the market will do quite well thank you and bring prosperity to all, is a dangerous canard.[15] Admittedly, this notion is true in the trivial sense that the market is always already doing the best that it can with the set of rules, institutions, players, and resource endowments in place at any particular time and in any particular area. However, the idea behind "left to its own devices" is really quite misleading. A market is never left to its own devices. It is always already constituted in part by the rules applicable to the players (with their existing resource endowments) in any institutionalized economic game. Some of these rules might be said to be customary in the sense that the operation of many institutions is significantly established by the recurrent actions of the participants engaged in the activities of that institution, their norms as it were. And only a committed legal imperialist would assert that since these norms are both tolerated by the state, by constituted political authority, and subject to replacement through the actions of that political authority, they are therefore legal norms.

Still, a significant portion of the rules applicable to the players in any economic game are anything but customary. The great silent work of the law of contract, tort, property, and crime is often spoken of as if it were customary in this sense. Such speech is profoundly wrong. While the details of contract, tort, property, and crime may properly be thought of as silent, in the sense of not being in the consciousness of but a few lawyers, it nevertheless is anything but customary in the sense of existing since time out of mind. These bodies of law have been the subject of refashioning by political authority since well before there was a State separable from the person of the monarch, either in court or with parliament.

Admittedly, ever since the separation of the person of the monarch from the State as a political entity, the body of rules and institutions that have been added to the great silent work of law has been growing apace. However, it would a mistake to argue that simply because some law is of more recent origin it is therefore more readily characterized as surplusage, not a proper part of the rules establishing the market. Rather, the proper constitution of markets is now, and long has been a subject for the exercise of political will and so of argument about appropriateness. Thus, it is not now and has not been the case for a very, very long time (perhaps forever) that the really important question is what rules are sufficient to constitute the "natural" market, one somehow pre-"customary" law. Rather, the question is who shall play in a given economic game and under what rules?

The question of what are to be the rules of the economic game is thus a moral question as much as an economic one. It is important to remember the dual nature—moral/economic—of questions about the structuring of markets because it is quite easy to assert morals are properly subordinated to that scientific reason to which economics aspires and then to smuggle morals back into scientific reason via the definition of what constitutes a market properly understood. This is of course what is being done when identifying what constitutes a natural or free (of law?) market, as discussed above.

Similarly misleading is the economic notion of moral hazard. A moral hazard is said to exist when a set of rules and institutions allow humans to act in a self-interested way, and to receive a benefit from doing so while shifting the cost, sometimes referred to as risk, to unknown others. The classic example is to allow the beneficiary on a life insurance policy to kill the insured in order to collect the death benefit. However, the notion of moral hazard, itself the attempt to distinguish bad self-interested behavior from good self-interested behavior by label and not argument, is not an observable entity.

A good example of this is the federal flood insurance program, a regular whipping boy of the moral hazard police, that forces homeowners who live in flood prone areas—hurricane prone coastal communities for example—to buy flood insurance, but then subsidizes part of the cost of such insurance. It is often said that the program is an example of legislation that creates a moral hazard because if people were forced to bear all the costs of their building on coastal property, they would not do so, or at least would do so less frequently, instead of shifting part of the cost of their choice to build to the great mass of taxpayers, the unknown others.

This labeling of the program is quite silly. First, forcing the owners of coastal property to bear all the cost of their behavior would mean that, in general, only the poorer citizens would be forced away from building there. Those with greater resource endowments would find it much easier to absorb the cost. It is doubtful that allowing only the wealthy to live on flood-prone coastal areas is a good social result; such areas are traditionally full of low-income communities. Second, all governmental expenditure programs benefit some at a cost to others. That is the nature of taxation. The beneficiaries are numerous, starting with legislators, other government employees, government contractors, and then moving on to farmers, users of various business tax credits, poor people, old people, sick people, and so forth. The point is not that all these things are bad, but that the label "moral hazard" could be applied to all of them and so that its use is designed to avoid actual substantive argument, and so political decision making with respect to the merits of the program in question. As such, it is hardly a concept worthy of any discipline that claims to be scientific.

What is the point of all this talk about "do nothing" economics, a patient reader may ask? It is important to understand why doing nothing might seem a good idea. Doing something sensible to aid a struggling economy is very complicated, as the eds and meds discussion makes modestly clear. Economies at any time and place are just too complicated, law, far too variously understood, and communities, far too different. In contrast, doing nothing seems very simple. Unfortunately, such simplicity is deceptive for it is brought at the cost of importing it into an assertedly objective science, implausible assumptions about the naturalness of the market, and the immorality of attempts to improve economic circumstances. Academic rigor aside, it is still easy to see the attractiveness of falling into the politics of drift and default that Willard Hurst derided as bastard pragmatism. If one believes that the problem of coping with economic change is significant enough to be worth thought that goes beyond doing what is easiest—doing nothing—one must at least understand in more detail why doing something is so hard.

Plato may or may not have been right when he asserted that Heraclitus said, "No man can ever step into the same river twice," but it seems quite likely that no nation has ever experienced the same economy twice. Economies are deeply lodged in the history of a nation as well as the communities that make it up. All these things change and there is no reason to believe that they march to the same cadence. Whether, like histories, economies may nevertheless rhyme, is a more difficult question, though where rhyming is concerned, one needs to remember that once one gets past the most simple of rhymes—Peep/sheep, Jill/hill, Hubbard/cupboard—rhyming becomes a matter of taste and so of careful judgment.

The necessity for careful judgment is easily shown by examining the history of two tax rate changes. Tax cuts made a positive economic difference in the Sixties, though it is most likely that what they did was simply to prolong the life of an economic structure in decline. Tax increases in the Nineties were accompanied by an expansion, though they probably made no difference to those years of dot.com euphoria, or if they did, it was to shorten the duration of the bit of economic froth that followed some real technological advance. But the key question in either case is not whether the change in taxes made a difference in growth, but whether prolonging a decline or limiting a bubble was a good thing for the economy at that time.

Arguably, the Kennedy-Johnson tax cut was not a good thing; it made it easier to believe that a policy of guns and butter could work as we began to take the Vietnam War seriously and, at the same time, it made the Great Inflation worse on the overall economy. And arguably, the increase was a good thing; on the theory that the longer the boom the harder the crash (the 2001 crash was hard enough as it was), a shorter boom is better for the economy. Though maybe, if the boom had lasted longer and the crash had been still harder, then some of what happened in the run-up to 2007–2008 might have been avoided and that crash might have been less devastating. On the third hand, maybe raising taxes decreased the deficit and the decrease in the deficit was what really extended the boom and so no tax increase would have shortened the boom that we had.

The point is not whether such speculation about either example of tax cuts or tax increases is correct, but rather whether the complexities of the actual situation can so overwhelm the actual decision to raise or lower taxes that prediction of the effect on the basis of prior circumstances is at best a dubious activity and at worst simply duplicitous. No one in his or her right mind could have predicted the exact consequences of either the choice to raise or lower taxes at the level of the national economy, though at a different level, some things might be rather firmly predicted.

For example, consider the choice to lower taxes in the Sixties. Some people were left undoubtedly wealthier, generally people with previously higher marginal tax rates. People with lower marginal tax rates most likely increase personal consumption more than personal savings. Some at the higher marginal tax rates may have done so as well, but the greater the income, the harder it is to avoid savings. What was done with such savings as each group kept is, however, the crucial question. At the margin, which is where growth happens, the people with lower tax rates put their savings in either savings and loan or savings bank accounts. That money was pushed back into home mortgages that financed home ownership on the part of people like themselves. Whether the increased savings created greater demand for housing, and so some modest inflation in housing prices, is hard to tell. It is equally difficult to tell what the relatively larger, on a per capita basis, savings of the people with higher marginal tax rates did with their savings. Some would have gone into commercial bank deposits where it might have fueled a bit of commercial lending. Some would have gone into stocks and bonds as well as mutual funds and paying off a mortgage—the latter two are what most middle-class men of the silent generation did with their savings—but to the extent that such funds were used to purchase existing securities, all that was being done was inflating stock prices and decreasing bond yields. Some was used for investments in new products and processes, but what percentage is hard to estimate. Still overall, wealth is likely to have increased among those with previously higher marginal tax rates; overall, consumption was increased among those with previously lower marginal tax rates. So consumption likely increased more than investment and drove the production of more consumer goods, rather than more investment in new products and processes.

Thus, the notion that seems to drive the idea behind tax cuts, that more disposable income being pumped into savings will bring forward a great show of productive investment is highly unlikely, given the way that such savings are recycled by upper-middle and lower upper-class taxpayers. Some will, because some people will choose to supply angel or venture capital because doing so is fun and perhaps profitable. But most will not, and so the effectiveness of the entire project will turn on whether a marginal decrease in taxes will cause more people to invest more of their own funds into more small economic ideas of their own design that will somehow exceed the success rate of new restaurants and thus drive economic development. A separate, equally tedious analysis would lead into another complex unraveling of the interaction between social class, economic position, and the range of possible skills likely to be held by the possible investors.

Even something as seemingly simple as raising the minimum wage is complex when tracing its economic impact. A conservative assumption would be that, at the margin, there would be a modest decrease in low-wage employment, a modest increase in the prices of the goods and services produced with low-wage labor, a modest decline in the production of those goods and services, and a modest increase in the wages of some low-wage labor. This set of assumptions implies absolutely nothing about anything other than the likelihood that the low-wage laborers whose wages were increased will spend their increased earnings on other goods and services that low-wage labor probably produces and sells, and that owners of enterprises that employ these low-wage laborers will see their profits diminish marginally as well. On the other hand, some portion of the economy that supplies goods and services consumed by these low-wage workers will find a marginal increase in the demand for their products and services and perhaps in their profits. So, what we can intuit is that some workers will gain some income from the change and some smaller number will lose, though whether as a result they will leave the workforce or remain in the workforce, but take longer to be hired, perhaps by the firms that experience an increase in a demand for their products, is unclear. Likewise, some employers will find profits decrease while others, perhaps a larger number, will see their profits increase. Each of these trade-offs will principally be felt within a single community, that of low-wage workers who tend to live together or employers who tend to live together. And when all of this is sorted out, the overall impact on the economy will be marginal in the extreme, except for the workers themselves.

There is a problem with both examples. They speak as if the effects of economic change created by law will be uniform across the entire country. At the level of how lives are lived, this is not likely to be true. Look at both examples again. First the tax cut. Poor communities or the poor portions of larger communities will experience the effect somewhat differently from other strata of the economy. In poor communities, even a proportional tax cut will be swallowed up in daily life—a little bit more money at the grocery store, a slightly better Christmas gift for each child, maybe a chance to eat out a McDonald's every few months. But poor communities are anything but equally distributed nationwide. They tend to be concentrated in parts of the South and the Appalachian range and in many rural areas. And even there, the absolute level of welfare and food stamp benefits has a significant impact on how poverty is experienced.

Once one gets into the various slices of the middle classes it all becomes more complicated. A middle-class farmer often has an economic profile that is remarkably like a bank—large assets supported by large debts and modest equity for a balance sheet and on the income side, relatively low income that, on top of everything else, is quite lumpy for "dirt farmers" and ranchers, though less so for dairy farmers or people in poultry. Still, the disparity between cash flow and the debt/equity ratio leads this piece of the middle class to following quite conservative consumption patterns, as compared with the consumption patterns of the salaried middle class or even the numerous owners of small retail businesses in almost any area. And let's face it; agriculture is hardly evenly spread throughout the country. Farming and ranching are heavily concentrated in the greater Midwest, Great Plains, and select portions of the South and West, in rural America. The salaried middle class is mostly found in urban areas.

At the level of the upper-middle and lower-upper classes of professionals and executives, tax matters become significantly more confusing because such people save a lot and much of it is in tax-preferred retirement funds of various kinds. Again, these people are anything but uniformly distributed nationally. Every modest town has at least one, two, or more. But again, such people are concentrated in urban areas as well as Sun Belt retirement communities. Saving through tax-preferred vehicles has two important properties. Such savings do not flow through to benefit any particular community, are most often realized many years in the future, and almost as often in other places than where the savings were earned. Some portion of the savings go to the benefit of the managers of the tax-preferred vehicle, be it a pension plan, mutual fund, or IRA, entities disproportionately located in the Northeastern states and, ultimately the funds deposited will flow to the seller of the actual securities that comprise the funds. Except for municipal bond funds, this flow of funds is likely to be disproportionately funneled through the same managing entities and then out to the same upper-middle and lower-upper class of savers, again disproportionately located in urban areas, but this time also in retirement communities.

A slightly clearer result follows from the other example, minimum wage increases. A significant proportion of minimum wage jobs are to be found in locally owned franchise facilities. Here, to the extent that patronage declines, any loss is likely to be borne by the local franchisee. Depending on how the franchise agreements are structured and how close the franchisee's income is to any minimum payment stipulated in that agreement, some of those losses will travel up to the franchisor in the form of diminished revenue, then turned into diminished income, and finally into diminished security prices, losses again distributed to the tax-preferred accounts of upper-middle and lower-upper individuals and their account managers, disproportionately located in urban areas and the Northeastern states respectively. This is also true with the gains that result from the increased patronage at franchise facilities by individuals whose income is increased by a rise in the minimum wage.

The same is true of those other minimum wage jobs that are at large nonfranchise businesses—for example Walmart, Staples, or Penney's. All that changes is that the loss or gain that is reported at the national level, then flows up the investment chain in the case with franchise facilities. For locally owned businesses, the real impact is local, for any loss or any gain is transferred directly to upper-middle class owners.

What is the point of these two examples? Simply this. Without making incredibly heroic assumptions, it is very difficult to identify the effect of legal change on economic change. When it comes to tax rate increases or decreases one must assume that social classes are uniformly distributed throughout the country as well as that the marginal impact will be the same across the various strata of social class. With respect to the minimum wage, one has to assume that nothing else matters other than the narrow question of the total number of low-wage workers employed. Once one begins to trace the results less simplistically, exactly where gains and losses will finally lie is not easy to identify and equally important, are anything but largely local. Thus, care in what one chooses to do in the direction of fostering economic change is important. Nothing in a modern economy is simple.

Now, of course, none of this is to say that the national government should do nothing about economic change. Rather, it suggests that when doing something, one needs to focus more clearly on exactly what doing something is likely to accomplish. As part of that focus, time might well be spent coming to understand more about the limits to the ability of governments to accomplish anything.

The number of ironic stories that include someone who says, "We're from the government and we're here to help you" is large for a reason. Delivering help is hard to do and governments are anything but omnicompetent. A good place to start understanding their limits is first to recognize that governments exist in large part to provide jobs for government workers. This surely is an ancient, if to some people, unpleasant truth. A particularly good example of the job-creating enterprise of government is from fiction—private investigator Marcus Didius Falco in Vespasian Rome, who as a reward for helping the emperor with a particularly difficult problem, was named procurator of the Sacred Geese of Juno, a modest sinecure of course, that gets this Bruce Willis knockoff into trouble, as expected, in Lindsey Davis's "One Virgin Too Many."[16] But still, it would be a mistake to ignore this enterprise and its relationship to its source of funds—taxation. If governments are going to help, a serious limit is their ability to do so will be the cost and limited skills of those employed to do something.

The point here is not to attack the honesty and industry of government employees generally. Most try hard to do their jobs and most are gravely hampered by the overlay of bureaucratic oversight that is deployed to protect partisan political actors from blame for the actions of those few employees who are not or that is designed to accomplish other collateral governmental objectives. But one needs to be honest here. If the topic is economic development, there is little reason to believe that a person who would be good at such an activity would likely chose government service helping others with just that task. Some, but not very many; most would use those skills for their own benefit or that of their friends. And so, the best that government is often able to do is to create a program that good, but not particularly entrepreneurial, government employees will administer, and that is hampered by being a program with the problems that "program" implies.

Second, hiring government employees requires raising taxes. Here the newspaper comic strip *Hagar the Horrible* best captures the enterprise. Whenever Hagar sees the tax collector coming, he quickly changes into his most tattered clothes and hides his best possessions somewhere away from his house. All of tax law can be found in this little story. The easiest way to collect large amounts of revenue is to tax those who can spare the wealth relatively painlessly, a principle that needs to be balanced against the cost collection. The income tax shows this balance quite wondrously. Withholding taxes from earned income is relatively inexpensive. And a broad middle class, if a nation has one, may actually supply more revenue than would be the case from taxing, even confiscatorilly, the income of those with more wealth, since relatively more of the income of the more wealthy is unearned, and so difficult to find. In contrast, taxes based on wealth are, when limited to real property, relatively easy to lay, but rather more difficult to collect, for most often there is no stream of income to capture the tax from, and even if there were, the notion of millions of people withholding part of their rent and remitting it quarterly to the Internal Revenue Service is quite silly. When it comes to income from investments in securities, the matter, while not as hard as the remission of withheld rent, is still quite difficult given that many remissions would be of small sums and that, when large sums are at issue, the temptation to play Hagar and stash assets overseas is likely to be overwhelming, as we have seen in recent years.

Caution ought to be exercised before suggesting that it is a very good use of hard-to-raise tax dollars, that likely come largely from the middle classes, on providing jobs for the various segments of the middle class, for that is what most government jobs are. It may well be, however, it may not, especially given the tendency of elected representatives to believe, for perfectly understandable reasons, that they are most likely to have an impact on economic change by seeing to it that the location of the facilities that will house new government employees are in their own cities, counties, districts, or states.

A lower cost alternative, at least for government, to hiring employees is misleadingly called "regulation."[17] The mere notion of regulation implies that there is some unregulated thing out there in the world on which government is intruding. This is a patently silly notion, as silly as the notion that the market can be "free." Free of what, is a good question. Surely, not of law. As noted above, it is through the law of contract, property, tort, and crime, not to mention partnership and corporation, as well as creditor's rights and procedural remedies, that markets and the players in them too, are constituted. This is the great silent work of law that we first encountered in Part I.[18]

There is nothing natural in any of these fields; they are creatures of governmental action and, from time to time, have been altered by such action. Indeed, price regulation in markets, an idea that these days is treated as anathema, is of far older provenance than the drivel about free markets that daily washes over public discourse. The question thus has always been how does governmental authority want markets to be structured and the only point of the rhetoric of the free market is to avoid the question of how to properly structure a given market.

A market is a very structured game. Games have rules, which law and other social norms imply is appropriate behavior by appropriate players. Thus, games also have to have players. Players come with resource endowments—money, friends, other relationships, expectations, dependencies, understandings of the rules both formal and social. More important, just because there are rules does not mean that there will be participants in the game thus defined. If a game is too stacked in favor of the House or particular players, other people will not play unless forced to do so, in which case "extortion" ought to be the word that first comes to mind. Similarly, because there are players does not mean that there will be a game either. Some combination of legal and social authority needs to come together to establish appropriate rules, including not just that there will be a game, but also who may play and what resource endowments players, may, must, and may not bring to the game.

Markets are thus both very robust human inventions when they are well designed for appropriately endowed players and very fragile human inventions when the rules establish play that is rigged to allow inappropriate players or discourage appropriate players. Markets may even be stillborn when the rules create a structure in which no one is willing to play. All of these possible outcomes suggest that again the structuring of markets is both a technical problem and a moral one as well, one about the proper treatment of some humans by other humans, a problem mediated, fairly or unfairly as it often is, by political authority.

Unfortunately, for all of the experience American government has had over well over two hundred years, it isn't very good at structuring. One reason is that law does not speak with a single voice. For example, the Sherman Act banning monopolistic behavior in interstate commerce was first interpreted not to touch manufacturing, because manufacturing was not commerce, and after that odd reading of the act was cleared up, it reappeared in a latter case when it was held that insurance was not commerce. Similarly, after the Clayton Act forbade the federal courts from enjoining strikes, the act was interpreted in a way that rendered it mostly a nullity and the federal courts returned to enjoining strikes until the Norris-LaGuardia Act enacted the ban again. But more importantly, law doesn't understand markets very well and is no better at predicting the future than anyone else, as is clear from some of the stories recounted in Part I.

The attempts to save the savings and loan industry from its problems brought on by the Great Inflation, of finding that its cost of funds was higher than the income derived for its portfolio of mortgages, managed to legislate the industry into oblivion, as it opened the door to the depredations of thieves and charlatans. The serial attempts to allow commercial banks to prosper in the wake of the savings and loan debacle may have saved the banks, but at the cost of ushering in the Great Recession. Even more astonishingly, the swarm of New Deal legislation restructuring the American economy during the Depression seemed not to work in the economy for which it was designed yet managed to work quite well in an economy it could not have foreseen, one where the country effectively had the only viable economy in the Northern Hemisphere.

Other dubious achievements are worth noticing. Abandoning the regulation of the airline industry in the name of creating competition brought not prosperity, but the gradual bankruptcy of all of the existing airlines. After thirty-five years, the industry may have settled into a perhaps stable four-party oligopoly, anything but the original objective of deregulation. Similar efforts at the state level allowed public utilities to shift the risk of energy price volatility from entities that had proven themselves not to be very good at the job of managing volatility, to consumers who had even less ability to, and no experience at all in doing so, and at the same time, allowed generators of electricity to escape regulation entirely. This deregulation was undertaken in the name of fostering competition; almost no competition appeared. In telecommunications and television, the cost of network expansion was shifted from debt-financed investments made by service providers to user-provided investments wrapped into the cost of service. Slowly but surely, relatively stable oligopolies seem to be emerging. Still, in neither of these areas has any real competition emerged, other than competition in obfuscating the actual marginal cost of service.

An actual success, at least on its own terms, bears mention too. There is a long and learned literature dating back into the Middle Ages about the nature of the corporation. By the Nineteenth Century, the question had devolved into arguments about who represented the corporation, which, in the case of the business corporation, boiled down to three possible parties—the officers, the directors, or the shareholders. The answer that law gives to this question is important because it is the basis for deciding who may have acted inappropriately when causing the corporation to act. This is because the traditional theory asserts that the responsible party needs to act in the best interest of the corporation. In the wake of an article by the renowned economist Milton Friedman, who asserted that the proper way to understand the corporation was that the appropriate point of reference was not the interest of the entity, but of the owner, it soon became the case that analysis of the appropriateness of corporate action could be decided by a single question, "Was the action taken in the interest of the shareholders?" Soon everywhere, one heard about the necessity for officers and directors to act in order to "improve shareholder value," by which was meant share price.

At the same time, another group of economists was worrying about "agency costs," the cost of assuring that the officers and directors acted in the interest of the shareholders and not of themselves. The answer given was that officers and directors needed to have their interests aligned with those of the corporation by paying such people based on a combination of bonuses measured by improving net income, and so share price, and of stock interests whose value was tied to share price.

The combination of these two developments was not optimum. The first brought a spate of bad officer behavior that demonstrated that shady accounting still might be in the interest of officers seeking to capture extra compensation dollars, but not the shareholders, a realization that brought forth the Sarbanes-Oxley Act. The second provided much evidence for the proposition that, even when the interests of the officers and the shareholders seemed well aligned, the powers of the officers and directors might be exercised in ways that were not in the interests of the corporation, its shareholders, its customers, or the economy as a whole, a realization that brought forth the Dodd-Frank Act.

Still, one of the astonishing things about the combination of the mantra about delivering shareholder value and that about aligning the interest of shareholders, directors, and officers is the degree to which together, they brought forth a bull market. This market filled the retirement accounts of many upper-middle and lower-upper class individuals, hardly a bad thing for the people concerned. Unfortunately, at the same time, this combination resulted in great pressure to reduce employee head count (cut costs) by outsourcing both production and other traditionally internal functions such as payroll or human resources, work staff harder, convert pension plans to IRAs of one kind or another, reduce health benefits, and limit internal product development—research budgets—in effect outsourcing the research and development function to the mergers and acquisitions market. The result for much of the middle class and the unionized working class has been an economic devastation. Whether the interest of the corporation (or of the nation) has benefitted is completely unclear since summing the lives of those improved by it all with those diminished is to treat neither group humanely.

There is a fourth way in which law has real limits to its effectiveness. It follows from the fact that since America is a middle-class democracy; it is politically implausible to suggest that law ever could do nothing. As noted in Part IV, no legislator or executive is likely to be reelected on the platform, "I will do nothing" when my constituents are in pain. It just doesn't work that way, as is best evidenced by all of the constituent service assistants there are on any elected official's staff. The problem, of course, is with the requests of constituents. It is easy to deliver help to one person with navigating a cranky bureaucracy, even easier if all that is needed is some information about a government program. The difficult problem comes when what is needed is legislation or maybe a rule changed or a rule created.

Of late, much has been said about this activity of legislators. Consider such mundane legislative action such as the odd little act from the Fifties extending price supports for rice growers to two counties in Arkansas that was mentioned in Part I. Or the recently much-maligned Export-Import Bank of the United States that provides payment guarantees for domestic sellers of goods to foreign buyers, and so helps foreign buyers of such goods finance these purchases. Or something possibly more nefarious, the exclusion of so-called end users of derivatives from having to post margin against their derivative positions entered into to protect against changes in the value of foreign earnings and or of raw materials.

All of these bits of law reduce the cost of production for some producers of goods. For the rice producers, it is the cost of credit for either the purchase of acreage or working capital by reducing the likelihood of default on either kind of credit. Similarly, the Export-Import Bank's program reduces the exporter's costs both by facilitating the buyers financing of the purchase and guaranteeing the sellers receipt of payment, generally reducing the seller's cost/amount of working capital. Avoiding the requirement of margin similarly reduces the effective cost of any derivative purchased, yet again by lessening the cost/amount of working capital. So much is clear. And in all three cases, at the margin, reducing costs probably increases sales. Endless arguments could be had over who benefits and by how much for each of these bits of law—farmer/banker/consumer, buyer/seller, producer/banker. But these arguments miss the impact on the costs of economic change. The first may possibly increase local prosperity; the second might possibly help expand a local economy or might instead, like various trade protection legislation mentioned in Part I, help to slow the demise of local industry or both; and the third may possibly expand an economy or slow its demise, but surely will reduce the cost of purchasing a derivative and so lead to increased fee income, and so increase the short-term bottom line of the sellers of such instruments.

One might run through the same kind of calculations with respect to various tax advantages bestowed on various parts of the American economy to the same indeterminate end, but the one thing that is clear is that the removal of such benefits, if benefits they are, would have a negative impact on identifiable pieces of local communities, just as their establishment had a positive benefit on those communities. However, as a matter of fostering or coping with economic change, it is hard to see much of either in any of these and similar provisions. There are of course, more extreme cases—both the programs encouraging the use of ethanol and the production and installation of solar panels and windmills. But, with apologies to environmentalist friends, even these larger programs disappear into a great mass of activities that is the American middle-class economy. Locally, they may be significant; but nationally, they are still noise.

To recognize that even the largest of these programs amount to no more than noise at the margin should not therefore imply that they are valueless. They can be very valuable to local economies; and after all the national economy is nothing but the sum of the multitude of local economies in their interactions with one another and the world outside this country's boundaries. And for most people, life is lived locally. As the story of Buffalo in Parts II and IV makes clear, booms that are not felt in local economies by local residents might as well be taking place in Patagonia, just as busts unfelt by others are mostly annoying stories on television news shows. Even worse, the degree to which a place is disconnected from booms and yet impacted by busts is a pretty good indication that such a place has slipped into advanced/backward trade relations and so evidence that the feeling of local prosperity is just that, a welcome, but implausible, feeling. Such feelings hide the likelihood of later, often regular disappointment, as is evident from the story of Buffalo in the years since the end of the Fifties boom.

The difficult question is how to respond to the political necessity to do something in response to economic change and, at the same time, to avoid doing something that will only bring eventual disappointment. Putting off the inevitable causes less human suffering than accelerating the inevitable but using law to lock in an old economic structure will simply increase costs, as law will regularly be enlisted to contain the eventual workarounds that humans always find. And, if these known limits on action were not enough, they all assume that the inevitable result is known beforehand, which is surely close to never the case. It is the lack of such foreknowledge that most strongly suggests that law's assistance be piecemeal and limited and offered knowing that the effectiveness of law is often overwhelmed by other social structures. Again, consider trade protection. While domestic production of radios, televisions, and related electronics eventually moved offshore, it is at least arguable that the complete disappearance to the American-made automobile was not similarly inevitable, though the move from complete dominance of the market by American manufacturers to present circumstances has been expensive, far more expensive than it needed to be, as management clung to an administrative and brand structure, employees clung to a work structure, and both to a labor relations structure, all of which made cost reduction and product change cumbrous in the extreme.

The foregoing discussion of the real limits on the ability of law to structure markets and direct economic change should not be taken to suggest that it is best that law do nothing, and not just because the exigencies of political life will bring action or because to refuse to act is, of course, the choice to do something. Rather, doing something is important because, in a democracy, humans deserve better from law than nothing, even if they seldom get equal benefit from action, as if citizens could know or agree on what equal required. And, as part of the better action that humans deserve is more careful action, though not in the sense of political CYA. Rather, they deserve more bold action, but bold action that is conscious of the limits to the effectiveness of law that comes from the fact that law is collective human action and humans are fallible creatures.[19]

What then, should law do that would be welcoming to the middle classes? When talking about what makes a community welcoming to the middle classes it is important to remember that seldom is this a matter of taxes and regulation, except possibly for the aging wealthy seeking to escape estate taxes and those investing in noxious industries, something no community, other than one so desperate for any shred of economic life as to find self-destructive backwards/advanced trade a desirable opportunity, would want in the first place. Rather, it is a simple question about whether one would like to live there. And the question of with whom one would like to live is always a matter of exclusion. The best evidence of this baseline is the list of people who advocate an inclusive community. Most often they wish to exclude (after all, silencing is a form of exclusion) racists, sexists, xenophobes, opponents of LBGT rights, opponents of abortion rights, opponents of teaching evolution in the schools, supporters of the NRA, and many other miscellaneous categories of people, and so to welcome only "people like us." Welcoming the middle class is never an unmixed blessing, but then again, the slow collapse of economic life is not much of an alternative either.

In addition to feeling welcomed, the middle classes want choice. As noted in Part IV, they want cars, houses, jobs, clothing and though, in the case of cars, as any large suburban parking lot will indicate, the choices the middle classes make turn out to be rather narrower than those available. With respect to housing, some like suburban single-family homes, others urban apartments; some, urban single-family houses, others suburban apartments. The list of possibilities could be longer and for many, the choice changes with age, family size, and station. For some, sprawl is great, for others, anathema; for some, old houses offer unparalleled possibilities, for others, only new construction will do. Walkable neighborhoods and small, hip shops; easily drivable neighborhoods and big chain stores. Shopping often; shopping seldom. Big gym, small gym, no gym, pool; public transportation, easy parking—preferably right near the door. But whatever the set of preferences at a time and place, the middle classes deeply dislike criticism of the choices they make, even if, and for some, especially if, such criticism comes from what objectively might be called "people like us."

In order to actually have any of those wants, the middle classes need economic stability. They are dependent on continuous employment, healthcare coverage, pensions, or private retirement funds, and where such are unavailable, Social Security benefits and Medicare. They may dislike funding such "entitlements" for others, but when shove comes, they need them for people like us. And they are formidable in pursuit of their wants and needs because they are so numerous and they vote.

Unfortunately, national governments can secure a reasonable amount of these needs of the middle classes, except for the key one—continuous employment. This the middle classes basically must do for themselves, but what such a government can do is to make it easier for local communities to welcome the middle class. It can help local governments—the only ones that make even modest economic sense; states are useless appendages of colonial history—supplement their meager resources from real estate and sales taxes—the former, a relic of the agricultural foundation of Western civilization and the latter, of the commercial foundation of modern capitalism—to provide the infrastructure necessary to secure the attention of the hoped for middle class—roads and bridges, water and sewers, public amenities such as parks and schools, and neighborhoods that are not an embarrassment. This is because it is only the nation, America, that has the ability to levy an effective, progressive income tax that recognizes that marginality applies, not just to ice cream cones, but also to extra income, and a large enough remit to redistribute it as needed.

Everyone knows that the middle classes hate taxes, or is it that they hate taxes that they do not see benefitting themselves, since in the end, they will be paying them? The latter is more likely. They did not complain about taxes when they paid for highways, or the cost of public higher education when they saw the opportunity it opened for their children. They only began to get stingy when taxes began to seem to them to benefit others more than themselves, when taxes began significantly to eat into marginal income and so into social position. And the national governmental apparatus cannot be expected to take over the infrastructure needs of every city, town, and hamlet in America, but at least it would help if that apparatus would place more dollars there and fewer in less plausible activities supposedly directed at economic development, such as intellectual property protection, sectorial support through tax preferences, and subsidies for emergent technology. Admittedly, much of this shift will not yield great sums for redistribution and so most will come from higher taxes. But government, which is to say law, has never been able to turn straw into gold or to feed multitudes on a few loaves and some fish.

There is another way of understanding what a national government might do to welcome the middle classes with all their different wishes for choices that they feel to be needs, not mere wants. It is a matter of an attitude toward its task: Maximize support for those activities that may possibly have the best chance to help the widest range of people. The idea would be that, given the limited ability of law to see, much less to understand the future, and the limited ability for it to design systems that will have their intended consequences, it is probably best to widen, rather than narrow, its targets. In this sense, helping finance investments in infrastructure is such a wider target. But even such an objective still calls for care in its pursuit. Waters and sewers are a wide target. All residents need clean, plentiful water and healthy sewerage disposal. Auditoria or stadia provide narrower targets. Significantly less than all residents will ever use an auditorium or stadium and claims to the contrary envision a fascist objective that is best not subsidized. Even such a simple object of national solicitation—roads and bridges—calls for careful efforts to separate needs from wishes, existing decrepitude from what would be nice to have, and even here it is important to be conscious that it is mighty easy to deploy the "only marginally more expensive" than the cost of repair argument to turn the former into the latter.

Even here, a real modesty is in order. New community centers will not transform neighborhoods; a single, even a large new employer or public facility (remember all the convention centers from the Eighties) or new bridge will not be a "game changer;" more libraries are not going to increase reading, though more books might help; and bringing high-speed internet into every home (and perhaps Wi-Fi for the homeless) is just not going to be "transformative." The more that infrastructure relates to "building our brand" or smells of entertainment, the less plausible it is for national support; brands die quickly and the entertainment that brings crowds too, as Rome of the Coliseum didn't understand.

Next, set aside building physical things and shift to more narrow economic matters, for example jobs. It is best to recognize that in general, "We are stuck with the peasants that we have, sire" as Sir Rodney said to the king of Id who had argued the need to replace his existing peasants who were revolting. The notion that, as a general matter, education is going to transform people into the workers who will fill the jobs they want or that others want them to want is implausible. An employment strategy that does not begin with the recognition that it has to include people of both genders who want to work with their hands is a fraud. An employment strategy that fails to recognize that some people will not want to work in the contemporary equivalent of the Fifties'-era gray flannel suit and a sea of cubicles, is built on fantasy. And in both cases, it will disappoint in a particular unfortunate way—disproportionately down the social ladder. Better for a nation not to do such things than to be seen as duplicitously favoring the already-favored classes.

Even more ephemeral in one sense and less in another, the national government can try to improve the structure of the economy. Not all such attempts have been failures. For example, the National Institutes of Health and the National Science Foundations may suffer from their bureaucratic rigidities, and in a different corner of the economic universe, the Defense Advanced Research Products Agency does too. However, all three have been modestly successful in advancing research in their respective fields. Similar research facilities might help the overall economy, especially if located somewhere other than the District of Columbia. In contrast, there are the recent disasters of Fannie Mae and Freddie Mac. Still, even here, "modest efforts" at structuring might help economic life. Fannie and Freddie could unwind the public objectives that it added to its more-narrow financing mandate while under a private ownership structure and these entities be returned to their mundane activity of using a government guarantee of simple mortgages as a way of making housing finance less expensive and less complicated, and so modestly reduce the cost of housing. Similarly, banking is crucial to any economy in its role as the provider of the utility services of moving money from place to place and making business and personal loans, the financial system's plumbing as it were. Changes that moved a portion of the industry away from that structure could be reversed and the rest of the industry left to go its merry way. Similarly, the structure of the securities law and taxes might be altered to increase internal investment, rather than distribution, of corporate earnings. Or the national government might try to make it difficult for local governments and developers to ignore the fact that, in most cases, any project that could not be undertaken without tax abatement is unlikely to be of more than marginal value and should be entered into very cautiously. Perhaps making such benefits fully taxable as ordinary income would do the trick.

Now, as the scare quotes around "modest" should indicate, none of these structural projects is politically modest, but it is important to understand that just because the legal structures that underpin any economy have often not worked out very happily does not mean that a nation must live with them for long periods of time. Of course, altering them will be costly, both for government and investors. Investments have been made in response to those structures; that was precisely what law hoped would take place when these structures were created. After all, it takes a lot of intellectual work to create a market; if no one comes to play, that is a dead weight loss. But remember that the capital recovery period for investments is seven or so years. That is a far shorter time than the capital recovery period for lives, much less communities. Investment can be worked down closer to zero, as was done through trade protection. Lawyers can easily figure out how to do it again and again.

In doing their work, lawyers need to remember some matters not yet attended to. Economic considerations can be overstressed when considering questions of economic development. They count more at the level of exports and imports than in more narrowly commercial contexts. They count more at the level of individual happiness and social welfare than most people would think. The same is true with cultural values/ideology. Americans' constant focus on price or worth, not value, inflects all sorts of things. It can be seen in such humble television programs as *Antiques Road Show*, the endless attention to raising shareholder value, the constant linear ranking of things as different colleges, cars, lipsticks, employees, and whatnot, from best to worst, without any sense of the smallness of differences in ordinal ranking. It makes results that can be understood as good seem deficient because they are not best. It makes it difficult to promote equality without making others on the social ladder feel that they have fallen behind. It makes invidious distinctions such as between "makers and takers" seem more plausible. It even makes hortatory concepts such as Richard Florida's Gay and Lesbian index seem threatening to other cultural values.[20]

Equally important, the social position of the interested parties makes a difference in what might be possible. Those who have modest power are less likely to be heard than those who have a stronger claim to be counted, especially if those with the stronger claim feel threatened by change or a possible response, or worse, both. Communities are much the same, and at the same time, feel the impact of change as well as the micro effects of development, differently. The latter is very, very hard to predict. And national governments whose problems are more difficult than the local ones, but whose powers are seemingly and in many ways actually greater, should have learned by now, but only sometimes attend to the fact that, where economies are concerned law can't make change happen, but can keep actions taken in response to change from being effective.

All of these concerns are important for they are relevant to what seems to be a good summary of law's difficult task, that is supporting economic development: avoid harm, offer help, promote change, and be sensitive to complexity. We have already seen the need for caution in matters of economic change. Execution of a do-no-harm-based strategy is even more complicated. Start with two rather easy cases that have been discussed before: the trade protection offered to declining consumer goods industries in the Sixties and Seventies through the quite hazy notion of "dumping," selling a product below cost. A similar program in the Eighties reduced auto imports through binational agreements. One might see this style of trade protection as a classic example of offering help while avoiding harm and promoting change. At the same time, it could be argued as insensitive to complexity, given that by ignoring the different capital recovery periods of capital and labor, it paid no attention to the impact on workers and the communities in which they lived.

The subsequent continuing attention to autos and steel are much harder to support. Initially, protection for the steel industry seemed to promote a shift to mini-mills, the basic oxygen furnace and continuous casting, as well as a decrease in the absolute size of the industry. Perhaps subsequent actions cover additional needs for a decrease in size. At the same time, it might well be argued that it is more likely an attempt to maintain an industry by continuously reducing the hourly cost of labor by increasing individual worker productivity, though not wages. Clearly this is not a case of do no harm.

Autos seem to have abandoned trade protection, difficult to defend given the continuously increasing presence of foreign manufacturers in America, and instead shifted to importing both parts and whole cars, increasing productivity through capital investment and focusing production on large, higher margin vehicles. Here too, productivity gains are not flowing through to employees. By avoiding a claim for trade protection, autos have shifted the question of harm to the larger issue of the structure of labor law. This is a complexity that everyone understands, some wish to do varying amounts about, but the political will necessary to do much of anything is clearly lacking. Such is a recurrent problem in a democracy that is based on inclusiveness, not ethnic fellow feeling, as much of Europe is increasingly realizing.

Whether the same analysis can be extended to products on the growth side of an economy is the old infant industry argument dragged from Hamilton's America to the Twenty-First Century. It is hard to tell how much, if any, evidence in the history of America since the Civil War will support or refute the argument, which is currently heard with respect to green technologies. However, intuitively, it seems likely that whether extending protection in this way is doing harm turns, not on the infant industry argument, but rather on the tendency of such an argument to be invoked where what is really being protected is plant location in the aid of growth strategies allied to advanced/backward trade. The failed placement of a large solar panel factory in Buffalo and earlier a computer chip plant in Albany are good examples of this kind of development, which is often fostered by entrepreneurs, academic or otherwise. They are at best building on educational resources alone but lack any other local resource base and so are essentially importing machinery and raw materials and exporting finished goods. Thus, they are unlikely to be fostering the local production of either the raw materials or the machinery. Such is a bad, but understandable, idea locally. Law's support for it on the national level would be even worse.

A topic discussed earlier—agricultural subsidy programs—is easy to reframe in terms of doing no harm. Agriculture has many parts. Cotton, sugar, and grains are commodities that are grown for both export markets and domestic consumption. There is even a small program covering wool. The existence of similar programs in the EU and Japan suggest some such programs in defense of food security would likely exist under any set of circumstances. Because market prices are significantly subject to worldwide crop/weather conditions, the obligation of law to help farm economies seems obvious. This is also one area where there have been enormous efforts directed toward promoting change. Farm bill after farm bill has attempted to do just that.

The complexities of doing anything are the real problem, as the enormous farm lobby has made clear. Crop subsidies may or may not increase prices to consumers, but they do increase land prices in farming communities, they do increase the market for very fancy machinery that is largely produced by a domestic farm implement industry, and they do support all sorts of allied seed production and animal breeding and fertilizer production industries as well. Large banks have no interest in, or ability to evaluate, farm mortgages. Most such mortgages are locally sourced. Most farmers are best described as "land poor," almost all of their wealth is tied up in an asset that is anything but liquid, and dependent on a cash flow cycle with a single peak followed by an ever-growing trough. Agricultural finance, except for chickens and eggs, which have a comparatively even cash flow, is just plain scary.

For law, the basic problem is simple. How does one promote change and avoid doing harm? Abrupt termination of crop subsidies would quickly bring the collapse of farm values and, as happened in the home mortgage market quite recently, defaults on farm mortgages (not to mention to secured finance of agricultural machinery), failure of the banks originating such mortgages and the collapse of a large number of the small towns that still survive in rural areas. This is not to say that, at a new, lower level of prices for agricultural products and farmland Americans would starve. Anything but. However, the carnage during the years between the subsidized regime and any new regime is close to unmentionable. At least the twenty to forty years (sensible estimate of the length of a working life) that it has taken Rust Belt communities to even partly absorb the changes in their economies from the movement of heavy manufacturing South, West, and overseas would be required for farm communities to absorb such a change as well. Many are probably too small to last that long.

It is not obvious which of the many possible designs for such subsidies would be least costly and would most likely lead toward a termination of subsidies. Even if one cares nothing about either corporate farms or the rural way of life, still on the basis of existing conditions, it is really hard to do no harm. A program designed to slowly wean farmers off existing subsidy programs would be of such duration that the notion of maintaining political support for such a long period of time seems fanciful. So, it is important to remember that sometimes law just can't fix things, even problems that law itself created.

Another example of the difficulty of avoiding harm, offering help, and promoting change, while law is sensitive to complexity, might be air transport deregulation discussed earlier. It is first necessary to reiterate a simple point. Deregulation was then, and is now, a misnomer. There are no unregulated markets. Even the market in illegal drugs is regulated, though poorly, by criminal sanctions and know your customer regulations governing banks and bank-like entities.

What airline deregulation did was respond to two things. The first was the general unhappiness with the high price of airfares and the limited scope of consumer options in the field. Many people agreed that the Civil Aeronautics Board was administering an oligopoly, as should have been expected of an agency that comes out of the Assocationalist ethos of the Twenties and Thirties. The second was a real lack of agreement about how the market in commercial flight ought to be structured. The language was of letting the market decide, but what was necessarily meant was that the structure of the industry would be created by the airlines, policed by the anti-trust laws, the bankruptcy code, the law of fraud, and misrepresentation and the hectoring of Congress.

Doing so was not stupid. Not knowing how to structure the industry, it was best to try not to do harm. Offering the possibility of lower fares was a real attempt at help to customers, if not to the industry that was somewhat scared of what the rigors of the marketplace would hold. And by not imposing a structure, deregulation was promoting change. Fares came down, new routes were opened, and new airlines appeared. Unfortunately, insufficient attention was paid to complexity. Airlines are somewhat like banks and farms. All three combine high fixed investments and real sensitivity to changes in both costs and price. This is a very scary place to be.

Rather quickly, bankruptcy, or its avoidance through merger, did its expensive work and soon an oligopoly was less stable and smaller. Innovation broke out in an attempt to remain solvent, though irregular changes in major costs, particularly fuel and downturns in economic life, nibbled away at the remaining members of the industry. Some routes were completely abandoned and some were contracted out to carriers with a lower labor cost structure; price discrimination became the key to maximizing revenue, more passengers were crammed into the same amount of space, and separate fees became a revenue source just as it had become for banks. The result has been an even smaller oligopoly that overall has reduced fares for some, but hardly all, passengers and has turned what was once a gracious mode of travel into the contemporary equivalent of the cattle car to the extent that the railroads that once went through the cattle car phase of passenger service, currently represented by Amtrak, now advertising its service by comparing it to air travel. The market's complexity is quite clearly as significant as law's or society's.

A common explanation for law's persistent failure to actually avoid harm, offer help, and promote change follows from an obvious proposition. No matter what the area is in question, it is reasonably predictable that that law is more likely to respond, and respond helpfully, based on social relations. The higher up the ladders that denote social and/or economic class, the more likely law will try. As the old saying goes, "Money talks." And in each of these three areas—trade protection, farm subsidies, and air travel—law's failures work largely for the benefit of embedded capital.

It thus would be silly to deny when law is relatively less effective, poor people are not likely to benefit. At the same time, one needs to remember that, "Prediction is difficult, especially of the future."[21] It is difficult for a polity and for its law, which is to say the government of the polity, to predict the future and to plan ahead for it. Predict a tsunami, something far less complex than the results of the deregulation of air travel and evacuate hundreds of thousands of people from coastal areas. If the tsunami doesn't come, the blame will far exceed any credit one might have garnered from having been right. It is thus hardly surprising, on independent grounds, that decisions will be biased in the direction do doing no harm to the people highest up on the relevant ladder.

Of course, this is precisely why economic development is so hard to do. If Jacobs is right and economic development cannot be predicted, though it can be kept from happening by taking actions that might make it more difficult, and only with difficulty can law plan ahead, indeed might better be seen as impotent in the face of an uncertain future, one would predict that such development as law attempts will be directed up the ladder and, for elected or appointed officials, to do pretty much what everyone else is doing. If everybody is doing eds and meds or nano technology or green energy, doing what everyone else is doing will provide the most protection from being blamed for the equivalent of dragging people out of their homes to protect them from the tsunami that did not come. And that is precisely what must be guarded against for economic development needs to be addressed to making individual places, and thus in sum, but not as a unity, America, a place that the middle classes will feel welcome in.

This is not a statement about immigration. Welcoming immigrants is much like providing a better life for the poor; it is an obligation that derives from their humanity. The idea that providing green cards to people who "invest" in America confuses an obligation toward others with portfolio investment, a category mistake and category mistakes are embarrassing as such. A place that welcomes the middle classes is one that believes that people who feel welcome are likely to come without a bribe and invest because they believe that they have something to offer to a nation's economy. Thus, for a nation, the reason to make their middle classes feel welcome is similar to the activity of city/regions when making their middle classes welcome, as discussed in Part IV. But it is more difficult for one who can't really design a national program since one size is not likely to fit all and notions of fairness between citizens and political entities always will push in the direction of one size. And yet, law cannot do nothing.

And Well Schooled

It is close to the truth to suggest that this section is included only as a matter of formal symmetry. Even closer to the truth would be to recognize that it would be embarrassing to have nothing even modestly interesting to say about this subject, but even more embarrassing to allow that to be fact to be made apparent by omission. What might best be said is that here, as everywhere, the law of unintended consequences/ineffectuality applies. For example, facilitating borrowing for college education, however well intended, seems to have done little else than increase individual indebtedness, give state legislatures an excuse for reducing support of public higher education, and give private higher education the ability to raise tuition. One might also note that the human capital theorists are correct in that they understand that education is absolutely crucial to economic growth, but at the same time it is equally clear that a world where everyone had a Ph.D. degree would not be any better, and just might be worse, than the one we have. And, to add to this mess despite its general value, there is a narrower sense of relevance and a greater demand for job readiness in higher education than in PreK-12 education. This may suggest that we have far too many people in higher education than we need and that such education costs far more than would be appropriate for job readiness. From these observations, it ought to be clear that job readiness is not what higher education is about. Better candidates for the purpose of these expenditures would include a reduction in unemployment, a modest increase in social skills, a way of helping employers choose employees who can endure the intense boredom of cubical/open office life and, as T. S. Eliot said, accumulating "fragments" to be "shored against my ruin." To me, all of these possible purposes are not obviously worth the cost imposed on families, though they may be worth enough if imposed on governments.

It is also quite clear that children, and young adults, are best taught in small groups by teachers who are deeply committed to their success, but that there is little agreement about what ought to be taught, what ought to be the object of that teaching, and therefore, what ought to be considered success. Recent efforts provide a good case for the proposition that national moneys for K-12 education only raise the pitch of the disputes over these three topics and bring far more bureaucratic oversight to educational practice, thus raising the cost of the education delivered so that it begins to approach the level of higher education where there are now more administrators than full-time faculty. And yet, it is clear that some oversight of the expenditure of the enormous amounts of money spent on K-12 education and on financing higher education is sensible. Ronald Reagan was not nuts when he said, "Trust, but verify."

More true than all of these statements is that there is absolutely no one with good evidence about how to get us out of this mess.

Et Cetera

Again, it would not be surprising if at this point, readers again expect to hear the suggestion that the residents of the nation called America ought to draw a nice warm bath, slide into its comfort, and slit their collective wrists. Such a suggestion is beyond imagination, because one can only be this despairing about someplace one loves. However, sometimes it takes a four-by-four straight to the temple to get the mule's attention and that is what this Part is meant to be. In these unpromising circumstances, there is no place for either nostalgia over, "the way we were," or for anger kept alive by picking at the scabs. So, review once more, this time with feeling.

It would be hard to maintain that the American economy did not fall apart between the late Sixties and the early Eighties or that three times we have tried to restart it, only to have it collapse, first in the savings and loan crisis, next in the dot.com boom and bust, and most recently in the real estate boom and bust that ushered in the Great Recession. The first and third were quite obviously brought on by a failure in market structure, banking in the former, and banking and mortgage finance in the latter. In the second, it is doubtful that there was a serious structural problem in the traditional legal sense, but the unwillingness of market regulators to use existing authority, the ability to raise or lower margin minima to control asset inflation, was a structural failure of a different type. Even closer related were the symptoms of these structural failures—dubiously priced assets, first real estate, next stock and most recently, debt instruments. In each case, at least some people identified the dubious pricing, but were unwilling or unable to do anything about it other than watch the crash from the sidelines. In one case, the chairman of the Federal Reserve Board called out the relevant market for tolerating "irrational exuberance" and was roundly criticized for doing so.

Hidden in these three stories are two problems with our economy that bear consideration. The first is in some sense, deeply intellectual—we have no way to understand value other than price. Value connotes intrinsic worth; price identifies what someone will pay today. It is an old problem that the medieval notion of fair price, of the tradesman's desert for the goods sold in the trade, attempted to solve by bridging value—the real, with price—the ephemeral. Contemporary economy reverses the ascription: price is the real and value is but a theoretician's model, an attempt to explain price that can be tested by comparison with actual prices. This choice is understandable as a part of the modern rejection of medieval understandings of the market, but it does have a particularly unfortunate aspect. Price is never just price, but also is position with respect to others in the market and those who are acting for the others.

For pure speculators, the nominal nature of price is just part of a game of "greater fool," at least unless the speculator's position is heavily leveraged and the provider of any necessary credit is not adequately hedged or sufficiently capitalized, conditions that often do not hold in rampaging markets. For the rest of the participants in the market, price is most often relevant to the return on a mutual fund or trust account or an endowment fund or a pension plan or insurance company assets. These returns then feed into the forward-looking plans of the beneficiary of the account as well as the earnings of the account's managers. To the extent that gains in a boom market are realized, the interests of the beneficiaries and the managers are reasonably congruent, but to the extent they are not, managers, who get paid in a shorter run have reason to run a position out for maximum return, especially if the position is leveraged, even if over the longer horizon of the beneficiaries, capturing a smaller gain would be a safer alternative. In a circumstance such as this, the choice of law to let a boom play itself out or to puncture the balloon is most often a choice between players with different interests, some of whom will be really angry and utter complaints about government picking winners and losers. This leads to caution on law's part, which may turn out to be unwarranted when the boom is over.

It is important to understand that exactly this problem can be identified in most any of law's programs suggested or offered for the benefit of the economy. The difficulty is that no matter which decision law makes—to act or not to act—law will be making a choice, picking winners and losers. Support producers, and consumers will lose; support consumers, and the producers will lose. This is true of bankers and depositors, auto dealers and auto manufacturers, shippers and railroads, and so forth. And that is the point of law . . . choosing, hopefully for better than for worse reasons.

It is at the time of choice that it is important for law to understand that what might be good for an industry or for consumers is not therefore good for the national economy. As usual, it all depends! But the one thing that isn't true is that an economy is the sum of whatever is good for every narrow economic interest.

And thus, it is essential that when choosing and when structuring markets, law exercise real care and develop a certain tough skin, for the interest hurt will be heard loudly and the interests helped will be smeared out in the great noise that is moving parts in any economy.[22]

Not only is it necessary to remember that what is good for a local economy is not necessarily good for the national economy, but this is just one difference between local and national entities that needs to be remembered. To follow the subtitle, start with "community." There is a concreteness to local communities that makes it relatively easy to identify segments of a local population and consider what might be done to help them. The abstractness of the notion of community at the national level makes it easy to confuse local situations with the nation situation, doing a disservice to both. A middle-class family in New York City or suburban Chicago or rural Iowa or a mining town in Arizona have so little in common as to render a national housing policy designed to address middle-class housing needs irrelevant. It could easily miss all four communities. That would be a waste of the tax dollars necessary to administer the program.

The situation is similar with respect to "economy." Silicon Valley's economy needs a better transportation network or more middle-class housing nearby, or better, both. Buffalo has a good transportation network and plenty of middle-class housing but suffers from a mismatch between available jobs and available employees. Tucson also has a remarkably effective transportation network, needs middle-class housing, but is not building any except multifamily, and generally suffers from a shortage of lower-middle class jobs. There is no possible national economic strategy that would cover all three places, and in most of America, the notion of helping Silicon Valley's economy would be taken as ludicrous.

And then there is "law." Localities are both dependencies of their states and dependent on their states because their source of financing is based on real estate taxation and fees for services. Both of these sources of resources are cyclical, rising in good times and falling in bad, when what localities need is a counter-cyclical source of revenue. The states that they are dependent on are often anything but plausible economic units, unlikely to be replaced any time soon with more plausible economic units, say Federal Reserve districts. Both of them have fairly good coercive powers, but not the money for an effective administration. In contrast, the federal government has rather weak coercive powers, but is capable of raising lots of funds. Surely no one expected that such would be the result of the Sixteenth Amendment.

At the national level, these differences translate into a need for widely flexible programs, which are hard to secure agreement on. There is very little likelihood of the cement and asphalt contractors in State A being willing to provide support for road building only in other states—and even harder to fund. Moreover, the lack of uniformity makes administration harder and the claims of political favoritism, often called corruption, easier to mount. Even worse is the willingness to see community development projects as aid to the economically marginalized and tax reduction as vehicles for economic development. All three targets turn on serious category mistakes as well as misunderstandings of what might help make any region, or the nation as a whole, attractive to the middle classes. As such, they suggest the need for extreme caution in choosing what to do.

Still, remember that doing nothing is just as much a choice as doing something that will, in the end, turn out to be unhelpful. Either choice will bring individuals to invest, maybe money, but surely a built life, based on the future that such choice envisions. And so, there is always the possibility, maybe even a likelihood, of real loss when the future turns out otherwise than envisioned. And if that isn't enough of a problem, much of the economic theory that will inevitably underlie the choice made will make assumptions about the educational capacity, as well as achievement—for that is what is the rock on which reason, and so a reasonable investor, in economics is built—that are probably wrong for a great proportion of the people whose lives will be affected by the choice. Even worse, the same thing is true of the savings decisions, for the limited spectrum of people may have the ability to save for eventual retirement, as part of building an estate beyond Social Security benefits, meager as they are.

Caution is not the half of it. Caution may be all of it, as there is no choice but to act in the face of our real inability to predict the, well any, future.

Once more, academics who publish observations related to current events are always asked, "Well, then, what should we do?" As if an education brings wisdom and not just perspective. It is in this circumstance with this past that the relevant question needs to be remembered: If economic development is something a nation can no more command than a farmer can command rain, what might be sensible advice to that nation to occupy its time while waiting for possible rain? Four suggestions come to mind; only one of them likely to be very popular.

First, "Grow up!" Americans are tired of being embarrassed by their governments and one another. Politicians wish to be reelected and so they need to deliver for their constituents. Representatives of industries, the public good, or just people who share the same problem, also wish to be employed and so need to deliver for their expected beneficiaries. Anyone who thinks otherwise is a fool. And in a world where delivering such is really, really hard, it is understandable that one might decide that a second-best alternative may be protecting such groups from what they fear. The fears of constituents or expected beneficiaries are often quite real, especially when they are a feeling that an accustomed world is crumbling and their place in it too. That feeling is what change brings, both economic and social. However, screaming that the world should be different is not a sensible strategy and blocking change is even worse. Both kinds of representatives need to help the people whom they represent to understand: one, that the Heraclitan river is not a tidal pool, but flows only one way; two, that the best strategy may be securing the support necessary to rebuild disrupted lives in way that will be different than before, but possibly in other ways comfortable going forward, all the time knowing that doing so will be expensive; and three, that there are always larger groups than their own to whom they owe allegiance that need their support too, groups at both the local and the national level whose strength is absolutely necessary for there to be a "United" States.

Second, "Do something," anything but tax cuts for which, on the basis of the past fifteen or so years, we have a good reason to believe will not work in the current economic circumstances. Try tax increases; they worked more recently; perhaps they will work again. Or try infrastructure investments or modest reductions is agricultural subsidies or increased aid for shop training in grades nine through twelve or universal healthcare (that would surely reduce an expense for most companies as well as spread the cost more widely) or weakened patent and copyright protections or increased the availability of national lands for natural resources recovery or increased defense spending on research and development or . . . or . . . or . . . or . . . . But don't lock in any change for a long period or, except for taxes, even for the whole country, because we have no reason to believe that any of these "somethings" will work.

Third, be humble. Once again remember that in the face of real uncertainty, shrill is unwarranted and political posturing really detrimental to America, which after all, is the entity that law on the national scale is responsive to. Don't fear change: welcome it and don't demonize, even the one percenters. Change cannot be reversed, but humans can tame it to a certain extent. Americans have done so before and they will do so again, as William Faulkner, as pessimistic a person about the potential of humans for cussedness as one could have, made clear.[23] Of course, it will be a different tame, though in no sense a devolved tame, but rather a tame as appropriate to the time and circumstance as Americans can make it.

Fourth, don't take academics, think-tank occupants, or other intellectuals too seriously.

Is Conclusion Even Possible?

Friends have suggested that it is Jane Jacobs's stubbornness that makes her work attractive to me. They may be right. Stubbornness comes as easy to me as to Jacobs. But conclusion does not. Let me start with a simple one. For many years, Buffalo was America written small. Then, starting sometime in the Sixties, Buffalo slowly lost this relatively direct relationship with the national economy.

America was there first, but once Buffalo got going, both part and whole created manufacturing economies based on transportation networks that, on the national scale, led to oligopolistic structures and, on the local scale, to becoming parts of a distributed structure. After World War I, existing transportation networks began to reconfigure themselves while both America and Buffalo grew quickly, then just as quickly fell into the Depression, an international phenomenon with no obvious singular cause. In response to the resulting economic devastation, Roosevelt's New Deal propped up the national and local economies modestly while enacting an economic model of a good economy called Associationalism, parts of which dated back to the turn of the century. While World War II pulled the national and Buffalo economies out of the Depression, after the war most of the rest of the world's economy was again no better than at the beginning of the Depression. In contrast, the American and Buffalo economies thrived in the nation's Associationalist structure.

By the middle of the Sixties, however, Buffalo's urban fabric was showing real wear, so that the suburban economy was dragging the political city along at a time when the national economy seemed to be doing better. Then, by the early Seventies both the national and the regional Buffalo economies were on the ropes as the Great Inflation destroyed economic expectations everywhere. In the following thirty-plus years the national Associationalist economy was slowly dismantled by a process called deregulation, though clearly it was more than just that. In time, the American economy improved, only to fall apart several times, always somehow, someway related to the financial markets. However, no one would say that the overall economy thrived as it had in the Fifties. In contrast, over these years, the economy of the region called Buffalo continued to slide downhill more extremely, and recover less completely, than the national economy. Then, in the Great Recession, the regional economy didn't collapse as did that of the rest of the country because the region had had no intervening boom, a clear, if odd example of coming off better because of having been worse. Buffalo had significantly decoupled its economy from the national one.

It is rather difficult to explain why the once tight part/whole relationship between Buffalo and the national economy fell apart, but there are several possibilities: the insularity of the Buffalo culture that came from the geographic structure of that place; the failure of the region to secure several corporate headquarters in the aftermath of the Great Merger Movement; the dependency that came ingrained from having developed a branch plant economy of advanced/backward transactions; the decline in the importance of railroad transportation and the increase in the importance of truck transportation that followed the construction of the interstate highway system; the culture of distanced portfolio capitalism among the families who liquidated their investments in the course of the Great Merger Movement and subsequently; and the risk adversity of labor that made it easy to look backward and so measure future possibilities in terms of real, or imagined, past lives.

What should one think about the decoupling of this part/whole relationship that Buffalo contributed to for so many years? Some people counsel that no one should care. Some might even read parts of this book as suggesting the plausibility of a distanced relationship to economic demise. In a cosmic sense it is doubtful that it matters if Buffalo grows or continues to decline. But damn few people live in the cosmic sense. Most people live anchored in a community, sometimes deeply, sometimes shallowly. In that community, survival, not to mention thriving, makes a difference. The coming apart of a way of life is sad. Community matters for those within it, because one of the ways that people build a hopeful, stable life is on the assumption of community's continued existence. Taking action that might help rebuild a declining community is thus also a very human activity. So too is waiting for rain, perhaps a hope against hope.

A second conclusion might note that it would be a great mistake to see this story about Buffalo's past, or the one about our nation's, as an occasion for wallowing in nostalgia. The past is past; there is no way to recreate it and, if there were, I doubt that many people would be happy living in whatever past was chosen. This is especially true of Buffalo in the Fifties—Klinkenborg's *Last Fine Time.* It was a fine time only in the sense that, at a party held on the night before Prohibition, people had a fine time. There was decay underneath both occasions and that decay had been growing for more than just a while. In addition, in both cases there was chaos and destruction in the offing.

All of which is not to say that good things did not happen in the Fifties. The creation of a large hourly or wage-earner middle class was an extraordinary achievement and its subsequent collapse, a terrible social and economic disaster.[1] It would not be wrong to say the anger at this disaster is what has motivated writing this book. Unfortunately, the Associationalist economy that supported the creation of an hourly middle class is very unlikely to be replicated, both because innovation is no longer done in the same way and because, if being the last man standing in the graveyard is a necessary part of the prescription, in an era with gobs and gobs of atomic weapons, the next aftermath will be far more horrifying than the aftermath of World War II. It will be something of which dystopian novels are made. The wage-earning middle class will be quite tiny and its wages, quite small.

Still, an attempt to rebuild a broader middle class could surely be undertaken. And the attempt would not be a waste of time and effort, at least if one takes democratic ideals seriously. If tried, it is quite likely that law would have some part of structuring the accompanying economy. At the same time, it is exceedingly unlikely that large amounts of government money would be what brings the onset of necessary growth, though political necessity guarantees that such will be spent. Instead, if successful, the result will be because some set of innovative technologies, "technologies of freedom," will interact with a return to significantly cheaper higher education to produce an economy that will be capable of using both highly skilled individuals and highly educated individuals and value both for their different abilities. Admittedly that is a tall order; there is no reason to believe that it has to be a pipe dream.

A third conclusion would start with the hope that no one who has read this far would come away with the idea that I believe that economy is in some sense a natural, unstoppable thing. Technology may be, but economy is not, except in the sense from the outdated anthropology of primitive peoples, of how these people do these things. As I said in the opening of Part I, "By the economy I mean *a persistent market structure that is the fusion of an understanding of economic life with the patterns of behavior within the economic, political, and social institutions that enact that understanding.*" Economic life thus may change, indeed does change all the time, without necessarily implying that there has been a change in "the economy," an enacted understanding of economic life. Thus, if one sees human action as outside of nature,[2] neither economy nor economic life can sensibly be seen as natural.

Nor are economy or economic life unstoppable. We regularly use law, as defined in the opening of Part I, "And by law, I mean *the many and variable actions undertaken by lawyers and other governmental officials, the formal and effective norms originating from the practices of these individuals, and the systematic presuppositions shared among them,*" in an attempt to, if not stop economic change, then at least alter, or deflect it from its present course. Sometimes this attempt has worked and sometimes it hasn't and sometimes it has worked, but not in the way it was supposed to. Law is not the Archimedean lever; there is no place to stand in the Heraclitan river and therefore, as noted, "Prediction is very difficult, especially about the future." In such a world, a certain real modesty is called for.

It is here that it seems to me that Jane Jacobs, a not particularly modest person,[3] seems to be helpful when she maintains that economic growth can best be seen as a matter of grace, a usage that I have altered to "rain" for previously stated reasons. Americans or Buffaloons can wait and watch, hope and pray, but predicting rain in a particular place, at a particular time, is iffy, even in a hurricane. And so, it is urgent that we reduce our vision to the question of what to do while waiting for rain. The answers that are offered here seem to respond best to the difficulty of prediction. Do not become members of a cargo cult expecting gifts to be showered on them by absent gods. Rather, use public funds to make a community better, as defined by the middle classes in this middle-class democracy. They are from whom innovation is more likely to come and whose staying in a place will most directly provide an economic return to that place for making innovation and innovators welcome.[4]

This is not a fancy argument; no argument under conditions of uncertainty could be. But it seems to me stronger than the arguments that come from either the Party of the Right or the Party of the Left. The former conflates the notion of deserving from past success and present resources, to argue that lower taxes on current income will allow entrepreneurs to invest more money in more innovative economic ideas. This idea ignores the regularly stated caution in mutual fund advertisements to the effect that past performance is no guarantee of future returns. It also ignores the lack of evidence of such investment practices both by successful entrepreneurs, who seemingly prefer personal real estate and portfolio investments, and of private equity and venture capital funds whose short-time horizon and rapaciousness are commonplaces.

The latter conflates the notion of deserving from of past deprivation and present need, to argue that funds spent for development in poor communities will bring economic development to the community at large. This idea shows a lack of understanding that, though effective economic development feeds back into a community through wages and profits, the important wages and profits are from exports to other communities, not from services delivered to all or any part of the community.

Both arguments tell us more about hopes and dreams than about any plausible relationship between law and economy, a relationship that, as far as I can tell, suggests the implausibility of putting much faith in enacted hopes and dreams.

The fourth conclusion derives from the quotation from Fernand Braudel's masterwork, *Capitalism and Material Life—1400–1800*, that begins this book and follows this conclusion—"Man lives from choice in the framework of his own making, trapped in his former achievements for generations on end." It is my recognition of the truth of Braudel's assertion that led me to begin this book with my two long stories about America and Buffalo. If one cannot order economic life going forward, but only recognize its coherence in the rearview mirror (and yet will live in the framework of that past for generations), one had better be pretty clear about what that framework was and why it continues to hold us in its thrall. If not, we will be less able modestly to steer economic life as we might wish because we will not recognize the time-boundedness of ideas that may appear to be hard constraints on action but may only be ghosts of economies past. Such an inability would not be a good state of affairs in this or any middle-class democracy, if only because it would accept as long lasting that which was both created for an economic world that has disappeared and also is unlikely to be even very loosely related to the economic world that is to come.

May 4, 2022

Man lives from choice in the framework of his own making, trapped in his former achievements for generations on end.

—Fernand Braudel, Civilization and Capitalism 15th–18th Century

Economic life develops by grace of innovating; it expands by grace of import-replacing.

—Jane Jacobs, Cities and the Wealth of Nations

A Note for Historians

It is odd, but useful, that the juxtaposition of the "old" growth theory of Robert Solow—labor and capital—and the New Growth theory of Robert Lucas and Paul Romer—labor, capital, and human capital—should be helpful in approaching the disputes about causation that have raged in the Academy since I have been a part of it. As I discussed in Part III, Lucas and Romer added human capital to Solow's equations that attempted to explain what caused economic development, because they believed and used mathematical methods to demonstrate that their three-factor model better explained causation than Solow's model. Their model allowed them to say "truer" things than Solow's. My suspicion is that they are correct.

At the same time, it is important to remember that economics, like the health sciences, most of the social sciences, and law suffers from physics envy. Physics can state true things; it can say definitely that this causes that, or at least, before Einstein and Heisenberg, it could and since none of the rest of us can understand contemporary physics, for us, it still does.[1] Historians have long talked and argued in terms of causation. Did slavery cause the Civil War or was it really New England capitalism? Law talked the same way. Did law cause economic change or vice versa; did changing understandings of the corporate form cause the development of industrial capitalism or vice versa?

Then in the Seventies, it quite suddenly became impossible to speak in terms of causation. Everything was too complicated. Telling stories was out, at least stories that had *a* meaning. The best that a historian could do was to thickly describe what had happened, but even that needed to be qualified by the limits of the author's research and perspective. Words like "explain or "understand' seemed to be the best a historian could do.

I came to do history because I liked to tell stories and thought that some of the stories I had been told were unlikely to be true. For me, the attempt to tell a story, to explain or come to understand what happened, implied that at least one of the parts of an explanation could be an answer to the question "Why"; a causal question that might be very hard, even impossible, to figure out, but that was not therefore unintelligible as a question. Thus, while I might not be able to "know" what happened and why, I was not limited to what I "believed" to have happened and why: there was a place in between.[2] That in-between place is where I have tried to work in this book.

I began with two stories, one about America and one about Buffalo, one less thickly described and one more thickly described. The former was relatively thinly described because I could not possibly complete a thicker description in my lifetime. The comparatively thicker one was written that way because I hope that such a presentation would help to understand the thinner one, and vice versa. I then explored Jane Jacobs's understanding of economic development and used it, with more success, to explain the thicker, Buffalo story. I had less success using Jacobs's work to explain the thinner, American story. It is here where old and new growth theory became helpful.

I never liked the Solow model. It left too much out. So, intuitively the Lucas and Romer's model seemed better, except that it seemed to me that "human capital" meant the same thing as labor and so they were counting the same thing twice or misnaming whatever they were counting or dividing labor into two segments—low skilled and high skilled. Such a choice conflated skill with years of education, a clean mistake. My preference is to believe that it is the second misnaming, though my fear is that it is the third. But whatever the reality, the important question is what would be a better name? If education is really what is being counted, then pretty much what is being measured is how economically advanced a country or place already is. Such an understanding is tautological. Not much of an advance on the Solow model. But human capital might be a placeholder for openness to the world that is sometimes said to follow from increasing education, a question of culture that economists would find really hard to quantify and so not disciplinarily attractive.

For historians, however, culture is in front of us all the time. And it is easier to see in the smaller unit of analysis, Buffalo, than in America. In Buffalo, one can see how geography can lead to insularity, not to the openness to the world implied by being a trading place; how employment in mass production industries can lead to both security and dependence, to an inability to recover from adverse economic effects; how capital is not fungible—that local capital reinvested creates a different social environment, one where capitalist elites care more about the community, not just more than distant capital, but also more than local portfolio capital; and how all three aspects of local culture work together to look backward not forward, to care more about defending a past, real or imagined, to treat as unwelcome opportunities that might be different from that past. It is in this sense that causation is an integral part of understanding or explanation.

Or consider the cultural understanding of value. In American culture, value has been pretty much equated it with price. The equation acts together with the cultural understanding that compensation, a measure of the value of services performed by managers of large business corporations, should be based on total return to shareholders from steadily increasing earnings per share; similarly, that the compensation of managers of investment funds should be based on the fund in question beating the relevant market return. The same logic explains how the need of corporate managers to show increasing returns and of managers of funds that hold securities that beat the market combine to drive innovation out of portfolio companies in order for them to save income and increase returns, while at the same time squeezing both labor and suppliers. Increased returns fatten the retirement accounts, full of shares in investment funds, of the upper-middle and lower-upper classes, themselves squeezed by the impermanence of employment quite similar, and at the same time, incredibly different, from that of the line worker. Again, this is an example of how causation is an integral part of understanding or explanation. And the entire mixture is shot through with law—contracts, corporations, estate planning, and securities—much of it of dubious efficacy.

Granted, this is not as simple and direct a causation as is implied by the old argument about whether the law drives capitalism or, more plausibly, capitalism drives law or whether capital causes labor's impoverishment or, less plausibly, labor's impoverishment is a result of its low value, statements that sound rather silly when put so bluntly. But it is still the case that causation is a central part of historical understanding. And so, a central part of why I believe that capital, not capitalism which, for me, is a separate concept,[3] is central to economic life and that the structuring of the institutions in which capital operates is thus central to the life that a community lives, and thus a central job for law, which is to say government, in any economy.

NOTES

Introduction

1. *Washington Post*, 11/23/08.

2. A word about periodization is in order. I am a legal and economic historian; I speak in historian's periods, not calendrical ones. I take the Eighteen Seventies to extend from 1865 to the Panic of 1884 and the Eighteen Eighties, to extend to the Panic of 1893. The Eighteen Nineties then extend until the Panic of 1907. That leaves little time for the Naughts, and it's an ugly word anyway, so I call the years after 1907 the Teens. The Nineteenth Century ends, and the Twentieth Century begins with the Twenties, which begin with the end of the postwar demobilization, about 1919, and extend until the stock market crash in 1929. The Thirties is a long period continuing until 1941 when, with the adoption of Lend-Lease, the U.S. economy was placed on a wartime footing. The Forties extend only to 1947, the end of the postwar inflation. Then came the Fifties. The Sixties begin late in 1962 and end with the rise in oil prices that accompanied the Yom Kippur War in 1973. The Seventies continue until the onset of the Reagan administration in 1981 or maybe until inflation finally turns down in the wake of the terrible recession of 1982. The Eighties begin thereafter or possibly in 1979 when the Federal Reserve Board moved to contract the money supply sharply and lasts until the end of the recession just before the start of the Clinton administration, that is the Nineties. The second, ugly Naughts unaccountably start on schedule with the new millennium. These are, I most emphasize, economic periods; I would identify social periods quite differently.

In contrast, I use ordinary Arabic numbers for all dates and periods before 1865 and for all calendrical references thereafter. For example, the Thirties covers economic events during the years between 1929 and 1941; the 1930s covers the period that includes 1930 through 1939.

Part I

1. Similarly, readers may be interested in knowing my specific positions on the twin issues of trade and inequality. I am a rabid free trader, believing that a country best serves its lower and middle classes by providing them with goods as cheaply as possible so that their

relatively limited resources stretch as far as possible. I also am in favor of a radical increase in the progressivity of the income tax and of an expansion, not contraction, of the estate tax together with an increase in the progressivity of that tax as well. My beliefs on these tax measures derive from the propositions that little good, other than charitable contributions, comes from income more than necessary to buy the "good Republican cloth coat" of Nixonian fame, and that children are best treated when they claim their own independence.

2. Joseph A. Schumpeter, *Capitalism, Socialism, and Democracy* (London: Routledge, 1942), 82–83.

3. As best as we can figure out, Fred Konefsky used the phrase in an exam question that he asked me to read in the late 1970s or early 1980s, but never used it in any publication. I like it because it captures what Marx was writing about—technologies that diminished the freedom for many.

4. Willard Hurst speaks of these things regularly: see *Law and the Conditions of Freedom in the Nineteenth Century United States* (Madison: University of Wisconsin Press, 1956); *Law and Social Process in United States History* (Ann Arbor: University of Michigan Law School, 1960); and *Law and the Social Order in the United States* (Ithaca, NY: Cornell University Press, 1977).

5. Alfred R. Konefsky, "Simon Greenleaf, Boston Elites, and the Social Meaning and Construction of the Charles River Bridge Case," in Daniel W. Hamilton and Alfred L. Brophy, eds., *2 Transformations in American Legal History: Essays in Honor of Professor Morton J. Horowitz* (Cambridge: Harvard University Press, 2010), 165–95.

6. Robert Wiebe, *The Search for Order, 1877–1920*. (New York: Hill & Wang, 1967.

7. However, it could be argued that this can be said only of the most narrowly economic notion of the demise of the archipelago. For the consumer/cultural aspect of an economy it was not until after the effective completion of the interstate highway system, the growth of television, and the malling of the countryside that the final unity of the American economy was complete.

8. My gorge rises whenever I hear or see the distinction between the financial and the real economy. There is nothing more real to humans than a collapse in the financial economy, as we have learned recently, and a real economy without financings would not be a capitalist one, as I have emphasized elsewhere. Still, I have fallen back on the old distinction because every alternative I could come up with—the tangible and the intangible economies (which has services on the wrong side of the line) or the material and the immaterial economies (which has a wonderful old Marxian ring to it that I do not mean) or the goods and nonfinancial services and the financial services economies (which is just plain ugly) or the productive and the financial economies (which only make explicit what is wrong with the distinction between the real and financial economies) or the old and the new economies (which is wrong on so many levels that I will not even start) are no better or even worse. For once I will settle for the old ways. I guess it is a symptom of age shifting from creeping to galloping.

9. Jeffry A. Frieden, *Global Capitalism: Its Fall and Rise in the Twentieth Century* (New York: W.W. Norton, 2007).

10. It did include the power to issue Federal Reserve Notes, the first national paper currency since the Civil War Greenbacks.

11. Naomi R. Lamoreaux, *The Great Merger Movement in American Business, 1895–1904* (New York: Cambridge University Press, 1985).

12. David A. Skeel, Jr., *Debt's Dominion: A History of Bankruptcy Law in America* (Princeton, NJ: Princeton University Press, 2004), 73–100.

13. It is important to understand the economics of railroading. It is relatively inexpensive to move a rail car from point A to point B, at least once the right of way and trackage are paid for. This fact led to Nineteenth Century railroads to build competing routes, however indirect, to capture/serve the business of users who paid per ton mile rates for carriage. Two consequences followed. First, the highest cost of any such movement was loading, assembling, and disassembling trains, activities that required large numbers of workers; so every stop added a disproportionate expense. Thus, the short line proverbial "milk train," serving dairy farmers daily that added cargo, even if the cargo was far more valuable than milk, added only marginally to overall profit for the trunk line. Second, the existence of lines brought industrialization to areas served by those lines and such increases in volume helped profits. Cessation of production, however, left "stranded costs" that symmetrically dragged down profits, a problem that became acute in the Thirties and thereafter.

14. Two exceptions need be noted. Western agriculture benefitted from continued Mexican immigration for agricultural work even after the cut off of European immigration. The Tens and Twenties saw the beginning of the Great Migration of Blacks both to the Northern industrial cities and to the Southwest.

15. Objection has been made to my preference for calling this school of thought, in part identified with the American "institutional" economists, "corporatism," because of that word's association with the forms of economic organization adopted in fascist countries, most explicitly Italy. I do not think that the association is wholly wrong. Corporatism was developed in Germany in the Nineteenth Century in part to stabilize preexisting class relationships that were threatened by industrialization in Europe. Italian corporatism had the effect of stabilizing traditional relationships in the face of later, but similar pressures. Such motives were also to be found in contemporaneous developments in the United States, and so I rather like the appellation *Corporatism*, and the adjectival form *Corporatist*, when dealing with similar American efforts. But disputes over the secondary meaning of words are unimportant to the story I am telling, and so I have adopted the more neutral usage. Rather, the important thing to note is that just as workers can be threatened by economic developments (including an outbreak of serious competition) and so seek to combine to resist them, so too may owners be threatened and seek to combine.

16. This line of thinking when combined with the notion of consumer fraud provided the impetus for the formation of Better Business Bureaus in the 1890s.

17. The fabled switch from an Associationalist to a competitive analysis of the economy, especially in antitrust enforcement, between the First New Deal and the Second is, I think, overdone, though I do not agree with my friend, Laura Kalman, that there

were not two New Deals. Self-regulation is not the only norm in the Associationalist model. That model expected that government would supply support for the eradication of "anti-competitive" practices—most often for the benefit of small producers—a classic form of regulation. And Associationalist forms were adopted during the Second New Deal; the Civil Aeronautics Board is a good example. It seems to me that it is better to recognize that both Associationalist and competitive strains of American economic thought and practice had existed side by side for a long time. Thus, it is the relative dominance of one or the other strain over an extended period that is important to keep in mind; generally, the occasional, even high-profile flip-flop, should be ignored. Therefore, it is not too simpleminded to say that the years before World War I were domináted by the competitive stream; the years after, by the Associationalist one.

18. Alan R. Kamp, "Uptown Act: A History of the Uniform Commercial Code: 1940–49," *Southern Methodist University Law Review* 359 (2001), 52.

19. These disputes are of course but a replay of the disputes that erupted first, when the Railway Express Company's railway package service, and then the United States Post Office's parcel post, brought an increasing range of goods from the national catalog houses, such as Sears, Roebuck and Montgomery Ward, to rural communities, thereby undercutting the prices of the local general store.

20. Paul Mahoney has indirectly suggested to me that there was a strong Associationalist and anticompetitive slant to the New Deal financial reforms. New York "wholesale" banks supported these reforms since they restructured the market to reduce competition among themselves, as did regional banks. New York brokers were reasonably supportive because the same reforms solidified the fixed commission system.

I am not surprised by his reading of the evidence. The New York banks surely would have required something in trade for their at least grudging support of the New Deal reforms. That something would likely have been delivered within the Associationalist model. Still, I believe that the dominant impulse for the reforms was part of the regulatory stream of Associationalist thought.

21. It is important to remember that Bretton Woods did not establish a "free trade" regime. It explicitly allowed national rules limiting foreign direct investment and assumed the existence of national tariff systems and preferences for colonial and formerly colonial countries. Freeing trade was a long slow process that began with the 1948 multilateral General Agreements on Tariffs and Trade and its successor agreements.

22. There were three functioning economies of note south of the equator—Argentina, South Africa, and Australia.

23. The notion of the family wage was not invented after World War II. It first appears in the mid-Nineteenth Century and was prominent in the struggle for the adoption of minimum wage laws starting late in that century and thereafter in Henry Ford's "five dollar" wage. A significant percentage of women, especially unmarried women, worked for wages outside the farm or home both before World War II and after it. But the important change here was the combination of this preexisting ideology with a sharp reduction in the marriage age and an increase in childbearing that together directed

women back home from the factories and offices they occupied during the war. This combination facilitated the explicit development of the postwar goal of providing a supra-minimum wage for each male worker, a wage that was more than just sufficient for him to support his family. This goal in turn underlay more general support of union demands for high blue-collar wages during these years. It would be a mistake not to notice that there was more than a hint of anti-Communism in all these ideas.

24. Adolph A. Berle and Gardner C. Means, *The Modern Corporation and Private Property* (New York: Macmillan, 1932).

25. Even before the building of the interstate highway system, moving freight by truck over short distances was cheaper than moving it by train because such travel saved the cost of train assembly and disassembly.

26. Unfortunately, the federally insured version was available only for new construction, a limit that pretty much guaranteed that it would only support suburban development.

27. The late Fred Hart reminded me of this apt description for the expanded Fifties middle class.

28. In small towns the tradition of home ownership extended down into the traditional bourgeois shopkeeper.

29. Two caveats are in order on this point. First, as Bert Westbrook and Amy Westbrook have pointed out to me, because there is no facility other than the New York Federal Reserve Bank with the capacity for clearing large transactions in dollars, it is not quite true that the Federal Reserve Board is without the ability to exercise some control over the Eurodollar market. What is important is that the Fed has not sought to do so by increasing or reducing transaction costs at the New York Fed, although it has used the bank to aid in the enforcement of economic sanctions imposed against various foreign governments.

Second, Ken Davidson reminds me that this development has not been an entirely bad one for our economy. In later years, the growth of the Eurodollar market financed our trade deficit with Europe as European companies that earned dollars chose to keep them invested, but not in the United States. In doing so, these companies created liquidity and stability in currency markets. Of course, what might happen if the holders of Eurodollars chose to seek to turn their investments into American goods or capital assets was another matter, as we shall see.

30. Of course, with the benefit of hindsight, the development of these industries was anything but the indication of a troubled economy, for they would eventually provide the basis for renewed growth. But at the time, they seemed to portend nothing in particular, much less the possibility of a renewed economic base.

31. The late Fred Hart suggests that malls solved a problem for the department stores that anchored them. In a pre-computer age, department stores could reduce the difficulties inherent in stocking and marketing a diverse range of goods simply by ceding some of that task to other, so-called specialty retailers and instead focusing their attention on the highest-margin goods.

32. George Dawson notes that agriculture was one of the few industries that was not dysfunctional in these years. America grew one hell of a lot of food. If there was a problem with agriculture, it was in the perverse incentives embedded in the various farm crop programs designed to help the smaller farmers that were then hijacked by the increasingly numerous larger ones.

33. This bit of law forbids companies from combining by means of asset purchase; the statute previously only forbid combining by means of stock acquisitions.

34. Ken Davidson reminds me that part of this work was done by the Cowles Foundation, initially headquartered at the University of Chicago, but later moved to Yale University, whose largess was directed toward economics departments, but naturally included the economics of finance.

35. Retained earnings are taxed once, at the corporate level; distributed earnings are taxed twice, once at the corporate level and once at the shareholder level. All things remaining equal, retained earnings, invested properly will increase the value of the common stock, the appreciation of which will be ultimately taxed upon sale, not at marginal individual rates, as would dividend distributions, but at lesser, capital gain rates.

36. Though quite obviously a decline in research and development spending is likely to be followed with a decline in productivity, in this period it appears that the reverse was also true. The reason is that in the economy of the Sixties and Seventies, increasing import penetration made investment in research and development, whether for new product development or old process improvement, seemed riskier than standing pat and investing retained earnings in the creation of conglomerate enterprises. The Associationalist ideal, which survived with diminished vigor in the thinking of American corporate officers well into the Eighties, was essentially a motto of caution, of avoiding risk on the part of management, a course not likely to be objected to by labor.

37. However obvious this fact may be, it never occurred to me until it was pointed out to me in Jonathan Levy, *Ages of American Capitalism: A History of the United States* (New York: Random House, 2021). His analysis throughout the book forced me to clear up my analysis at several places in Part I.

38. Tom Headrick reminds me of the contribution to inflation in these years by the then-contemporary understandings of proper labor-management relations: the necessity that wage increases match price increases via the periodic negotiation of a "new" contract.

39. Other factors acting at the time were rising demand for oil and the increasing technical competence of the Arab operators of the oil fields. Thus, Arab outrage at the results of the Yom Kippur War led to a willingness to break away from the traditional position of supporting the West by selling oil cheaply, a willingness aided by the knowledge that demand would support such a price and that the Arab countries could operate the oil fields independently.

40. It should be noted that the rise of the deficit after Reagan lowered taxes and the fall of the deficit after Clinton raised taxes, but in a generally upward trending economy, suggest that the relationship between taxes and economic growth is anything but obvious. For example, complicating both decisions is the steep decline in defense spending

in the final years of the Reagan administration and the early years of the years of the Clinton administration, resulting from the trumpeted "peace dividend" that followed after the collapse of the Soviet Union. *Ceteris* is almost never *paribus*.

41. As Bert Westbrook reminds me, automation of production processes, even though sold based on their potential to raise industrial productivity, at least so far seem not to have done so very much, except in the computer industry itself.

42. Fred Hart suggests that the growth of consumer legislation is a direct response to the replacement of Main Street retailers, who had reason to satisfy their customers, by the mass-merchandising retailers, for whom product claims were a nuisance since they competed solely on price.

43. Seldom counted in the balances toted up by the participants in this debate are the industries that both kinds of regulation spawned. American environmental technology is sold around the world. My guess is that our occupational safety technology will come to be the basis of a significant international industry as well.

44. Ken Davidson insists that I make explicit, what seems to me implicit in the text. So here goes. The combination of a neoclassical microeconomics that assumes perfect competition in the face of anything but, deregulation that assumes that there is such a thing as an natural/other than structured by law market, and "supply side" economics that asserts on the basis of a single example undermined by many contrary examples that tax cuts generate economic growth, has been a sham and a delusion, which is not to say it has been an ineffective political program.

45. Alfred E. Kahn, *The Economics of Regulation: Principles and Institutions* (New York: Wiley, 1970).

46. Tom Headrick reminds me that the discovery of the stock market in the Fifties by the upper-middle class, which began to spread beyond that class in the Sixties and early Seventies, ran into higher interest rates and slower growth in the later Seventies. These new, middle-class investors were, at the margin, more significantly impacted by these changes than the older, upper-middle class investors and so were easily encouraged to support deregulation and the accompanying restructuring on Wall Street as a way of lowering their cost of investing.

47. As the late Marty Lybecker explained to me, when corporate treasurers switched from bank borrowings to issuing debt to money market funds, the banks were losing both their most stable source of funds and their shortest term, and thus least risky, high-quality loans. Both sides of the balance sheet were being hammered simultaneously.

48. It is about this time that the already common credit cards begin to coalesce into a few national brands.

49. Earlier examples of the socialization of the losses (but of course, not of the profits) of a private business can be seen in the bailouts of Boeing and Chrysler, and in the similar rescue of Continental Illinois Bank and Trust when its solvency was threatened by the failure of its small bank borrowers who in turn lent too much to the oil industry wildcatters just before a downturn in oil prices. Beginning in 2007, we experienced another.

50. Both Avi Soifer and Bert Westbrook insist that I make the following qualification. As the German example indicates, the Associationalist model does not require that interest rates be low. The participants in an Associationalist economy might decide that interest rates should be kept high, as the Germans had done, and to great success between, say 1969 and 1989. High wages and high prices may be maintained at the same time as high interest rates, if the goods produced in such an economy are of high value and the participants in that economy are willing to accept a smaller basket of goods and services than the one to which Americans in the Fifties had become accustomed.

51. Here, the possible breakout of professional services beyond national borders, particularly law, accounting, and financial engineering, is a caution, as is the processing of credit card accounts and medical claims abroad. And then there is the call center.

52. I am somewhat appalled that I have come this far in my story without mentioning the growth of female participation in the professional and managerial work force or the growth of relatively better jobs for African Americans as a result of thirty-five years of affirmative action policies. As noted in the text above, the growth of female participation in the workforce made it possible for families to maintain a middle-class standard of living in the face of significant inflation and declining real wages by shifting from the one to the two-wage-earner family norm. I rather doubt that this use of female labor power is what the early feminists had in mind in the Sixties. I am reluctant to conclude that, despite its positive effect on some members of the African American community, the growth of relatively better jobs for African Americans has had any significant effect on the American economic life, but that seems to be the case.

53. The real appeal of the conglomerate model may well have been the relatively linear relationship between assets under management and executive pay. Such a model was hard pressed to survive against a model of executive pay based on whopping capital gains at the end of the line. This shift is likewise a reflection of management school instruction on executive compensation as influenced by agency cost theory coming from economists.

54. I have buried a very complicated problem of monetary policy theory and practice in the text. Orthodox theory holds that the actions of the Federal Reserve can only influence short-term interest rates because long-term rates are influenced not by the money supply, but by expectations for inflation over the long term. I rather doubt that this neat academic distinction holds true in practice, however. In this case there is an alternative explanation for the plunge in long-term rates: Chinese policy called for the use of its great and rapidly increasing trade surplus to purchase US Treasury bonds across maturities, a practice that also drove down long-term rates. Which aspect of the decline in rates—the increase in monetary aggregates or Chinese purchases—was in fact more important is here unimportant.

55. Federal law defines "bank" as a "deposit taking institution." Any entity that does not accept deposits may, however, act as if it were a bank by delivering banklike services, including making loans, provided that it has some other way of securing capital than accepting deposits. Such entities are called "non-bank banks."

56. In synthetic versions of these instruments neither party needed to own actual securities. Thus, they were essentially contracts that paid off as if they contained actual enumerated securities. They were often used to facilitate bets against CMOs. Phil Halpern aptly calls this activity as "fantasy baseball played with real money."

57. Buying their own would have caused the entire original issuance of the securities to fail for complicated and tedious legal reasons related to bankruptcy law.

58. I suppose that at this point readers may be bewildered that I have not mentioned the "subprime crisis" or the Community Reinvestment Act (CRA). There is a reason for my omission. There was a subprime crisis, but it was a humanitarian crisis, not an economic one. Thousands of people had such poor credit that it was impossible to secure a "prime" mortgage, that is one that was capable of being purchased as a "confirming" mortgage by Fannie Mae or Freddie Mac, or at least they were convinced that they had such poor credit. Most of these people were "sold" mortgages that they could not afford, often on homes with serious problems. They lost their homes when they defaulted on mortgages that shouldn't have been issued in the first place. However, in the overall scheme of things, subprime mortgages, like the "Alt-A" mortgages that were issued with little or no documentation of income or assets of the borrowers, only meant that the securities into which they were packaged were "private label," not issued in the name of Fannie or Freddie, and so without a federal guarantee. There were all sorts of conforming mortgages issued on homes that in the aftermath of the housing bust ended up in default because their owners could not maintain their mortgage payments for all sorts of reasons. The securities that these conforming loans were packaged into also lost value in the aftermath of the housing bust. It is thus a mistake to suggest that blame for the crisis was the actions of subprime borrowers, implicitly poor people, much less on bank regulator pressure to meet CRA obligations. If blame there is, and there is plenty to go around, it was systemwide, and so I refuse to use the standard terminology.

59. Lehman failed for numerous reasons including a political objection to bailing out another investment bank after having bailed out Bear Stearns by facilitating its sale to JP Morgan Chase. One of the most curious is that Lehman owned the losing end of many synthetic CMOs/CLOs/CDOs, essentially betting that the mortgage market would strengthen.

60. The acronyms these programs spawned were wonderful: consider, in alphabetical order: AMLF (Asset-Backed Commercial Paper Money Market Liquidity Facility), CPFF (Commercial Paper Funding Facility), PDCF (Primary Dealer Credit Facility), TALF (Term Asset-Backed Securities Lending Facility), and TSLF (Term Securities Lending Facility).

61. Dodd-Frank was essentially a grab bag of ideas about strengthening the financial system. Among the other provisions in the act that have created continuing controversy were the creation of a Consumer Financial Protection Bureau and the requirement that large banks undergo yearly "stress tests" designed to test the adequacy of a bank's capital structure.

62. The proper name for "most favored nation."

63. Several readers express surprise that I make no mention of the September 11 tragedy and the military activities that followed it. Wars are always good for reducing unemployment. The preceding tragedy did the same thing by increasing the number of low-wage government workers whose job is addressing potential security threats at airports and elsewhere, though with poorer benefits than are provided to members of the armed forces some of whom seem to pay for those better benefits with an incredible need for services after discharge, need that gives new, and again unfortunately ironic, meaning to the idea of serving ones country. Beyond this modest support for employment, I find that both sets of events had little to no impact on the overall economy.

64. Careful structuralist readers will expect that at this point I will take up the question of what law has to do with it. Unfortunately, such is the one thing I cannot do. There has been plenty of going to law by those who have been unhappy with the way that changes in economic life have impacted them and law has responded in its usual, often erratic ways, but one needs to get somewhere before this implicit question can be answered. I quite doubt that the American economy has reached any *there* for now over thirty years. This is the essence of our present situation. If we know where *there* was, we would know better what we should do in our present circumstances.

65. Many of those with seven-figure incomes came to understand what it is to be "land poor," as Midwestern farmers laconically put it.

66. Ironically, though Schumpeter was right about the creative destruction of capitalism, he was wrong in seeing that the result of that process would be the end of the entrepreneur. That character thrives in Silicon Valley and the biotechnology industries to an extent that hasn't been seen in perhaps one hundred years. Bert Westbrook provided this observation. Some people think that the same is true of the financial cowboys in $3,000 suits: I am not convinced this is so.

67. It is less that they are being rolled back, than it is that our hopes for what they were meant to be are being extinguished. Reform is always contestable.

68. My dear former student, Abbie Gorin, to whom I owe much of my understanding of Marxism, made sure that I did not forget this possibility.

69. I say "seems," because on one view what has departed are the corporate giants and their "satanic mills" that are popularly associated with industrial production. In fact, there remains a great deal of industrial production in the United States. It is just small scale or, if large scale, no longer employs hordes of employees whose arrival at work reminds one of Eisenstein's vision of the storming of the Winter Palace. What have disappeared are the satanic mills, victims of changes in production methods and, I suspect, increasing pollution and workplace safety controls. It is not clear to me why we do not exult in the disappearance of these large industrial production facilities. Few, other than the capitalists themselves, thought that they were good for their employees or the surrounding area.

70. Laura Kalman provided me with the odd but telling fact.

Part II

1. The other objective of the Erie Canal project was to lower the cost of shipping agricultural goods from the Genesee Valley, spreading south of modern-day Rochester, that was the breadbasket of the state.

2. Though I am a railroad freak, there is a limit to such obscure passions. For this reason, I will save my readers from the trouble of following the endless name changes of the railroads that have reached Buffalo. Instead, I stick to the names they were known by after World War II. Purists can always go to Edward T. Dunn's detailed work, *A History of Railroads in Western New York*, 2nd ed. (Buffalo: Canisius College Press, 2000) to secure the blow-by-blow details.

3. Of course, geographic considerations need appropriate conditions to demonstrate their economic importance. There was no great growth in grain storage on the waterfront until the Eighteen Seventies.

4. Buffalo has a complicated relationship with Black Rock. Politically, the Village of Buffalo was a part of the Town of Buffalo, an entity that encompassed almost all of the present City of Buffalo. The Village was located above the marshland along Buffalo Creek and Lake Erie through which the most westerly leg of the canal would be built. Black Rock was similarly located, but about one-and-a-half miles north of the creek at a point where Lake Erie emptied into the Niagara River. Black Rock was named for a nearby outcropping of a very dark limestone the river had exposed when cutting its channel; a remnant of this outcropping had fallen into the lake at that point; it was *the* Black Rock. Both the Village of Buffalo and the hamlet of Black Rock sought to be the terminus of the Erie Canal.

In 1832, the village was incorporated as a city and expanded its boundaries to include the entire waterfront north of Buffalo Creek and areas to the north and east, including part of the hamlet of Black Rock but still was no bigger than the southwestern corner of the Town of Buffalo. Five years later the Town of Buffalo was renamed the Town of Black Rock. At the same time, some of the area north of the city to the northern boundary of the Town of Black Rock was incorporated as the Village of Black Rock. This logomachical mess was mostly cleaned up in 1853 when the city absorbed all of the Town of Black Rock, including the Village of Black Rock; but not completely, for thereafter a neighborhood along the Niagara River north of Scajaquada Creek became known as Black Rock, a neighborhood in the city.

5. This spatial density is also true of the several Orthodox Jewish *shul*s located cheek by jowl along Hickory Street in the near east side neighborhood. I have been unable to identify what differentiated individual congregations, but my guess is that it was tied to particular old countries, or even to particular communities, as was the case in the Italians in Buffalo.

6. Sometimes very large schools. At one point Saint Ann's, once the center of an early, vibrant German neighborhood, had a school that enrolled two thousand students, all taught in German.

7. It is asserted that at one point in time a single Lebanese clothing manufacturer employed the entire Lebanese community in the city.

8. The first hospital in the city was Catholic. A fight over hospital privileges led to the formation of a separate Protestant hospital. When the Protestants moved to establish a medical school that ultimately became part of the nucleus of the University of Buffalo, the Catholic doctors moved to establish a medical school at Niagara University, north of Niagara Falls. Of course, the ethnic overlay only made such things worse. The first Catholic church in the city was Saint Louis, a French congregation that was pushed out of its church by later immigrant German parishioners and forced to form its own congregation—Our Lady of Lourdes—about half a mile away.

9. Interestingly, Olmsted saw the system as helping speed the carriages of the elite men to the place of business. Ari Goldberg discovered this fact and shared it with me.

10. Here it is probably sensible to clear up a few bits of basic New York State local government law. The basic unit of local government in the state is not the county, much less the city or village, but the town. Towns are not made up of cities, villages, and unincorporated hamlets; they are made up of school districts. Incorporation of a city or village is a way of gaining a certain amount of political independence from the town, and in the case of cities, of gaining control of a school district.

11. The precise significance of Queen City remains obscure. It is not a reference to the city's gay population and though it might seem an appropriate, if ironic and obscene, reference to the city's treatment by the downstate dominated by the New York State Legislature, this is not the case either. I doubt that it contrasts with King's County, as Brooklyn once was known.

12. It is my periodization, and so my use of capitalized words denoting such, in this part remains the same as used in Part I.

13. The village was named for Chauncy Depew, president of the New York Central. Sloan, the village to the west of Depew, was named for Samuel Sloan, president of the DLW.

14. Pittsburgh, though nominally smaller, was effectively larger than Buffalo and had been for most of the Nineteenth Century. However, for all of that century its metropolitan area was composed to two cities, Pittsburgh and Allegheny. The cities were merged in 1907.

15. Robert M. Fogelson, *Downtown: Its Rise and Fall: 1880–1950* (New Haven: Yale University Press, 2001), 14.

16. The oddness of the failure of a builder of trucks at a time when all production was directed to war work points out the difficulty of documenting when firms fail. Unless a firm has a big role in a community it is unlikely to make more than a column inch or two in a newspaper; many more disappear without even that limited trace. It is obvious that many small firms failed during the Depression. I doubt that Buffalo was hit any harder than similar cities, but it experienced no less of a decline in economic activity than others, either. However, most bankruptcies leave little trace and so history needs stand mute about their passing.

17. It is possible that some of the support for the Securities Acts of 1933 and 1934 might have come from such persons.

18. A third possibility was the one that the Wendt family did with Buffalo Forge. In 1940, they took the company public and kept some interest in the new public entity. Why other owners did not undertake similar transactions is unclear, to me at least.

19. "September Song," is a Kurt Weill tune with lyrics by Maxwell Anderson. My reference is to the chorus as sung by Frank Sinatra on his 1965 album, "September of My Years." It goes "Oh, the days dwindle down to a precious few / September, November /And these few precious days I'll spend with you / These precious days I'll spend with you." It has long struck me that Buffalo holds ON to its vision of the glorious Fifties as an aging lover would a new younger partner, knowing full well that the relationship cannot last, but nevertheless determined to believe in that possibility.

20. An odd, clearly collateral fact needs to be remembered. During the war a housing project known as Ti-O-Run-Da was built in Cheektowaga at a location that would have made it easy for workers at either the Curtiss-Wright plant at the airport or the Spencer Lens factory to live nearby. The project mixed apartments, two different sizes of single-family houses, a school, two churches—one Catholic and the other Protestant, park space, and a small shopping center. Over time, a freeway was built along one edge of the development, the school closed, the apartments became more than a bit shoddy, and the shopping center lost all of its tenants. Around 2010, a developer came forward with a plan to develop the area. To his and pretty much everyone else's surprise, the surviving residents of the area threw such a fit that the developer gave up. Ti-O-Run-Da, "the place where two streams meet," remained a real community as today's New Urbanists would predict; what had happened is that changes in living patterns that accompanied the decline in public transportation had made the place less viable as an economic unit, but not less valuable as a neighborhood. Along the way an important lesson was lost as zoning laws made creating such neighborhoods impossible.

21. Regulatory accounting under the Interstate Commerce Commission was an obscure art form, entirely devoid of any notion of marginal cost, so trying to understand the cost of any service cost was a dubious activity. And the railroads played this obscurity for all it was worth. For example, all during the Fifties and Sixties, they complained that truckers and barge operators had the right of way paid for and maintained by the federal government while the railroads had to pay for and maintain their own right of way. It is telling that no railroader ever suggested that railroad right of way be nationalized to equalize competitive position.

In any case, the real problem was a competitive one. No railroad, not even a commuter railroad, could possibly offer service as flexible in terms of time and destination as could the automobile. Which is not to say that the railroads tried; they regularly worked to cut service to stations between large cities. It is likely that a problem equally significant to the one of cost was that providing passenger service interfered with the provision of rapid long distance freight service. This observation is supported by the dogged attempts by major trunk line carriers to eliminate short line service. Short line service that yielded cars that needed switching to mainline trains similarly interfered with the provision of rapid long distance freight service. The cost of such service may have been marginally remunerative, but it was systematically costly.

22. Unaccountably, but fortunately, it also moved into auto safety systems.

23. Endless arguments can be had as to what constitutes a "first-class" hotel. My locution avoids this argument.

24. It is likely that J. N. Adam's parent, Associated Dry Goods, which also owned Hengerer's, decided that one department store in Buffalo was enough, itself a far more ominous conclusion than that J. N. Adam was being shut down. The store had not failed; the parent was taking an opportunity to disinvest.

25. A modest note is appropriate here. The problem that the railroads faced was not the cost of any particular service, but of the operation of a system sensible when there were few competitive alternatives for other than local transportation, but that turned out to be far too large and far too fragmented for a time when competition was driving price down. Though it took more than eighty years, countless rail mergers, endless local agonies, and the development of first piggy-back (trailer on flatcar) and then containerization of goods, railroading is once again a fairly robust business for long-distance travel of heavy goods. It should be noticed however that the railroads are still dependent on local transport to get a significant proportion of the goods carried to a destination, except that now the local transport is no longer provided by a teamster with a horse and wagon moving goods from boxcars located on "team" tracks, but by a trucker with a truck to pull a piggy-backed trailer or a truck to pull a trailer designed to haul containers. The lesson here is most general. Economists are right that sunk costs are sunk and should be ignored going forward; however, sunk costs are seldom experienced as such by the people who live by administering them and places where they have been sunk.

26. Natives call themselves "Buffalonians." That word sounds ugly and shows a real lack of humor. I prefer the obvious self-mocking construction in the text. The ability to laugh at oneself is an important part of that self-knowledge that makes possible the ability to change ingrown habits.

27. Verlyn Klinkenborg, *The Last Fine Time* (New York: Alfred Knopf, 1992).

28. The reference here is to William Butler Yeats' poem, "The Second Coming." I recognize, and perhaps intend, that there is a certain irony in this reference, for there was no "second coming" in Buffalo's future, nor "rough beast," slouching to be born. If there were this book would not have been written.

29. Or maybe because the city could no longer finance the continuing stream of capital improvements that airports seem to require.

30. Walter S. Dunn Jr., *History of Erie County: 1870–1970* (Buffalo, NY: Buffalo and Erie County Historical Society, 1972), 217–30.

31. As should be obvious from these observations, my wife and I moved to Buffalo in 1973.

32. Utilities merit no mention.

33. Laura Kalman and my good editor object to my implication that the appearance the "two-wage earner" family made community impossibly hard. I know that, except at

the top of the social pyramid, women have always done "housework," and often much more. At the same time, the Mid-Nineteenth century social norm, established even before the disappearance of servants, that saw a woman's not being gainfully employed outside of the home as a major mark of a family's middle-class status, lasted a long time. It also implied a social structure that influenced how life, including housing, was experienced.

Three things are important here. First, Jane Jacobs in *The Death and Life of Great American Cities* (New York: Random House, 1961), makes clear that in the Fifties community was built from eyes on the street. Eyes on the street make community maintenance easier, even in income-segregated suburban neighborhoods. Second, the people whom I am talking about, people clinging onto middle-class status, one of whom was often employed in the industries mentioned in the text, mostly worked out of economic necessity or occasionally boredom. They thought of themselves as workers; for them only professionals had careers. Third, I am thus not discussing the two-career families of today. Their single-minded focus on schools and home value creates different problems for community maintenance.

34. This piece will be discussed in greater detail in Part IV.

35. Of late, I have wondered why the city moved from being the country's eighth largest in 1900 to tenth largest in 1910. I have no answer.

36. Tom Headrick did ask this exact question.

37. Jim Gardner supplied this apt word.

38. Jacobs, *Death and Life.*

39. Private schools have not proven to be a viable option. Four quite different, quite good schools serve a relatively elite part of the population. The Catholic population supports some quite good schools as well, especially at the high school level. The Black population in the area has not begun to take advantage of this resource until quite recently, and then only to a limited extent. Whether this is because such a small percentage of the Black population is Catholic or because the larger portion does not feel welcome, I do not know, but it is not because there were no Catholic churches in Black neighborhoods.

40. Richard L. Florida, *The Rise of the Creative Class: And How It's Transforming Work, Leisure, and Everyday Life* (New York: Basic Books, 2002).

41. Economic localism usually comes with the word "green" attached. This is a good, short-term idea, especially for encouraging skill acquisition that might lead to hourly middle-class jobs. However, until there is serious evidence that solar panels and other green hardware are likely to be replaced like refrigerators, stoves, dishwashers and clothes washers and dryers, green is a one-trick pony, not the basis for building a stable economic life.

42. I say nothing about architectural tourism. It is a silly idea, not because the local architecture is unworthy of aesthetic appreciation, but because anyone who has looked at the result of tourism in Niagara Falls ought to have figured out that the result of such a strategy is not beautiful to behold.

43. The lack of a common campus that in Claremont's case is a real drawing card, makes such a solution harder in Buffalo. Still, together the six schools have an enrollment

of over fourteen thousand students, as big as the University of Rochester or the Rochester Institute of Technology, and bigger than Buffalo State College. Such combined heft might make possible their securing students from outside Western New York. After spending more than forty years watching these small enterprises struggle, the solution is so obvious that the fact that no one takes it seriously is quite painful.

44. Or maybe the other way around; it makes no difference.

Part III

1. A structurally inclined reader may now suspect that this book does not inscribe an arc, but rather a V shape, and that Part III is the inflection point of the V. Thus, the two Parts following this one can be expected to mirror the movement already experienced from the more general to the more particular as this book goes from the more particular—Buffalo—to the more general—the America. Such a reader should expect that, having explored the context described by community, economy, and change, and the why of economic change, these latter two parts will explicitly bring law into the discussion to the extent that such is possible. Hopefully, such a reader will not feel disappointed.

2. John Henry Schlegel, "On the Many Flavors of Capitalism, or Reflections on Schumpeter's Ghost," *Buffalo Law Review* 56 (2009): 965–1025.

3. Jane Jacobs, *The Death and Life of Great American Cities* (New York: Random House, 1961).

4. *The Economy of Cities.* (New York: Random House, 19690; Jane Jacobs, *Cities and the Wealth of Nations* (New York: Random House, 1984).

5. Jacobs, *Cities and Wealth*, 3.

6. Ibid.

7. Stated somewhat differently, the city as an economic unit is taking advantage of elimination of transportation costs, and possibly the existence of lower labor and/or resource costs, to reduce the price to it (and to any place it sells these new goods as exports) by undercutting the price charged by the existing exporter. These are nickel-and-dime savings, but in a large enough economy, they add up to real dollars.

8. Jane Jacobs, *The Economy of Cities* (New York: Random House 1969).

9. Jacobs, *Cities and Wealth*, 39.

10. Robert E. Lucas, "On the Mechanics of Economic Development," *Journal of Monetary Economics* 22 (1988): 3–42.

11. A more complete exploration of the work of Lucas and Romer can be found in David Warsh, *Knowledge and the Wealth of Nations* (New York: W. W. Norton, 2006).

12. Jacobs, *Cities and Wealth*.

13. Ibid., 47.

14. Ibid., 59.

15. Ibid., 68.

16. Ibid. 97.

17. Ibid., 119.

18. The relationship between Jacobs's summary of her understanding of capital financed economic expansion—"Development cannot be given. It has to be *done*."—and her understanding of why such expansion begins—"Economic life develops by grace of innovating; it expands by grace of import-replacing."—is interesting. The notion that the origins of a process are mysterious, but that the success of that process is human is very Protestant, reflecting perhaps Jacobs's upbringing as a minority Protestant in a predominantly Catholic community that would be attuned to the idea that grace is more likely to descend upon the heart of the well-prepared through doing good works. A Weberian understanding of capitalism would thus find Jacobs's position significant.

I am not a Weberian in these matters and so am more interested in the relationship between "grace" and "doing" largely because of Jacobs almost virulent discussion of the effects of the Tennessee Valley Administration's program on that region's economy (*Cities and Wealth,* 110–11.) and her more sympathetic, but still negative, discussion of the impact of migrant worker remittances on their home countries (*Cities Wealth,* 74–77.) She lumps both discussions with those on the impact of crash industrialization programs in Russia, Iran under the Shah, and Ghana. Grace, even transient grace, may improve the lives of humans, although it may not start the process of economic development. Jacobs seems to denigrate such improvement, however modest, and thus seems to share the values of the economists whose work she criticizes. Ah, the joy of irony discovered. Equally ironic is the unwillingness of those who object to Jacobs's work on political grounds to recognize that transient grace is a least a good second best to their preferred political solution to problems of powerlessness and attendant poverty. The choice to disparage the good in pursuit of the excellent in both academic and political discourse is an aspect of the life of the mind in America that deserves much scholarly attention.

19. Jacobs, *Cities and Wealth,* 140–41.

20. Ibid., 182.

21. It surely identifies Buffalo as a declining region at least as early as World War II.

22. Jacobs, *Cities Wealth,* 221–22.

23. W. H. Auden, "Law, Says the Gardeners, Is the Sun," in *Another Time* (London: Farber & Farber, 1940).

24. David Bender, "Jane in the Cities," in *The Nation*, June 2, 1984, 238:677–69.

25. Ibid.

26. Ibid., 278.

27. Ibid.

28. Robert F. Wagner, Jr., "City Lights," in 191 *The New Republic* 191:29–32 (July 2, 1984).

29. Adam Smith, *An Inquiry into the Nature and Causes of the Wealth of Nations* I.i:25. (London: W. Strahan, 1776).

30. Thorstein Veblen, *The Engineers and the Price System* (New York: B. W. Huebsch, 1921).

31. Irus Braverman, *Wild Life: The Institution of Nature* (Palo Alto, CA: Stanford University Press, 2015) explores this topic with great care.

32. Pierre Schlag, *The Enchantment of Reason* (Durham, NC: Duke University Press, 1998).

33. "Book Review," *Harvard Business Review* 63, May 1, 1985, 50.

34. Betty Mensch pointed out the following example.

35. Fernand Braudel, *Civilization and Capitalism 15th–18th Century: The Wheels of Commerce*, trans. Sian Reynolds (New York: Harper and Roe Publishers, 1982).

36. D. W. Meinig, *The Shaping of America, A Geographical Perspective on 500 Years of History: Global America, 1915–2000* (New Haven: Yale University Press, 2004).

37. Jacobs, *Death and Life*, 153.

38. Ibid., 193.

39. Ibid., 161.

40. Ibid., 162.

41. Ibid.

42. Jacobs, *Cities and Wealth*, 39.

43. Ibid.

44. I have chosen not to discuss classic comparative advantage theory, though I mention it later, not because I think it silly; on the contrary, it underpins Jacobs's work on trade, but because it does not speak to changes in trade that are central to Jacobs's work and derivatively to mine. Comparative advantage is essentially an argument against trade barriers. Unfortunately, this argument ignores the question of who benefits from and is harmed by such barriers, questions that are quite important to development practice, if not theory.

45. The possibility that any correlation is spurious is the bane of statistical social science research. Unfortunately, taking this possibility seriously is likely to be paralyzing. Paralyzed scholars do not publish and therefore do not earn tenure and promotion. So, in some sense, ignoring this possibility is understandable . . . except when it is not.

46. Richard L. Florida, *The Rise of the Creative Class: And How It's Transforming Work, Leisure, Community, and Everyday Life* (New York: Basic Books, 2004).

47. Michael E. Porter, *The Competitive Advantage of Nations* (New York: The Free Press, 1990).

48. Annalee Saxenian, *Regional Advantage: Culture and Competition in Silicon Valley and Route 128* (Cambridge: Harvard University Press, 1994), interestingly argues that the more open social environment of California, as against the more closed social environment of Massachusetts, can explain the differing fates of these two areas. Her explanation for the origin of these social differences seems to me to be less persuasive than her documentation of their existence. Michael Storper, Thomas Kemeny, Naji Philip Markarem and Taner Osman, *The Rise and Fall of Urban Economies: Lessons from Los Angeles and San Francisco* (Palo Alto, CA: Stanford University Press, 2015), is a fine attempt to do a similar analysis that comes to remarkably similar conclusions.

49. Edward L. Glaeser, "Reinventing Boston: 1630–2003," *Journal of Economic Geography* 5 (2004): 119.

50. Edward L. Glaeser, "Can Buffalo Ever Come Back?" *City Journal* 17 (August 2007): 94–99.

51. This is a historical question that, at least in principle, is answerable.

52. Edward L. Glaeser, Heidi D. Kallal, Jose A. Scheinkman, and Andrei Shleifer, "Growth in Cities," *Journal of Political Economy* 100 (1992): 1126–52.

53. Veblen, *Engineers and the Price System.*

54. Sidney Ratner, James H. Soltow, and Richard Sylla, *The Evolution of the American Economy: Growth, Welfare, and Decision Making* (New York: Basic Books, 1979).

55. This is a problem with all of Jacobs's writing about economics, though such was not the case in *The Death and Life of Great American Cities.*

56. Jacobs, *Cities and Wealth,* 222.

57. Willard Hurst speaks of these things regularly: see *Law and the Conditions of Freedom in the Nineteenth Century United States* (Madison: University of Wisconsin Press, 1956); *Law and Social Process in United States History* (Ann Arbor: University of Michigan Law School, 1960); and *Law and the Social Order* (Ithaca, NY: Cornell University Press, 1977).

58. "Rain" is a locution I came to with the help of colleagues, especially Jim Gardner.

59. "Thou Art Indeed Just, Lord, If I Contend" *Gerard Manley Hopkins: A Selection of His Poetry and Prose,* ed. W. H. Gardner (Baltimore: Penguin, 1962), 67.

Part IV

1. Jane Jacobs, *Cities and the World Economy* (New York: Random House 1984), 183.

2. Edward Glaeser, "Reinventing Boston: 1630–2003," *Journal of Economic Geography* 5 (2005): 119.

3. Ibid., 123.

4. Ibid., 129.

5. Glaeser does not identify a starting date. I have supplied one, but given my limited knowledge of Boston's economic history, it could be wildly incorrect.

6. Glaeser, 132.

7. Ibid, 144.

8. A word might be offered about the relationship of technology, economy, and competition. As best I can tell, economies are built on a stable set of technologies and sometimes technologies disrupt economies, though when and why they do and when and why they don't is quite a mystery. As should be obvious, I am not a scholar of technology. As for competition, I am fairly sure that oligopolies are both maintained with technology and disrupted by it too. Whether more competitive economies bring forward more disruptive technologies is unclear to me, but it is clear to me that the urge to escape from

the competition that follows the introduction of a disruptive technology generally leads to attempts to establish an effective oligopoly.

9. Glaeser, 121.

10. The precise extent of the region's growth is difficult to gauge. There are, of course, the decennial census reports, which have the great advantage of being accurate and the great disadvantage of needing to be adjusted for changes in political boundaries over time. Recently the Census Bureau has attempted to address this difficulty in a publication that at least highlights the differences that careful investigators might find sensible to account for: http://www.census.gov/population/www/documentation/twps0027/twps0027.html. This source indicates that the city doubled in size every decade from 1830 to 1860. The difficulty with this adjustment is that it fails to account for growth outside of the city, but within the region. Another source, http://www.peakbagger.com/pbgeog/histmetropop.aspx, attempts to account for this difference by retrospectively calculating population for what might possibly have been the effective urbanized area surrounding the political city at a given point in time. It makes modest attempts to expand the scope of this urbanized area over time. I prefer this source because of the urbanization adjustment, however, as my argument does not turn on precise population figures at given points in time, but only general level of change over time, the differences are not significant for present purposes.

11. Buffalo is still a small place. Even after living here forty nine years, longer than anywhere else, I am still from Chicago. For a person of my age to be able to claim to be a native Buffaloon, one needs to be able to answer the question, "What was your (elementary, middle, and high) school" appropriately, and in certain circles, "What was your parish"? It does not help that I live in a first-ring suburb.

12. Mark J. Stern, *Society and Family Strategy: Erie County, New York 1850–1920* (Albany: State University of New York Press, 1987).

13. Allan Rogers, "Some Aspects of Industrial Diversification in the United States," *Economic Geography* 33 (1957): 16–30.

14. John Kort, "Regional Economic Instability and Industrial Diversification in the United States," *Land Economics* 57 (1981): 596–608. It also finds the area's economy among the most stable, giving one pause about method.

15. There is a fourth, fanciful possibility. Buffalo was doomed from the beginning by the geography that it shared with the rest of the Rust Belt. The Ohio River and the Appalachians pretty much dictated that the axis of the area north of the river would be east-west. When the gasoline engine finally made it easy to cross that river, an entire area south of the river was newly opened for industrial investment. Had the Ohio River drained south, Buffalo might have had north-south commercial relations to fall back on when the lake/canal and lake/rail axis began to dry up.

16. Even if one ignores that the convention center is too small and poorly located, the casino is too small and without facilities for the regular concerts that are used to draw people to such places, the season for tourists is basically from late spring through early fall.

17. It is surprising that given that the University at Buffalo's great strength is its engineering school, that no one ever suggests that the region try to become a center of

engineering talent. After all, engineering services are easily exported and produce good, clean middle-class jobs. A community of engineers might be a bit strange, but then again it might be quite interesting.

18. Michael Rose, *The Mind at Work* (New York: Viking, 2004).

19. There are good contemporary examples provided by the destructive activities of young males that would suggest such is the case.

20. There is a massive problem here that I am intentionally avoiding. Some of the working class, the hourly middle class that I talk of from time to time, overlaps with the middle classes. The size of the overlap has changed over time. Indeed, it is the shrinking of the overlap that I focus on in this Part IV. In the late Fifties and Sixties, the overlap was large and meant that a reasonable percentage of the hourly working class was part of the central core of the middle classes, the group I sometime denote as the middle-middle class. That is no longer true. Still, for my work precision here is of little importance. This is not an example of sociology by the numbers, but as I said in the introduction, a work of political economy.

21. For a different but similar understanding of these years read Judith Stein, *Running Steel, Running America: Race, Economic Policy, and the Decline of Liberalism* (Chapel Hill: University of North Carolina Press, 1998); and *Pivotal Decade: How the United States Traded Factories for Finance* (New Haven: Yale University Press, 2010).

22. Richard L. Florida, *The Rise of the Creative Class: And How It's Transforming Work, Leisure, Community, and Everyday Life* (New York: Basic Books, 2004).

23. Jacobs, *Cities and the Wealth of Nations*. New York: Random House, 1984, 183.

24. Ibid.

25. Ibid.

26. I admit to both humility and arrogance. I have no credentials that would qualify me to have done what has come before and what will follow. Though I firmly believe that credentials are wildly overvalued, that the distinction between professional and amateur, credentialed and not, has ruined the university as a place for thought, except possibly in the hard sciences, I recognize that many, perhaps most of my readers think otherwise. Still, as I admit to the limited basis for the conclusions that follow, I offer them based on at least fifty years of observation and thought. I think that counts for a lot, not just something.

27. I intentionally avoid the problem of what to do where residents feel harassed by the police. All I know is that policing is most effective where its presence is welcomed. I have no idea how to escape from a place where the residents fear the police and the police fear the residents.

28. This is the silliest thing that Buffalo boosters (and also architects and planners in their renderings of streetscapes) do. No intelligent person will forget the massive snowstorms that occasionally come to the region, any more than the huddled masses often to be found in the Bills' stadium at the last game of the year. Why would Buffalo even want to attract someone who would mistake this region for San Diego and why would we want to offend intelligent people by suggesting that they make such a mistake? Moreover, any site plan that does not first consider where the snow is going to be piled is courting disaster.

29. Here one might need to be reminded that the first book about law written in English was about permissible delay, about the pleas that would allow a defendant to delay appearing in court to answer the writ served upon him.

30. One of the good things the charter school movement has done for the Buffalo schools is to act as a kind of teacher training program. Perhaps, after being in such a program, new teachers are better prepared for the more difficult problems that await them in many of the city's public schools.

31. The university regularly produces studies that attempt to quantify its economic impact on the region. These studies seem to me to confuse money spent with impact. A little bit of butter improves the taste of nut bread but does not improve the nut bread at all.

32. Thomas E. Headrick and John Henry Schlegel, "Understanding Buffalo's Economic Development," *Buffalo Review* 54 (2007): 1537–53.

33. The architect and planner Andres Duany has quite sensibly suggested that local governments in depressed areas ought to enforce regulations lightly in ways that might make establishing marginal economic enterprises more affordable. It would be hard to identify an idea better designed to improve such depressed areas that was also politically problematic both by providing an occasion for graft and an occasion for claims of fairness to lead to the migration of such an approach up the food chain. Sad but true. See: https://www.strongtowns.org/journal/2013/10/23/duany-from-detroit.html.

Part V

1. A multinational currency, as the euro, may seem to be even more complicated to manage; and in one sense it is. Cities are subordinate governmental units in the United States, while the countries of the euro zone assert their sovereign equality, whatever may be their actual degree of economic sovereignty. The varying degrees of economic sovereignty in the euro zone may create all sorts of political problems for the euro zone, still the member states can be easily and fruitfully analyzed as if they were cities within a nation-state, just as Buffalo can be easily and fruitfully analyzed as a city within a nation-state. The differences are far more political than economic, to the extent that the two can be distinguished.

2. The reader may be happy to know that Part V is presented in the same sequence as Part IV—Some Perspectives; Strengths, Problems, and Political Context; Making American Attractive to the Middle Class; And Well Schooled, and Et Cetera. Yes, there are surprisingly many structuralist bones in my body.

3. Robert L. Gordon, *The Rise and Fall of American Growth: The U. S. Standard of Living since Civil War* (Princeton: Princeton University Press, 2016).

4. I would be remiss if I did not remind my readers that the producers of today's consumer goods have produced these goods in the same way that Americans did in the

Twentieth Century—with vast armies of poorly paid, semiskilled labor happy to do this work because it was less backbreaking and better paid than was labor in the rural areas from which they came.

5. Much depends on how sector importance is measured. If the measure is GDP unadjusted for inflation, the manufacturing's share of the economy has experienced an almost linear decline since World War II. Adjusted for inflation manufacturing's share of the economy has been stable for the past thirty years.

6. Niccolo Machiavelli, *The Prince*, eds. Quentin Skinner and Russell Price (Cambridge: Cambridge University Press, 1988), 59. Thanks to Jim Gardner for reminding me of this long-lost piece of my college education.

7. Ibid., 60.

8. In the long run law has regularly been more indulgent of capital's fears than of labor's. This bias can be most recently seen in the continuing fight to maintain the enlarged middle class that was the result of the Associationalism of the Fifties.

9. I occasionally wonder what might be learned about the efficacy of law from our experience with public accommodations law and equal employment opportunity law. On the whole, both became tolerably effective after a bit of real reluctance. Why would one expect more from a human institution? That school integration has been much less successful may also speak of the limits of legal institutions in the face of real social opposition or maybe just of the differing social meaning of hotels and restaurants and places of employment as against local schools. In either case, it is probably a mistake to expect law to be effective in the way that law thinks of itself as being so.

10. The choice to shift investment to index funds turns out to result in quite similar problems. Just exactly what index should one choose? If the answer is not obvious and so one relies on a fee-based financial advisor to suggest answers, this person is likely to have incentives much like other money managers.

11. My good copyeditor asked whether losing "their social place" might include losing their place in the racial hierarchy. For some that is of course true. But the real question is how large the proportion of that is "some." I honestly don't know, but I am pretty sure that that both sides of the racial divide see the proportion differently.

12. Jane Jacobs, *Cities and the Wealth of Nations* (New York: Random House, 1984), 183.

13. I have absolutely no interest in debating whether the money poured into our financial system during the Great Recession was a subsidy. If one understands how close we came to destroying the plumbing of that system as a result of lax regulation and unbridled optimism, one will not see these funds as a subsidy. If one does not, no amount of my rhetoric will convince. General Motors and Chrysler clearly rode banker coattails as a sop to blue-collar America. Their assistance is best argued as one would about the propriety of playing "pin the tail on the donkey" at a PETA meeting.

14. David Warsh, *Knowledge and the Wealth of Nations* (New York: W. W. Norton, 2006).

15. The material that follows in this and the next five paragraphs is presented in more detail in John Henry Schlegel, "On the Many Flavors of Capitalism, or Reflections on Schumpeter's Ghost," *Buffalo Law Review* 56 (2009): 965–1025.

16. Lindsey Davis, *One Virgin Too* Many (New York: Mysterious Press, 2000).

17. Tom Headrick regularly reminds me that for the smallest firms the regulation that bites is state and local, not federal.

18. I am sure that the players in none of the markets that we "deregulated" in the Seventies and Eighties would have been happy had such action had deprived them of any of the forgoing bits of law.

19. Some of my readers will hear echoes of two of my least favorite bits of legal in scholarship in this paragraph—see Roscoe Pound, "The Limits of Effective Legal Action," *American Bar Association Journal* 3 (1917): 55–70; as well as Lon Fuller, "The Forms and Limits of Adjudication" *Harvard Law Review* 92 (1978):353–409—and hopefully be surprised by it. There is a big difference between Pound's and Fuller's point and mine. They see limits to law's effectiveness and so argue it is inappropriate to act; I see limits to effectiveness but argue that the existence of such limits does not discharge the need for law to act. Rather these limits only establish the need to understand that any action taken needs be taken with the understanding that it is likely to be only modestly effective. Law is a human institution; it cannot but be flawed.

20. Richard L. Florida, *The Rise of the Creative Class: And How It's Transforming Work, Leisure, Community, and Everyday Life* (New York: Basic Books, 2004).

21. There are many people who are alleged to have said this. I am unable to referee the fight. The quotation marks are here only for the purpose of indicating to my readers that I know I was not the first person.

22. I am aware that in this paragraph I might be seen as a partisan of so-called Public Choice economics. Such would be a mistake. I know that choice is necessary and so wish it to be careful and conscious, not to avoid choice as a principle.

23. William Faulkner, "William Faulkner's Nobel Prize Acceptance Speech," *Southern Cultures* 12 (Spring 2006):71.

Is Conclusion Even Possible?

1. The modest national commitment to greater civil rights for Blacks and other American minorities that progressed much more slowly and experienced much more, and continuing overt opposition, seems to have had more staying power, at least among the more traditional middle classes. The entrenchment of feminism and the somewhat surprising opening to the LGBT community offer another cause for a bit of hope.

2. I do not, but for the purposes of this book I have chosen to avoid the complexities that my understanding introduces into any discussion of the economy.

3. But then again, I am not a particularly modest person, either.

4. I wish to note that I think that my analysis holds, whatever might be the resolution of the dispute over the correctness of Robert J. Gordon's estimate of American growth going forward, *The Rise and Fall of American Growth: The U.S. Standard of Living since Civil War* (Princeton: Princeton University Press, 2016), a question that would be foolish for me to comment upon, except to note that his lower boundary makes it rather clear the need for caution in choosing economic development strategies. In such circumstances, it would be best not to enact the definition of insanity as doing the same thing that repeatedly has failed and expecting a different result.

A Note for Historians

1. I have wondered what might be the case if we were we able to talk with atomic entities. It is at least possible that some such entities, whether in the form of particles or waves, hate cats and others do not, and so that is the real dilemma for Schrodinger's cat.

2. John Henry Schlegel, "If the Music Hadn't Stopped, or Reflections on the Great Kerfuffle: Historicism's Continuing Grasp for Truth," *Yale Journal of Law and Humanities* 31 (2021): 276.

3. John Henry Schlegel, "On the Many Flavors of Capitalism, or Reflections on Schumpeter's Ghost," *Buffalo Law Review* 56 (2009): 965–1025.

ACKNOWLEDGMENTS

Reading Jane Jacobs helped focus this project, but eight other people were particularly helpful. Mark Goldman's three books about Buffalo made my task in writing Part II not impossible. Many of the ideas in Parts II, III and IV were fleshed out in a course at the Buffalo Law School called Regional Economic Development. The late Bill Greiner, a friend from back when I started at Buffalo who left teaching for an administrative career, started the course when he returned to teaching and put up with my tagging along. As the course grew, first the late Jim Allen, who ran a local economic development agency, and later Rich Tobe, who long worked at economic development from the governmental side, joined us. All three shared their experience in local and state affairs and so helped me try to bring theory down to earth. Fred Konefsky, my historian buddy here at the Law School, taught me a lot about the Nineteenth Century economy and law's place in it. Perhaps more importantly, he was always willing to read and talk about any scrap of this project that I was willing to share. At some point along the way, Guyora Binder took on the absolutely essential role of gentle goad, endlessly reminding me that this project was worth being completed.

The seventh is the avatar of my longtime friend and colleague, Jan Lindgren, that has perched on my shoulder whenever I began to write saying, "Keep the structure clean and the prose clear, Schlegel!" It also would remind readers that, "If you can't understand a Schlegel sentence, read it out loud and it all becomes clear." Each and every reader should separately thank her for this service. My editor, Elizabeth Demers, not only accepted my manuscript after many editors passed, but also made all my prose clearer and my arguments sharper. Her old-fashioned handwritten manuscript editing fit well with my old-fashioned mind. Sherondra Thedford made my pushing to the end easier.

Thanks, of course, needs to be distributed to many, many other people. Today, I can remember Jim Atleson, Ken Davidson, Chris Dawson, George Dawson, Richard Deitz, Tom Disare, Jose Gabilondo, Jim Gardner, Abbie Gorin, Phil Halpern, Fred Hart, Tom Headrick, Bruce Jackson, Karl Klare, the late Marty Lybecker, the late Jim Magavern, Paul Mahoney, Steve Marshall, Martha McCluskey, Frank Munger, Athena Mutua, Phil Perry, Gail Radford, Pierre Schlag,

Steve Schlegel, Chris Tomlins, Amy Westbrook, Bert Westbrook, and Jim Wooten. Many of these people attended Buffalo Law School Faculty seminars where all attendees helped me make sense out of my mess.

Next, thanks needs be given to those people who read and commented on the whole megillah—Tom Disare, Tom Headrick, Laura Kalman, Fred Konefsky, Rich Schragger, and Avi Soifer, two anonymous readers for the Michigan Press, as well as a faithful research assistant Zac Persichini who proofreads far better than I do. Former student, Paul LaCapruccia and the late Tom Schofield, separately read the history portions of the manuscript. Former research assistants Jonathan Falk and Joseph Fabian spent hours creating a wonderful database of manufacturing firms in Buffalo; it is not their fault that in the end my estimate of the usefulness of their project was mistaken.

Thanks also go to Guyora Binder, Bob Gordon, Laura Kalman, Fred Konefsky, Bruce Mann, and Ted White who did their best at various times to help me secure financial support and publisher interest for this project.

Then there are the various people who supported work that has been incorporated in this effort in many different ways: Bruce Jackson, Tom Headrick, Chris Tomlins and the editors of the *Buffalo Law Review*. Then there is the novelist, Elizabeth Hyde, who at an otherwise dismal dinner party, asked that we not talk about her work and so forced me to lay out a structure for this book. The guys at the Buffalo Harbor Museum supplied a map that was crucial to understanding the structure of Buffalo's waterfront. Twenty-four volumes of the *Western New York Heritage* magazine were even more helpful than the evidence of my continuing subscription would indicate.

No self-respecting historian would get anything done without the help of librarians. Special thanks thus goes to Mary K. Demont, former archivist at Buffalo State College, Cynthia Van Ness, former librarian in Special Collections at the Buffalo and Erie County Library and now librarian at the Buffalo History Museum, and Marsha Zubrow, of the Law School's Charles B. Sears Library, who has really been my personal law librarian for more years than she and I wish to account for.

And last, but therefore most, to Jo and Liz and Steven who knew enough not to ask and cared enough not to complain; they therefore provided more support than they ever could know.

As the title asserts, this is a book about community, economy, and law. I have previously written about this topic in the context of the role of law seen primarily in activity during times of economic decline. See "Unfortunately, White-Collar Is the Default Setting: Boys and Higher Education," *Buffalo Law Review* 53 (2005): 1035–58; "Like Crabs in a Barrel: Economy, History, and Redevelopment in Buffalo," 2005, http://csac.buffalo.edu/centerworkingpapers.html; "More Crabs, Still No Barrel," 2008, https://www.law.buffalo.edu/faculty/facultyDirectory/SchlegelJohn.html; "Understanding Buffalo's Economic Development," *Buffalo Law Review* 54 (2007): 1537–53; the review, with Thomas E. Hedrick, of Diana Dillaway's, *Power Failure: Politics, Patronage, and the Economic Future of Buffalo, New York.*

Part I is based in large part on an early version of the story told there, which examined the United States economy in the years following the end of the First World War: "Law and Economic Change in the Short Twentieth Century" in C. Tomlins and M. Grossberg, eds., *Cambridge History of Law in America* 3: 563–612, © Cambridge University Press 2008, used by permission. I especially thank the press for permission to use this material.

Part II contains material from "An Oblique Perspective," a paper I prepared for the conference, "Redescribing the Sacred-Secular Divide: The Legal Study" in 2009 at the request of my former colleague, Winnifred Fallers Sullivan.

Parts IV and V include ideas first explored in a piece about law and capitalism, "On the Many Flavors of Capitalism, or Reflections on Schumpeter's Ghost," *Buffalo Law Review* 56 (2009): 965–1025.

Bruce Jackson supplied the cover art and many stories about living in Buffalo.

SUGGESTED READINGS

I have chosen not to supply the traditional bibliography that I have collected over the twenty plus years I have worked on this project. First, it is very long and completely uninformative; making it more informative would make it longer still. In addition, a bibliography seems somehow inappropriate for an essay. Instead, I have chosen to offer a set of suggestions for further reading including all of the works cited in the text. I have commented on individual works when I had something specific to say; the absence of such commentary should be understood as my indication that my readers should sample as they see fit.

Overviews

If seriously interested in community, law, and economy start with—

Braudel, Fernand. *Civilization and Capitalism 15th–18th Century*. 3 vols. Translated by Sian Reynolds. New York: Harper & Row, 1981–1984.

If reading Braudel is too daunting and one wishes to stick with American history, there are two possible places to start—

Levy, Jonathan. *Ages of Capitalism: A History of the United States*. New York: Random House, 2021; focused on finance, not industry.

Meinig, D. W. *The Shaping of America*. 4 vols. New Haven: Yale University Press, 1986–1998; easy, gracious reading by a geographic historian.

If a focus on economic history is desired, here are three possible places to start

Bruchey, Stuart. *The Wealth of the Nation: An Economic History of the United States*. New York: Harper & Row, 1988.

Engerman, Stanley L., and Robert E. Gallman, eds. *The Cambridge Economic History of the United States*. 3 vols. Cambridge: Cambridge University Press, 2000; articles directed at graduate students seeking an introduction to a topic written by experts in the topic covered.

Ratner, Sidney, James H. Soltow, and Richard Sylla. *The Evolution of the American Economy: Growth, Welfare and Decision-Making*. 2nd ed. New York: Basic Books, 1993; old but dependable.

If a focus on law is desired there are two places to start—

Grossberg, Michael, and Christopher Tomlins, eds. *The Cambridge History of Law in America*. 3 vols. New York: Cambridge University Press, 2008; articles directed at graduate students seeking an introduction to a topic written by experts in the topic covered.

Hurst, James Willard. *Law and Social Process in United States History*. Ann Arbor: University of Michigan Law School, 1960.

———. *Law and Markets in United States History: Different Modes of Bargaining*. Madison: University of Wisconsin Press, 1982.

———. *Law and the Social Order in the United States*. Ithaca, NY: Cornell University Press, 1977.

———. *A Legal History of Money in the United States, 1774–1970*. Lincoln: University of Nebraska Press, 1973.

———. *The Legitimacy of the Business Corporation in the Law of the United States, 1780–1970*. Charlottesville: University Press of Virginia, 1970; five sets of lectures that together paint a wonderful whole.

If a focus on Buffalo's history is desired—

Older resources:

Hill, Henry Wayland, ed. *Municipality of Buffalo, New York: A History*. 4 vols. New York: Lewis Historical Company, 1923.

Larned, J. N. *A History of Buffalo*. New York: The Progress of the Empire State Company, 1911; best early version.

Smith, H. Perry. *History of Buffalo and Erie County*. 2 vols. Syracuse, NY: D. Mason, 1884.

Newer resources:

Goldman, Mark. *City on the Edge*. Amherst, NY: Prometheus Books, 2007.

———. *City on the Lake: The Challenge of Change in Buffalo*. Amherst, NY: Prometheus Books, 1990; focus on the 1970s and1980's.

———. *High Hopes*. Albany: State University of New York Press, 1983; though with some overlap, together absolutely basic for any understanding the Buffalo's history.

A more regional point of view—

Dunn, Walter S., ed. *History of Erie County 1870–1971*. Buffalo: Buffalo and Erie County Historical Society, 1972.

Jackson, John N. *The Mighty Niagara: One River—Two Frontiers*. Amherst, NY: Prometheus Press, 2003.

Percy, John W. *Buffalo Niagara Connections: A New Regional History of the Niagara Link*. Buffalo: New York Western New York Heritage Press, 2007.

Narrower Topics

If interested in Jane Jacobs's work—

Start with her publications:

The Death and Life of Great American Cities. New York: Random House, 1961.

Cities and the Wealth of Nations. New York: Random House, 1984.

The Economy of Cities. New York: Random House, 1969.

And then move on to commentary on her work:

Reviews of *Cities and the Wealth of Nations*:

Anonymous. "Book Review." *Harvard Business Review* 63:650 (1985).

Bender, Thomas. "Book Review." *The Nation* 238:677 (June 2, 1984).

Wagner, Jr., Robert F. "City Lights." *The New Republic* 191: 29–32 (July 2, 1984).

Other commentary—

Glaeser, Edward L., Heidi D. Kallal, Jose A. Scheinkman, and Andrei Shleifer. Growth in Cities." *Journal of Political Economy* 100:1126 (1992); an empirical search for validation of Jacobs's theories.

Lucas, Robert E. "On the Mechanics of Economic Development." *Journal of Monetary Economics* 22:3 (1988); Nobel Prize lecture.

Page, Max, and Timothy Mennel, eds. *Reconsidering Jane Jacobs*. Chicago: American Planning Association, 2011.

If interested in details of Buffalo's history—

Anonymous. "Made in Buffalo." *Fortune* 44:91 (July 1951); review and pictures of Buffalo manufacturing.

Buffalo Chamber of Commerce. *The Niagara Area*. Buffalo: *The Buffalo Journal of Commerce*, 1930; special edition; illuminating puff piece.

Davis, Clyde Brion. "Buffalo." *Holiday* 18:94 (August 1955); pictures of places to go when visiting the city.

Dunn, Edward T. *A History of Railroads in Western New York*. 2nd ed. Buffalo: Canisius College Press, 2000.

Ederer, Martin. *Buffalo's Catholic Churches*. Buffalo: Bates Jackson Press, 2003.

Glaeser, Edward L. "Can Buffalo Come Back?" *City Journal* 17:94 (Autumn 2007); not terribly accurate rant, but still illuminating.

Graebner, William. *Coming of Age in Buffalo*. Philadelphia: Temple University Press, 1990.

Headrick, Thomas E., and John Henry Schlegel. "Understanding Buffalo's Economic Development." *Buffalo Review* 54:1537–53 (2007); book review.

International Geographical Union. *Industrial Cities Excursion Guidebook*. 17th International Geographical Congress, United States, 1952; Publication 2.

Klinkenborg, Verlyn. *The Last Fine Time*. New York: Alfred Knopf, 1992; Buffalo in the Fifties; deeply understood and beautifully written.

Stern, Mark J. *Society and Family Strategy*. Albany: State University of New York Press, 1987; Italian Buffalo.

If interested in economic/political history for limited times or specific topics—

The long Nineteenth Century

Berk, Gerald. *Alternative Tracks: The Constitution of American Industrial Order: 1865–1917*. Baltimore: Johns Hopkins University Press, 1994.

Chandler, Jr., Alfred D. "The Structure of American Industry in the Twentieth Century." *Business History Review* 43:255 (1969).

———. *The Visible Hand: The Managerial Revolution in American Business*. Cambridge, MA: Belknap Press, 1977; classic.

———. *Scale and Scope: The Dynamics of Industrial Capitalism*. Cambridge, MA: Belknap Press, 1990; classic.

Green, Hardy. *The Company Town: The Industrial Edens and Satanic Mills That Shaped the American Economy*. New York: Basic Books, 2010; a topic seldom addressed.

Kolko, Gabriel. *Railroads and Regulation, 1877–1916*. Princeton: Princeton University Press, 1965; insightfully opinionated.

———. *The Triumph of Conservatism*. New York: The Free Press, 1963; insightfully opinionated.

Lamoreaux, Naomi R. *The Great Merger Movement in American Business, 1895–1904*. New York: Cambridge University Press, 1985; basic.

Noble, David F. *America by Design: Science, Technology, and the Rise of Corporate Capitalism*. New York: Cambridge University Press, 1977.

Sklar, Martin. *The Corporate Reconstruction of American Capitalism, 1890–1916*. New York: Cambridge University Press, 1988.

Wiebe, Roger H. *The Search for Order, 1877–1920*. New York: Hill & Wang 1967; basic.

The 1920s

Barber, William J. *From New Era to New Deal: Herbert Hoover, the Economists and American Economic Policy, 1921–1933*. New York: Cambridge University Press, 1985.

Hawley, Ellis W. Murray N. Rothbard, Robert F. Himmelberg, and Gerald D. Nash. *Herbert Hoover and the Crisis of American Capitalism*. Cambridge, MA: Schenkman Publishing, 1973.

The 1930s

Barber, William J. *Designs within Disorder: Franklin D. Roosevelt, the Economists, and the Shaping of American Economic Policy, 1933–1945*. New York: Cambridge University Press, 1996.

Berle, Adolf A. *The American Economic Republic.* New York: Harcourt, Brace & World, 1963; a defense of business regulation based on an Associationalist understanding of the American economy.
Hawley, Ellis W. *The New Deal and the Problem of Monopoly: A Study in Economic Ambivalence.* Princeton: Princeton University Press, 1966.
Leuchtenburg, William E. *Franklin D. Roosevelt and the New Deal, 1932–1940.* New York: Oxford University Press, 1963; basic introduction.
Radford, Gail. *Modern Housing for America: Policy Struggles in the New Deal Era.* Chicago: University of Chicago Press, 1996; a unique perspective.
Tobey, Ronald C. *Technology as Freedom: The New Deal and Electrical Modernization of the American Home.* Berkeley: University of California Press, 1996.

The 1940s

Atleson, James B. *Labor and the Wartime State: Labor Relations during World War II.* Urbana: University of Illinois Press, 1998; the centrality of the wartime experience for labor relations.
Graebner, William. *The Age of Doubt: American Thought and Culture in the 1940s.* Prospect Heights, IL: Waveland Press, 1991.
Hamby, Alonzo L. *Harry Truman and the Fair Deal.* Lexington, MA: D.C. Heath, 1974.
Matusow, Allen J. *Farm Policies and Politics in the Truman Years* Cambridge: Harvard University Press, 1967.
Nash, Gerald D. *World War II and the West: Reshaping the Economy.* Lincoln: University of Nebraska Press, 1990.

The 1950s

Behrman, Greg. *The Most Noble Adventure: The Marshall Plan and the Time When America Helped Save Europe.* New York: The Free Press, 2007.
Bennett, Michael J. *When Dreams Came True: The GI Bill and the Making of Modern America.* Washington, DC: Brassey's, 1996.
Coontz, Stephanie. *The Way We Never Were: American Families and the Nostalgia Trap.* New York: Basic Books, 1992; important insight.
Daniel, Pete. *Lost Revolutions: The South in the 1950s.* Chapel Hill: University of North Carolina Press, 2000.
Diggins, John Patrick. *The Proud Decades: America in War and Peace, 1941–1960.* New York: W.W. Norton, 1988; truly insightful work.
Donaldson, Gary A. *Abundance and Anxiety: America, 1945–1960.* Westport, CT: Praeger, 1997.
Halberstam, David. *The Fifties.* New York: Ballantine Books, 1994; a standard work.
Hogan, Michael J. *The Marshall Plan: America, Britain, and the Reconstruction of Western Europe, 1947–52.* Cambridge: Cambridge University Press, 1987.

Martinson, Tom. *American Dreamscape: The Pursuit of Happiness in Postwar Suburbia*. New York: Carroll & Graf, 2000; hard to find, but well worth any effort.
Meyer, Michael S. *The Eisenhower Presidency and the 1950s*. Boston: D.C Heath, 1998.
Miller, Douglas T., and Marion Nowak. *The Fifties: The Way We Really Were*. Garden City, NY: Doubleday, 1977.
O'Neill, William L. *American High: The Years of Confidence: 1945–1960*. New York: The Free Press, 1986.
Oakley, J. Ronald. *God's Country: America in the* Fifties. New York: Dembner Books, 1986.
Perrett, Geoffrey. *A Dream of Greatness: The American People, 1945–63*. New York: Coward, McCann & Goheagan, 1979.
Vatter, Harold G. *The U.S. Economy in the 1950s*. New York: Norton, 1963.

The 1960s, 70s, and 80s
Alesina, Alberto, and Geoffrey Carliner, eds. *Politics and Economics in the Eighties*. Chicago: University of Chicago Press, 1999.
Bruck, Connie. *The Predators' Ball: The Junk Bond Raiders and the Man Who Stalked Them*. New York: American Lawyer, 1988.
Lowenstein, Roger. *When Genius Failed*. New York: Random House, 2000; makes the finance very clear.
Mayer, Martin. *The Greatest Bank Robbery: The Collapse of the Savings and Loan Industry*. New York: C. Scribner's Sons, 1990; a good case made for simple outrage.
Stein, Judith. *Pivotal Decade: How the United States Traded Factories for Finance in the Seventies*. New Haven: Yale University Press, 2010.

The postwar years generally
Collins, Robert M. *More: The Politics of Economic Growth in Postwar America*. New York: Oxford University Press, 2000.
Elliott, Michael. *The Day Before Yesterday: Reconsidering America's Past, Rediscovering the Present*. New York: Simon & Schuster, 1996; a different, but fine telling of my story.
French, Michael. *U. S. Economic History Since 1945*. Manchester: Manchester University Press, 1997; an unusual perspective.
Leuchtenburg, William E. *A Troubled Feast: American Society Since 1945*. Boston: Little Brown, 1983.
Solomon, Robert. *The International Monetary System, 1945–1981*. New York: Harper & Row, 1982; U.S. participation in international finance as seen by an insider; beautifully written.
———. *Money on the Move*. Princeton: Princeton University Press, 1999; U.S. participation in international finance as seen by an insider; beautifully written.
Spigel, Lynn. *Make Room for TV: Television and the Family Ideal in Postwar America*. Chicago: University of Chicago Press, 1992; understanding a crucial change in family life.

Vietor, Richard H. K. *Energy Policy in America Since 1945: A Study of Business-Government Relations*. New York: Cambridge University Press, 1984.

Wells, Wyatt. *Anti-Trust and the Formation of the Postwar World*. New York: Columbia University Press, 2002.

Zinn, Howard. *Postwar America: 1945–1971*. Cambridge, MA: South End Press, 2002; insightful rant.

The 90s and 2000s

Blinder, Alan S. *After the Music Stopped: The Financial Crisis, the Response and the Work Ahead*. New York: Penguin Books, 2013; the best of a large pile of books.

Giffels, David. *The Hard Way on Purpose: Essays and Dispatches from the Rust Belt*. New York: Scribner, 2014; accumulated economic damage made clear.

Lowenstein, Roger. *The End of Wall Street*. New York: Penguin Press, 2010.

Shiller, Robert J. *The Subprime Solution: How Today's Global Financial Crisis Happened, and What to Do About It*. Princeton: Princeton University Press, 2008; a fine economist working at his best.

Historical periodizations other than my own

Chernov, Ron. *The House of Morgan: An American Banking Dynasty and the Rise of Modern Finance*. New York: Atlantic Monthly Press, 1990; well argued.

Frieden, Jeffry A. *Global Capitalism: Its Fall and Rise in the Twentieth Century*. New York: W.W. Norton, 2007.

Galambos, Louis, and Joseph Pratt. *The Rise of the Corporate Commonwealth: U.S. Business and Public Policy in the Twentieth Century*. New York: Basic Books, 1988; classic.

Gordon, Robert J. *The Rise and Fall of American Growth: The U.S. Standard of Living Since the Civil War*. Princeton: Princeton University Press, 2016; the charts are annoying, but the text is really insightful.

Keller, Morton. *Regulating a New Economy: Public Policy and Economic Change in America, 1900–1933*. Cambridge: Harvard University Press, 1990.

Manchester, William. *The Glory and the Dream: A Narrative History of America 1932–1972*. Boston: Little Brown, 1973; a good read.

McCraw, Thomas K. *American Business, 1920–2000: How It Worked*. Wheeling, IL: Harlan Davidson, 2000; excellent retelling.

Mitchell, Lawrence E. *The Speculation Economy: How Finance Triumphed Over Industry*. San Francisco: Berrett-Koehler, 2007.

Patterson, James T. *Grand Expectations: The United States, 1945–1974*. New York: Oxford University Press, 1996; sensible.

Stein, Herbert. *The Fiscal Revolution in America: Policy in Pursuit of Reality*. 2nd rev. ed. Washington, DC: AEI Press, 1996; astute views from an insider.

Tomlins, Christopher. *The State and the Unions: Labor Relations, Law, and the Organized Labor Movement in America, 1880–1960*. New York: Cambridge University Press, 1985; makes labor history clear.

Vietor, Richard H. K. *Contrived Competition: Regulation and Deregulation in America*. Cambridge, MA: Belknap Press, 1994.

Wells, Wyatt. *American Capitalism 1945–2000: Continuity and Change from Mass Production to the Information Society*. Chicago: Ivan R. Dee, 2003.

Woeste, Victoria Saker. *The Farmers Benevolent Trust: Law and Agricultural Cooperation in Industrial America, 1865–1945*. Chapel Hill: University of North Carolina Press, 1998.

Wright, Gavin. *Old South, New South: Revolutions in the Southern Economy Since the Civil War*. New York: Basic Books, 1986; an opening to understanding complicated questions.

Railroads—

Daughen, Joseph R. *The Wreck of the Penn-Central*. Boston: Little, Brown, 1971.

Grant, H. Roger. *Erie Lackawanna: Death of an American Railroad, 1938–1992*. Palo Alto, CA: Stanford University Press, 1994.

Salsbury, Stephen. *No Way to Run a Railroad: The Untold Story of the Penn Central Crisis*. New York: McGraw Hill, 1982.

Stover, John F. *American Railroads*. 2nd ed. Chicago: University of Chicago Press, 1997.

———. *The Routledge Historical Atlas of the American Railroads*. New York: Routledge, 1999; brief, but incredibly insightful.

Steel—

Leary, Thomas E., and Elizabeth C. Sholes. *From Fire to Rust: Business, Technology and Work at the Lackawanna Steel Plant, 1899–1983*. Buffalo: Buffalo and Erie County Historical Society, 1987; absolutely essential for understanding what collapsed in the 1980s.

Hall, Christopher G. L. *Steel Phoenix: The Fall and Rise of the U.S. Steel Industry*. New York: Saint Martin's Press, 1997.

Plowden, David. *Steel*. New York: Viking, 1981.

Reutter, Mark. *Sparrows Point: Making Steel—The Rise and Ruin of American Industrial Might*. New York: Summit Books, 1988.

Stein, Judith. *Running Steel, Running America: Race, Economic Policy, and the Decline of Liberalism*. Chapel Hill: University of North Carolina Press, 1998; an important aspect of steel making that is usually ignored.

Downtown

Fogelson, Robert M. *Downtown: Its Rise and Fall, 1890–1950*. New Haven: Yale University Press, 2001.

Isenberg, Alison. *Downtown America: A History of the Place and the People Who Made It*. Chicago: University of Chicago Press, 2004.

The middle class—

Bledstein, Burton J., and Robert D. Johnston, eds. *The Middling Sorts: Explorations in the History of the American Middle Class*. New York: Routledge, 2001.

Cohen, Lizabeth. *A Consumers' Republic: The Politics of Mass Consumption in Postwar America*. New York: Knopf, 2003.

Malamud, Deborah C. "Engineering the Middle Classes: Class Line-Drawing in the New Deal Hours Legislation." *Michigan Law Review* 96: 2212 (1998).

———. "Who Are—or Were: Middle Class Welfare in the Early New Deal." *University of Pennsylvania Law Review* 151: 2019 (2003).

Regularly, and unfairly, neglected topics—

Harris, Alice Kessler. *Out to Work: A History of Wage-Earning Women in the United States*. New York: Oxford University Press, 1982.

Rose, Michael. *The Mind at Work: Valuing the Intelligence of the American Worker*. New York: Penguin, 2004; a defense of trades people.

If interested in economic development in specific places or for narrower time periods—

Florida, Richard L. *The Rise of the Creative Class: And How It's Transforming Work, Leisure, and Everyday Life*. New York: Basic Books, 2002; social groups a source of economic change.

Glaeser, Edward L. "Reinventing Boston 1630–2003." *Journal of Economic Geography* 5:119 (2004); innovation as a basis for economic change.

Kort, John. "Regional Economic Instability and Industrial Diversification in the United States." *Land Economics* 57:596 (1981).

Rogers, Allan. "Some Aspects of Industrial Diversification in the United States." *Economic Geography* 33:16 (1957).

Krugman, Paul. "History and Industry Location: The Case of the Manufacturing Belt." *The American Economic Review* 81:80 (1991).

Safford, Sean. *Why the Garden Club Couldn't Save Youngstown*. Cambridge: Harvard University Press, 2009; an insightful comparison of two Rust Belt economies.

Saxenian, AnnaLee. *Regional Advantage: Culture and Competition in Silicon Valley and Route 128*. Cambridge: Harvard University Press, 1994; social life as an explanation for economic difference.

Schragger, Richard. *City Power: Urban Governance in a Global Age*. New York: Oxford University Press, 2016; urban renewal as economic development.

Storper, Michael, Thomas Kemeny, Naji Philip Markarem and Taner Osman. *Economic Growth and Development: Lessons from Los Angeles and San Francisco*. Palo Alto, CA: Stanford University Press, 2015; social life as an explanation for economic difference.

Weaver, Russell, Sharmista Bagchi-Sen, Jason Knight, and Amy Fraszier. *Shrinking Cities: Understanding Urban Decline in the United States*. New York: Routledge, 2016.

If interested in specific bits of law related to economy—

Berle, Adolph A., and Gardner C. Means, *The Modern Corporation and Private Property*. New York: Macmillan, 1932; the basic understanding of corporate behavior.

Brownlee, W. Elliot. *Federal Taxation in America: A Short History*. Washington, DC: Woodrow Wilson Center Press, 1996.

Carruthers, Bruce G., and Terrence C. Halliday. *Rescuing Business: The Making of Corporate Bankruptcy Law in England and the United States*. New York: Oxford University Press, 1998.

Kamp, Alan R. "Between the Wars Social Thought: Karl Llewellyn, Legal Realism, and the Uniform Commercial Code in Context." *Albany Law Review* 59:327 (1995).

———. "Uptown Act: A History of the Uniform Commercial Code: 1940–49." *Southern Methodist University Law Review* 52:275 (1998).

Konefsky, Alfred R. "Simon Greenleaf, Boston Elites, and the Social Meaning and Construction of the Charles River Bridge Case." In *Transformations in American Legal History: Essays in Honor of Professor Morton J. Horowitz*. Edited by Daniel W. Hamilton and Alfred L. Brophy. Cambridge: Harvard University Press, 2010, 165; elegant.

Radford, Gail. *The Rise of the Public Authority: State building and Economic Development in Twentieth Century America*. Chicago: University of Chicago Press, 2013; a far more important topic than commonly understood.

Skeel, David A., Jr. *Debt's Dominion: A History of Bankruptcy Law in America*. Princeton: Princeton University Press, 2004.

If interested in economic theory generally—

Baumol, William J., Robert E. Litan, and Carl Schramm. *Good Capitalism, Bad Capitalism, and the Economics of Growth and Prosperity*. New Have: Yale University Press, 2007.

Davidson, Kenneth M. *Reality Ignored: How Milton Friedman and Chicago Economics Undermined American Institutions and Endangered the Global Economy*. Arlington, VA: Kenneth M. Davidson, 2011.

Denning, Steven. "The Origin of the World's Dumbest Idea, Milton Friedman." *Forbes* 191:57 (June 26, 2013).

Galbraith, John Kenneth. *Economics in Perspective: A Critical History*. Boston: Houghton Mifflin, 1987; intellectual history of economic thought.

Hall, Peter A., and David Soskice. "An Introduction to Varieties of Capitalism." In Peter A. Hall and David Soskice, eds. *Varieties of Capitalism: The Institutional Foundations of Comparative Advantage* 1. New York: Oxford University Press, 2001; clear contrast to Baumol et al.

Kahn, Alfred E. *The Economics of Regulation: Principles and Institutions*. New York: Wiley, 1970); fundamental textbook on utility regulation.

Lindbloom, Charles E. *Politics and Markets*. New York: Basic Books, 1977; unfortunately, regularly underrated.

Porter, Michael E. *The Competitive Advantage of Nations*. New York: The Free Press, 1990.

Schumpeter, Joseph A. *Capitalism, Socialism, and Democracy*. London: Routledge, 1942.

Smith, Adam. *An Inquiry into the Nature and Causes of the Wealth of Nations*, 1776. London: W. Srahan. The urtext.

Taleb, Nassim Nicholas. *AntiFragile: Things That Gain from Disorder*. New York: Random House, 2012.

Veblen, Thorstein. *The Engineers and the Price System*. New York: B. W. Huebsch, 1921.

Warsh, David. *Knowledge and the Wealth of Nations*. New York: W. W. Norton, 2006; intellectual history of New Growth theory.

Yergin, Daniel, and Joseph Stanislaw. *The Commanding Heights: The Battle Between Government and the Marketplace That Is Remaking the Modern World*. New York: Simon & Schuster, 1998.

If interested in legal theory—

Fuller, Lon L., and Kenneth I. Winston. "The Forms and Limits of Adjudication." *Harvard Law Review* 92:353 (1978); procedural understanding of legality.

Pound, Roscoe. "The Limits of Effective Legal Action." *International Journal of Ethics* 27:150 (1917); social understanding of legality.

Schlag, Pierre. *The Enchantment of Reason*. Durham, NC: Duke University Press, 1998; critique of the notion of law as an exercise reason.

Attempting to put it all together—

Westbrook, David A. *City of Gold: An Apology for Global Capitalism in a Time of Discontent*. New York: Routledge, 2003; a complex, but rewarding read.

Less Directly Relevant

Miscellaneous—

Braverman, Irus. *Wild Life: The Institution of Nature*. Palo Alto, CA: Stanford University Press, 2015; good discussion of the concept of "nature."

Machiavelli, Niccolo. *The Prince*. Edited by Quentin Skinner and Russell Price. Cambridge: Cambridge University Press, 1988; classic text on political life.

Modestly relevant novels and poetry—

Auden, W. H. "Law, Says the Gardeners, Is the Sun." In *Another Time*. London: Farber & Farber, 1940, 1.

Davis, Lindsey. *One Virgin Too Many*. New York: Mysterious Press, 2000.

Faulkner, William. "William Faulkner's Nobel Prize Acceptance Speech." *Southern Cultures* 12:71 (Spring 2006).

Hopkins, Gerard Manley. "Thou Are Indeed Just Lord." In *Gerard Manley Hopkins: A Selection of His Poetry and Prose*. Edited by W. H. Gardner. Baltimore: Penguin Books, 1962, 67.

Anyone who has not read enough of John Henry Schlegel's prose yet might try—

"On the Many Flavors of Capitalism, or Reflections on Schumpeter's Ghost." *Buffalo Law Review* 56:965 (2009).

"Unfortunately, White-Collar Is the Default Setting: Boys and Higher Education." *Buffalo Law Review* 53:1035 (2005).

INDEX

Page numbers in italics represent figures.